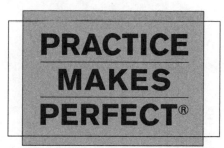

**PRACTICE
MAKES
PERFECT®**

French Vocabulary Building with Suffixes and Prefixes

PRACTICE MAKES PERFECT®

French Vocabulary Building with Suffixes and Prefixes

Eliane Kurbegov

New York Chicago San Francisco Athens London Madrid
Mexico City Milan New Delhi Singapore Sydney Toronto

1 2 3 4 5 6 7 8 9 0   QVS/QVS   1 0 9 8 7 6 5 4

ISBN   978-0-07-183620-3
MHID   0-07-183620-9

e-ISBN   978-0-07-183621-0
e-MHID   0-07-183621-7

Library of Congress Control Number 2014933902

McGraw-Hill Education, the McGraw-Hill Education logo, Practice Makes Perfect, and related trade dress are trademarks or registered trademarks of McGraw-Hill Education and/or its affiliates in the United States and other countries and may not be used without written permission. All other trademarks are the property of their respective owners. McGraw-Hill Education is not associated with any product or vendor mentioned in this book.

Interior design by Village Bookworks, Inc.

McGraw-Hill Education products are available at special quantity discounts to use as premiums and sales promotions or for use in corporate training programs. To contact a representative, please visit the Contact Us pages at www.mhprofessional.com.

This book is printed on acid-free paper.

Contents

Preface ix

Introduction xi

How to use this book xiii

2 Intermediate/advanced suffixes 83

Preface

A French word may be a basic word, like English *soft*, or a word with a prefix and/or a suffix, like *presoftened* and *softly*. These two words are part of a family of words that have the base word *soft*. In a family of words, the base word is the common element and contains the main idea of the word. Knowing the meaning of the base word (*soft*) and the meanings of the prefix (*pre-*) and the suffixes (*-en, -ed,* and *-ly*) helps you recognize or infer the meaning of a word like *presoftened* or *softly*.

To know the meaning of an affixed base word requires that you be familiar with the possible meanings of prefixes like *pre-* and suffixes like *-ly*. Fortunately, most French prefixes have recognizable English counterparts. Suffixes, however, differ quite a bit between French and English and require careful study.

A prefix is a letter or group of letters affixed to the beginning of a base word to add to or otherwise modify the base word's meaning. For example, the adjective *amoral* is composed of the base word *moral* and the prefix *a-*, which adds the concept of *not* to the meaning of the adjective. The word *moral* means being concerned with right and wrong; the word *amoral* means *not* being concerned with right and wrong. A prefix does not change the function of the base word: *moral* and *amoral* are both adjectives.

A suffix is a letter or group of letters affixed to the end of a base word to form a new, related word. For example, the suffix *ity* added to the base word *moral* changes the adjective *moral* to the noun *morality*. A suffix may change the function of a word; for example, *fear* is a noun, but *fearful* is an adjective. Some French suffixes are grammatical, including endings to mark infinitives, present participles, past participles, and adverbs. These suffixes and their uses are explained in Appendix A.

Introduction

The French language relies on suffixes to mark parts of speech and gender. It relies on both suffixes and prefixes to modify base words and convey nuances of meaning. *Practice Makes Perfect: French Vocabulary Building with Suffixes and Prefixes* will help you expand your vocabulary and comprehension, as well as gain an appreciation of the language through awareness of French suffixes and prefixes.

In this age of information and technology, it is easy to look up vocabulary and get translations online. You may even find lists of suffixes and prefixes; unfortunately, they are rarely accompanied by enough examples and they never offer in-depth analysis. By contrast, this book focuses on individual suffixes and prefixes, providing charts of words, along with their base words and the English equivalents of both. Of course, these charts are not exhaustive—there are simply too many suffixes and prefixes. You will, however, be exposed to about 4,000 words, and you will learn to modify many of the base words you already know and become an artisan of language as a result.

The 160 suffixes and prefixes in this book deliver the most potential for expanding your vocabulary. They also provide insight into families of words. The base words you have learned in your introductory French courses are but the stem of a flower. Starting with this stem, you can sketch out a beautifully blooming flower composed of many petals; these petals are the suffixed and prefixed words. The stem may be the root of the flower (frequently a Latin or Greek root), but more often, the stem is a French base word that grew out of a Latin or Greek root. This is why the term *base word* is used instead of *root* in the vocabulary charts.

Practice Makes Perfect: French Vocabulary Building with Suffixes and Prefixes presents 100 suffixes and 60 prefixes, selected on the basis of their frequency and usage. Some affixes are more common than others, but all are found in words you encounter in everyday conversation and reading, from magazine articles and newspapers to literature.

Both suffixes and prefixes are grouped as beginning or intermediate/advanced. Each entry is presented with its basic meaning, its English equivalent if one exists, its part(s) of speech, and its gender if it is a noun. A short paragraph then explains and analyzes the suffix or prefix, specifying how it is used to form new words and providing other important information. At least one chart follows, presenting a list of words formed with the affix, their base words, and the English equivalents of both. If an affix appears predominantly in nouns, a chart of nouns is presented, followed by a list of related verbs and/or adjectives that are derived from the same base words as the nouns. If an affix appears in nouns, adjectives, and verbs, the chart may be comprised of words that function as two parts of speech, for example, nouns and adjectives. Every chart is followed by at least one exercise aimed at testing your comprehension of the affixed words; there are more than 200 exercises in all. The number of exercise items depends on the frequency of the words formed with a given suffix or prefix, as well as on their degree of difficulty for the learner of French.

Two appendixes are provided. Appendix A presents a crash course in French verbs (specifically, infinitives, present participles, and past participles) and adverbs. Appendix B presents a list of all 160 affixes in this book, each with its reference number, meaning(s), and at least one example word.

Enjoy the art of sketching delightful word flowers and appreciating their bloom!

How to use this book

The base words for affixed words are usually French, but they may also be Latin roots or words from another language, such as Greek or Italian. These languages are indicated in square brackets in the charts.

[DUTCH]	Dutch
[ENG.]	English
[FRANKISH]	Frankish
[GER.]	German
[GRK.]	Greek
[HEBREW]	Hebrew
[ITAL.]	Italian
[LAT.]	Latin
[MED. LAT.]	Medieval Latin
[OLD FR.]	Old French
[ROMANSH]	Romansh
[SP.]	Spanish

Square brackets are also used to indicate grammatical functions and usage status.

[ADJ.]	Adjective
[ADV.]	Adverb
[M.]	Masculine noun
[F.]	Feminine noun
[M.F.]	Masculine and feminine noun
[PL.]	Plural
[PAST PART.]	Past participle
[ARCHAIC]	Archaic
[FAMILIAR]	Familiar
[PEJORATIVE]	Pejorative
[SLANG]	Slang

An asterisk (*) is used in certain charts to mark one of the following terms.

- A noun with a related adjective under another affix (see page 43)
- An adjective that also functions as a noun (see page 47)
- A noun with a pejorative connotation (see page 87)
- A masculine noun that has a feminine counterpart (see page 144)

French Vocabulary Building with Suffixes and Prefixes

French suffixes

A suffix is a letter or group of letters affixed to the end of a base word to form a new, related word. The suffix may also change the part of speech of the base word. For example, a base word that is a verb may become a noun or an adjective, depending on the suffix attached to it. Part I presents charts of suffixed words with their English equivalents and base words, grouped as nouns, adjectives, or verbs. If a suffix appears extensively in two or three of these categories, multiple charts, organized by grammatical function, are provided.

Learners of French know all too well the challenge of identifying the gender of a noun that does not represent a person. The good news is that a noun's suffix not only gives a broad or precise indication of who or what is denoted by the noun, but also indicates the gender of the noun. For example, nouns ending in **-ation** are feminine, whereas nouns ending in **-ment** are masculine. The suffix of an adjective, provided in its masculine form, usually indicates its feminine form as well. For verbs, this book focuses on the impact of suffixes on infinitive forms and on present and past participles; these verbal forms are explained and analyzed in Appendix A.

Many suffixed words can be classified thematically; for example, feminine nouns ending in **-esse** denote titled or powerful females, like **princesse**. Other suffixed words, such as **courageux**, are grouped under a broader descriptive theme.

1
Beginning suffixes

 **-ain/-aine**

MEANING	Citizen, inhabitant
ENGLISH EQUIVALENT	*-an*
PART OF SPEECH	Noun, adjective
GENDER	Masculine/feminine

A French noun or adjective ending in the suffix **-ain** (feminine: **-aine**) often denotes a person's nationality or place of origin. The base word may be a city, region, province, state, country, or even a continent. For example, the base word for **Cubain** *a Cuban man* or **Cubaine** *a Cuban woman* is **Cuba**. If the suffixed word is a noun, it is capitalized; if the suffixed word is an adjective, it is not capitalized. **Les Américains** are *Americans*, but in the phrase **mes amis américains** *my American friends*, **américains** is an adjective.

NOUN/ADJECTIVE ENDING IN **-ain/-aine**	ENGLISH EQUIVALENT	BASE WORD	ENGLISH EQUIVALENT
Africain	*African*	Afrique	*Africa*
Américain	*American*	Amérique	*America*
Costaricain	*Costa Rican*	Costa Rica	*Costa Rica*
Cubain	*Cuban*	Cuba	*Cuba*
Dominicain	*Dominican*	République Dominicaine	*Dominican Republic*
Marocain	*Moroccan*	Maroc	*Morocco*
Mexicain	*Mexican*	Mexique	*Mexico*
Portoricain	*Puerto Rican*	Porto Rico	*Puerto Rico*
Romain	*Roman*	Rome	*Rome*
Tibétain	*Tibetan*	Tibet	*Tibet*
Toulousain	*from Toulouse*	Toulouse	*city of Toulouse*

EXERCICE
1·1

Vrai ou faux? *Indicate whether each statement is true or false, using* **V** *for* **vrai** *true or* **F** *for* **faux** *false.*

1. _____ Une Dominicaine parle espagnol.

2. _____ Les Tibétains ont beaucoup de montagnes dans leur pays.

3. _____ La langue maternelle des Costaricains est le Français.

4. _____ Les Marocains habitent sur une île.

5. _____ Les Mexicains habitent en Amérique du sud.

6. _____ Les Américains adorent le football américain.

7. _____ Les Africains sont les habitants d'un continent.

8. _____ Les Portoricains habitent tous à San Juan.

9. _____ Les Toulousains sont des Suisses.

10. _____ Les Romains sont des Italiens.

 # -ais/-aise

MEANING	Citizen, inhabitant
ENGLISH EQUIVALENT	—
PART OF SPEECH	Noun, adjective
GENDER	Masculine/feminine

A French noun or adjective ending in the suffix **-ais** (feminine: **-aise**) often denotes a nationality or place of residence. The base word may be a city, region, province, state, or country. For example, the base word for **Anglais** *Englishman* or **Anglaise** *Englishwoman* is **Angleterre** *England*. If the suffixed word is a noun, it is capitalized; if the suffixed word is an adjective, it is not capitalized. **Les Anglais** are *English people*, but in the phrase **mes amis anglais** *my English friends*, **anglais** is an adjective.

NOUN/ADJECTIVE ENDING IN **-ais/-aise**	ENGLISH EQUIVALENT	BASE WORD	ENGLISH EQUIVALENT
Anglais	*English person*	Angleterre	*England*
Antillais	*from the Antilles*	Antilles	*Antilles*
Écossais	*Scot/Scotch*	Écosse	*Scotland*
Français	*French*	France	*France*
Martiniquais	*from Martinique*	Martinique	*Martinique*
Montréalais	*from Montreal*	Montréal	*Montreal*
New Yorkais	*New Yorker*	New York	*New York*
Polonais	*Pole*	Pologne	*Poland*
Portugais	*Portuguese*	Portugal	*Portugal*
Sénégalais	*Senegalese*	Sénégal	*Senegal*

EXERCICE
2·1

Les personnes célèbres! *Complete each sentence with the appropriate noun of nationality.*

1. Le compositeur Chopin était un _____ d'origine.

2. Gustave Eiffel est un _____ célèbre parce qu'il a construit la Tour Eiffel.

3. Aimé Césaire est des Antilles; c'est un _____ célèbre pour sa poésie.

4. Christophe Colomb est un _____ célèbre pour sa découverte du « Nouveau Monde ».

5. L'écrivain Senghor est un _____ qui était aussi président du Sénégal.

6. Frantz Fanon, né en Martinique, était psychiatre et militant; c'est un

_____ important.

7. Michael Bloomberg et Rudy Giuliani sont des _____ importants puisqu'ils étaient maires de la ville de New York.

8. Mary Stuart est bien connue par les _____; elle est devenue reine d'Écosse à l'âge de six jours.

9. Les _____ habitent dans la deuxième plus grande ville francophone.

10. Les _____ aiment traverser la Manche pour visiter la Normandie.

◆ 3 ◆ -ois/-oise

MEANING	Citizen, inhabitant
ENGLISH EQUIVALENT	—
PART OF SPEECH	Noun, adjective
GENDER	Masculine/feminine

A French noun or adjective ending in the suffix **-ois** (feminine: **-oise**) often denotes a nationality or place of residence. The base word may be a city, region, province, state, or country. For example, the base word for **Québécois** *man from Quebec* or **Québécoise** *woman from Quebec* is **Québec.** If the suffixed word is a noun, it is capitalized; if the suffixed word is an adjective, it is not capitalized. **Les Québécois** are *people from Quebec,* but in the phrase **une ville québécoise** *a city in the province of Quebec,* **québécoise** is an adjective.

NOUN/ADJECTIVE ENDING IN **-ois/-oise**	ENGLISH EQUIVALENT	BASE WORD	ENGLISH EQUIVALENT
Berlinois	*from Berlin*	Berlin	*Berlin*
Bruxellois	*from Brussels*	Bruxelles	*city of Brussels*
Champenois	*from Champagne*	Champagne	*Champagne*
Chinois	*Chinese*	Chine	*China*
Danois	*Dane*	Danemark	*Denmark*
Hongrois	*Hungarian*	Hongrie	*Hungary*
Luxembourgeois	*from Luxembourg*	Luxembourg	*Luxembourg*
Québécois	*from Quebec*	Québec	*Quebec*
Strasbourgeois	*from Strasbourg*	Strasbourg	*Strasbourg*
Suédois	*Swede*	Suède	*Sweden*

Faites votre choix! *Choose the best completion for each sentence.*

1. _____ Les Suédois habitent
2. _____ Les Danois habitent
3. _____ Les Chinois habitent
4. _____ Les Hongrois habitent
5. _____ Les Luxembourgeois habitent
6. _____ Les Québécois habitent
7. _____ Les Strasbourgeois habitent
8. _____ Les Champenois habitent
9. _____ Les Bruxellois habitent
10. _____ Les Berlinois habitent

a. près de la Pologne.

b. la capitale de la Belgique.

c. la capitale de l'ancienne Allemagne de l'est.

d. près du Pôle Nord.

e. la région connue pour le Champagne.

f. en Asie.

g. le Danemark.

h. un petit pays européen voisin de la Belgique.

i. à la frontière allemande.

j. en Amérique du nord.

4 ▸ -ien/-ienne

MEANING	Citizen, inhabitant
ENGLISH EQUIVALENT	*-ian*
PART OF SPEECH	Noun, adjective
GENDER	Masculine/feminine

A French noun or adjective ending in the suffix **-ien** (feminine: **-ienne**) often denotes a nationality or place of residence. The base word may be a city, region, province, state, country, or even a continent. For example, the base word for **Italien** *Italian man* or **Italienne** *Italian woman* is **Italie** *Italy*. If the suffixed word is a noun, it is capitalized; if the suffixed word is an adjective, it is not capitalized. **Les Italiens** are *Italians*, but in the phrase **une actrice italienne** *an Italian actress*, **italienne** is an adjective.

NOUN/ADJECTIVE ENDING IN **-ien/-ienne**	ENGLISH EQUIVALENT	BASE WORD	ENGLISH EQUIVALENT
Alsacien	*from Alsace*	Alsace	*Alsace*
Australien	*Australian*	Australie	*Australia*
Brésilien	*Brazilian*	Brésil	*Brazil*
Canadien	*Canadian*	Canada	*Canada*
Colombien	*Colombian*	Colombie	*Colombia*
Égyptien	*Egyptian*	Égypte	*Egypt*
Éthiopien	*Ethiopian*	Éthiopie	*Ethiopia*
Floridien	*Floridian*	Floride	*Florida*
Haïtien	*Haitian*	Haïti	*Haiti*
Israélien	*Israeli*	Israël	*Israel*

NOUN/ADJECTIVE ENDING IN -ien/-ienne	ENGLISH EQUIVALENT	BASE WORD	ENGLISH EQUIVALENT
Italien	*Italian*	Italie	*Italy*
Ivoirien	*from the Ivory Coast*	Côte d'Ivoire	*Ivory Coast*
Parisien	*Parisian*	Paris	*Paris*
Tunisien	*Tunisian*	Tunisie	*Tunisia*
Ukrainien	*Ukrainian*	Ukraine	*Ukraine*
Vénézuélien	*Venezuelan*	Venezuela	*Venezuela*
Vietnamien	*Vietnamese*	Vietnam	*Vietnam*

EXERCICE 4·1

Qui sont-ils? *Identify each group of people by nationality or place of residence.*

1. Ce peuple africain est mentionné dans l'*Iliade* et l'*Odyssée*.

   a. les Éthiopiens   b. les Haïtiens

2. Les résidents de cet état américain profitent du soleil toute l'année.

   a. les Canadiens   b. les Floridiens

3. Gabriel García Márquez est un romancier issu de cette culture latine.

   a. les Brésiliens   b. les Colombiens

4. Ils habitent à Strasbourg, à Colmar, à Nancy, à Belfort etc.

   a. les Alsaciens   b. les Parisiens

5. Ils habitent un pays qui est maintenant indépendant de l'ancienne Union Soviétique.

   a. les Roumains   b. les Ukrainiens

6. Leur première langue est l'hébreu.

   a. les Tunisiens   b. les Israéliens

7. Ils ont beaucoup de vestiges anciens dans leur pays comme des théâtres et des aqueducs.

   a. les Italiens   b. les Vénézuéliens

8. Ils ont des pyramides très visitées.

   a. les Australiens   b. les Égyptiens

9. Ce sont les habitants de l'est de la péninsule indochinoise.

   a. les Ivoiriens   b. les Vietnamiens

10. Ils ont accès à un des musées les plus visités du monde.

   a. les Parisiens   b. les Tunisiens

5 ▸ -ien/-ienne

MEANING	Expert, specialist
ENGLISH EQUIVALENT	*-ian*
PART OF SPEECH	Noun
GENDER	Masculine/feminine

If a French noun ending in the suffix **-ien** (feminine: **-ienne**) does not denote a place of origin or residence (see No. 4), it identifies a person who has a specific expertise. The base word is the noun that represents the field of expertise. For example, the noun **musicien** *male musician* or **musicienne** *female musician* is a person whose specialty is **musique** *music*. This suffix is not limited to professions; it is also used to describe a person who specializes in the study of a writer or artist: **un(e) proustien(ne)** is a specialist in the French writer Proust's work.

NOUN ENDING IN **-ien/-ienne**	ENGLISH EQUIVALENT	BASE WORD	ENGLISH EQUIVALENT
académicien	*academician*	académie	*academy*
acousticien	*acoustician*	acoustique	*acoustics*
chirurgien	*surgeon*	chirurgie	*surgery*
collégien	*junior high student*	collège	*junior high*
comédien	*comedian*	comédie	*comedy*
électricien	*electrician*	électricité	*electricity*
gardien	*guard*	garde	*watch, guard*
généticien	*geneticist*	génétique	*genetics*
grammairien	*grammarian*	grammaire	*grammar*
historien	*historian*	histoire	*history*

EXERCICE
5·1

Que font ces gens? *Complete each sentence with the appropriate masculine or feminine noun.*

1. C'est une spécialiste de la génétique; elle est _____.

2. C'est un élève de douze ans; il est _____.

3. C'est un homme qui surveille ce qui se passe dans un musée; il est

   _____.

4. Cette dame voit des patients qui n'entendent pas bien; elle est

   _____.

5. Ce monsieur écrit des livres de grammaire; il est _____.

6. Marguerite Yourcenar a été élue à l'Académie Française en 1980; elle est

   _____.

7. Plutarque, Grec d'origine, a étudié la Rome antique; il est _____.

8. C'est une femme qui joue des rôles dans des pièces ou des films; elle est

   _____.

9. C'est un homme qui vient en aide quand il y a des problèmes d'électricité; il est

   _____.

10. C'est une femme qui fait des opérations chirurgicales; elle est _____.

NOUN ENDING IN **-ien/-ienne**	ENGLISH EQUIVALENT	BASE WORD	ENGLISH EQUIVALENT
informaticien	*computer specialist*	information	*information, data*
logisticien	*logician*	logique	*logic*
lycéen	*high school student*	lycée	*high school*
magicien	*magician*	magie	*magic*
mathématicien	*mathematician*	mathématiques	*mathematics*
mécanicien	*mechanic*	mécanique	*field of mechanics*
musicien	*musician*	musique	*music*
pharmacien	*pharmacist*	pharmacie	*pharmacy*
proustien	*Proust specialist*	Proust	*Marcel Proust* (writer)
tragédien	*tragedian*	tragédie	*tragedy*

EXERCICE
5·2

Qui sont ces experts? *Complete each sentence with the appropriate masculine plural noun.*

1. Les _____ travaillent avec les ordinateurs et les logiciels.

2. Les _____ sont des spécialistes des mathématiques.

3. Les _____ connaissent l'art de l'illusion.

4. Les _____ dispensent des médicaments.

5. Les _____ réparent les voitures.

6. Les _____ gèrent les méthodes d'organisation d'une entreprise.

7. Les _____ jouent ou composent de la musique.

8. Les _____ français terminent leurs études avec le baccalauréat.

9. Les _____ sont de grands admirateurs du romancier Proust.

10. Les _____ jouent dans des pièces dramatiques.

6 ◆ -al/-ale

MEANING	Like, pertaining to
ENGLISH EQUIVALENT	*-al*
PART OF SPEECH	Adjective
GENDER	Masculine/feminine

A French adjective ending in the suffix **-al** (feminine: **-ale**) denotes a characteristic related to manner, time, or place. The base word is typically a noun that represents the characteristic. For example, the base word for **amical** is **ami** *friend*, and this suffixed adjective means *friendly*. The regular formation for this type of adjective consists in adding the suffix to a noun (**nation** yields **national**) or replacing the **-e** ending of a noun with **-al** (**colosse** yields **colossal**), but there are many slightly irregular formations, especially if the base word is a Latin root. Since many of these French adjectives have English cognates, they tend to be easily recognized.

ADJECTIVE ENDING IN **-al/-ale**	ENGLISH EQUIVALENT	BASE WORD	ENGLISH EQUIVALENT
amical	*friendly*	ami	*friend*
amoral	*amoral*	[a-] + mœurs	*not + morals*
ancestral	*ancestral*	ancêtre	*ancestor*
annal	*yearly*	année	*year*
bifocal	*bifocal*	[bi-] + focus [LAT.]	*two + hearth*
collégial	*collegial, collegiate*	collège	*college*
colossal	*colossal*	colosse	*colossus*
équatorial	*equatorial*	équateur	*equator*
international	*international*	[inter-] + nation	*between + nation*
médiéval	*medieval*	medius + aevum [LAT.]	*middle + age*
mondial	*global*	monde	*world*
musical	*musical*	musique	*music*
natal	*natal*	natus [LAT.]	*born*
naval	*naval*	navalis [LAT.]	*naval*
normal	*normal*	norme	*norm*
oriental	*oriental*	orient	*orient*
pluvial	*pluvial*	pluie	*rain*
végétal	*vegetal*	vegetare [LAT.]	*to invigorate*

EXERCICE 6·1

Vrai ou faux? *Indicate whether each statement is true or false, using* **V** *for* **vrai** *true or* **F** *for* **faux** *false.*

1. _____ On se fait une accolade amicale entre ennemis.

2. _____ Rectifier les problèmes climatiques est une entreprise colossale.

3. _____ Médecins sans Frontières est une organisation internationale.

4. _____ Les États-Unis n'ont pas de flotte navale.

5. _____ Critiquer ses collègues est très collégial.

6. _____ La Chine est un pays oriental.

7. _____ Les symphonies sont des compositions musicales.

8. _____ Faire du sport est une activité saine et normale.

9. _____ Le désert du Sahara a un climat pluvial.

10. _____ L'inceste est amoral.

11. _____ Les Africains apprécient beaucoup les traditions ancestrales.

12. _____ Les végétariens ne mangent pas beaucoup de plats de sources végétales.

13. _____ Les forêts équatoriales du Brésil ne sont pas en danger.

14. _____ Une procuration annale se termine après deux ans.

15. _____ Les lentilles bifocales sont prescrites pour la presbytie.

16. _____ Un Festival de la Renaissance est un festival médiéval.

17. _____ L'endroit natal d'Einstein est en France.

18. _____ La faim est un problème mondial.

7 ◆ -el/-elle

MEANING	Referring to, pertaining to
ENGLISH EQUIVALENT	—
PART OF SPEECH	Adjective
GENDER	Masculine/feminine

A French adjective ending in the suffix **-el** (feminine: **-elle**) denotes a characteristic of the base word, which is a noun. For example, the base word for the adjective **présidentiel** is the noun **président**, and the meaning of this suffixed adjective is *presidential*. The regular formation for this type of adjective consists in adding the suffix to the noun (for example, **accident** yields **accidentel**) or replacing the **-e** ending of a noun with the suffix **-(i)el** (for example, **artifice** yields **artificiel**), but there are many slightly irregular formations, especially if the base word is Latin. If the suffix is attached to a noun ending in **-n**, the **n** is doubled (for example, **nutrition** yields **nutritionnel**). In the following chart, an adjective marked by an asterisk (*) may also function as a noun; for example, in the phrase **une occupation professionnelle** *a professional occupation*, the suffixed word is an adjective, but in the sentence **C'est un vrai professionnel** *He is a real professional*, it is a noun. Since these French adjectives have English cognates, they are easily recognized.

ADJECTIVE ENDING IN **-el/-elle**	ENGLISH EQUIVALENT	BASE WORD	ENGLISH EQUIVALENT
accidentel	*accidental*	accident	*accident*
annuel	*annual*	année	*year*
artificiel	*artificial*	artifice	*artifice*
conventionnel	*conventional*	convention	*convention*
éternel	*eternal*	éternité	*eternity*
exceptionnel	*exceptional*	exception	*exception*
exponentiel	*exponential*	exposant	*exponent*
fraternel	*fraternal*	frater [LAT.]	*brother*

▶

ADJECTIVE ENDING IN -el/-elle	ENGLISH EQUIVALENT	BASE WORD	ENGLISH EQUIVALENT
◄ habituel	*habitual*	habitude	*habit*
immortel*	*immortal*	[im-] + mort	*not + death*
intellectuel*	*intellectual*	intellect	*intellect*
maternel	*maternal*	mater [LAT.]	*mother*
nutritionnel	*nutritional*	nutrition	*nutrition*
paternel	*paternal*	pater [LAT.]	*father*
présidentiel	*presidential*	président	*president*
professionnel*	*professional*	profession	*profession*
textuel	*textual*	texte	*text*
traditionnel	*traditional*	tradition	*tradition*
transitionnel	*transitional*	transition	*transition*

EXERCICE 7·1

Quelques fait divers *Complete each sentence with the correct form of the appropriate adjective.*

1. Un président se déplace dans une voiture _____.

2. Quelquefois un fils ou une fille hérite de la maison _____.

3. L'étude d'œuvres littéraires est un travail _____.

4. Le dieu mythologique Zeus est _____ contrairement aux humains.

5. La fête du 14 juillet est une fête _____ en France.

6. Un plat de pâtes et de viande est _____.

7. Ce monsieur a une table _____ dans son café favori.

8. J'aime recevoir un message _____ sur mon smartphone.

9. Il y a une période _____ quand le régime de gouvernement doit changer.

10. Le robot et l'ordinateur ont une intelligence _____.

11. L'amitié entre deux hommes est parfois _____.

12. Une faute de grammaire ou d'orthographe est souvent _____.

13. Une négociation entre employés et employeurs est _____ avant un nouveau contrat.

14. Un électricien a généralement un diplôme d'aptitude _____.

15. L'augmentation de salaire est une valeur _____ de l'expérience et de la compétence.

16. Le compositeur Mozart était un enfant _____.

17. Le festival des Arts dramatiques est un événement _____ dans la ville d'Avignon.

18. Notre vie est d'autant plus précieuse qu'elle n'est pas _____.

8 ◆ -if/-ive

MEANING	Referring to, pertaining to
ENGLISH EQUIVALENT	*-ive*
PART OF SPEECH	Adjective
GENDER	Masculine/feminine

A French adjective ending in the suffix **-if** (feminine: **-ive**) usually denotes a characteristic pertaining to attitude, behavior, emotion, or function. The base word is typically a noun. For example, the base word for the adjective **abusif** is the noun **abus** *abuse*, and the suffixed adjective means *abusive*. The regular formation for this type of adjective consists in adding the suffix **-if/-ive** to a noun, as in the previous example, or replacing the **-ion** ending of a noun with the suffix (for example, **attention** yields **attentif**). Slight irregularities may occur, as in **excessif** in the following chart. Since most of these French adjectives have English cognates, they tend to be easily recognized.

ADJECTIVE ENDING IN **-if/-ive**	ENGLISH EQUIVALENT	BASE WORD	ENGLISH EQUIVALENT
abusif	*abusive*	abus	*abuse*
adoptif	*adoptive*	adoption	*adoption*
attentif	*attentive*	attention	*attention*
combatif	*combative*	combat	*combat*
compréhensif	*understanding*	compréhension	*understanding*
émotif	*emotional*	émotion	*emotion*
évasif	*evasive*	évasion	*evasion*
excessif	*excessive*	excès	*excess*
exécutif	*executive*	exécution	*execution*
expansif	*expansive, effusive*	expansion	*expansion*
explosif	*explosive*	explosion	*explosion*
incisif	*incisive*	incision	*incision*
instinctif	*instinctive*	instinct	*instinct*
maladif	*sickly*	maladie	*sickness*
objectif	*objective*	objet	*object*
offensif	*offensive*	offense	*offense*
pensif	*pensive*	pensée	*thought*
persuasif	*persuasive*	persuasion	*persuasion*
productif	*productive*	production	*production*
répulsif	*repulsive*	répulsion	*repulsion*
subjectif	*subjective*	sujet	*subject*

EXERCICE

8·1

À garder ou à congédier? *Indicate whether you would keep or fire each employee, using* **G** *for* **garder** *to keep or* **C** *for* **congédier** *to fire.*

1. _____ Une employée aux manières répulsives

2. _____ Une employée attentive

3. _____ Un employé au regard évasif

4. _____ Un employé à l'intelligence instinctive

5. _____ Une employée à l'odeur offensive

6. _____ Un employé à l'humeur explosive

7. _____ Un employé productif

8. _____ Une employée persuasive

9. _____ Un employé à la curiosité incisive

10. _____ Un employé à l'attitude objective

EXERCICE

8·2

En un mot! *Provide the correct form of the appropriate adjective for each person's description.*

1. Elle pleure constamment; elle s'énerve pour un rien. _____

2. Il contrôle tout d'une manière irrationnelle et excessive. _____

3. Elle est souvent malade. _____

4. Il voit rouge et veut se battre. _____

5. Elle a des réactions basées purement sur ses opinions. _____

6. Il insulte les gens. _____

7. Elle a adopté ses enfants: c'est leur mère. _____

8. Il agit spontanément et suit ses instincts. _____

9. Elle aime réfléchir et rêver. _____

10. Il parle et exprime ses sentiments avec abandon. _____

11. Elle n'est ni têtue ni intolérante. _____

12. Il n'est ni lent ni mou. _____

13. Elle est directrice d'école. _____

9 ◆ -atif/-ative

MEANING	Characterized by a tone/manner
ENGLISH EQUIVALENT	*-ative*
PART OF SPEECH	Adjective
GENDER	Masculine/feminine

A French adjective ending in the suffix **-atif** (feminine: **-ative**) often denotes a characteristic related to tone or manner, in a look, an attitude, or behavior. The base word is generally a noun ending in **-ation**. For example, the base word for the suffixed adjective **accusatif** is the noun **accusation**, and the suffixed adjective denotes an accusatory tone or manner. The regular formation for this type of adjective consists in replacing the **-ation** ending of a noun with the suffix **-atif/-ative**, but there are slightly irregular formations for some words. Since most of these French adjectives have English cognates, they tend to be easily recognized.

ADJECTIVE ENDING IN **-atif/-ative**	ENGLISH EQUIVALENT	BASE WORD	ENGLISH EQUIVALENT
accusatif	*accusatory*	accusation	*accusation*
admiratif	*admiring*	admiration	*admiration*
approximatif	*approximate*	approximation	*approximation*
consultatif	*consultative*	consultation	*consultation*
démonstratif	*demonstrative*	démonstration	*demonstration*
estimatif	*estimated*	estimation	*estimation*
imaginatif	*imaginative*	imagination	*imagination*
informatif	*informative*	information	*information*
narratif	*narrative*	narration	*narration*
rébarbatif	*off-putting*	se rebarber [OLD FR.]	*to push back*
récapitulatif	*summary*	récapitulation	*recapitulation*
récitatif	*recitative*	récitation	*recitation*
représentatif	*representative*	représentation	*representation*
vindicatif	*vindictive*	vindicare [LAT.]	*to punish*

EXERCICE

9·1

Les antonymes *Provide the masculine form of the antonym of each adjective.*

1. Précis _____

2. Naturel/spontané _____

3. Amusant _____

4. Exceptionnel _____

5. Réconciliant/doux _____

6. Critique _____

7. Réservé _____

8. Factuel _____

9. Défensif _____

10. Exécutif _____

Complétez! *Complete each sentence with the correct form of the appropriate adjective.*

1. Ce paragraphe _____ fait le résumé de l'essai.

2. Ce projet est _____ de la qualité de notre travail.

3. Une personne intravertie n'est pas _____ de ses pensées ou de ses sentiments.

4. Cette présentation, avec ses statistiques et ses données, est excellente et

   _____ .

5. La personne soumise à des accusations devient naturellement

   _____ .

6. Une réponse _____ n'est pas suffisante.

7. Une attitude _____ envers d'autres étudiants ou envers les collègues n'est pas appréciée.

10 ◆ -eux/-euse

MEANING	Exhibiting a trait
ENGLISH EQUIVALENT	—
PART OF SPEECH	Adjective
GENDER	Masculine/feminine

A multitude of French adjectives ending in the suffix **-eux** (feminine: **-euse**) denote personality traits. The base word is generally a noun that represents the specific quality or trait. For example, the base word for the suffixed adjective **ambitieux** is the noun **ambition**, and the suffixed adjective denotes an ambitious personality. The regular formation for this type of adjective depends on the type of base noun. If the base noun ends in **-tion** (for example, **ambition**), the **-on** ending is replaced by the suffix **-eux/-euse**. If the base noun ends in **-e**, the ending **-e** becomes **-ieux/-ieuse**; for example, the noun **astuce** yields the adjective **astucieux** *clever*. (An exception is **scrupuleux** *scrupulous*, from **scrupule**.) There are irregular formations with base nouns ending in **-tion**; for example, **affection** yields **affectueux** *affectionate*—the Latin root has the letter **u**, which appears in the French adjective. In other cases, the suffix is simply attached to the base noun; for example, **amour** yields **amoureux** *in love*. Since most of these French adjectives have English cognates, they tend to be easily recognized.

The following chart features adjectives with the suffix **-eux/-euse** that refer to a personality trait.

ADJECTIVE ENDING IN -eux/-euse	ENGLISH EQUIVALENT	BASE WORD	ENGLISH EQUIVALENT
affectueux	*affectionate*	affection (affectus [LAT.])	*affection*
ambitieux	*ambitious*	ambition	*ambition*
amoureux	*in love*	amour	*love*
astucieux	*clever*	astuce	*trick, cleverness*
audacieux	*audacious*	audace	*audacity*
avaricieux	*miserly*	avarice	*miserliness*
consciencieux	*conscientious*	conscience	*conscience*
courageux	*courageous*	courage	*courage*
généreux	*generous*	générosité	*generosity*
heureux	*happy*	heur [ARCHAIC]	*good luck*
impétueux	*impetuous*	impétuosité	*impetuosity*
malheureux	*unhappy*	[mal-] + heureux	*not + happy*
pointilleux	*fastidious*	pointiller	*to contest*
présomptueux	*presumptuous*	présomption	*presumption*
prétentieux	*pretentious*	prétention	*pretentiousness*
respectueux	*respectful*	respect	*respect*
scrupuleux	*scrupulous*	scrupule	*scruple*
soucieux	*worried*	souci	*worry*
valeureux	*brave*	valeur	*value*
vicieux	*vicious*	vice	*vice*

EXERCICE
10·1

Bien ou pas bien? *Indicate whether each quality or trait is good or not good, using* **B** *for* **bien** *good or* **PB** *for* **pas bien** *not good. You do not need to know the individual characters in order to complete this exercise.*

A. Pinnochio

1. _____ Impétueux comme Pinnochio

2. _____ Présomptueux comme le renard

3. _____ Généreux comme Gepetto

4. _____ Valeureux comme Pinnochio quand il sauve Gepetto

5. _____ Heureux comme Pinnochio quand il devient un vrai garçon

B. Bilbo le Hobbit

1. _____ Astucieux comme Gandalf

2. _____ Courageux comme Bilbo

3. _____ Amoureux comme Legolas

4. _____ Affectueux comme Kili

5. _____ Vicieux comme Smaug

C. Harry Potter

1. _____ Courageux comme Harry
2. _____ Consciencieuse comme Hermione
3. _____ Respectueux comme Slytherin
4. _____ Vicieux comme Voldemort
5. _____ Prétentieux comme Draco Malfoy
6. _____ Pointilleuse comme Hermione
7. _____ Scrupuleux comme Hagrid
8. _____ Soucieux comme Neville
9. _____ Suspicieux comme Snape
10. _____ Audacieux comme Dumbledore

 # -eux/-euse

MEANING	Possessing a quality
ENGLISH EQUIVALENT	—
PART OF SPEECH	Adjective
GENDER	Masculine/feminine

Many French adjectives ending in the suffix **-eux** (feminine **-euse**) denote qualities of objects or ideas. The base word is a noun that represents the quality. For example, the base word for **boueux** is the noun **boue** *mud*, and the suffixed adjective denotes a muddy quality or condition. The regular formation for this type of adjective consists in replacing the **-e** ending of the base noun with **-eux/-euse**, as in the previous example, or simply adding the suffix to the noun; for example, **douleur** *pain* yields **douloureux** *painful*. There are, however, slightly irregular formations, especially with Latin roots.

ADJECTIVE ENDING IN -eux/-euse	ENGLISH EQUIVALENT	BASE WORD	ENGLISH EQUIVALENT
avantageux	*advantageous*	avantage	*advantage*
boueux	*muddy*	boue	*mud*
broussailleux	*bushy*	broussaille	*bush*
caillouteux	*rocky*	caillou	*pebble*
cireux	*waxy*	cire	*wax*
copieux	*copious*	copiosus [LAT.]	*copious*
dangereux	*dangerous*	danger	*danger*
douloureux	*painful*	douleur	*pain*
ennuyeux	*boring*	ennui	*boredom*
hasardeux	*hazardous*	hasard	*chance*

Soyons logiques! *Choose the best completion for each sentence.*

1. _____ Une jambe cassée est   a. copieux.

2. _____ Après la pluie ou la neige, la rue est   b. dangereux.

3. _____ A Noël, on a tendance à avoir des repas   c. douloureuse.

4. _____ Une promotion est une situation   d. broussailleux.

5. _____ Un petit sentier de montagne est souvent   e. cireuse.

6. _____ Un jardin abandonné est   f. avantageuse.

7. _____ Sauter d'un avion sans parachute est   g. boueuse.

8. _____ Attendre des heures sans rien faire est   h. hasardeux.

9. _____ Une bougie ou une chandelle est   i. caillouteux.

10. _____ Le destin d'un aventurier est   j. ennuyeux.

ADJECTIVE ENDING IN **-eux/-euse**	ENGLISH EQUIVALENT	BASE WORD	ENGLISH EQUIVALENT
lumineux	*luminous*	luminosus [LAT.]	*bright*
merveilleux	*marvelous*	merveille	*marvel*
monstrueux	*monstrous*	monstre	*monster*
nuageux	*cloudy*	nuage	*cloud*
odieux	*odious*	odium [LAT.]	*hatred*
poreux	*porous*	pore	*pore*
savonneux	*soapy*	savon	*soap*
somptueux	*sumptuous*	sumptuosus [LAT.]	*lavish*
tumultueux	*tumultuous*	tumulte	*tumult*
vertigineux	*dizzy*	vertige	*dizziness*

Complétez! *Complete each sentence with the appropriate choice of adjectives in parentheses.*

1. Le ciel est _____; il va pleuvoir. (nuageux | odieux)

2. Quelle classe _____! Tout le monde parle et fait du bruit. (merveilleuse | tumultueuse)

3. Le bal de Nouvel An est toujours une affaire _____. (somptueuse | odieuse)

4. Le corail au fond de l'océan est _____. (vertigineux | poreux)

5. L'eau du bain est _____. (lumineuse | savonneuse)

6. Le saut d'une grande altitude est _____. (vertigineux | odieux)

7. Dans les contes mythologiques, il y a toujours une créature _____.
   (monstrueuse | poreuse)

8. Le ciel est plein d'étoiles _____. (lumineuses | nuageuses)

 **-in/-ine**

MEANING	Referring to, pertaining to
ENGLISH EQUIVALENT	*-ine*
PART OF SPEECH	Adjective
GENDER	Masculine/feminine

A French adjective ending in the suffix **-in** (feminine: **-ine**) usually denotes a characteristic represented by the base word, which is typically a noun. For example, the base word for **adultérin/ adultérine** is the noun **adultère** *adultery*, and therefore **un enfant adultérin** is *a child born from an adulterous relationship*. The regular formation for this type of adjective consists in replacing the **-e** ending of the base noun with the suffix **-in/-ine**, as in the previous example, or adding the suffix directly to the noun. There are, however, many irregular formations.

Note that **chauvin** can function both as a noun and as an adjective in the following sentences. In **Je n'aime pas les chauvins** *I do not like bigots*, **chauvin** is a noun; in **Quelle attitude chauvine!** *What a bigoted attitude!*, **chauvin** is an adjective. (The related noun **chauvinisme** is explained in No. 63.) Also note that the adjectives **féminin** and **alpin** are related to the nouns **féministe** and **alpiniste**, respectively. (See Nos. 68 and 69 for an explanation of these nouns.) Since most of these French adjectives have English cognates, they tend to be easily recognized.

ADJECTIVE ENDING IN **-in/-ine**	ENGLISH EQUIVALENT	BASE WORD	ENGLISH EQUIVALENT
adultérin	*born from an adulterous relationship*	adultère	*adultery*
alpin	*alpine*	Alpes	*Alps*
anodin	*harmless, mild*	anodynus [LAT.]	*painkiller*
bovin	*bovine*	bœuf	*ox*
canin	*canine*	canis [LAT.]	*dog*
chauvin	*chauvinistic*	Chauvin	*Nicolas Chauvin*
chevalin	*equine*	cheval	*horse*
cristallin	*crystalline*	cristal	*crystal*
estudiantin	*student-related*	étudiant	*student*
féminin	*feminine*	femme	*woman*
masculin	*masculine*	masculinus [LAT.]	*masculine*
salin	*saline*	sal [LAT.]	*salt*

Définitions! *Provide the appropriate feminine adjective to describe each item.*

1. La race du bœuf: la race _____

2. L'espèce du chien: l'espèce _____

3. L'espèce du cheval: l'espèce _____

4. Une attitude extrêmement patriotique: une attitude _____

5. Une personne née d'une union adultère: une personne _____

6. Une rencontre sans importance: une rencontre _____

7. La transparence du cristal: la transparence _____

8. L'injection du sel: l'injection _____

9. Une allure d'homme: une allure _____

10. Une toilette de femme: une toilette _____

11. Une vie d'étudiant: une vie _____

12. Une randonnée dans les Alpes: une randonnée _____

Less frequently, an adjective ending in the suffix **-in/-ine** denotes the origin or nationality of a person. The word may also function as a noun. For example, the noun **un Argentin** denotes a man from Argentina, while **une Argentine** denotes a woman from Argentina; in **une ville argentine** *an Argentine city*, **argentine** is an adjective. These words may also denote faith- or order-based clerical persons, in both adjective and noun functions. The noun **un capucin** denotes a Capuchin monk, while **une capucine** denotes a Capuchin nun; in **l'ordre capucin** *the Capuchin order*, **capucin** is an adjective.

ADJECTIVE ENDING IN **-in/-ine**	ENGLISH EQUIVALENT	BASE WORD	ENGLISH EQUIVALENT
argentin	*Argentine*	Argentine	*Argentina*
bénédictin	*Benedictine*	Benoît	*Benedict* (Catholic saint)
byzantin	*Byzantine*	Byzance	*Byzantium*
capucin	*Capuchin*	capuce	*(monk's) hood*
jacobin	*Jacobin, Dominican*	Jacobus [LAT.]	*St. Jacques* (street in Paris where the Jacobins met; church to which the Dominicans' convent was attached)
périgourdin	*from Périgord*	Périgord	*Périgord* (former French province)
poitevin	*from Poitiers*	Poitiers	*Poitiers* (French town)

Devinez! *Choose the phrase in the second column that corresponds to the sentence in the first column.*

1. _____ Il vient d'une région française.

2. _____ C'est un religieux dans l'ordre des Capucins.

3. _____ C'est une spécialité de la ville de Poitou.

4. _____ C'est un moine dans l'ordre Jacobin.

5. _____ C'est un religieux dans l'ordre des Bénédictins.

6. _____ Il habitait l'ancienne Byzance.

7. _____ Il habite en Argentine.

a. Un frère capucin

b. Un frère bénédictin

c. Un personnage byzantin

d. Un plat poitevin

e. Un touriste argentin

f. Un moine jacobin

g. Un voyageur périgourdin

13 ◆ -ation

MEANING	Action, result of an action, condition
ENGLISH EQUIVALENT	*-ation*
PART OF SPEECH	Noun
GENDER	Feminine

A French noun ending in the suffix **-ation** denotes the action, result of an action, or condition expressed in the base word, which is a verb. For example, **abdication** indicates the action of abdicating or its end result; the base word is the verb **abdiquer** *to abdicate*. The regular formation for this type of noun consists in replacing the **-er** infinitive ending of a verb with **-ation**. Note that some verbs, like **attirer** *to attract* and **arrêter** *to arrest*, undergo minor changes before the suffix is attached. Since nearly all French nouns of this type have English cognates, they are easily recognized.

NOUN ENDING IN -ation	ENGLISH EQUIVALENT	BASE WORD	ENGLISH EQUIVALENT
abdication	*abdication*	abdiquer	*to abdicate*
accusation	*accusation, prosecution*	accuser	*to accuse*
activation	*activation*	activer	*to activate*
agitation	*agitation, excitement*	agiter	*to agitate, excite*
alimentation	*food*	alimenter	*to feed*
annulation	*cancellation*	annuler	*to cancel*
argumentation	*argumentation*	argumenter	*to argue*
arrestation	*arrest*	arrêter	*to arrest*
attraction	*attraction*	attirer	*to attract*
augmentation	*augmentation*	augmenter	*to augment*

EXERCICE 13·1

Le bon mot! *Complete each sentence with the appropriate noun.*

1. L'_____ d'une carte de crédit est nécessaire avant son usage.

2. Une _____ végétarienne est bonne pour la santé.

3. Une _____ de salaire est toujours bien reçue.

4. Une _____ de mariage est difficile à obtenir.

5. Une _____ très longue précède un jugement de justice.

6. Une _____ touristique célèbre est Disney World.

7. L'_____ d'un espion attire l'attention du public.

8. L'_____ d'un dictateur est une bonne nouvelle.

9. L'_____ d'une personne suspecte doit être basée sur des faits.

10. Une grande _____ suit une victoire au football.

NOUN ENDING IN **-ation**	ENGLISH EQUIVALENT	BASE WORD	ENGLISH EQUIVALENT
calcination	*calcination*	calciner	*to burn*
collaboration	*collaboration*	collaborer	*to collaborate*
documentation	*documentation*	documenter	*to document*
émigration	*emigration*	émigrer	*to emigrate*
fracturation	*fracturing*	fracturer	*to fracture*
globalisation	*globalization*	globaliser	*to globalize*
infestation	*infestation*	infester	*to infest*
numérisation	*digitization*	numériser	*to digitize*
palpitation	*palpitation*	palpiter	*to palpitate, beat*
usurpation	*usurpation*	usurper	*to usurp*

EXERCICE 13·2

Vrai ou faux? *Indicate whether each statement is true or false, using* **V** *for* **vrai** *true or* **F** *for* **faux** *false.*

1. _____ Une infestation de termites peut dévaster la structure d'une maison.

2. _____ Les palpitations de cœur sont fréquentes lors d'une grande émotion.

3. _____ La globalisation du commerce est un phénomène américain.

4. _____ L'émigration illégale n'est pas un problème.

5. _____ La calcination des arbres et du terrain après des feux de forêt entraîne des inondations.

6. _____ La fracturation hydraulique entraîne des tremblements de terre.

7. _____ La documentation des sans-papiers est estimative.

8. _____ La numérisation des textes littéraires avance bien.

9. _____ L'usurpation est un procédé légitime.

10. _____ La collaboration entre les membres d'une équipe permet une meilleure performance.

14 ▸ -ateur/-atrice

MEANING	Possessing a quality/purpose
ENGLISH EQUIVALENT	*-ator*
PART OF SPEECH	Adjective, noun
GENDER	Masculine/feminine

An adjective ending in the suffix **-ateur** (feminine: **-atrice**) denotes a special quality or purpose in a person or thing. The base word is almost always a verb that represents the nature of the quality or purpose. For example, the base word for **admirateur** is the verb **admirer**, and the suffixed adjective denotes an admiring quality. Similarly, the purpose of an **accompagnateur** *guide* is indicated in the base verb **accompagner** *to accompany*. The regular formation for this type of adjective consists in replacing the **-er** ending of the base verb with **-ateur/-atrice**. Most irregular formations involve Latin roots or base verbs other than regular **-er** verbs.

The adjectives in the following chart also function as nouns. In the phrase **un regard admirateur** *an admiring look*, **admirateur** is an adjective, but in the sentence **Elle a un admirateur** *She has an admirer*, it is a noun.

ADJECTIVE/NOUN ENDING IN **-ateur/-atrice**	ENGLISH EQUIVALENT	BASE WORD	ENGLISH EQUIVALENT
accompagnateur	*guide, accompanist*	accompagner	*to accompany*
accusateur	*accusing/accuser*	accuser	*to accuse*
admirateur	*admiring/admirer*	admirer	*to admire*
adorateur	*adoring/worshipper*	adorer	*to adore*
appréciateur	*appreciative/estimator*	apprécier	*to appreciate*
approbateur	*approving/superior*	approuver	*to approve*
dénonciateur	*denunciatory/informer*	dénoncer	*to denunciate*
exportateur	*exporting/exporter*	exporter	*to export*
formateur	*formative/trainer*	former	*to train*
médiateur	*intermediary/mediator*	mediator [LAT.]	*mediator*
provocateur	*provocative/agitator*	provoquer	*to provoke*
purificateur	*purifying/purifier*	purifier	*to purify*

Définissez la qualité! *Complete each sentence with the correct form of the appropriate adjective.*

1. L'avocat général lance un regard _____ à l'accusé.

2. Quand il corrige un excellent essai, le professeur a une mine _____ .

3. L'assistant _____ pour ces nouveaux employés est merveilleux.

4. Les accros des nouvelles technologies ont une fascination _____ pour les smartphones.

5. Le rôle du critique gastronomique est un rôle _____ .

6. Dans les régimes tyranniques, un agent _____ va en prison.

7. L'action de la filtration de l'eau est _____ .

8. Une lettre _____ vient d'arriver chez le commissaire de police.

9. L'action _____ de l'ambassadeur a porté des fruits.

10. Le guide _____ de ce groupe d'élève a beaucoup d'expérience.

11. La France n'est pas le seul pays _____ de vin.

12. Un sourire _____ vaut mille compliments.

The words in the following chart function only as nouns. Those ending in the suffix **-ateur** refer to males, while those ending in the suffix **-atrice** refer to females. Note that some masculine **-ateur** forms have, because of their historical contexts, no feminine **-atrice** counterparts; examples are **gladiateur** *gladiator* and **dictateur** *dictator*. In the chart, the base words are verbs except for **avion**, which is the base noun for **aviateur/aviatrice**, and **gladiateur** and **spectateur**, which have Latin roots.

NOUN ENDING IN -ateur/-atrice	ENGLISH EQUIVALENT	BASE WORD	ENGLISH EQUIVALENT
adjudicateur	*adjudicator*	adjuger	*to adjudicate*
aviateur	*aviator*	avion	*plane*
blasphémateur	*blasphemer*	blasphémer	*to blaspheme*
conjurateur	*conjurer*	conjurer	*to conjure*
conspirateur	*conspirator*	conspirer	*to conspire*
démonstrateur	*demonstrator*	démontrer	*to demonstrate*
dictateur	*dictator*	dicter	*to dictate*
évangélisateur	*evangelist*	évangéliser	*to evangelize*
gladiateur	*gladiator*	gladiator [LAT.]	*gladiator*
préparateur	*assistant*	préparer	*to prepare*
présentateur	*presenter*	présenter	*to present*

▶

NOUN ENDING IN -ateur/-atrice	ENGLISH EQUIVALENT	BASE WORD	ENGLISH EQUIVALENT
procurateur	*procurator*	procurer	*to provide*
programmateur	*programmer*	programmer	*to program*
réformateur	*reformer*	réformer	*to reform*
spectateur	*spectator*	spectator [LAT.]	*spectator*
usurpateur	*usurper*	usurper	*to usurp*
utilisateur	*user*	utiliser	*to use*

EXERCICE
14·2

Un rébus *Label each person, using the correct form of the appropriate noun.*

1. Il fait un coup d'état et prend la place d'un monarque. _____

2. Il se battait contre d'autres esclaves sous l'empire romain. _____

3. Elle montre comment utiliser un appareil. _____

4. Elle complote contre les autorités. _____

5. Il regarde une pièce ou un autre type de spectacle. _____

6. Il gouverne avec une autorité absolue. _____

7. Elle programme les logiciels. _____

8. C'est le magistrat d'une cour de justice. _____

9. Elle aide le pharmacien à faire des préparations. _____

10. Il s'inscrit à des blogs ou des réseaux sociaux. _____

11. Il profère des propos injurieux, des blasphèmes. _____

12. Elle est chargée des adjudications. _____

13. Il propose ou mène des réformes. _____

14. Elle prêche l'Évangile. _____

15. Elle pilote des avions. _____

15 ▸ -ition

MEANING	Action, result of an action, condition
ENGLISH EQUIVALENT	*-ition*
PART OF SPEECH	Noun
GENDER	Feminine

A French noun ending in the suffix **-ition** denotes the action, result of an action, or condition expressed in the base word, which is a French or Latin verb. For example, **composition** *composition* indicates the action of **composer** (*composing*) or its result (*the composition*). The regular formation for this type of noun consists in replacing the **-er**, **-ir**, or **-re** infinitive ending of the base verb with the suffix **-ition**. Since nearly all French nouns with the suffix **-ition** have English cognates, they are easily recognized.

NOUN ENDING IN **-ition**	ENGLISH EQUIVALENT	BASE WORD	ENGLISH EQUIVALENT
abolition	*abolition*	abolir	*to abolish*
addition	*addition*	additionner	*to add*
apparition	*(supernatural) appearance*	apparaître	*to appear*
audition	*audition*	auditionner	*to audition*
coalition	*coalition*	coalescere [LAT.]	*to grow together*
composition	*composition*	composer	*to compose*
définition	*definition*	définir	*to define*
démolition	*demolition*	démolir	*to demolish*
disparition	*disappearance*	disparaître	*to disappear*
expédition	*expedition*	expédier	*to expedite*
malnutrition	*malnutrition*	mal + nourrir	*badly + to nourish*
prédisposition	*predisposition*	prédisposer	*to predispose*
proposition	*proposition*	proposer	*to propose*
punition	*punishment*	punir	*to punish*
transition	*transition*	transiter	*to cross, transit*

EXERCICE

15·1

Complétez! *Choose the best completion for each sentence.*

1. _____ Le suffixe d'un mot peut aider

2. _____ Les changements climatiques peuvent causer

3. _____ L'emprisonnement est

4. _____ L'addition de miel

5. _____ Une proposition sérieuse

6. _____ Une audition réussie

7. _____ La coalition des partis politiques

8. _____ Il y a une phase de transition

9. _____ L'abolition de la peine de mort

10. _____ La démolition du mur de Berlin

11. _____ Une prédisposition génétique peut

12. _____ La malnutrition existe surtout

13. _____ La composition de l'équipe

14. _____ Une expédition lunaire

a. se fait par contrat.

b. est en place dans plusieurs états.

c. à comprendre sa définition.

d. une punition.

e. avoir une influence sur la santé physique et psychique.

f. dans les pays pauvres.

g. demande des compétences spécifiques de chacun.

h. a été annulée à cause des conditions atmosphériques.

i. est récompensée par un rôle.

j. sera suivie d'une bonne collaboration politique.

k. rend le gâteau plus sucré.

l. la disparition de certaines espèces animales.

m. a marqué la réunification des deux Allemagnes.

n. après l'élection du nouveau président.

16 ▸ -tion

MEANING	Action, result of an action, condition
ENGLISH EQUIVALENT	*-tion*
PART OF SPEECH	Noun
GENDER	Feminine

A French noun ending in the suffix **-tion** denotes the action, result of an action, or condition expressed in the base word, which is usually a French or Latin verb. For example, **désertion** indicates the action of deserting or its result. The formation of these nouns is diverse due to the variety of base verbs and their irregular patterns. Since most French nouns with the suffix **-tion** have English cognates, they tend to be easily recognized.

NOUN ENDING IN **-tion**	ENGLISH EQUIVALENT	BASE WORD	ENGLISH EQUIVALENT
abduction	*abduction*	abducere [LAT.]	*to lead away*
action	*action*	agir	*to act*
addiction	*addiction*	addictus [LAT.]	*addicted*
affection	*affection*	affectus [LAT.]	*affection*
affliction	*affliction*	affliger	*to afflict*
attraction	*attraction*	attirer	*to attract*
bénédiction	*blessing*	benedictus	*blessed*
collection	*collection*	collectionner	*to collect*
confection	*making, preparation*	conficere [LAT.]	*to compose, prepare*
contradiction	*contradiction*	contredire	*to contradict*

EXERCICE 16·1

Des synonymes! *Match each noun in the first column with its synonym in the second column.*

1. _____ Affection   a. Activité

2. _____ Contradiction   b. Tendresse

3. _____ Addiction   c. Enlèvement

4. _____ Bénédiction   d. Symptôme

5. _____ Abduction   e. Fabrication

6. _____ Collection   f. Grâce

7. _____ Affliction   g. Désaccord

8. _____ Action   h. Amassement

9. _____ Confection   i. Attirance

10. _____ Attraction   j. Dépendance

NOUN ENDING IN **-tion**	ENGLISH EQUIVALENT	BASE WORD	ENGLISH EQUIVALENT
désertion	*desertion*	déserter	*to desert*
dilution	*dilution*	diluer	*to dilute*
élocution	*speech*	[e-] + locutus [LAT.]	*out + spoken*
éviction	*eviction*	evictus [LAT.]	*prevailed over*
induction	*induction*	inductus [LAT.]	*led into*
résolution	*resolution*	résoudre	*to solve*
rétraction	*retraction*	retractus [LAT.]	*withdrawn*
rétribution	*retribution*	rétribuer	*to remunerate*
substitution	*substitution*	substituer	*to substitute*
suggestion	*suggestion*	suggérer	*to suggest*
traduction	*translation*	traduire	*to translate*

EXERCICE
16·2

Action et réaction! *For each set of words, identify the action with* **A** *and the reaction or follow-up with* **R**.

1. _____ Rétribution   _____ Désertion

2. _____ Suggestion   _____ Résolution

3. _____ Éviction   _____ Induction

4. _____ Dilution   _____ Création chimique

5. _____ Élocution   _____ Traduction

6. _____ Substitution   _____ Attribution

17 ◆ -ant/-ante

MEANING	Effect
ENGLISH EQUIVALENT	*-ing*
PART OF SPEECH	Adjective
GENDER	Masculine/feminine

An adjective ending in the suffix **-ant** (feminine: **-ante**) denotes an effect. The base word is a verb that represents the nature of the effect. For example, the base word for the adjective **amusant** is the verb **amuser** *to amuse*, and the suffixed adjective takes on the meaning *amusing, fun*. The most common formation for such an adjective consists in replacing the **-er** infinitive ending of the base verb with the suffix **-ant/-ante**, as in the **amuser ~ amusant** example. With other types of verbs, such as regular **-ir** verbs and irregular verbs, the stem of the base is altered before the suffix is attached. This type of adjective is consistent with the present participle formation of a verb; see Appendix A for information on the use of present participles as adjectives.

ADJECTIVE ENDING IN **-ant/-ante**	ENGLISH EQUIVALENT	BASE WORD	ENGLISH EQUIVALENT
accablant	*oppressive*	accabler	*to oppress*
amusant	*amusing, fun*	amuser	*to amuse*
attirant	*attractive*	attirer	*to attract*
bienfaisant	*beneficial*	bien faire	*to do good*
calmant	*calming*	calmer	*to calm*
charmant	*charming*	charmer	*to charm*
cinglant	*scathing*	cingler	*to whip*
dégradant	*degrading*	dégrader	*to degrade*
éblouissant	*dazzling*	éblouir	*to dazzle*
édifiant	*edifying*	édifier	*to edify*

EXERCICE
17·1

Complétez l'image! *Complete each description with the correct form of the appropriate adjective.*

1. Un succès surprenant et _____

2. Un don généreux et _____

3. Un petit garçon mignon et _____

4. Une blague drôle et _____

5. Une lumière brillante et _____

6. Une chaleur torride et _____

7. Une musique douce et _____

8. Une femme belle et _____

9. Une remarque insultante et _____

10. Un vent froid et _____

ADJECTIVE ENDING IN **-ant/-ante**	ENGLISH EQUIVALENT	BASE WORD	ENGLISH EQUIVALENT
gênant	*embarrassing*	gêner	*to embarrass*
malfaisant	*harmful*	mal faire	*to do harm*
menaçant	*menacing*	menacer	*to threaten*
méprisant	*spiteful*	mépriser	*to despise*
moralisant	*moralizing*	moraliser	*to moralize*
passionnant	*exciting*	passionner	*to excite*
plaisant	*pleasing*	plaire	*to please*
pressant	*pressing*	(se) presser	*to rush*
séduisant	*seductive*	séduire	*to seduce*
terrifiant	*terrifying*	terrifier	*to terrify*

Un conte *To reconstitute this short version of* A Christmas Carol, *fill in each blank with the correct form of the appropriate adjective.*

Il y avait une fois un homme (1) _____ envers les pauvres:

il s'appelait M. Scrooge. Il était (2) _____ et

(3) _____ envers son employé. L'idée de la richesse était

(4) _____ et même (5) _____ pour lui.

Mais un esprit bienfaisant s'est présenté à M. Scrooge. D'abord l'apparition de l'esprit était

(6) _____, mais bientôt M. Scrooge a compris que son obsession

pour la richesse matérielle était (7) _____. Un changement était

(8) _____. La fin de l'histoire se termine en une épiphanie:

elle est (9) _____ et (10) _____.

18 ◆ -ance

MEANING	Action, result of an action, state
ENGLISH EQUIVALENT	*-ance, -ence, -ency*
PART OF SPEECH	Noun
GENDER	Feminine

A French noun ending in the suffix **-ance** denotes the action, result of an action, or state expressed in the base word, which is usually a verb. For example, the base word for **abondance** *abundance* is the verb **abonder** *to abound*, and the suffixed noun indicates the action or result of abounding. A few of these suffixed nouns are derived from adjectives; for example, **aisance** *ease* comes from **aisé** *at ease*. For some nouns ending in the suffix **-ance**, the base word is a Latin word; an example is **ambiance**, from the Latin verb **ambire** *to go around*. Since many of these French words have English cognates, they tend to be easily recognized.

Note that a noun ending in the suffix **-ance** is a variant of the present participle form of a verb, which ends in **-ant** in French and is the equivalent of a verb form ending in *-ing* in English. The present participle of the verb **attirer** *to attract* is **attirant** *attracting*, which can be used as an adjective meaning *attractive*; the noun derived from the verb **attirer** is **attirance** *attraction*. (See No. 17, as well as the section on present participles used as adjectives in Appendix A.)

NOUN ENDING IN **-ance**	ENGLISH EQUIVALENT	BASE WORD	ENGLISH EQUIVALENT
abondance	*abundance*	abonder	*to abound*
aisance	*ease*	aisé	*at ease*
alliance	*alliance*	allier	*to unite*
ambiance	*ambiance*	ambire [LAT.]	*to go around*
assurance	*insurance*	assurer	*to insure*

NOUN ENDING IN -ance	ENGLISH EQUIVALENT	BASE WORD	ENGLISH EQUIVALENT
attirance	*attraction*	attirer	*to attract*
bienveillance	*benevolence*	bien + veiller	*well + to watch over*
condescendance	*condescension*	condescendre	*to condescend*
délinquance	*delinquency*	delinquere [LAT.]	*to fail in duty*
désobéissance	*disobedience*	désobéir	*to disobey*
extravagance	*extravagance*	extra + vagari [LAT.]	*beyond + to wander*
exubérance	*exuberance*	exuberare [LAT.]	*to abound*

EXERCICE
18·1

Vrai ou faux? *Indicate whether each statement is true or false, using* **V** *for* **vrai** *true or* **F** *for* **faux** *false.*

1. _____ La délinquance est souvent une conséquence de la pauvreté.

2. _____ L'extravagance est souvent attribuée aux artistes.

3. _____ La désobéissance d'une enfant n'est jamais punie.

4. _____ L'abondance d'un aliment dans les marchés mène à un prix plus haut.

5. _____ L'alliance entre deux pays rivaux peut mettre fin à une guerre.

6. _____ L'exubérance des enfants est maladive.

7. _____ L'aisance avec laquelle certains athlètes performent est admirable.

8. _____ La condescendance est mal vue.

9. _____ L'ambiance dans une salle de classe devrait être amicale.

10. _____ La bienveillance des grands-parents envers les petits est ennuyeuse.

11. _____ L'attirance physique entre deux personnes vient de leurs sentiments.

12. _____ L'assurance médicale n'est jamais nécessaire.

NOUN ENDING IN -ance	ENGLISH EQUIVALENT	BASE WORD	ENGLISH EQUIVALENT
imprévoyance	*lack of foresight*	[im-] + prévoir	*not + to foresee*
insignifiance	*insignificance*	[in-] + signifier	*not + to signify*
malveillance	*malevolence*	mal + veiller	*badly + to watch over*
mésalliance	*misalliance*	[més-] + allier	*wrongly + to unite*
ordonnance	*prescription*	ordonner	*to prescribe*
persévérance	*perseverance*	persévérer	*to persevere*
reconnaissance	*recognition, gratitude*	reconnaître	*to recognize*
ressemblance	*resemblance*	ressembler	*to resemble*
subsistance	*subsistence*	subsister	*to subsist*
tendance	*tendency*	tendre	*to extend*
tolérance	*tolerance*	tolérer	*to tolerate*
vigilance	*vigilance*	vigilare [LAT.]	*to be watchful*

Des synonymes! *Match each noun in the first column with its synonym in the second column.*

1. _____ Imprévoyance   a. Méchanceté

2. _____ Insignifiance   b. Gratitude

3. _____ Malveillance   c. Similitude

4. _____ Mésalliance   d. Persistance

5. _____ Ordonnance   e. Insouciance

6. _____ Persévérance   f. Mauvaise union

7. _____ Reconnaissance   g. Respect

8. _____ Ressemblance   h. Alimentation

9. _____ Subsistance   i. Prescription

10. _____ Tendance   j. Attention

11. _____ Tolérance   k. Futilité

12. _____ Vigilance   l. Inclination

19 ▸ -ité

MEANING	State, condition
ENGLISH EQUIVALENT	*-ity*
PART OF SPEECH	Noun
GENDER	Feminine

A French noun ending in the suffix **-ité** denotes the state or condition expressed in the base word, which is an adjective. For example, the base word for the noun **absurdité** *absurdity* is the adjective **absurde**, and the suffixed noun denotes an absurd state. A regular formation for this type of noun consists in replacing the **-e** ending of an adjective with the suffix, as in the **absurde ~ absurdité** example, or adding the suffix directly to an adjective that ends in **-al**; for example, the adjective **banal** yields the noun **banalité**. If the base adjective ends in **-if**, the suffix is attached to the adjective's feminine form; thus, the feminine form of **agressif**—**agressive**—yields the noun **agressivité**. Since most French nouns with this suffix have English cognates, they tend to be easily recognized.

NOUN ENDING IN **-ité**	ENGLISH EQUIVALENT	BASE WORD	ENGLISH EQUIVALENT
absurdité	*absurdity*	absurde	*absurd*
acidité	*acidity*	acide	*acid*
affinité	*affinity*	affinis [LAT.]	*connected*
agilité	*agility*	agile	*agile*
agressivité	*aggressiveness*	agressif/agressive	*aggressive*

▸

NOUN ENDING IN **-ité**	ENGLISH EQUIVALENT	BASE WORD	ENGLISH EQUIVALENT
austérité	*austerity*	austère	*austere*
banalité	*banality*	banal	*banal*
collégialité	*collegiality*	collégial	*collegial*
efficacité	*efficiency, efficacy*	efficace	*efficient*
égalité	*equality*	égal	*equal*

EXERCICE 19·1

Des antonymes! *Provide the antonym for each noun.*

1. Extravagance _____

2. Inégalité _____

3. Passivité _____

4. Alacrité _____

5. Improductivité _____

6. Douceur _____

7. Bon sens _____

8. Maladresse _____

9. Individualisme _____

10. Absence de rapport _____

NOUN ENDING IN **-ité**	ENGLISH EQUIVALENT	BASE WORD	ENGLISH EQUIVALENT
énormité	*enormity*	énorme	*enormous*
exclusivité	*exclusivity*	exclusif/exclusive	*exclusive*
générosité	*generosity*	généreux	*generous*
impétuosité	*impetuosity*	impétueux	*impetuous*
lucidité	*lucidity*	lucide	*lucid*
médiocrité	*mediocrity*	médiocre	*mediocre*
moralité	*morality*	moral	*moral*
ténacité	*tenacity*	tenace	*tenacious*
unité	*unity*	un	*one*
vulgarité	*vulgarity*	vulgaire	*vulgar*

EXERCICE 19·2

Complétez! *Complete each sentence with the appropriate noun.*

1. Les philanthropes font preuve de _____ envers les individus dans le besoin.

2. L'_____ peut faire faire des choses regrettables.

3. La _____ en public est choquante.

4. Il est difficile d'imaginer l'_____ de l'univers.

5. La nouvelle collection va être présentée en _____ dans notre boutique.

6. Il y a des témoins de _____ pour l'accusé pendant le procès.

7. Il faut toujours prendre des décisions importantes en toute _____.

8. La _____ au travail n'ouvre pas beaucoup de portes à de bons emplois.

9. L'_____ monétaire européenne est l'euro.

10. La _____ face aux obstacles montre la force de caractère d'une personne.

◆ 20 ◆ -bilité

MEANING	Possibility of a state/condition
ENGLISH EQUIVALENT	*-bility*
PART OF SPEECH	Noun
GENDER	Feminine

A French noun ending in the suffix -**bilité** denotes the hypothetical but realizable state or condition expressed in the base word, which is an adjective ending in -**able** or -**ible**. For example, the base word for the noun **accessibilité** *accessibility* is the adjective **accessible**. The regular formation for these nouns consists in replacing the ending -**ble** of the base adjective with the suffix -**bilité**. (For more information on adjectives ending in -**able** or -**ible**, see Nos. 21 and 22.) Since many nouns ending in this suffix have English cognates, they tend to be easily recognized.

NOUN ENDING IN -**bilité**	ENGLISH EQUIVALENT	BASE WORD	ENGLISH EQUIVALENT
acceptabilité	*acceptability*	acceptable	*acceptable*
accessibilité	*accessibility*	accessible	*accessible*
admissibilité	*admissibility*	admissible	*admissible*
amabilité	*amiability*	aimable	*amiable*
audibilité	*audibility*	audible	*audible*
comestibilité	*edibility*	comestible	*edible*
digestibilité	*digestibility*	digestible	*digestible*
disponibilité	*availability*	disponible	*available*
flexibilité	*flexibility*	flexible	*flexible*
imperméabilité	*impermeability*	imperméable	*impermeable*
imprévisibilité	*unpredictability*	imprévisible	*unpredictable*
insatiabilité	*insatiability*	insatiable	*insatiable*

Complétez! *Choose the best completion for each sentence.*

1. _____ En gymnastique, il faut

2. _____ Un gros pourboire à un serveur

3. _____ Il y a une condition d'admissibilité

4. _____ Ce patient ne mange pas; il a des problèmes

5. _____ Il faut vérifier la disponibilité

6. _____ L'imperméabilité des chaussures

7. _____ L'imprévisibilité du temps

8. _____ L'accessibilité du sommet de la montagne

9. _____ L'audibilité est améliorée

10. _____ Une insatiabilité constante peut causer

11. _____ La comestibilité des aliments en conserve

12. _____ L'acceptabilité de cette offre d'emploi

a. dépend des conditions météorologiques.

b. rend difficile la planification des activités.

c. par les haut-parleurs.

d. de digestibilité.

e. à ce club.

f. l'obésité.

g. est une marque d'amabilité et de gratitude.

h. beaucoup de flexibilité.

i. dépend de leur date d'expiration.

j. dépend de la rémunération.

k. des chambres dans cet hôtel.

l. est une nécessité en montagne.

NOUN ENDING IN **-bilité**	ENGLISH EQUIVALENT	BASE WORD	ENGLISH EQUIVALENT
inséparabilité	*inseparability*	inséparable	*inseparable*
instabilité	*instability*	instable	*unstable*
invisibilité	*invisibility*	invisible	*invisible*
irritabilité	*irritability*	irritable	*irritable*
perfectibilité	*perfectibility*	perfectible	*perfectible*
possibilité	*possibility*	possible	*possible*
probabilité	*probability*	probable	*probable*
respectabilité	*respectability*	respectable	*respectable*
réversibilité	*reversibility*	réversible	*reversible*
sociabilité	*sociability*	sociable	*sociable*
susceptibilité	*susceptibility*	susceptible	*susceptible*
vulnérabilité	*vulnerability*	vulnérable	*vulnerable*

Des synonymes! *Provide the noun that is synonymous with each phrase.*

1. Tendance à se mettre en colère _____

2. Possibilité de rendre parfait _____

3. Capacité à vivre en société   _____

4. Honorabilité   _____

5. Sensibilité   _____

6. Manque de constance   _____

7. Option   _____

8. Grande possibilité   _____

9. Effet de ne rien voir   _____

10. Qui admet un retour en arrière   _____

11. État qui n'admet pas la séparation   _____

12. État de faiblesse   _____

21 ◆ -able

MEANING	Likely to be, worthy of being
ENGLISH EQUIVALENT	-able
PART OF SPEECH	Adjective
GENDER	Masculine/feminine

Many French adjectives ending in the suffix **-able** denote the likeliness or worthiness of an occurrence or condition being realized. The base word is a verb that represents what is likely or worthy. For example, the base word for **adorable** is the verb **adorer,** and the suffixed adjective denotes that something or someone is likely to be adored or worthy of being adored. The regular formation for this type of adjective consists in replacing the **-er** ending of the base verb with **-able**. These adjectives have the same ending in the masculine and feminine forms. Since many of them have English cognates, they tend to be easily recognized. (See No. 20 for nouns related to these adjectives.)

ADJECTIVE ENDING IN **-able**	ENGLISH EQUIVALENT	BASE WORD	ENGLISH EQUIVALENT
abordable	*approachable*	aborder	*to approach*
admirable	*admirable*	admirer	*to admire*
adorable	*adorable*	adorer	*to adore*
appréciable	*considerable*	apprécier	*to appreciate*
blâmable	*blameworthy*	blâmer	*to blame*
buvable	*drinkable*	boire	*to drink*
consommable	*consumable*	consommer	*to consume*
désirable	*desirable*	désirer	*to desire*
détestable	*detestable*	détester	*to detest*
discutable	*debatable*	discuter	*to discuss*
durable	*durable*	durer	*to last*
fiable	*trustworthy*	se fier	*to trust*

Qu'ont-ils en commun? *Provide two adjectives to describe what the three items in each line have in common.*

1. Picasso, Renoir, Monet _____ _____

2. Les voleurs, les assassins, les meurtriers _____ _____

3. Les jolis bébés, les beaux bijoux, les belles coiffures _____ _____

4. Les films, les livres, les pièces _____ _____

5. Le vin, la bière, la limonade _____ _____

6. Un bon mariage, une bonne relation, un rapport amoureux _____ _____

In the following chart, the prefixes **im-** and **in-** give the adjectives ending in **-able** the opposite meaning of feasibility. For example, the base word for the adjective **impensable** is the verb **penser** *to think*; with its prefix **im-** *not* and suffix **-able**, the adjective has the meaning *unthinkable*. (See No. 120 for more information about the prefixes **im-** and **in-** meaning *not*.)

ADJECTIVE ENDING IN **-able**	ENGLISH EQUIVALENT	BASE WORD	ENGLISH EQUIVALENT
imbuvable	*undrinkable*	[im-] + boire	*not + to drink*
immangeable	*inedible*	[im-] + manger	*not + to eat*
impensable	*unthinkable*	[im-] + penser	*not + to think*
imprésentable	*unpresentable*	[im-] + présenter	*not + to present*
incassable	*unbreakable*	[in-] + casser	*not + to break*
incomparable	*incomparable*	[in-] + comparer	*not + to compare*
incontestable	*incontestable*	[in-] + contester	*not + to contest*
indiscernable	*indiscernible*	[in-] + discerner	*not + to discern*
indispensable	*indispensable*	[in-] + dispenser	*not + to dispense*
ingonflable	*not inflatable*	[in-] + gonfler	*not + to inflate*
inimaginable	*unimaginable*	[in-] + imaginer	*not + to imagine*
invariable	*invariable*	[in-] + varier	*not + to vary*

Quelle est la caractéristique? *Provide the adjective(s) characteristic of each item.*

1. Une marmite en fer _____

2. La forme d'un adverbe _____

3. Un monde en paix _____ _____

4. Un ballon troué _____

5. Une boisson amère _____

6. L'eau propre   _____

7. Une baguette d'il y a quinze jours   _____

8. Un discours exceptionnel   _____

9. Une vérité prouvée   _____

10. Une idée terriblement obscène et immorale   _____   _____

11. Un objet informe à travers la pluie et le brouillard   _____

12. Mal soigné, mal habillé, dépeigné, malodorant   _____

Sometimes, an adjective ending in the suffix **-able** denotes a realized state or condition. The base word is a Latin root. Since most of these French adjectives have English cognates, they tend to be easily recognized.

ADJECTIVE ENDING IN -able	ENGLISH EQUIVALENT	BASE WORD	ENGLISH EQUIVALENT
abominable	*abominable*	abominabilis [LAT.]	*abominable*
affable	*affable*	affabilis [LAT.]	*affable*
capable	*capable*	capabilis [LAT.]	*capable*
impeccable	*impeccable*	impeccabilis [LAT.]	*impeccable*
probable	*probable*	probabilis [LAT.]	*probable*
stable	*stable*	stabilis [LAT.]	*stable*
serviable	*helpful*	servilis [LAT.]	*servile*
variable	*variable*	variabilis [LAT.]	*variable*

22 ▸ -ible

MEANING	Feasible
ENGLISH EQUIVALENT	*-ible*
PART OF SPEECH	Adjective
GENDER	Masculine/feminine

Many French adjectives ending in the suffix **-ible** denote that something is feasible or can be done. The base word is a verb that represents what can be done. For example, the base word for the adjective **lisible** is the verb **lire** *to read*, and the suffixed adjective means *readable*. Note that the prefix **in-** gives these adjectives the opposite meaning of feasibility. The adjective **invincible** has for its base word the verb **vaincre** *to vanquish*; with its prefix **in-** and suffix **-ible**, the adjective has the meaning *invincible*. (See No. 120 for more information about the prefixes **im-** and **in-** meaning *not*.) The regular formation for this type of adjective consists in replacing the **-er** ending of the base verb with **-ible**; most of these adjectives, however, are formed irregularly. These adjectives have the same ending in the masculine and feminine forms. Since many of them have English cognates, they tend to be easily recognized. (See No. 20 for nouns related to these adjectives.)

ADJECTIVE ENDING IN -ible	ENGLISH EQUIVALENT	BASE WORD	ENGLISH EQUIVALENT
accessible	*accessible*	accéder	*to access*
admissible	*admissible*	admettre	*to admit*
audible	*audible*	audire [LAT.]	*to hear*
combustible	*combustible*	comburere [LAT.]	*to burn*
comestible	*edible*	comesse [LAT.]	*to consume*
compatible	*compatible*	compati [LAT.]	*to suffer with*
compréhensible	*comprehensible*	comprendre	*to comprehend*
corrigible	*correctable*	corriger	*to correct*
crédible	*credible*	croire	*to believe*
destructible	*destructible*	détruire	*to destroy*
diffusible	*diffusible*	diffuser	*to diffuse, broadcast*
disponible	*available*	disposer	*to dispose*

EXERCICE

22·1

Qu'ont-ils en commun? *Provide two adjectives to describe what the two items in each line have in common.*

1. Une phrase correcte et bien écrite, un livre simple et bien organisé

   _____ _____

2. Une voix claire et forte, une chanson *a capella*

   _____ _____

3. Un but raisonnable, une éducation de base

   _____ _____

4. Une bûche, un arbre

   _____ _____

5. Une promesse bien intentionnée, un documentaire avec des sources fiables

   _____ _____

6. Un sandwich frais au frigo, un poulet rôti prêt à être mangé

   _____ _____

ADJECTIVE ENDING IN -ible	ENGLISH EQUIVALENT	BASE WORD	ENGLISH EQUIVALENT
invincible	*invincible*	[in-] + vaincre	*not + to conquer*
irréductible	*irreducible*	[ir-] + réduire	*not + to reduce*
lisible	*readable*	lire	*to read*
ostensible	*conspicuous*	ostensibilis [LAT.]	*conspicuous*
paisible	*peaceful*	paix	*peace*
pénible	*painful*	poenalis [LAT.]	*punitive*
possible	*possible*	possibilis [LAT.]	*possible*

ADJECTIVE ENDING IN **-ible**	ENGLISH EQUIVALENT	BASE WORD	ENGLISH EQUIVALENT
réversible	*reversible*	reversibilis [LAT.]	*reversible*
sensible	*sensitive*	sensibilis [LAT.]	*perceptible*
tangible	*tangible*	tangere [LAT.]	*to touch*
traduisible	*translatable*	traduire	*to translate*
visible	*visible*	voir	*to see*

EXERCICE
22·2

Quelle est la caractéristique? *Provide the adjective characteristic of each item.*

1. Facilement ému _____

2. Difficile à supporter _____

3. Qui se voit immédiatement _____

4. Qu'on peut lire _____

5. Qu'on peut toucher _____

6. Qu'on peut traduire _____

7. Qu'on peut voir _____

8. Calme, tranquille _____

9. Qui peut se passer _____

10. Qu'on peut retourner ou remettre à son état d'origine _____

11. Qu'on ne peut pas changer ou diminuer _____

12. Qu'on ne peut pas vaincre _____

23 ◆ -té

MEANING	Abstract concept, state, condition
ENGLISH EQUIVALENT	*-ty*
PART OF SPEECH	Noun
GENDER	Feminine

A French noun ending in the suffix **-té** denotes the abstract state or quality expressed in the base word, which is usually an adjective. The regular formation for these nouns consists in adding the suffix **-té** to the masculine form of the base adjective; for example, the adjective **beau** *beautiful* yields **beauté** *beauty.* A notable exception is the noun **naïveté**, which is based on the feminine form, **naïve**, of the adjective **naïf**. Some nouns ending in **-té** are derived from Latin nouns; in this case, the Latin ending **-tas** becomes the suffix **-té** in the French noun.

NOUN ENDING IN -té	ENGLISH EQUIVALENT	BASE WORD	ENGLISH EQUIVALENT
beauté	*beauty*	beau	*beautiful*
bonté	*goodness*	bon	*good*
chasteté	*chastity*	chaste	*chaste*
cruauté	*cruelty*	cruel	*cruel*
ébriété	*intoxication*	ebrietas [LAT.]	*intoxication*
équité	*equity, fairness*	aequitas [LAT.]	*justice*
fermeté	*firmness*	ferme	*firm*
fierté	*pride*	fier	*proud*
honnêteté	*honesty*	honnête	*honest*
liberté	*liberty*	libre	*free*

Quel concept est évoqué? *Provide the noun associated with the two items in each line.*

1. Un prêtre, un ministre _____

2. Une œuvre d'art, un modèle _____

3. Un professeur strict, une mère exigeante _____

4. Un pays démocratique, la statue de Marianne _____

5. La jeune fille du Moyen Âge, la virginité _____

6. La belle-mère de Cendrillon, l'oppression _____

7. Abus d'alcool, intoxication _____

8. La justice, le respect de tous _____

9. La charité, les dons _____

10. Le patriotisme, l'amour-propre _____

NOUN ENDING IN -té	ENGLISH EQUIVALENT	BASE WORD	ENGLISH EQUIVALENT
majesté	*majesty*	majestas [LAT.]	*majesty*
méchanceté	*meanness*	méchant	*mean*
naïveté	*naiveté*	naïf/naïve	*naive*
parenté	*kinship*	parent	*relative, kin*
piété	*piety*	pietas [LAT.]	*piety*
propreté	*cleanliness*	propre	*clean*
santé	*health*	sain	*healthy*
variété	*variety*	varié	*varied*
vérité	*truth*	veritas [LAT.]	*truth*
volupté	*sensual pleasure*	voluptas [LAT.]	*pleasure*

Complétez! *Choose the best completion for each sentence.*

1. _____ Respecter les règles de l'hygiène   a. de naïveté.

2. _____ Un lien de parenté était   b. est une preuve de méchanceté.

3. _____ Un régime alimentaire équilibré   c. aux saints.

4. _____ On parle parfois de la majesté   d. de bien-être.

5. _____ La piété est surtout attribuée   e. demande une variété d'aliments.

6. _____ On dit que la vérité sort   f. pour rester en bonne santé.

7. _____ Il faut faire beaucoup d'exercice   g. de la bouche des enfants.

8. _____ La volupté est un sentiment   h. des grands arbres des parcs naturels.

9. _____ L'innocence est souvent synonyme   i. demande la propreté.

10. _____ Faire du mal aux êtres faibles   j. important dans les familles royales.

24 ◆ -ie

MEANING	State, genre, field
ENGLISH EQUIVALENT	-y
PART OF SPEECH	Noun
GENDER	Feminine

The suffix **-ie** is extremely common in French nouns. A French noun ending in the suffix -ie can denote a state of political turmoil (**anarchie** *anarchy*), a state or condition (**agonie** *pain* and **allergie** *allergy*), a genre (**comédie** *comedy*), or a field (**astronomie** *study of stars*). Many of these nouns have related adjectives ending in **-ique** (see Nos. 25 and 26); these are indicated by an asterisk (*) in the following charts. The base words for most of the suffixed nouns are Latin and Greek words. Since these French nouns have English cognates, they are easily recognized. (See Nos. 27 and 31 for related nouns ending in **-sie** (state or condition) and **-tie** (state or skill), respectively.)

NOUN ENDING IN -ie	ENGLISH EQUIVALENT	BASE WORD	ENGLISH EQUIVALENT
agonie	*agony*	agonia [GRK.]	*struggle*
alchimie	*alchemy*	alchemia [LAT./ARABIC]	*study of black earth*
allergie*	*allergy*	allos + ergon [GRK.]	*other + action/force*
anarchie*	*anarchy*	anarchia [GRK.]	*lack of a leader*
anatomie*	*anatomy*	anatomia [LAT.]	*dissection*
anémie*	*anemia*	[an-] + haima [GRK.]	*not + blood*
anomalie	*anomaly*	anomalia [GRK.]	*irregularity*
anorexie*	*anorexia*	anorexia [GRK.]	*anorexia*
apoplexie*	*apoplexy*	apoplexia [LAT.]	*apoplexy*
astrologie*	*astrology*	astrologia [LAT.]	*astronomy*

EXERCICE 24·1

Vrai ou faux? *Indicate whether each statement is true or false, using* **V** *for* **vrai** *true or* **F** *for* **faux** *false.*

1. _____ L'agonie est une grande souffrance.

2. _____ Certaines maladies proviennent d'une anomalie génétique.

3. _____ L'anémie provient d'un manque d'alcool.

4. _____ L'alchimie est une science du futur.

5. _____ L'anorexie est un trouble de l'alimentation.

6. _____ L'anatomie des oiseaux est semblable à l'anatomie humaine.

7. _____ La boule de cristal et les cartes sont des instruments en astrologie.

8. _____ L'anarchie mène à l'ordre civil.

9. _____ Beaucoup de gens ont une allergie aux cacahuètes.

10. _____ Une crise d'apoplexie peut être due au stress.

NOUN ENDING IN -ie	ENGLISH EQUIVALENT	BASE WORD	ENGLISH EQUIVALENT
bigamie	*bigamy*	bigamia [LAT.]	*bigamy*
biologie*	*biology*	bios + logia [GRK.]	*life + study*
chimie*	*chemistry*	alchemia [LAT./ARABIC]	*study of black earth*
comédie	*comedy*	comoedia [LAT.]	*comedy*
décennie	*decade*	decem + annus [LAT.]	*ten + year*
dynastie*	*dynasty*	dynasteia [GRK.]	*dynasty*
économie*	*economy*	oeconomia [LAT.]	*economy*
géographie*	*geography*	geographia [LAT.]	*study of the earth*
tragédie*	*tragedy*	tragoedia [LAT.]	*tragedy*
vilenie	*vileness*	vilain	*vile*

EXERCICE 24·2

Un rébus *Provide the noun that describes each item.*

1. Celle de la famille autrichienne des Habsburg _____

2. Quand elle est bonne, les gens ont des emplois _____

3. L'étude de la terre _____

4. Un acte méprisable et cruel _____

5. Une période de dix ans _____

6. Une pièce qui doit amuser et divertir _____

7. Science des molécules _____

8. Pièce au dénouement dramatique   _____

9. État de la personne mariée à deux personnes   _____

10. Science de la vie   _____

 **-ique**

MEANING	Pertaining to a field/skill
ENGLISH EQUIVALENT	*-ic, -ical*
PART OF SPEECH	Adjective
GENDER	Masculine/feminine

A French adjective ending in the suffix **-ique** usually denotes a characteristic inherent in a field or skill, which is represented by the base word. For example, the adjective **acrobatique** describes a person or thing that has the characteristics one would expect to find in the area of **acrobatie** *acrobatics*. The regular formation for this type of adjective consists in replacing the **-ie** ending of the base noun with the suffix **-ique**. Adjectives ending in **-ique** have the same ending in the masculine and feminine forms. Since most of them have English cognates, they tend to be easily recognized. (See Nos. 24 and 31 for related nouns ending in **-ie** and **-tie**, respectively.)

ADJECTIVE ENDING IN **-ique**	ENGLISH EQUIVALENT	BASE WORD	ENGLISH EQUIVALENT
acrobatique	*acrobatic*	acrobatie	*acrobatics*
anatomique	*anatomical*	anatomie	*anatomy*
anorexique	*anorexic*	anorexie	*anorexia*
biologique	*biological*	biologie	*biology*
calligraphique	*calligraphic*	calligraphie	*calligraphy*
comique	*comic*	comédie	*comedy*
cosmique	*cosmic*	kosmos [GRK.]	*universe*
dynastique	*dynastic*	dynastie	*dynasty*
économique	*economical*	économie	*economy*
endémique	*endemic*	endémie	*endemic disease*
extatique	*ecstatic*	extase	*ecstasy*
gastronomique	*gastronomical*	gastronomie	*gastronomy*

EXERCICE
25·1

Complétez! *Complete each sentence with the correct form of the appropriate adjective.*

1. L'écriture est un exercice _____ .

2. La grippe est une affliction _____ .

3. Une farce a un effet _____ .

4. La boulimie est liée au trouble _____ .

5. Le chômage est lié à une crise _____.

6. Les empires chinois sont des exemples de tradition _____.

7. Il y a beaucoup de critiques _____ en France et aux États-Unis.

8. Un professionnel de la santé doit avoir des connaissances _____.

9. Le tissu humain est une matière _____.

10. Une très grande joie produit un effet _____.

11. On voit des changements climatiques à l'échelle _____.

12. Les gymnastes olympiques atteignent la perfection _____.

ADJECTIVE ENDING IN -ique	ENGLISH EQUIVALENT	BASE WORD	ENGLISH EQUIVALENT
géométrique	*geometric*	géométrie	*geometry*
informatique	*computing*	information	*information, data*
ludique	*playful*	ludus [LAT.]	*play*
magique	*magical*	magie	*magic*
pathologique	*pathological*	pathologie	*pathology*
philosophique	*philosophical*	philosophie	*philosophy*
technologique	*technological*	technologie	*technology*
théologique	*theological*	théologie	*theology*
tragique	*tragic*	tragédie	*tragedy*
zoologique	*zoological*	zoologie	*zoology*

EXERCICE
25·2

Quelle caractéristique est évoquée? *Provide the adjective associated with the two items in each line.*

1. L'effet d'un jeu, l'effet d'un puzzle _____

2. Aspect d'un ordinateur, but d'un logiciel _____

3. Triste, morbide _____

4. Effet de l'enchantement, effet d'une illusion _____

5. Aspects d'un carré, aspect d'un rectangle _____

6. Pensée de Descartes, écrits de Pascal _____

7. Pensées de Luther, activités de Calvin _____

8. Expositions, présentations d'animaux exotiques _____

9. La maladie, les afflictions psychiques _____

10. Les inventions informatiques, les progrès robotiques _____

26 ◆ -ique

MEANING	Possessing a quality/belief
ENGLISH EQUIVALENT	*-ic*
PART OF SPEECH	Adjective
GENDER	Masculine/feminine

Many French adjectives ending in the suffix **-ique** denote a particular quality or a personal belief. For example, the base word for **agnostique** is the Greek prefix **a-** *not* plus the Greek noun **gnosis** *knowledge*, and the suffixed adjective describes a person who claims no knowledge of the existence or nonexistence of a divine power. Similarly, the base word for **lunatique** is the French noun **lune** *moon*, and the suffixed adjective describes a person whose mood is affected by the phases of the moon. These adjectives have the same ending in the masculine and feminine forms. Since most of them have English cognates, they tend to be easily recognized. (See Nos. 31 (**-tie**) and 63 and 64 (**-isme**) for related nouns.) Some of the adjectives in the following chart also function as masculine and feminine nouns; these are indicated by an asterisk (*). In the sentence **C'est un agnostique** *He is an agnostic*, **agnostique** is a noun, but in the sentence **C'est une perspective agnostique** *It is an agnostic perspective*, **agnostique** is an adjective.

ADJECTIVE ENDING IN **-ique**	ENGLISH EQUIVALENT	BASE WORD	ENGLISH EQUIVALENT
aéronautique*	*aeronautical*	aéronaute	*balloonist*
agnostique*	*agnostic*	[a-] + gnosis [GRK.]	*not + knowledge*
antagonique	*antagonistic*	[ant-] + agon [GRK.]	*against + struggle*
antipathique	*disagreeable*	antipathie	*antipathy*
apathique	*apathetic*	apathie	*apathy*
fanatique*	*fanatic*	fanaticus [LAT.]	*fanatic*
linguistique	*linguistic*	linguiste	*linguist*
lunatique*	*lunatic*	lune	*moon*
magnifique*	*magnificent*	magnificence	*magnificence*
photogénique	*photogenic*	photo + gène	*photo + productive*
romantique*	*romantic*	romance	*romance*
stoïque*	*stoic*	stoicus [LAT.]	*stoic*
sympathique	*likeable*	sympathie	*sympathy*

EXERCICE

26·1

Quelle caractéristique est évoquée? *Provide the adjective associated with the two items in each line.*

1. Changements d'humeur, caprices _____

2. Faiblesse, passiveté _____

3. Passion, obsession _____

4. Photographiable, belle apparence _____

5. Avions, pilotage _____

6. Sans croyance, rejet de la religion   _____

7. Sentiments, sensibilité   _____

8. Superbe, somptueux   _____

9. Courageux, ferme   _____

10. Aversion, répulsion   _____

11. Opposition, contradiction   _____

12. Compréhension d'autrui, compatibilité   _____

13. Langue, langage   _____

 **-sie**

MEANING	State, condition
ENGLISH EQUIVALENT	*-sia, -sy*
PART OF SPEECH	Noun
GENDER	Feminine

A French noun ending in the suffix **-sie** denotes a state or condition. For example, the noun **amnésie** *amnesia* denotes a state of forgetfulness. Many of the nouns with this suffix are related to adjectives ending in **-ique**: **amnésie**, **anesthésie**, **antisepsie**, **hérésie**, and **télékinésie**. (See Nos. 25 and 26 for more information on these adjectives.) Since the French nouns have English cognates, they are easily recognized.

The base words for the nouns in the following chart are Greek words. Some ancient Greek words became French prefixes long ago; for example, the Greek noun **bios** *life* is the prefix **bio-** in many French words. In these cases, returning to the ancient Greek root helps explain the meaning of the French noun.

NOUN ENDING IN **-sie**	ENGLISH EQUIVALENT	BASE WORD	ENGLISH EQUIVALENT
amnésie	*amnesia*	amnesia [GRK.]	*forgetfulness*
anesthésie	*anesthesia*	[an-] + aisthesis [GRK.]	*no + sensation*
antisepsie	*antisepsis*	[anti-] + sepsis [GRK.]	*against + putrefaction*
autopsie	*autopsy*	autopsia [GRK.]	*seeing with one's own eyes*
biopsie	*biopsy*	bios + ops [GRK.]	*life + eye*
euthanasie	*euthanasia*	[eu-] + thanatos [GRK.]	*good + death*
hérésie	*heresy*	hairesis [GRK.]	*option*
hypocrisie	*hypocrisy*	hypokrisis [GRK.]	*stage acting, pretense*
synesthésie	*synesthesia*	[syn-] + aisthesis [GRK.]	*together + sensation*
télékinésie	*telekinesis*	tele + kinesis [GRK.]	*at a distance + movement*

EXERCICE

27·1

Vrai ou faux? *Indicate whether each statement is true or false, using* **V** *for* **vrai** *true or* **F** *for* **faux** *false.*

1. _____ L'hérésie religieuse est encore condamnée de nos jours.

2. _____ La biopsie révèle parfois un tissu cancéreux.

3. _____ Des magiciens prétendent transporter des personnes par télékinésie.

4. _____ L'autopsie d'un cadavre peut donner des indices sur la cause de la mort d'une personne.

5. _____ La synesthésie consiste à percevoir deux sensations à partir d'une seule stimulation.

6. _____ L'amnésie consiste à ne rien comprendre.

7. _____ L'anesthésie est nécessaire pour nettoyer les dents.

8. _____ L'hypocrisie est synonyme de sincérité.

9. _____ L'antisepsie est un ensemble de méthodes pour tuer les microbes.

10. _____ Tous les médecins pratiquent l'euthanasie.

 # 28 -gramme

MEANING	Tool for print/visual/graphic representation
ENGLISH EQUIVALENT	*-gram*
PART OF SPEECH	Noun
GENDER	Masculine

A French noun ending in the suffix **-gramme** may denote a visual or graphic representation. Such nouns often appear in the nomenclature of health sciences and medicine; many pertain to medical evaluations. The noun **cardiogramme**, based on the Greek word **kardia** *heart*, denotes a graphic representation of heart activity. The base words for most of the nouns ending in **-gramme** are Greek words.

NOUN ENDING IN -**gramme**	ENGLISH EQUIVALENT	BASE WORD	ENGLISH EQUIVALENT
adénogramme	*adenogram*	aden [GRK.]	*gland*
audiogramme	*audiogram*	audire [LAT.]	*to hear*
cardiogramme	*cardiogram*	kardia [GRK.]	*heart*
encéphalogramme	*encephalogram*	enkephalos [GRK.]	*brain*
hémogramme	*hemogram*	haima [GRK.]	*blood*
myogramme	*myogram*	mys [GRK.]	*muscle*
oscillogramme	*oscillogram*	osciller	*to oscillate*
spermogramme	*spermogram*	sperma [GRK.]	*sperm*

Définitions! *Provide the noun that matches each description.*

1. Diagramme des différences de potentiel électrique entre _____
   les cellules du cerveau

2. Étude des globules contenus dans le sang _____

3. Courbe visuelle sur l'écran d'un oscillographe _____

4. Diagramme représentant la sensibilité de l'oreille au son _____

5. Diagramme représentant les contractions musculaires _____

6. Tracé graphique des mouvements du cœur _____

7. Analyse du sperme _____

8. Examen des cellules prélevées sur un ganglion lymphatique _____

A French noun ending in the suffix **-gramme** may also denote a type or style of writing, as well as one of several other visual representations. For example, the base word for **anagramme** (rearrangement of letters to form a new word) is the Greek root **ana** *bottom to top*, and the suffixed noun **anagramme** means presenting letters in an unconventional order. Similarly, the base word for **monogramme** is the Greek word **monos**; this prefix of Greek origin is found in many French and English words and means *one, only, unique*. The suffixed noun **monogramme** denotes a unique symbol made of overlapping or combined letters. Each of the words in the following chart engages in wordplay involving the meaning of the base word and that of the suffix. Use your imagination when decoding them.

NOUN ENDING IN **-gramme**	ENGLISH EQUIVALENT	BASE WORD	ENGLISH EQUIVALENT
anagramme	*anagram*	ana [GRK.]	*bottom to top*
calligramme	*poem shaped like a picture*	kallos [GRK.]	*beauty*
diagramme	*diagram*	diagramma [GRK.]	*marked out in lines*
épigramme	*epigram*	epigramma [GRK.]	*inscription*
histogramme	*histogram*	histos [GRK.]	*mast*
hologramme	*hologram*	holos [GRK.]	*entire*
idéogramme	*ideogram*	idea [GRK.]	*visible aspect*
monogramme	*monogram*	monogrammos [GRK.]	*drawn with a single line*
organigramme	*flow chart*	organiser	*to organize*
pictogramme	*pictogram*	pictus [LAT.]	*painted, colored*

De quel type de représentation s'agit-il? *Provide the noun that represents each type of graphic representation.*

1. La structure d'une organisation _____

2. Un graphique représentant la répartition statistique d'une variable à l'aide de barres verticales _____

3. Un symbole consistant de plusieurs lettres _____

4. Un jeu de mots basé sur la permutation des lettres _____

5. Un symbole représentant un mot ou une idée _____

6. Une image en trois dimensions _____

7. Anciennement, inscription sur une pierre tombale _____

8. Dessin stylisé ayant fonction de signe _____

9. Poème dont la disposition graphique fait un dessin _____

10. Représentation visuelle qui simplifie des concepts ou des données _____

29 ◆ -graphie

MEANING	Art of print/visual/graphic representation
ENGLISH EQUIVALENT	*-graphy*
PART OF SPEECH	Noun
GENDER	Feminine

A French noun ending in the suffix **-graphie** denotes a type of writing or drawing; the base word represents the subject of the writing or drawing. For example, the base word for **biographie** *biography* is the Greek noun **bios** *life*, and the suffixed noun is a written work about someone's life.

NOUN ENDING IN -**graphie**	ENGLISH EQUIVALENT	BASE WORD	ENGLISH EQUIVALENT
biographie	*biography*	bios [GRK.]	*life*
calligraphie	*calligraphy*	kallos [GRK.]	*beauty*
cartographie	*cartography*	carte	*map*
chorégraphie	*choreography*	choreia [GRK.]	*dance*
cinématographie	*cinematography*	cinema	*cinema*
démographie	*demography*	demos [GRK.]	*people*
échographie	*sonogram*	echo	*echo*
mammographie	*mammography*	mamma [LAT.]	*breast*
orthographie	*spelling*	orthos [GRK.]	*correct*
photographie	*photography*	phos/photos [GRK.]	*light*

Vrai ou faux? *Indicate whether each statement is true or false, using* **V** *for* **vrai** *true or* **F** *for* **faux** *false.*

1. _____ Les frères Lumière ont joué un rôle important dans les débuts de la cinématographie.

2. _____ La chorégraphie s'applique exclusivement aux danses modernes.

3. _____ La démographie n'a pas changé en France depuis cinquante ans.

4. _____ La cartographie est un jeu de cartes.

5. _____ Les Français Niépce et Daguerre sont des pionniers de la photographie.

6. _____ On trouve les biographies d'auteurs et d'artistes célèbres sur Internet.

7. _____ On peut voir l'image d'un fœtus grâce à l'échographie.

8. _____ Il n'y a pas de logiciels pour l'orthographie en ligne.

9. _____ La mammographie permet de détecter des anomalies des seins.

10. _____ La calligraphie va être plus importante dans le monde informatique de demain.

30 ◆ -pathie

MEANING	Illness, affliction
ENGLISH EQUIVALENT	*-pathy*
PART OF SPEECH	Noun
GENDER	Feminine

A French noun ending in the suffix -**pathie** denotes an illness or affliction; the base word represents the part of the anatomy affected. For example, the noun **hémopathie** refers to a blood disease, because the base word, **haima**, means *blood*. Most of the base words for the medical words in the following chart are Greek. Related nouns ending in -**pathe** (for example, **cardiopathe** and **hémopathe**) refer to people who suffer from these afflictions.

Returning to the Greek root of one of these French nouns helps explain its meaning. As an example, **cardio-** derives from the Greek word **kardia** *heart*.

NOUN ENDING IN -**pathie**	ENGLISH EQUIVALENT	BASE WORD	ENGLISH EQUIVALENT
arthropathie	*arthropathy*	arthron [GRK.]	*joint*
cardiopathie	*cardiopathy*	kardia [GRK.]	*heart*
coronaropathie	*coronary artery disease*	coronarius [LAT.]	*of a crown*
hémopathie	*hemopathy*	haima [GRK.]	*blood*
myopathie	*myopathy*	mys [GRK.]	*muscle*
névropathie	*neuropathy*	neuron [GRK.]	*sinew, tendon*
ostéopathie	*osteopathy*	osteon [GRK.]	*bone*
psychopathie	*psychopathy*	psyche [GRK.]	*mind, soul*

La médecine! *Provide the name of the affliction for each part of the anatomy.*

1. Le cœur   _____

2. Les muscles   _____

3. Le cerveau / l'esprit   _____

4. Le sang   _____

5. Les nerfs   _____

6. Les os   _____

7. Les artères du cœur   _____

8. Les articulations   _____

31 ◆ -tie

MEANING	State, skill
ENGLISH EQUIVALENT	*-ty*
PART OF SPEECH	Noun
GENDER	Feminine

A French noun ending in the suffix **-tie** denotes a state (for example, amnesty) or a skill (for example, diplomacy). The base word represents the state or skill, or the possessor of the skill. The base word for **modestie** *state of modesty* is the adjective **modeste** *modest*, while the base word for **acrobatie** *acrobatics* is the noun **acrobate** *acrobat*. The regular formation for this type of noun consists in replacing the **-e** ending of the base word with the suffix **-ie**. Since many of these French nouns have English cognates, they tend to be easily recognized.

NOUN ENDING IN **-tie**	ENGLISH EQUIVALENT	BASE WORD	ENGLISH EQUIVALENT
acrobatie	*acrobatics*	acrobate	*acrobat*
amnistie	*amnesty*	amnestia [GRK.]	*amnesty*
calvitie	*baldness*	calvus [LAT.]	*bald*
diplomatie	*diplomacy*	diplomate	*diplomat*
minutie	*meticulousness*	minutieux	*meticulous*
modestie	*modesty*	modeste	*modest*
orthodontie	*orthodontics*	orthos + odous [GRK.]	*straight + tooth*
prophétie	*prophecy*	prophète	*prophet*
répartie	*quick response*	repartir	*to get going*
suprématie	*supremacy*	suprême	*supreme*

Complétez! *Complete each sentence with the appropriate noun.*

1. Un travail artisanal se fait avec _____ .

2. Une trêve entre deux ennemis se fait par le biais de la _____ .

3. Les personnes spirituelles ont souvent une _____ quand on leur parle.

4. La _____ afflige les hommes même jeunes.

5. Certains criminels reçoivent l'_____ à la fin du mandat présidentiel.

6. Les _____ de Nostradamus l'ont rendu célèbre.

7. L'_____ est essentielle pour la bonne position des dents.

8. La _____ est une des vertus du pape François.

9. Des nageurs comme Phelps affirment la _____ des champions olympiques de natation américains.

10. Les trapézistes font preuve d'agilité et de courage en _____ .

32 ◆ -crate

MEANING	Dedicated to power, seeking power
ENGLISH EQUIVALENT	*-crat*
PART OF SPEECH	Noun
GENDER	Masculine/feminine

The French suffix **-crate** derives from a Greek word meaning *force, power*. A noun ending in this suffix identifies a person who believes that power resides in the essence of the base word, or who represents that power. For example, the base word for **démocrate** *democrat* is the Greek noun **demos** *people*, and a **démocrate** is dedicated to, and seeks power for, the people. Nouns with the suffix **-crate** may be of either gender, with exceptions like **phallocrate** *phallocrat*, which is masculine due to its meaning. Some of these nouns may also function as adjectives. In the sentence **C'est un aristocrate** *He is an aristocrat*, **aristocrate** is a noun, but in the sentence **C'est une attitude aristocrate** *This is an aristocratic attitude*, it is an adjective; dual-function words ending in **-crate** are indicated by an asterisk (*). Since many of these French nouns have English cognates, they tend to be easily recognized. (For related nouns ending in **-cratie** that describe the field of values or beliefs of the people identified with the suffix **-crate**, see No. 33.)

NOUN ENDING IN **-crate**	ENGLISH EQUIVALENT	BASE WORD	ENGLISH EQUIVALENT
aristocrate*	*aristocrat*	aristos [GRK.]	*best*
autocrate*	*autocrat*	autos [GRK.]	*oneself*
bureaucrate	*bureaucrat*	bureau	*office*

NOUN ENDING IN -crate	ENGLISH EQUIVALENT	BASE WORD	ENGLISH EQUIVALENT
démocrate*	democrat	demos [GRK.]	people
eurocrate	eurocrat	euro	euro (European Union)
phallocrate*	male chauvinist	phallos [GRK.]	penis
physiocrate	physiocrat	physis [GRK.]	nature
ploutocrate	plutocrat	ploutos [GRK.]	wealth
technocrate	technocrat	techne [GRK.]	art, skill
théocrate*	theocrat	theos [GRK.]	god

EXERCICE 32·1

De quel passionné s'agit-il? *Provide the noun that best describes what the two items in each line have in common.*

1. La noblesse, les titres _____

2. Le sentiment de dominance, fierté masculine _____

3. L'amour des richesses, la puissance par les finances _____

4. Technicien, pouvoir administratif _____

5. Constitution naturelle, gouvernement _____

6. Souverain, pouvoir absolu _____

7. Souci du people, équité sociale _____

8. L'Europe, l'union des pays d'Europe _____

9. Bureau, travail administratif _____

10. Partisan des prêtres, ami de l'Église _____

33 ◆ -cratie

MEANING	Ruling/governing power
ENGLISH EQUIVALENT	-cracy
PART OF SPEECH	Noun
GENDER	Feminine

A French noun ending in the suffix **-cratie** denotes a principle or power related to ruling and governing. The base word represents the principle or power. (For related nouns ending in **-crate** that denote people with specific beliefs in such powers, see No. 32.) The regular formation for this type of noun consists in replacing the suffix **-crate** of the base word with the suffix **-cratie**. Since these French nouns have English cognates, they are easily recognized.

NOUN ENDING IN -cratie	ENGLISH EQUIVALENT	BASE WORD	ENGLISH EQUIVALENT
aristocratie	*aristocracy*	aristocrate	*aristocrat*
autocratie	*autocracy*	autocrate	*autocrat*
bureaucratie	*bureaucracy*	bureaucrate	*bureaucrat*
démocratie	*democracy*	démocrate	*democrat*
eurocratie	*eurocracy*	eurocrate	*eurocrat*
phallocratie	*male chauvinism*	phallocrate	*male chauvinist*
physiocratie	*physiocracy*	physiocrate	*physiocrat*
ploutocratie	*plutocracy*	ploutocrate	*plutocrat*
technocratie	*technocracy*	technocrate	*technocrat*
théocratie	*theocracy*	théocrate	*theocrat*

EXERCICE
33·1

Des synonymes! *Match each noun in the first column with a corresponding descriptive phrase in the second column.*

1. _____ Autocratie

2. _____ Eurocratie

3. _____ Phallocratie

4. _____ Bureaucratie

5. _____ Physiocratie

6. _____ Ploutocratie

7. _____ Aristocratie

8. _____ Technocratie

9. _____ Théocratie

10. _____ Démocratie

a. Gestion par les administrateurs des bureaux

b. La classe noble, gouvernement par les nobles

c. Gouvernement par des représentants ecclésiastiques

d. Système politico-économique qui donne le pouvoir aux spécialistes

e. Gouvernement par les riches

f. Système de gouvernement basé sur la souveraineté du peuple

g. Gouvernement par l'union européenne

h. Gouvernement d'un souverain absolu

i. Dominance du sexe masculin

j. Doctrine économique qui ne considère que les ressources naturelles de la terre

34 ◆ -ier

MEANING	(Fruit) tree
ENGLISH EQUIVALENT	—
PART OF SPEECH	Noun
GENDER	Masculine

A French noun ending in the suffix **-ier** may denote a specific fruit tree. The base word is a noun that represents the fruit borne by the tree. The regular formation for this type of noun consists in replacing the **-e** ending of the base word with the suffix **-ier**. For example, the base noun for **pom-**

mier *apple tree* is **pomme** *apple*. This suffix is modified to **-er** in the nouns **oranger** *orange tree* and **pêcher** *peach tree*. Note that the names of other trees may end in this suffix, for example, **palmier** *palm tree*.

NOUN ENDING IN **-ier**	ENGLISH EQUIVALENT	BASE WORD	ENGLISH EQUIVALENT
abricotier	*apricot tree*	abricot	*apricot*
amandier	*almond tree*	amande	*almond*
avocatier	*avocado tree*	avocat	*avocado*
bananier	*banana tree*	banane	*banana*
cerisier	*cherry tree*	cerise	*cherry*
citronnier	*lemon tree*	citron	*lemon*
figuier	*fig tree*	figue	*fig*
manguier	*mango tree*	mangue	*mango*
olivier	*olive tree*	olive	*olive*
oranger	*orange tree*	orange	*orange*
pamplemoussier	*grapefruit tree*	pamplemousse	*grapefruit*
pêcher	*peach tree*	pêche	*peach*
poirier	*pear tree*	poire	*pear*
pommier	*apple tree*	pomme	*apple*
prunier	*plum tree*	prune	*plum*

EXERCICE

34·1

Quel arbre fruitier est-ce? *Provide the name of the fruit tree described in each sentence.*

1. Cet arbre porte le fruit qui représente la Floride. _____

2. Cet arbre porte de petits fruits verts ou noirs qu'on met dans une salade. _____

3. Cet arbre porte des agrumes plus gros que les oranges. _____

4. Cet arbre tropical porte des fruits qu'on trouve dans la glace et dans des boissons exotiques. _____

5. Cet arbre porte des fruits que les singes adorent, mais attention à ne pas glisser sur leurs peaux. _____

6. Cet arbre porte un fruit vert dont la chair fond comme du beurre dans la bouche. _____

7. Cet arbre provençal et méditerranéen porte des fruits très sucrés. _____

8. Cet arbre porte de jolies fleurs roses ou blanches qui se transforment en petits fruits rouges ou jaunes. _____

9. Cet arbre porte des fruits violets qui traitent la paresse intestinale. _____

10. Cet arbre porte des fruits oranges qui ressemblent un peu aux pêches. _____

11. Cet arbre porte les fruits dont on fait de la limonade. _____

12. Cet arbre porte de délicieuses noix dont on fait souvent _____
une pâte pour les desserts.

13. Cet arbre porte des fruits dont on se sert pour faire _____
beaucoup de desserts en France, par exemple la Poire
Belle Hélène.

14. Cet arbre porte le fruit qu'on utilise pour la tarte favorite _____
des Américains.

-(r)aie

MEANING	Patch, orchard, plantation, grove
ENGLISH EQUIVALENT	—
PART OF SPEECH	Noun
GENDER	Feminine

A French noun ending in the suffix **-(r)aie** denotes a patch or orchard of flowers, trees, or other plants. For example, the base word for **cerisaie** is the noun **cerise** *cherry*, and the suffixed noun is a *cherry orchard*. Similarly, the base word **banane** *banana* yields **bananeraie** *banana plantation*.

NOUN ENDING IN -(r)aie	ENGLISH EQUIVALENT	BASE WORD	ENGLISH EQUIVALENT
bananeraie	*banana plantation*	banane	*banana*
cerisaie	*cherry orchard*	cerise	*cherry*
châtaigneraie	*chestnut grove*	châtaigne	*chestnut*
chênaie	*oak grove*	chêne	*oak tree*
cocoteraie	*coconut plantation*	cocotier	*coconut tree*
fraiseraie	*strawberry patch*	fraise	*strawberry*
hêtraie	*beech grove*	hêtre	*beech tree*
oliveraie	*olive grove*	olive	*olive*
palmeraie	*palm grove*	palmier	*palm tree*
ronceraie	*bramble patch*	ronce	*bramble*
roseraie	*rose garden*	rose	*rose*
saulaie	*willow grove*	saule	*willow*

EXERCICE 35·1

Où les trouve-t-on? *Provide the name of the patch, orchard, grove, or plantation associated with each plant or fruit.*

1. Les olives _____

2. Les rosiers _____

3. Les hêtres _____

4. Les bananes _____

5. Les palmiers   _____

6. Les saules   _____

7. Les cocotiers   _____

8. Les chênes   _____

9. Les cerises   _____

10. Les fraises   _____

11. Les ronces   _____

12. Les châtaignes   _____

36 ◆ -culture

MEANING	Cultivation, raising
ENGLISH EQUIVALENT	*-culture*
PART OF SPEECH	Noun
GENDER	Feminine

A French noun ending in the suffix **-culture** denotes the cultivation of plants or raising of animals or children. The base word represents what or who is being cultivated or raised. For example, the base word for **arboriculture** is the Latin word **arbor** *tree*, and the suffixed noun denotes the growing of trees. Many of the Latin roots that serve as base words for this type of noun are also prefixes in French, some of which are included in Part II.

NOUN ENDING IN **-culture**	ENGLISH EQUIVALENT	BASE WORD	ENGLISH EQUIVALENT
agriculture	*agriculture*	ager/agris [LAT.]	*field*
apiculture	*bee farming*	apis [LAT.]	*bee*
aquaculture	*aquaculture*	aqua [LAT.]	*water*
arboriculture	*arboriculture*	arbor [LAT.]	*tree*
aviculture	*poultry farming*	avis [LAT.]	*bird*
floriculture	*floriculture*	flos/floris [LAT.]	*flower*
horticulture	*horticulture*	hortus [LAT.]	*garden*
puériculture	*child care*	puer [LAT.]	*child*
riziculture	*rice growing*	riz	*rice*
saliculture	*salt farming*	sal [LAT.]	*salt*
salmoniculture	*salmon farming*	saumon	*salmon*
sériciculture	*silkworm farming*	sericus [LAT.]	*made of silk*
sylviculture	*forestry*	silva [LAT.]	*forest*
viticulture	*vine growing*	vitis [LAT.]	*vine*

Nommez la culture! *Provide the noun associated with each person or animal being raised or plant being cultivated.*

1. La forêt _____

2. Les arbres _____

3. Les fleurs _____

4. Le sel _____

5. L'eau _____

6. Le riz _____

7. Les enfants _____

8. La volaille _____

9. Le saumon _____

10. Le vin _____

11. La soie _____

12. Les légumes, les fleurs, les arbres _____

13. Les champs _____

14. Les abeilles _____

37 ▸ -ier/-ière

MEANING	Worker
ENGLISH EQUIVALENT	*-er*
PART OF SPEECH	Noun
GENDER	Masculine/feminine

A French noun ending in the suffix **-ier** (feminine: **-ière**) denotes a person who is involved in some form of work. Sometimes, the base word indicates where a person works; for example, the base word for **cuisinier** *cook* is **cuisine** *kitchen*. Often, the base word indicates with whom or what the person works; for example, the base word for **infirmier/infirmière** *nurse* is the adjective **infirme** *ill*, and a nurse cares for ill people. Similarly, **aumônier** *chaplain* takes care of people who ask for **aumône** *alms*. Since the noun **aumônier** is rooted in the Catholic religion, which limits this type of service to men, it has no feminine form. The regular formation of these nouns consists in adding the suffix **-ier/-ière** directly to the base word (for example, **plomb** *lead* yields **plombier** *plumber*) or in replacing the **-e** ending of the base word with the suffix (see the **cuisinier** ~ **cuisine** example).

NOUN ENDING IN **-ier/-ière**	ENGLISH EQUIVALENT	BASE WORD	ENGLISH EQUIVALENT
ambulancier	*ambulance driver*	ambulance	*ambulance*
aumônier (M.)	*chaplain*	aumône	*alms*
bachelier	*high school graduate*	baccalauréat	*French diploma*
chansonnier	*songwriter*	chanson	*song*
contrebandier	*smuggler*	contrebande	*smuggled goods*
couturier	*fashion designer*	couture	*fashion design*
créancier	*creditor*	créance	*credit*
cuisinier	*cook*	cuisine	*kitchen, cooking*
douanier	*customs officer*	douane	*customs office*
gondolier	*gondolier*	gondoliere [ITAL.]	*gondolier*
infirmier	*nurse*	infirme	*infirm*
ouvrier	*factory worker*	operarius [LAT.]	*worker*
plombier	*plumber*	plomb	*lead*
romancier	*novelist*	roman	*novel*

EXERCICE
37·1

Vrai ou faux? *Indicate whether each statement is true or false, using* **V** *for* **vrai** *true or* **F** *for* **faux** *false.*

1. _____ Les pirates des Caraïbes étaient des contrebandiers.

2. _____ La couturière Coco Chanel a inventé le corset.

3. _____ Un bachelier est quelqu'un qui a réussi à son baccalauréat.

4. _____ Une ambulancière conduit l'ambulance.

5. _____ Paul Bocuse est un grand cuisinier canadien.

6. _____ Un créancier est une personne qui vous doit de l'argent.

7. _____ Il y a trop de gondoliers à Paris.

8. _____ On appelle un plombier pour réparer des fuites d'eau.

9. _____ Le chansonnier interprète des chansons satiriques.

10. _____ Victor Hugo était un grand romancier.

11. _____ L'infirmière peut prescrire des médicaments.

12. _____ L'aumônier est un prêtre.

13. _____ Il faut des ouvriers pour construire une maison.

14. _____ Le douanier donne des amendes pour excès de vitesse.

A French noun ending in the suffix **-ier** (feminine: **-ière**) may denote a salesperson or a manager or owner of a store. The base word represents what is sold in the store. **Épicier** *male grocer* or **épicière** *female grocer* sells food in general; once upon a time, these were mostly **épices** *spices* from distant lands. (See No. 38 for stores and shops.) Note that the suffix is modified to **-er/-ère** for **boucher/bouchère** *butcher* and **boulanger/boulangère** *baker*.

NOUN ENDING IN -ier/-ière	ENGLISH EQUIVALENT	BASE WORD	ENGLISH EQUIVALENT
banquier	*banker*	banque	*bank*
bijoutier	*jeweler*	bijou	*jewel*
boucher	*butcher*	bouc	*goat*
boulanger	*baker*	bolla [FRANKISH]	*round bread*
boutiquier	*shop owner*	boutique	*shop*
caissier	*cashier*	caisse	*cash register*
charcutier	*deli owner/manager*	charcuterie	*deli meats*
chocolatier	*chocolate maker*	chocolat	*chocolate*
cordonnier	*shoemaker*	cordon	*lace*
crémier	*dairyperson*	crème	*cream*
épicier	*grocer*	épice	*spice*
poissonnier	*fishmonger*	poisson	*fish*

EXERCICE
37·2

Qui le fait? *Provide the masculine or feminine form of the person who performs each activity.*

1. Elle vend le chocolat. _____

2. Il vend le poisson. _____

3. Il fait ou répare les chaussures. _____

4. Il fait le pain. _____

5. Elle vend la viande. _____

6. Elle travaille dans un petit magasin d'alimentation. _____

7. Il possède une banque. _____

8. Elle fait ou vend des bijoux. _____

9. Il travaille à la caisse. _____

10. Elle vend le jambon, la saucisse etc. _____

11. Il vend du lait, des œufs, de la glace et du fromage. _____

12. Il a une petite boutique. _____

38 ▸ -erie

MEANING	Store, shop, factory
ENGLISH EQUIVALENT	*-ry*
PART OF SPEECH	Noun
GENDER	Feminine

A French noun ending in the suffix **-erie** often denotes a store or shop (infrequently, a factory). The base word is a noun depicting the product sold there (or for a factory, the product made there). For example, **biscuiterie** *cookie factory* is the place where **biscuits** *cookies* are produced and sold. There are noteworthy exceptions: the base word for **blanchisserie** *dry cleaner's* is the verb **blanchir** *to whiten* (by extension, *to clean*), and the base word for **confiserie** *candy store* is the verb **confire**, which means to crystallize fruit in order to preserve it.

NOUN ENDING IN **-erie**	ENGLISH EQUIVALENT	BASE WORD	ENGLISH EQUIVALENT
bijouterie	*jewelry store*	bijou	*jewel*
billetterie	*ticket office*	billet	*ticket*
biscuiterie	*cookie factory*	biscuit	*cookie*
blanchisserie	*dry cleaner's*	blanchir	*to whiten*
boucherie	*butcher shop*	bouc	*goat*
boulangerie	*bakery*	bolla [FRANKISH]	*round bread*
bouquinerie	*used-book store*	bouquin	*book*
brasserie	*brewery*	brasseur	*brewer*
charcuterie	*deli shop*	chair cuite	*cooked meat*
chocolaterie	*chocolate shop*	chocolat	*chocolate*
confiserie	*candy store*	confire	*to preserve* (fruit)
crémerie	*dairy store*	crème	*cream*

EXERCICE 38·1

Où va-t-on? *Provide the noun for the store or factory where each activity occurs.*

1. Pour acheter des bonbons et des sucreries _____

2. Pour faire nettoyer une chemise _____

3. Pour acheter quelques caisses de bonne bière _____

4. Pour acheter du lait frais _____

5. Pour acheter un beau collier _____

6. Pour commander un panier de chocolat _____

7. Pour acheter du jambon et du pâté _____

8. Pour acheter des baguettes _____

9. Pour trouver un bon livre d'occasion _____

10. Pour voir comment on fabrique les biscuits _____

11. Pour commander des billets de théâtre _____

12. Pour acheter du poulet et un gigot d'agneau _____

NOUN ENDING IN **-erie**	ENGLISH EQUIVALENT	BASE WORD	ENGLISH EQUIVALENT
crêperie	*crêpe shop/restaurant*	crêpe	*crêpe*
épicerie	*grocery store*	épice	*spice*
fromagerie	*cheese shop*	fromage	*cheese*
ganterie	*glove factory*	gant	*glove*
glacerie	*ice cream shop*	glace	*ice cream*
herboristerie	*herbal shop*	herbe	*herb*
maroquinerie	*leather shop*	maroquin	*leather*
parfumerie	*perfume store*	parfum	*perfume*
pâtisserie	*pastry shop*	pâte	*pastry*
poissonnerie	*fish shop*	poisson	*fish*
quincaillerie	*hardware store*	quincaille	*hardware*
sucrerie	*sugar refinery*	sucre	*sugar*

EXERCICE
38·2

Où trouve-t-on ces choses? *Provide the noun for the store or factory where the two elements in each line are made or sold.*

1. Sac à main, valise _____

2. Plantes médicinales, tisanes _____

3. Filet de sole, saumon _____

4. Lancôme, Chanel _____

5. Sucre en poudre, sucre raffiné _____

6. Baba au rhum, éclairs au chocolat _____

7. Ustensiles ménagers, outils _____

8. Crêpes, café _____

9. Camembert, Brie _____

10. Sel et poivre, eau minérale _____

11. Gants de cuir, gants de travail _____

12. Sorbet, glaces _____

39 ▸ -erie

MEANING	Collection
ENGLISH EQUIVALENT	*-ry*
PART OF SPEECH	Noun
GENDER	Feminine

A French noun ending in the suffix **-erie** may be a collective noun for items such as silverware and sweets. The base word represents the commonality among the items represented by the collective noun. For example, **argenterie** *silverware* comprises items made of **argent** *silver*. The regular formation for this type of noun consists in adding **-erie** directly to a noun ending in a consonant or replacing the **-e** ending of the base noun with **-erie**. Note that the nouns **charcuterie**, **confiserie**, and **pâtisserie** have double meanings. They denote shops (see No. 38), but they are also collective nouns; for example, **charcuterie** denotes a deli shop, as well as the deli meats that are sold there.

NOUN ENDING IN **-erie**	ENGLISH EQUIVALENT	BASE WORD	ENGLISH EQUIVALENT
argenterie	*silverware*	argent	*silver*
armurerie	*armory*	armure	*armor*
boiserie	*woodwork*	bois	*wood*
carrosserie	*body* (of a car)	carrosse	*coach*
charcuterie	*deli meats*	chair cuite	*cooked meat*
confiserie	*candy*	confire	*to preserve* (fruit)
coutellerie	*cutlery*	couteau	*knife*
ferronnerie	*ironware*	fer	*iron*
lingerie	*lingerie*	linge	*linen*
maçonnerie	*masonry*	maçon	*bricklayer*
pâtisserie	*pastry*	pâte	*dough*
soierie	*silkware*	soie	*silk*
sucrerie	*candy*	sucre	*sugar*
tapisserie	*tapestry*	tapis	*rug*
verrerie	*glassware*	verre	*glass*

EXERCICE 39·1

De quoi s'agit-il? *Provide the collective noun associated with the two items in each line.*

1. Foulards, robes _____

2. Tenture, petit point _____

3. Pierres, briques _____

4. Sous-vêtements, chemise de nuit _____

5. Décoration de fer, grillage en fer _____

6. Cadre en bois de la porte, portes des placards _____

7. Fourchettes, candélabres _____

8. Couteaux, instruments tranchants _____

9. Bonbons, caliçons _____

10. Pistolets, sabres _____

11. Structure extérieure de la voiture, capot _____

12. Tartes, gâteaux _____

13. Verres, vases _____

14. Pâtes d'amande, fruits confits _____

15. Salami, foie gras _____

 **-erie**

MEANING	Display of behavior, condition
ENGLISH EQUIVALENT	*-ry*
PART OF SPEECH	Noun
GENDER	Feminine

A French noun ending in the suffix **-erie** may denote a type of behavior. The base word is usually an adjective or a verb, but it may also be a noun. For example, the base word for **coquetterie** *flirtatiousness* is the feminine form of the adjective **coquet** *flirtatious*. The base word for **ânerie** *silliness* is the noun **âne** *donkey*, due to the stereotypical dumbness attributed to that animal.

NOUN ENDING IN **-erie**	ENGLISH EQUIVALENT	BASE WORD	ENGLISH EQUIVALENT
ânerie	*silliness*	âne	*donkey*
bouderie	*sulkiness*	bouder	*to sulk*
brusquerie	*rudeness*	brusque	*rude*
cajolerie	*cajolery*	cajoler	*to cajole*
camaraderie	*camaraderie*	camarade	*buddy*
chicanerie	*niggling*	chicaner	*to quibble*
coquetterie	*flirtatiousness*	coquet(te)	*flirtatious*
duperie	*trickery*	dupe	*dupe*
effronterie	*insolence*	effronté	*insolent*
flatterie	*flattery*	flatter	*to flatter*
niaiserie	*foolishness*	niais	*foolish*
pleurnicherie	*whining*	pleurnicher	*to whine*
pruderie	*prudishness*	prude	*prudish*
rêverie	*daydreaming*	rêver	*to dream*
sorcellerie	*witchcraft*	ensorceler	*to cast a spell*

EXERCICE

40·1

Complétez! *Complete each sentence with the appropriate noun.*

1. Il a vendu ce tableau pour plus que sa valeur. Quelle _____!

2. Elle marchande sans arrêt. Quelle _____!

3. Il répond impoliment. Quelle _____!

4. Elle pense devenir super riche. Quelle _____!

5. Ce qu'il fait est très stupide. Quelle _____!

6. Elle ne veut pas se mettre en maillot de bains. Quelle _____!

7. Il ne fait que se plaindre de tout. Quelle _____!

8. Elle lui dit qu'il est magnifique. Quelle _____!

9. Il ne fait que la caresser et lui dire des mots doux. Quelle _____!

10. Il parle comme un bébé. Quelle _____!

11. Elle fait disparaître tout ce qu'elle touche. Quelle _____!

12. Elle se fait aussi jolie que possible. Quelle _____!

13. Il est fâché; il ne veut parler à personne. Quelle _____!

14. Elle est amie avec moi depuis des années. Quelle _____!

15. Elle pousse tous les gens dans son passage. Quelle _____!

41 -ée

MEANING	Action, result of an action
ENGLISH EQUIVALENT	—
PART OF SPEECH	Noun
GENDER	Feminine

The suffix **-ée** is an extremely common ending for French nouns. Many of the nouns that use this suffix may be grouped by theme.

A French noun ending in the suffix **-ée** frequently denotes the action or result of an action expressed in the base word, which is, predictably, an action verb. In the following chart, the nouns represent simple results of actions; for example, **rentrée** denotes the first day back to school, based on the verb **rentrer** *to go back*.

NOUN ENDING IN **-ée**	ENGLISH EQUIVALENT	BASE WORD	ENGLISH EQUIVALENT
armée	*army*	armer	*to arm*
bouffée	*breath*	bouffer	*to puff out*
dictée	*dictation*	dicter	*to dictate*
donnée	*fact*	donner	*to give*
enjambée	*stride*	enjamber	*to stride*
fumée	*smoke*	fumer	*to smoke*
montée	*ascent*	monter	*to go up*
portée	*range, reach*	porter	*to carry*
rangée	*row* (of objects)	ranger	*to tidy up*
rentrée	*beginning of the school year*	rentrer	*to go back*
retombée	*fallout, consequence*	retomber	*to fall back down*
ruée	*rush*	ruer	*to rush*

EXERCICE
41·1

Soyons logiques! *Choose the best completion for each sentence.*

1. _____ Dans la forêt, il faut faire de grandes enjambées

2. _____ Mes parents sont sûrs que mes buts

3. _____ Il y a une ruée de gens à l'heure d'ouverture

4. _____ Il nous faut une bouffée d'air frais

5. _____ Toute cette fumée

6. _____ La rentrée des classes est

7. _____ La retombée radioactive

8. _____ La dictée rapide d'aujourd'hui

9. _____ L'armée française actuelle est

10. _____ La donnée que j'ai trouvée sur Internet

11. _____ La montée à pied jusqu'au cinquième étage

12. _____ Je voudrais m'asseoir

a. composée de volontaires.

b. m'a fait faire des fautes.

c. est fausse.

d. dans la première rangée.

e. est très pénible pour les personnes âgées.

f. inquiète tout le monde.

g. plus tôt que d'habitude cette année.

h. sont à ma portée.

i. par-dessus des troncs d'arbre à terre.

j. les jours de solde.

k. nous suffoque et nous donne la migraine.

l. après avoir été enfermés dans ce bureau.

42 ◆ -ée

MEANING Place, location
ENGLISH EQUIVALENT —
PART OF SPEECH Noun
GENDER Feminine

A French noun ending in the suffix -**ée** may denote a place. The base word may be a verb or a noun; for example, the base word for **entrée** *entrance* is the verb **entrer** *to enter*. Gender exceptions in the following list are **lycée** *high school* and **musée** *museum*, which are masculine.

NOUN ENDING IN -ée	ENGLISH EQUIVALENT	BASE WORD	ENGLISH EQUIVALENT
allée [F.]	*alley*	aller	*to go*
chaussée [F.]	*pavement, road*	calceata [LAT.]	*road made with lime*
entrée [F.]	*entrance*	entrer	*to enter*
jetée [F.]	*jetty*	jeter	*to throw*
lycée [M.]	*high school*	lyceum [LAT.]	*school, lecture hall*
mosquée [F.]	*mosque*	mousquaie [OLD FR.]	*mosque*
musée [M.]	*museum*	museum [LAT.]	*museum*
vallée [F.]	*valley*	vallis [LAT.]	*valley*

EXERCICE
42·1

Où est-ce? *Complete each sentence with the appropriate noun of place.*

1. Les musulmans vont à la _____ pour prier.

2. Nous laissons nos manteaux dans l'_____.

3. Il y a une nouvelle collection au _____.

4. On peut pêcher sur la _____.

5. Il faut aller au _____ pour préparer le baccalauréat.

6. Il faut mettre les poubelles dans l'_____.

7. Entre ces deux montagnes, il y a une très belle _____.

8. Les piétons doivent faire très attention en traversant la _____.

 **43 ◆ -ée**

MEANING	Physical/natural condition, thought
ENGLISH EQUIVALENT	—
PART OF SPEECH	Noun
GENDER	Feminine

A French word ending in the suffix -**ée** sometimes denotes a physical condition such as **nausée** *nausea*, a natural condition such as **rosée** *dew*, or a thought such as **idée** *idea*. The base word is usually a Latin or Greek word.

NOUN ENDING IN -**ée**	ENGLISH EQUIVALENT	BASE WORD	ENGLISH EQUIVALENT
apnée	*apnea*	[a-] + pnoia [GRK.]	*not + breath*
idée	*idea*	idea [LAT.]	*aspect*
marée	*tide*	mare [LAT.]	*sea*
nausée	*nausea*	nausea [LAT.]	*nausea*
odyssée	*odyssey*	Odyssea [LAT.]	*Odyssey*
pensée	*thought*	penser	*to think*
risée	*laughing stock*	risus [LAT.]	*laughter*
rosée	*dew*	ros [LAT.]	*water*

A French word ending in the suffix -**ée** is sometimes a noun derived from another noun; it has the same meaning as the base word. The base word is masculine, but the suffixed noun is feminine. For example, **journée** is based on **jour**; the masculine base noun represents a generic division of time, whereas the feminine suffixed noun emphasizes the duration of time. In the sentence **Le soir est mon moment favori de la journée** *The evening is my favorite time of the day*, **le soir** represents a portion of **la journée** *the entire day*.

NOUN ENDING IN -**ée**	ENGLISH EQUIVALENT	BASE WORD	ENGLISH EQUIVALENT
année	*year*	an	*year*
journée	*day*	jour	*day*
matinée	*morning*	matin	*morning*
soirée	*evening*	soir	*evening*

EXERCICE
43·1

Vrai ou faux? *Indicate whether each statement is true or false, using* **V** *for* **vrai** *true or* **F** *for* **faux** *false.*

1. _____ Une année a douze mois.

2. _____ C'est toujours une bonne idée de payer ses factures.

3. _____ Il est amusant d'être la risée de ses camarades.

4. _____ Un film en matinée coûte moins cher.

5. _____ L'odyssée du héros mythologique Hercule est une histoire contemporaine.

6. _____ Une journée à Tahiti n'est jamais possible pour les non-francophones.

7. _____ Une robe de soirée doit être courte.

8. _____ La marée dépend des phases de la lune.

9. _____ Quand on a la grippe, on peut avoir la nausée.

10. _____ La plongée en apnée peut durer des heures.

11. _____ La rosée a lieu le matin.

12. _____ Les mauvaises pensées peuvent être déprimantes.

 **-ée**

MEANING	Quantity that fills
ENGLISH EQUIVALENT	-ful
PART OF SPEECH	Noun
GENDER	Feminine

A French noun ending in the suffix **-ée** may denote a quantity that would fill a container or enclosure, for example, a mouthful, fistful, or spoonful. The suffixed noun is derived from a base noun that represents the container or enclosure; the exception is **pincée** *pinch,* which is derived from the verb **pincer** *to pinch.* The regular formation for this type of noun consists in replacing the **-e** ending of the base noun with **-ée**.

NOUN ENDING IN **-ée**	ENGLISH EQUIVALENT	BASE WORD	ENGLISH EQUIVALENT
assiettée	*plateful*	assiette	*plate*
bouchée	*mouthful*	bouche	*mouth*
brassée	*armful*	bras	*arm*
brouettée	*wheelbarrowful*	brouette	*wheelbarrow*
cuillcréc	*spoonful*	cuillère	*spoon*
fourchetée	*forkful*	fourchette	*fork*
gorgée	*sip, gulp*	gorge	*throat*
pelletée	*shovelful*	pelle	*shovel*
pincée	*pinch*	pincer	*to pinch*
poignée	*fistful*	poing	*fist*

EXERCICE
44·1

Qu'est-ce qui le plus probable? *Complete each sentence with the appropriate noun.*

1. Mets une _____ de sel dans la soupe.

2. Mets une _____ de brindilles dans le feu.

3. Mange ça en une seule _____ .

4. Prends juste une _____ de ce vin pour le goûter.

5. Mets une _____ de sable sur l'escalier couvert de neige.

6. Apporte-moi une _____ de bonne terre pour mon jardin.

7. Sers-moi une bonne _____ de cette délicieuse lasagna.

8. Regarde. Il arrive avec une grande _____ de fleurs sauvages.

9. Prends une _____ de ces spaghettis et dis-moi s'ils sont prêts.

10. Donne-moi une _____ de cette sauce.

45 ▸ -esse

MEANING	State of being, characteristic
ENGLISH EQUIVALENT	*-ness*
PART OF SPEECH	Noun
GENDER	Feminine

A French noun ending in the suffix **-esse** denotes the state of being or the characteristic expressed in the base word, which is an adjective. For example, the base word for **bassesse** *lowness, baseness* is the feminine adjective **basse** *low, base*. The regular formation for this type of noun consists in replacing the **-e** ending of the feminine adjective with the suffix **-esse**; for this reason, the following charts also give the feminine forms of the base words if they differ from the masculine forms.

Irregular formations include the nouns **adresse**, **promesse**, **politesse**, and **altesse** (which is based on a Latin root). The noun **vitesse** is derived from the adverb **vite** *fast* rather than from an adjective. The base word for **prouesse** is not a feminine adjective: the adjective **preux** exists only in the masculine form, because it dates to the Middle Ages and the Age of Chivalry, when bravery was associated with knighthood. (See No. 46 for nouns ending in **-esse** that are derived from nouns.)

NOUN ENDING IN **-esse**	ENGLISH EQUIVALENT	BASE WORD	ENGLISH EQUIVALENT
adresse	*dexterity*	adroit/adroite	*dexterous*
allégresse	*joy*	allègre	*joyful*
altesse	*highness*	altus [LAT.]	*high*
bassesse	*lowness, baseness*	bas/basse	*low, base*
gentillesse	*niceness*	gentil/gentille	*nice*
grossesse	*pregnancy*	gros/grosse	*big, fat*
jeunesse	*youth*	jeune	*young*
largesse	*generosity*	large	*wide*
noblesse	*nobility*	noble	*noble*
politesse	*politeness*	poli/polie	*polite*

De quoi s'agit-il? *Provide the noun associated with the two items in each line.*

1. Faire des choses méprisables, faire du mal à des gens vulnérables _____

2. Être heureux, état de joie _____

3. Bonnes manières, respect des autres _____

4. Grandeur, distinction _____

5. Amabilité, sympathie _____

6. Classe sociale, titres _____

7. Dons, cadeaux généreux _____

8. État prénatal, attente de la naissance _____

9. Dextérité, agilité _____

10. Période précédant l'âge adulte, après l'enfance _____

NOUN ENDING IN **-esse**	ENGLISH EQUIVALENT	BASE WORD	ENGLISH EQUIVALENT
promesse	*promise*	promis/promise	*promised*
prouesse	*bravery*	preux/—	*brave*
richesse	*richness*	riche	*rich*
sagesse	*wisdom, good behavior*	sage	*wise, well behaved*
sécheresse	*drought*	sec/sèche	*dry*
tendresse	*tenderness*	tendre	*tender*
vieillesse	*old age*	vieux/vieille	*old*
vitesse	*speed*	vite	*fast*

Complétez! *Complete each sentence with the appropriate noun.*

1. La _____ de la terre empêche toute végétation de pousser.

2. Cette enfant est d'une _____ exemplaire.

3. Toute _____ devrait être tenue.

4. Les mamans et les papas tiennent leurs nouveaux-nés avec _____.

5. Les pompiers et les agents de police font souvent preuve de _____ au travail.

6. La locution « troisième âge » décrit aussi la _____.

7. Un excès de _____ sur l'autoroute est risqué.

8. On dit que la _____ ne fait pas toujours le bonheur.

46 ▸ -esse

MEANING	Power, title, position
ENGLISH EQUIVALENT	-ess
PART OF SPEECH	Noun
GENDER	Feminine

A French noun ending in the suffix **-esse** may denote a female in a position of power and influence (benevolent or malevolent). The base word is the noun's masculine counterpart; for example, the masculine noun **prince** is the base word for the suffixed noun **princesse**. The regular formation for this type of noun consists in replacing the **-e** ending of the base noun with the suffix **-esse**. Note that the **-eur** ending of a base noun becomes **-er** in the feminine noun.

NOUN ENDING IN -esse	ENGLISH EQUIVALENT	BASE WORD	ENGLISH EQUIVALENT
comtesse	*countess*	conte	*count*
décsse	*goddess*	dieu	*god*
diablesse	*she-devil*	diable	*devil*
doctoresse	*female doctor*	docteur	*doctor*
duchesse	*duchess*	duc	*duke*
enchanteresse	*enchantress*	enchanteur	*enchanter*
hôtesse	*hostess*	hôte	*host*
maîtresse	*mistress, teacher*	maître	*master*
ogresse	*female ogre*	ogre	*ogre*
pécheresse	*female sinner*	pécheur	*sinner*
poétesse	*female poet*	poète	*poet*
prêtresse	*priestess*	prêtre	*priest*
princesse	*princess*	prince	*prince*
tigresse	*tigress*	tigre	*tiger*
traîtresse	*female traitor*	traître	*traitor*

EXERCICE
46·1

Vrai ou faux? *Indicate whether each statement is true or false, using* **V** *for* **vrai** *true or* **F** *for* **faux** *false.*

1. _____ Maya Angelou était une poétesse américaine.

2. _____ Kate Middleton est une duchesse anglaise.

3. _____ Il y a des prêtresses dans l'église catholique.

4. _____ On appelle une femme qui a toutes sortes de vices une diablesse.

5. _____ Une ogresse est une ménagère.

6. _____ L'hôtesse accueille les invités de son lit.

7. _____ Pendant la seconde guerre mondiale, on appelait les femmes qui fraternisaient avec les nazis des traîtresses.

8. _____ Les maîtresses des jeunes enfants de maternelle doivent être méchantes.

9. _____ La femele du tigre est une tigresse.

10. _____ Mora l'enchanteresse est un personnage de fiction dans une bande dessinée américaine.

11. _____ La bible mentionne Marie la Magdaléenne comme pécheresse.

12. _____ Dans la mythologie grecque, il y a des déesses.

13. _____ La femme d'un prince est automatiquement une duchesse.

14. _____ Une doctoresse est toujours une obstétricienne.

15. _____ La comtesse écrit des contes.

47 ◆ -issime

MEANING	Possessing a superlative quality (formal and literary registers)
ENGLISH EQUIVALENT	—
PART OF SPEECH	Adjective
GENDER	Masculine/feminine

A French adjective ending in the suffix **-issime** denotes a superlative quality. The base word is an adjective that represents the quality, such as looks or age, that is enhanced by the suffix **-issime**. For example, the base word for **richissime** is the adjective **riche** *rich*, and the suffixed adjective means *extremely rich*. The regular formation for this type of adjective consists in replacing the **-e** ending of the feminine form of the base adjective with **-issime**, as in the **riche ~ richissime** example, or adding the suffix **-issime** to an adjective ending in **-d** (for example, **grand**) or **-t** (for example, **urgent**). The masculine and feminine forms of the suffixed adjective are identical.

An **-issime** adjective can be used with sincere reverence: **votre altesse sérénissime** *Most Serene Highness* was used under the monarchy and may still be used in very formal occasions with royalty. The same can be said of the adjective **illustrissime** found in literature featuring noble or ecclesiastical personages. Because of their pedantic tone in modern times, however, these adjectives may be used in a mocking manner: **C'est un succès rarissime** *It is an extremely rare success* could be used ironically to point out a general lack of success.

ADJECTIVE ENDING IN -issime	ENGLISH EQUIVALENT	BASE WORD	ENGLISH EQUIVALENT
bellissime	*extremely beautiful*	beau/belle	*beautiful*
célébrissime	*extremely famous*	célèbre	*famous*
éminentissime	*extremely eminent*	éminent	*eminent*
grandissime	*extremely great*	grand	*great*
gravissime	*extremely serious*	grave	*serious*
illustrissime	*extremely illustrious*	illustre	*illustrious*
rarissime	*extremely rare*	rare	*rare*
richissime	*extremely rich*	riche	*rich*
sérénissime	*extremely serene*	serein/sereine	*serene*
urgentissime	*extremely urgent*	urgent	*urgent*

La meilleure description! *Provide the appropriate adjective for each item.*

1. La première édition d'un livre ancien _____

2. Warren Buffett _____

3. Une crise cardiaque _____

4. Gandi le pacifiste _____

5. Mandela le réformateur _____

6. Angelina Jolie _____

7. Le philosophe Pascal _____

8. La réputation du pape _____

9. Un génocide _____

10. Michael Jackson _____

48 ◆ -ment

MEANING	Action, result of an action
ENGLISH EQUIVALENT	*-ment*
PART OF SPEECH	Noun
GENDER	Masculine

A French noun ending in the suffix **-ment** denotes an action or the result of an action. The base word is a verb. The regular formation for this type of noun consists in replacing the **-r** ending of the base verb with **-ment**; thus, the verb **bercer** *to rock* yields the noun **bercement** *the act of rocking*. If the verb's stem ends in **-y**, the **y** changes to **i** in forming the noun. Note the slightly irregular formation of the noun **mouvement** in the second chart.

NOUN ENDING IN **-ment**	ENGLISH EQUIVALENT	BASE WORD	ENGLISH EQUIVALENT
aboiement	*barking*	aboyer	*to bark*
abonnement	*subscription*	abonner	*to subscribe*
accouchement	*delivery, birth*	accoucher	*to give birth*
bercement	*rocking*	bercer	*to rock*
commencement	*beginning*	commencer	*to begin*
contentement	*contentment*	contenter	*to please*
dénouement	*unraveling* (plot)	dénouer	*to untie, unravel*
déplacement	*displacement*	déplacer	*to displace*
dérangement	*disturbance*	déranger	*to disturb*
développement	*development*	développer	*to develop*
empoisonnement	*poisoning*	empoisonner	*to poison*
emprisonnement	*imprisonment*	emprisonner	*to imprison*

Complétez! *Complete each sentence with the appropriate noun.*

1. La période historique où les Acadiens ont quitté le Canada pour la Louisiane s'appelle

   « Le grand _____ ».

2. On savoure le _____ d'une mission accomplie.

3. Pendant la Renaissance, les Italiens étaient les experts des _____
   surtout dans les cercles des familles royales.

4. Le _____ du bateau a rendu les passagers malades.

5. Le _____ de ce film est plutôt ennuyeux.

6. Je ne peux plus supporter l'_____ de ce chien.

7. La promotion de ce cadre exige son _____ dans un pays étranger.

8. L'_____ de Napoléon Bonaparte sur l'île d'Elbe n'a pas duré très
   longtemps.

9. Le _____ de l'intrigue est vraiment banal.

10. Les pays en voie de _____ ont besoin de s'industrialiser.

NOUN ENDING IN **-ment**	ENGLISH EQUIVALENT	BASE WORD	ENGLISH EQUIVALENT
enlèvement	*kidnapping*	enlever	*to kidnap*
fonctionnement	*functioning*	fonctionner	*to function*
licenciement	*dismissal*	licencier	*to dismiss*
mouvement	*movement*	mouvoir	*to move*
paiement	*payment*	payer	*to pay*
plissement	*crinkling*	plisser	*to crease*
sentiment	*sentiment*	sentir	*to feel*
surpeuplement	*overpopulation*	surpeuplé	*overpopulated*
tremblement	*trembling*	trembler	*to tremble*
tutoiement	*using "tu"*	tutoyer	*to use "tu"*
vouvoiement	*using "vous"*	vouvoyer	*to use "vous"*

Des antonymes! *Provide the antonym for each item.*

1. Immobilité _____

2. Tutoiement _____

3. Banqueroute _____

4. Indifférence _____

5. Panne _____

6. Embauche   _____

7. Fermeté, calme   _____

8. Dépeuplement   _____

9. Retour sain et sauf   _____

10. Assouplissement   _____

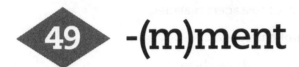

49 ◆ -(m)ment

MEANING	In a manner pertaining to
ENGLISH EQUIVALENT	—
PART OF SPEECH	Adverb

A French word ending in the suffix **-ment** or **-mment** is often an adverb. The base word is the feminine form of an adjective; for example, the adjective **abusif/abusive** yields the adverb **abusivement** *abusively*. Similarly, the adjective **ambitieux/ambitieuse** yields the adverb **ambitieusement** *ambitiously*. The feminine form is added to the base adjective in the following charts if the feminine form differs from the masculine form. The suffix **-ment** is attached directly to the masculine form of an adjective that ends in **-i** or **-u**; for example, the adjective **absolu** *absolute* yields the adverb **absolument** *absolutely*. An adverb in **-(m)ment** is formed differently if the base adjective ends in **-ant** and **-ent**; for example, the adjective **élégant** yields the adverb **élégamment** *elegantly* and the adjective **éloquent** yields the adverb **éloquemment** *eloquently*. (For more information about adverbs, see Appendix A.)

ADVERB ENDING IN -(m)ment	ENGLISH EQUIVALENT	BASE WORD	ENGLISH EQUIVALENT
abondamment	*plentifully*	abondant	*plentiful*
absolument	*absolutely*	absolu	*absolute*
abusivement	*abusively*	abusif/abusive	*abusive*
activement	*actively*	actif/active	*active*
ambitieusement	*ambitiously*	ambitieux/ambitieuse	*ambitious*
amoureusement	*lovingly*	amoureux/amoureuse	*in love*
catégoriquement	*categorically*	catégorique	*categorical*
curieusement	*curiously*	curieux/curieuse	*curious*
cyniquement	*cynically*	cynique	*cynical*
éloquemment	*eloquently*	éloquent	*eloquent*
fièrement	*proudly*	fier/fière	*proud*
finement	*finely*	fin/fine	*fine*
fréquemment	*frequently*	fréquent	*frequent*

Des synonymes! *Provide the appropriate synonym for each phrase.*

1. Très souvent _____

2. D'une manière distinguée et délicate _____

3. Avec du scepticisme _____

4. Beaucoup _____

5. Sans souci d'égalité ni respect _____

6. Avec amour _____

7. Avec effort et énergie _____

8. Avec fierté _____

9. Avec une compétence communicative brillante _____

10. D'une manière inquisitive _____

11. Sans aucun doute _____

12. Sans aucune contestation _____

ADVERB ENDING IN -(m)ment	ENGLISH EQUIVALENT	BASE WORD	ENGLISH EQUIVALENT
follement	*madly*	fou/folle	*mad*
fraîchement	*freshly*	frais/fraîche	*fresh*
froidement	*coldly*	froid/froide	*cold*
furieusement	*furiously*	furieux/furieuse	*furious*
harmonieusement	*harmoniously*	harmonieux/harmonieuse	*harmonious*
innocemment	*innocently*	innocent	*innocent*
insolemment	*insolently*	insolent	*insolent*
mollement	*softly, half-heartedly*	mou/molle	*soft, half-hearted*
naïvement	*naively*	naïf/naïve	*naive*
simplement	*simply*	simple	*simple*
verbalement	*verbally*	verbal/verbale	*verbal*
virtuellement	*virtually*	virtuel/virtuelle	*virtual*

Complétez! *Complete each sentence with the appropriate adverb.*

1. Elle travaille _____ car elle est déprimée.

2. Il parle _____ car il est en colère.

3. Elle parle _____ quand elle est avec des enfants.

4. Il blague _____ pour ne pas choquer son entourage.

5. Elle préfère communiquer _____ plutôt que par courriel.

6. Il a _____ répondu: « Non ».

7. Elle s'est _____ jetée dans les bras de son amant retrouvé.

8. Il a _____ perdu la tête dans le brouhaha.

9. Les intrus ont _____ bu tout le vin qu'ils ont trouvé.

10. Les chanteurs ont _____ interprété leur nouvelle chanson.

50 ◆ -cide

MEANING	Killing, killer
ENGLISH EQUIVALENT	*-cide*
PART OF SPEECH	Noun
GENDER	Masculine

The French suffix **-cide** derives from a Latin word that means *to kill*. French and English words ending in this suffix denote people or things that kill what is represented by the base word; for example, a fungicide kills fungus. These suffixed words may also denote the act of killing. Since these nouns are cognates in English and French, they are easily recognized.

NOUN ENDING IN **-cide**	ENGLISH EQUIVALENT	BASE WORD	ENGLISH EQUIVALENT
fongicide	*fungicide*	fungus [LAT.]	*fungus*
fratricide	*fratricide*	frater [LAT.]	*brother*
génocide	*genocide*	genus [LAT.]	*race*
germicide	*germicide*	germe	*germ*
herbicide	*herbicide*	herbe	*grass*
homicide	*homicide*	homo [LAT.]	*human being*
infanticide	*infanticide*	enfant	*child*
insecticide	*insecticide*	insecte	*insect*
matricide	*matricide*	mater [LAT.]	*mother*
parricide	*parricide*	parent	*parent, relative*
pesticide	*pesticide*	peste	*pest*
suicide	*suicide*	sui [LAT.]	*oneself*

EXERCICE 50·1

La définition! *Provide the noun that is synonymous with each phrase.*

1. Qui tue les insectes nocifs _____

2. Qui tue sa mère _____

3. Qui élimine l'herbe _____

4. Qui se tue lui/elle-même _____

5. Qui tue son père   _____

6. Qui tue un être humain   _____

7. Qui détruit une race   _____

8. Qui tue un enfant   _____

9. Qui tue son frère   _____

10. Qui élimine les champignons parasites   _____

11. Qui détruit les germes   _____

12. Qui tue les pestes   _____

2
Intermediate/advanced suffixes

 **-ade**

MEANING	Action, result of an action
ENGLISH EQUIVALENT	—
PART OF SPEECH	Noun
GENDER	Feminine

A French noun ending in the suffix **-ade** denotes an action or the result of an action. The base word is typically a verb. The regular formation for this type of noun consists in replacing the **-er** ending of the base verb with **-ade**; for example, the verb **promener** *to take for a walk* yields the noun **promenade** *walk*. Note that some base words in the following charts are not verbs; instead, they are Latin or Italian words, or even other French nouns, like **barrique** *barrel*, which is the base word for **barricade** due to its common use in forming a barricade in earlier times.

NOUN ENDING IN **-ade**	ENGLISH EQUIVALENT	BASE WORD	ENGLISH EQUIVALENT
ambassade	*embassy*	ambasciata [ITAL.]	*diplomatic mission*
baignade	*bathing*	baigner	*to bathe*
balade	*stroll*	(se) balader	*to stroll*
barricade	*barricade*	barrique	*barrel*
bousculade	*rush, scramble*	bousculer	*to shove*
brimade	*bullying*	brimer	*to bully*
camarade	*roommate, friend*	camera [LAT.]	*room*
cavalcade	*stampede*	cavalcare [ITAL.]	*to ride*
citronnade	*lemonade*	citron	*lemon*
colonnade	*colonnade*	colonne	*column*
dérobade	*evasion, dodging*	dérober	*to steal*
embuscade	*ambush*	imboscare [ITAL.]	*to hide*

EXERCICE
51·1

Des synonymes! *Provide the noun that is synonymous with each phrase.*

1. L'entrée d'un temple grec   _____

2. Une attaque surprise   _____

3. Celui ou celle qui partage votre chambre   _____

4. Ce qui se passe quand tout le monde pousse   _____

5. Une petite promenade sans but précis   _____

6. Une fuite pour ne pas faire face à un rival   _____

7. Une petite nage dans la piscine ou le lac _____

8. La représentation diplomatique d'un pays _____
   dans un autre état

9. Une boisson rafraîchissante _____

10. Une chevauchée bruyante _____

NOUN ENDING IN **-ade**	ENGLISH EQUIVALENT	BASE WORD	ENGLISH EQUIVALENT
esplanade	*promenade area*	planus [LAT.]	*level, flat*
fusillade	*shootout*	fusiller	*to shoot to death*
galopade	*romp*	galoper	*to gallop*
grillade	*barbecue*	griller	*to grill*
malade	*patient*	malus [LAT.]	*bad*
nomade	*nomad*	Nomades [LAT.]	*name of wandering people*
orangeade	*orangeade*	orange	*orange*
parade	*parade*	parada [SP.]	*horse exhibition*
peuplade	*tribe*	peupler	*to populate*
promenade	*walk*	promener	*to take for a walk*
rigolade	*laugh*	rigoler	*to laugh*
tornade	*tornado*	tornado [SP.]	*turned*

EXERCICE
51·2

Complétez! *Complete each sentence with the appropriate noun.*

1. Il y a eu beaucoup de _____, de cyclones et d'ouragans cette
   année.

2. Allons faire une _____ au parc! Il fait beau.

3. Donne-moi un verre d'_____. J'ai très soif.

4. Il y a toujours une belle _____ Macy's à New York.

5. Dans certains quartiers, il y a des _____ entre différents gangs.

6. Ses histoires drôles sont toujours accompagnées de _____.

7. Les enfants vont toujours jouer sur l'_____ voisine.

8. Les langages de certaines _____ africaines sont très anciens.

9. Les _____ sont en quarantaine pour quelques jours.

10. Quand on a tiré le coup de feu du départ de la course, il y a eu une
    _____ effrénée.

11. On va faire une _____ pour la famille sur la terrasse cet après-midi.

12. Il y a encore des _____ qui se déplacent régulièrement dans le
    Sahara.

52 ◆ -age

MEANING	Action, result of an action
ENGLISH EQUIVALENT	—
PART OF SPEECH	Noun
GENDER	Masculine

A French noun ending in the suffix **-age** denotes an action or the result of an action. The base word is a verb. The infinitive ending of the base word is replaced by **-age**; for example, the verb **aborder** *to reach land, attack a ship* yields the noun **abordage** *boarding/attacking a ship*.

NOUN ENDING IN **-age**	ENGLISH EQUIVALENT	BASE WORD	ENGLISH EQUIVALENT
abordage	*boarding/attacking a ship*	aborder	*to reach land, attack a ship*
arbitrage	*refereeing*	arbitrer	*to referee*
atterrissage	*landing*	atterrir	*to land*
bavardage	*chatting*	bavarder	*to chat*
braconnage	*poaching*	braconner	*to poach*
bronzage	*tanning*	bronzer	*to tan*
cambriolage	*robbery*	cambrioler	*to rob*
chauffage	*heating*	chauffer	*to heat*
décodage	*decoding*	décoder	*to decode*
grignotage	*snacking*	grignoter	*to nibble*
lavage	*washing*	laver	*to wash*
maquillage	*putting on makeup*	maquiller	*to put on makeup*
ravage	*ravage, devastation*	ravager	*to ravage*
surdosage	*overdose*	[sur-] + doser	*over + to measure out*
témoignage	*testimony*	témoigner	*to testify*

EXERCICE
52·1

Vrai ou faux? *Indicate whether each statement is true or false, using* **V** *for* **vrai** *true or* **F** *for* **faux** *false.*

1. _____ Le bronzage donne une peau mate.

2. _____ Le braconnage est légal en toute saison.

3. _____ L'arbitrage peut influencer le résultat d'un match.

4. _____ Dans une action juridique, il faut souvent des témoignages.

5. _____ Les modèles n'ont pas besoin de maquillage.

6. _____ Les professeurs stricts ne punissent pas le bavardage en classe.

7. _____ Le surdosage d'un somnifère est dangereux.

8. _____ Quand les pirates de Somalie prennent un bateau, l'abordage se fait sans violence.

9. _____ Les cambriolages ont surtout lieu dans les quartiers défavorisés.

10. _____ Il faut le chauffage dans un appartement floridien en hiver.

11. _____ Attention au grignotage! Cela peut faire grossir.

12. _____ Les passagers aiment bien un atterrissage doux.

13. _____ Le décodage de jeux de mots est mauvais pour la matière grise.

14. _____ Les femmes abusées ont généralement subi un lavage de cerveau.

15. _____ Les ravages de l'abus des drogues sont difficiles à supporter.

 **53** ◆ **-aille**

MEANING	Action, result of an action
ENGLISH EQUIVALENT	—
PART OF SPEECH	Noun
GENDER	Feminine

A French noun ending in the suffix **-aille** denotes an action or the result of an action. The base word is usually a verb. In some cases, the suffix **-aille** remains after the **-r** ending of the infinitive is dropped: the verb **(se) batailler** *to fight* yields the noun **bataille** *battle*. In other cases, the suffix **-aille** replaces the **-er** ending of the infinitive: the verb **trouver** *to find* yields the noun **trouvaille** *find, invention*. Some base words are nouns; for example, the base word for **canaille** is the Italian noun **canaglia** *scoundrel*. Note that **canaille** can not only represent an individual, but can also be a collective noun and, therefore, represent a group of scoundrels (see the second chart of nouns in **-aille**). The same is true of **broussaille**, which can be a single scrub or, as a collective noun, undergrowth.

NOUN ENDING IN **-aille**	ENGLISH EQUIVALENT	BASE WORD	ENGLISH EQUIVALENT
bataille	*battle*	(se) batailler	*to fight*
broussaille	*undergrowth, scrub*	broussailler	*to plant bushes*
canaille	*scoundrel*	canaglia [ITAL.]	*scoundrel*
entaille	*nick, cut*	entailler	*to nick, cut*
maille	*link, stitch*	mailler	*to mesh*
taille	*size*	tailler	*to carve*
trouvaille	*find, invention*	trouver	*to find*
victuailles	*food*	victus [LAT.]	*food supply*

Complétez! *Choose the best completion for each sentence.*

1. _____ Les fanas des marchés aux puces   a. est extraordinaire.

2. _____ La taille de ce diamant   b. au frigo.

3. _____ On ne peut pas faire d'entaille   c. les batailles de polochon.

4. _____ Dans les histoires d'enfant, il y a toujours   d. une canaille.

5. _____ Les enfants adorent   e. un certain nombre de mailles.

6. _____ Il faut mettre les victuailles pour le pique-nique   f. font de bonnes trouvailles.

7. _____ Ce jardin abandonné est plein de   g. dans un vrai diamant.

8. _____ On commence à tricoter un pull avec   h. broussaille.

The suffix **-aille** may impart a collective quality to a noun. It may also give a depreciative or pejorative nuance to the suffixed noun; these nouns are indicated by an asterisk (*) in the following chart. The base word may be a noun, an adjective, or a verb. The base word for **fiançailles** is the verb **(se) fiancer** *to get engaged*, and **fiançailles** denotes the act and rituals of an engagement without a pejorative connotation—the focus is on the proceedings and formalities. The noun **antiquaille**, however, is based on the adjective **antique** and is definitely pejorative; **antiquailles** have little or no value.

NOUN ENDING IN **-aille**	ENGLISH EQUIVALENT	BASE WORD	ENGLISH EQUIVALENT
antiquailles*	*old junk*	antique	*antique*
blanchaille	*school of white fish*	blanc/blanche	*white*
bouffaille*	*food*	bouffe [SLANG]	*food*
brumaille	*fog, mist*	brume	*fog, mist*
canaille*	*(bunch of) scoundrel(s)*	canaglia [ITAL.]	*scoundrel*
épousailles	*wedding*	épouser	*to marry*
ferraille	*scrap iron*	ferrailler	*to cross swords*
fiançailles	*engagement*	(se) fiancer	*to get engaged*
grisaille	*grayness*	gris	*gray*
marmaille*	*brats*	marmot	*kid*
muraille	*(big) wall*	mur	*wall*
pierraille	*loose stones*	pierre	*stone*
quincaille*	*hardware, junk*	clincaille [OLD FR.]	*stuff that clinks*
rocaille	*rocky ground*	roche	*rock*
verraille	*glassware*	verre	*glass*
volaille	*poultry*	voler	*to fly*

Vrai ou faux? *Indicate whether each statement is true or false, using **V** for **vrai** true or **F** for **faux** false.*

1. _____ Les mousquetaires du dix-septième siècle adoraient la marmaille.

2. _____ Un fermier donne de la viande à sa volaille tous les jours.

3. _____ Dans le dépôt d'une gare, on trouve de la ferraille.

4. _____ Sur un chantier de construction, il y a beaucoup de pierraille et de rocaille.

5. _____ Quand il y a du soleil, il y a aussi de la grisaille.

6. _____ Les maisons américaines ont souvent une muraille qui entoure leur jardin.

7. _____ On trouve de la quincaille et de l'antiquaille à une brocante.

8. _____ Les fiançailles d'un couple sont la déclaration de l'intention de mariage.

9. _____ Les épousailles du prince William d'Angleterre avec Kate Middleton se sont faites incognito.

10. _____ Les pêcheurs détestent la blanchaille car elle baisse la visibilité.

11. _____ Il faut faire attention quand on conduit dans la brumaille.

12. _____ Il y a de la verraille partout quand on cuisine un grand repas.

13. _____ Les membres des familles de crime forment une canaille bien organisée.

14. _____ On ne manque pas de bouffaille quand chacun apporte quelque chose.

54 ◆ -fère

MEANING	Carrying, containing
ENGLISH EQUIVALENT	*-ferous*
PART OF SPEECH	Adjective
GENDER	Masculine/feminine

A French adjective ending in the suffix **-fère** denotes carrying or containing an item represented by the base word. The base word for the adjective **salifère** is the Latin word **sal** *salt*, and the suffixed adjective indicates that an item contains salt. These adjectives have the same form, whether masculine or feminine.

ADJECTIVE ENDING IN -**fère**	ENGLISH EQUIVALENT	BASE WORD	ENGLISH EQUIVALENT
alifère	*winged*	ala [LAT.]	*wing*
calorifère	*conveying heat*	calor [LAT.]	*heat*
carbonifère	*carboniferous*	carbo [LAT.]	*coal*
florifère	*floriferous*	flos/floris [LAT.]	*flower*
fructifère	*fruit-bearing*	fructus [LAT.]	*fruit*
humifère	*containing humus*	humus [LAT.]	*organic matter*
papillifère	*with taste buds*	papille	*taste bud*
salifère	*containing salt*	sal [LAT.]	*salt*
somnifère	*soporific*	somnus [LAT.]	*sleep*
vaccinifère	*vaccine-carrying*	vaccin	*vaccine*

Complétez! *Complete each sentence with the correct form of the appropriate adjective.*

1. La partie de l'anatomie qui porte des papilles est _____ .

2. De la terre riche en humus est _____ .

3. Pour dormir après une opération, il faut parfois une substance

   _____ .

4. Un insecte qui porte des ailes est _____ .

5. Le Gulf Stream a une influence _____ .

6. Il y a des dépôts _____ sur le littoral marin.

7. On se sert de chèvres, de vaches et de volaille comme animaux _____
   pour préparer des vaccins.

8. On plante de nouveaux arbres fruitiers en espérant qu'ils seront _____ .

9. Il y a une abondance de plantes _____ et odorantes dans ce parc
   naturel.

10. Les bassins houillers de l'ère primaire étaient _____ .

55 ▸ -forme

MEANING	Of a shape
ENGLISH EQUIVALENT	*-form*
PART OF SPEECH	Adjective
GENDER	Masculine/feminine

A French adjective ending in the suffix -**forme** denotes a characteristic based on the shape represented by the base word. For example, the base word for **aliforme** is the Latin word **ala** *wing*, and the suffixed adjective means *wing-shaped*. The formation of some of the adjectives in the following chart consists in attaching the suffix -**forme** directly to a prefix; for example, the prefix **multi-** with this suffix forms the adjective **multiforme** *multiform*.

ADJECTIVE ENDING IN -**forme**	ENGLISH EQUIVALENT	BASE WORD	ENGLISH EQUIVALENT
aliforme	*wing-shaped*	ala [LAT.]	*wing*
conforme	*in conformity*	[con-]	*with, together*
difforme	*deformed*	[de-]	*away from*
digitiforme	*finger-shaped*	digitus [LAT.]	*finger*
filiforme	*long and thin, spindly*	fil	*thread*
informe	*shapeless*	[in-]	*not*
multiforme	*multiform*	[multi-]	*many*
serpentiforme	*snake-shaped*	serpent	*snake*
uniforme	*uniform, identical*	[uni-]	*one*
vermiforme	*vermiform*	vermis [LAT.]	*worm*

EXERCICE
55·1

Vrai ou faux? *Indicate whether each statement is true or false, using* **V** *for* **vrai** *true or* **F** *for* **faux** *false.*

1. _____ Il y a des espèces marines qui sont vermiformes.

2. _____ On laisse une empreinte digitiforme sur le verre dans lequel on boit.

3. _____ Le cœur est multiforme.

4. _____ Une ombre bien visible est informe.

5. _____ Une batte de baseball est serpentiforme.

6. _____ Une décision uniforme a l'accord de tous.

7. _____ L'aspect difforme d'un objet est généralement hideux.

8. _____ La Guadeloupe est souvent appelée île-papillon à cause de son aspect aliforme.

9. _____ Un document photocopié n'est pas conforme à l'original.

10. _____ Les antennes de certains insectes sont filiformes.

56 ◆ -ateur/-atrice

MEANING	Worker, performer
ENGLISH EQUIVALENT	*-ator, -atrix*
PART OF SPEECH	Noun
GENDER	Masculine/feminine

A French noun ending in the suffix **-ateur** (feminine: **-atrice**) denotes a person engaged in the occupation, career, or activity represented by the base word. For example, the base word for **accompagnateur/accompagnatrice** *male/female guide* is the verb **accompagner** *to accompany*, and the occupation or activity of the suffixed word is to accompany or guide people. The base word is usually a verb; sometimes, however, it is a Latin root: **spectator** *observer* is the Latin root for the suffixed noun **spectateur/spectatrice** *spectator*. The regular formation for this type of noun consists in replacing the **-er** ending of the verb with the suffix **-ateur/-atrice**; for example, the verb **administrer** *to administer* yields the noun **administrateur** *male administrator* or **administratrice** *female administrator*.

NOUN ENDING IN **-ateur/-atrice**	ENGLISH EQUIVALENT	BASE WORD	ENGLISH EQUIVALENT
accompagnateur	*guide*	accompagner	*to accompany*
accusateur	*accuser*	accuser	*to accuse*
administrateur	*administrator*	administrer	*to administer*
admirateur	*admirer*	admirer	*to admire*
agitateur	*agitator*	agiter	*to agitate*
animateur	*host, presenter*	animer	*to host, animate*
calomniateur	*slanderer*	calomnier	*to slander*

▶

NOUN ENDING IN **-ateur/-atrice**	ENGLISH EQUIVALENT	BASE WORD	ENGLISH EQUIVALENT
collaborateur	*collaborator*	collaborer	*to collaborate*
communicateur	*communicator*	communiquer	*to communicate*
conspirateur	*conspirator*	conspirer	*to conspire*
coordinateur	*coordinator*	coordonner	*to coordinate*
cultivateur	*grower*	cultiver	*to cultivate*

EXERCICE
56·1

Complétez! *To elaborate on Madame D.'s portrait, complete each sentence with the feminine form of the appropriate noun.*

1. Madame D. est la meilleure _____ pour planifier les activités communes des membres d'un groupe.

2. C'est ma _____ préférée; nous travaillons très bien ensemble.

3. Elle a des _____ dans notre société qui voudraient toutes lui ressembler.

4. Il y a bien sûr une exception; Élise n'aime pas du tout Madame D. Mais peu importe car Élise est une _____ qui dit des mensonges.

5. Élise ferait mieux de retourner à sa ferme faire son ancien travail de _____ .

6. Il paraît même qu'Élise a faussement accusé une collègue d'avoir defraudé la société; c'est une _____ de premier ordre mais on ne la croit pas.

7. Élise a une co-_____ qui s'appelle Éloïse. Elles se ressemblent!

8. Éloïse est une bonne _____ de jeux; c'est pour cela qu'on la garde.

9. Mais c'est une _____ et une provocatrice au même degré que sa complice Élise.

10. Elle trouve toujours moyen de mettre la pagaille! Quelle _____ experte mais pénible!

11. Heureusement que Madame D. est toujours l'_____ quand on dirige un voyage organisé.

12. Madame D. est une excellente _____ dans plusieurs langues!

NOUN ENDING IN **-ateur/-atrice**	ENGLISH EQUIVALENT	BASE WORD	ENGLISH EQUIVALENT
dénonciateur	*informer*	dénoncer	*to denounce*
dessinateur	*designer*	dessiner	*to design*
explorateur	*explorer*	explorer	*to explore*
narrateur	*narrator*	narrer	*to narrate*
navigateur	*navigator*	naviguer	*to navigate*

NOUN ENDING IN -ateur/-atrice	ENGLISH EQUIVALENT	BASE WORD	ENGLISH EQUIVALENT
négociateur	*negotiator*	négocier	*to negotiate*
observateur	*observer*	observer	*to observe*
organisateur	*organizer*	organiser	*to organize*
présentateur	*presenter*	présenter	*to present*
prestidigitateur	*prestidigitator*	preste + digitus [LAT.]	*nimble + finger*
spectateur	*spectator*	spectator [LAT.]	*observer*
utilisateur	*user*	utiliser	*to use*

EXERCICE

56·2

Complétez! *Choose the best completion for each sentence.*

1. _____ L'organisateur de l'exposition

2. _____ L'utilisateur de cette messagerie

3. _____ La narratrice de ce roman

4. _____ Pour faire une bande dessinée,

5. _____ Houdini était un

6. _____ Chaque guerre a ses héros et

7. _____ L'explorateur Samuel Champlain

8. _____ Les spectateurs des matchs de football

9. _____ Amerigo Vespucci était

10. _____ Certains étudiants vont à des cours

11. _____ Il y a une nouvelle présentatrice

12. _____ Hillary Clinton est une

a. en simples observateurs.

b. a fondé la ville de Québec.

c. ses dénonciateurs ainsi que ses traîtres.

d. sont souvent des fanas du sport.

e. pour cette émission.

f. crée des personnages intrigants.

g. doit avoir un mot de passe.

h. il faut un dessinateur ou une dessinatrice.

i. négociatrice brillante.

j. a trouvé des tableaux exceptionnels.

k. prestidigitateur audacieux.

l. un grand navigateur italien.

57 ◆ -eur/-euse ~ -rice

MEANING	Engaged in, occupied with
ENGLISH EQUIVALENT	*-er* or *-or*
PART OF SPEECH	Noun
GENDER	Masculine/feminine

French words ending in the suffix **-eur** are numerous. (See Nos. 58, 60, 61, and 62 for other words that have this suffix.) The feminine form of these nouns ends in either **-euse** or **-rice**.

A French noun ending in the suffix **-eur** denotes a person engaged in the occupation, career, or activity represented by the base word. The regular formation for this type of noun consists in replacing the **-er** ending of the verb with the suffix **-eur**; for example, the verb **chanter** *to sing* yields **chanteur** *male singer* and **chanteuse** *female singer*. Similarly, a **farceur** or **farceuse** is a person who regularly jokes or tricks people, like the **Schtroumpf farceur** also known as **Jokey Smurf**.

In the following two charts, all base words are verbs except for **auto-stop**, **farce**, and the Latin word **professor**. Many dictionaries indicate a masculine form only for the noun **professeur**, even though it is becoming common to call a female professor **professeure** (using an irregular feminine ending). Some of the people listed are not involved in earning a living (for example, *bather*) or winning accolades (for example, *profiteer* and *thief*). Words that function both as nouns and as adjectives are indicated by an asterisk (*).

Note that the nouns **chasseur** *hunter* and **pécheur** *sinner* have irregular feminine endings (**chasseresse** and **pécheresse**, respectively). (See No. 46.)

NOUN ENDING IN **-eur/-euse**	ENGLISH EQUIVALENT	BASE WORD	ENGLISH EQUIVALENT
acheteur	*buyer*	acheter	*to buy*
auto-stoppeur	*hitchhiker*	auto-stop	*hitchhiking*
baigneur	*bather*	baigner	*to bathe*
balayeur	*sweeper*	balayer	*to sweep*
bricoleur*	*tinkerer/tinkering*	bricoler	*to tinker*
chanteur	*singer*	chanter	*to sing*
chasseur	*hunter*	chasser	*to hunt*
danseur	*dancer*	danser	*to dance*
dompteur	*tamer*	dompter	*to tame*
éclaireur	*scout*	éclairer	*to light up*
farceur	*joker*	farce	*farce*
flatteur*	*flatterer/flattering*	flatter	*to flatter*
grogneur	*grouch*	grogner	*to grumble*

EXERCICE
57·1

Définitions! *Provide the masculine or feminine form of the noun that denotes the person described in each sentence.*

1. Il travaille avec les animaux sauvages dans un cirque.   Le _____

2. Elle a l'habitude de protester et de se plaindre.   La _____

3. Il nettoie les rues, les cours, les trottoirs ou les couloirs.   Le _____

4. Elle fait des achats.   L'_____

5. Il a l'habitude de flatter les gens.   Le _____

6. Elle interprète des chansons.   La _____

7. Il est membre d'une association de scoutisme.   L'_____

8. Elle essaie de faire arrêter les autos pour se faire conduire quelque part.   L'_____

9. Il fait de petits projets de rénovation ou de réparations.   Le _____

10. Elle nage dans le lac.   La _____

11. Il interprète une composition chorégraphique.   Le _____

12. Elle n'agit jamais sérieusement.   La _____

NOUN ENDING IN **-eur/-euse**	ENGLISH EQUIVALENT	BASE WORD	ENGLISH EQUIVALENT
pécheur	*sinner*	pécher	*to sin*
professeur	*teacher, professor*	professor [LAT.]	*professor*
profiteur	*profiteer*	profiter	*to profit*
programmeur	*programmer*	programmer	*to program*
rêveur	*dreamer*	rêver	*to dream*
ronfleur	*snorer*	ronfler	*to snore*
serveur	*server*	servir	*to serve*
tatoueur	*tattoo artist*	tatouer	*to tattoo*
troqueur	*barterer*	troquer	*to trade, swap*
vendeur	*salesperson*	vendre	*to sell*
visiteur	*visitor*	visiter	*to visit*
voleur	*thief*	voler	*to steal*
voyageur	*traveler*	voyager	*to travel*

EXERCICE

57·2

Charade! *Provide the masculine noun associated with the two items in each line.*

1. Dessin, cutané   _____

2. Boissons, pourboires   _____

3. Dérober, cambrioler   _____

4. Respirer par le nez, congestion   _____

5. Prendre le train, voir le monde   _____

6. Enseigner, instruire   _____

7. Échanger, faire du troc   _____

8. Rester chez des amis, explorer la ville   _____

9. Jouir d'un avantage, satisfaire un désir   _____

10. Rêverie, pensées chimériques   _____

11. Écriture informatique, ordinateur   _____

12. Chaussures, vêtements   _____

Most masculine nouns ending in the suffix **-eur** have a feminine form ending in **-euse**, for example, **acheteur**, **chanteur**, **dompteur**, **flatteur**, **profiteur**, and **visiteur**. Some, however, have a feminine form ending in **-rice**. All nouns in the following chart have the irregular feminine ending **-rice**. The base words are verbs except for the Latin noun **actor**. Nouns that may also function as adjectives are indicated by an asterisk (*).

NOUN ENDING IN **-eur/-rice**	ENGLISH EQUIVALENT	BASE WORD	ENGLISH EQUIVALENT
acteur	*actor*	actor [LAT.]	*actor*
compositeur	*composer*	composer	*to compose*
conducteur*	*driver, conductor/driving*	conduire	*to drive*
constructeur	*constructor, builder*	construire	*to construct*
destructeur*	*wrecker/wrecking*	détruire	*to destroy*
éditeur*	*publisher/publishing*	éditer	*to edit*
instructeur	*instructor*	instruire	*to instruct*
lecteur	*reader*	lire	*to read*
moniteur	*(camp) instructor*	monere [LAT.]	*to advise*
persécuteur	*persecutor*	persécuter	*to persecute*
protecteur	*protector*	protéger	*to protect*
rédacteur	*editor*	rédiger	*to write*
sculpteur	*sculptor*	sculpter	*to sculpt*
séducteur*	*seducer/seductive*	séduire	*to seduce*

EXERCICE

57·3

Complétez! *Choose the best completion for each sentence.*

1. _____ La rédactrice de cet article
2. _____ Une tempête de vent
3. _____ Don Juan était un
4. _____ Gustave Eiffel était
5. _____ Auguste Bartholdi était
6. _____ Audrey Tautou est
7. _____ Une instructrice de yoga
8. _____ Le roi Louis XIV était
9. _____ Claude Debussy était
10. _____ Une bonne conductrice
11. _____ Un éditeur web produit
12. _____ Les Romains étaient les
13. _____ Il faut faire des stages de formation
14. _____ Il y a beaucoup de lectrices

a. un contenu adapté à Internet.
b. doit être flexible.
c. pour devenir moniteur ou monitrice.
d. est prudente et vigilante.
e. pour ce blog dédié aux femmes.
f. un grand compositeur français.
g. est une grande destructrice.
h. une actrice française.
i. persécuteurs des chrétiens.
j. un constructeur brillant.
k. est une journaliste-enquêteuse.
l. un protecteur des arts et des lettres.
m. charmant séducteur.
n. le sculpteur de la Statue de la Liberté.

58 ◆ -eur

MEANING	Physical state, quality
ENGLISH EQUIVALENT	—
PART OF SPEECH	Noun
GENDER	Feminine

A French noun ending in the suffix **-eur** may denote a state or quality represented by an adjective; the state is typically physical (for example, size, weight, color, taste, temperature, or speed). The regular formation for this type of noun consists in adding the suffix **-eur** to the masculine form of the adjective that serves as the base word. The **-e** ending of a base adjective is replaced by **-eur**; for example, the adjective **aigre** *bitter* yields **aigreur** *bitterness*. Irregular formations of this type of noun often require dropping the final **-e** of the feminine form of the adjective and adding **-eur**; for example, the adjective **douce** *sweet* yields **douceur** *sweetness*. In the following chart, the feminine form of the adjective is provided if it is used to form the suffixed noun.

NOUN ENDING IN -eur	ENGLISH EQUIVALENT	BASE WORD	ENGLISH EQUIVALENT
aigreur	*bitterness*	aigre	*bitter*
ampleur	*breadth, scope*	ample	*loose, wide*
apesanteur	*weightlessness*	[a-] + pesanteur	*not + weight*
blancheur	*whiteness*	blanc/blanche	*white*
blondeur	*blondness*	blond	*blond*
candeur	*candor*	candide	*candid*
chaleur	*heat*	chaud	*hot*
douceur	*sweetness*	doux/douce	*sweet*
douleur	*pain*	dolor [LAT.]	*pain*
grandeur	*greatness, height*	grand	*great, big, tall*
grosseur	*size, weight*	gros/grosse	*large*
hauteur	*height*	haut	*high*

EXERCICE
58·1

Complétez! *Complete each sentence with the appropriate noun.*

1. La _____ d'une personne est aussi sa taille.

2. La _____ d'une orange peut varier.

3. La _____ de la peau d'un bébé est adorable.

4. Seuls les astronautes font l'expérience de l'_____.

5. La _____ des cheveux fait penser au maïs.

6. La _____ du lait est appétissante.

7. La piqûre pour la grippe cause parfois une petite _____.

8. La _____ de la Tour Eiffel est impressionnante.

9. Peu de gens aiment l'_____ du lait tourné.

10. La voix d'un chanteur d'opéra a une grande _____.

11. La _____ de cette jeune fille en fait une ingénue.

12. La _____ tropicale est pleine d'humidité.

NOUN ENDING IN -eur	ENGLISH EQUIVALENT	BASE WORD	ENGLISH EQUIVALENT
largeur	width	large	wide
lenteur	slowness	lent	slow
longueur	length	long/longue	long
lourdeur	heaviness	lourd	heavy
maigreur	thinness	maigre	thin
minceur	slimness	mince	slim
pâleur	paleness	pâle	pale
pesanteur	gravity	pesant	heavy
profondeur	depth	profond	deep
raideur	stiffness	raide	stiff
rougeur	redness	rouge	red
vigueur	vigor	vigor [LAT.]	vigor

EXERCICE
58·2

Des antonymes! *Provide the antonym(s) for each item.*

1. Blancheur _____

2. Grosseur _____ _____

3. Vitesse _____

4. Longueur _____

5. Apesanteur _____

6. Apathie _____

7. Flexibilité _____

8. Couleur _____ _____

9. Légèreté _____

10. Superficialité _____

MEANING	Device, appliance
ENGLISH EQUIVALENT	*-ator*
PART OF SPEECH	Noun
GENDER	Masculine

A French noun ending in the suffix **-ateur** may denote a device or appliance used for a particular purpose. The base word, which is a verb, represents that purpose. The regular formation for this type of noun consists in replacing the **-er** ending of the verb with **-ateur**; for example, the verb **aspirer** *to aspirate* is the base word for **aspirateur** *vacuum*. Several of these suffixed words denote automobile parts, such as **alternateur** and **carburateur**. Since most of these French nouns have English cognates, they tend to be easily recognized.

NOUN ENDING IN **-ateur**	ENGLISH EQUIVALENT	BASE WORD	ENGLISH EQUIVALENT
accélérateur	*accelerator*	accélérer	*to accelerate*
adaptateur	*adapter*	adapter	*to adapt*
alternateur	*alternator*	alterner	*to alternate*
applicateur	*applicator*	appliquer	*to apply*
aspirateur	*vacuum*	aspirer	*to aspirate*
carburateur	*carburetor*	carburer	*to speed along*
commutateur	*switch*	commuter	*to switch*
congélateur	*freezer*	congeler	*to freeze*
générateur	*generator*	générer	*to generate*
ordinateur	*computer*	ordonner	*to put in order*
purificateur	*purifier*	purifier	*to purify*
ventilateur	*ventilator, fan*	ventiler	*to ventilate*

EXERCICE
59·1

De quoi s'agit-il? *Provide the noun associated with each set of items.*

1. Pureté, filtration _____

2. Deux pièces, unir _____

3. Énergie, moteur _____

4. Lumière, bouton _____

5. Internet, logiciel _____

6. Nettoyer, par terre _____

7. Déplacer l'air, courants d'air _____

8. Pédale, vitesse _____

9. Crème solaire, maquillage _____

10. Moteur à essence, injection _____

11. Produits gelés, glaçons _____

12. Dynamo, source d'énergie _____

60 ◆ -eur

MEANING	Equipment, machinery
ENGLISH EQUIVALENT	-or, -er
PART OF SPEECH	Noun
GENDER	Masculine

A French noun ending in the suffix -**eur** may denote a piece of machinery or equipment used for a particular purpose. The base word, which is typically a verb, represents that purpose. The regular formation for this type of noun consists in replacing the -**er** ending of the verb with -**eur**; for example, the verb **classer** *to file* is the base word for **classeur** *binder, file cabinet.*

NOUN ENDING IN -**eur**	ENGLISH EQUIVALENT	BASE WORD	ENGLISH EQUIVALENT
ascenseur	*elevator*	ascendere [LAT.]	*to go up*
autocuiseur	*pressure cooker*	[auto-] + cuire	*by itself + to cook*
classeur	*binder, file cabinet*	classer	*to file*
climatiseur	*air conditioner*	climatiser	*to air-condition*
compacteur	*compactor*	compacter	*to compact*
conducteur	*conductor* (electricity)	conduire	*to conduct*
diffuseur	*diffuser*	diffuser	*to diffuse*
disjoncteur	*circuit breaker*	disjoncter	*to break*
moteur	*motor*	movere [LAT.]	*to move*
projecteur	*projector*	projeter	*to project*
réacteur	*reactor*	réagir	*to react*
tracteur	*tractor*	trahere [LAT.]	*to pull*

EXERCICE
60·1

Que faut-il? *Provide the noun denoting the equipment or machinery required to perform each activity.*

1. Pour baisser la température dans cette maison _____

2. Pour faire marcher la voiture _____

3. Pour travailler dans les champs _____

4. Pour réduire les déchets de la cuisine _____

5. Pour organiser les notes de cours _____

6. Pour monter au cinquième étage _____

7. Pour couper le courant en cas de surcharge _____

8. Pour cuire sous pression _____

9. Pour permettre un ensemble de réactions en chaîne _____

10. Pour laisser passer le courant électrique _____

11. Pour projeter une image sur un écran _____

12. Pour diffuser des huiles ou des parfums _____

61 ◆ -euse

MEANING	Equipment, furniture
ENGLISH EQUIVALENT	—
PART OF SPEECH	Noun
GENDER	Feminine

A French noun ending in the suffix **-euse** may denote home, yard, or office equipment or furniture used for a particular purpose. The base word, which is typically a verb, represents that purpose. The regular formation for this type of noun consists in replacing the **-er** or **-re** ending of the verb with **-euse**; for example, the verb **agrafer** *to staple* is the base word for **agrafeuse** *stapler*. A few of these suffixed nouns denote large equipment, for example, **dépanneuse** *tow truck*.

NOUN ENDING IN -euse	ENGLISH EQUIVALENT	BASE WORD	ENGLISH EQUIVALENT
agrafeuse	*stapler*	agrafer	*to staple*
balayeuse	*sweeper*	balayer	*to sweep*
berceuse	*rocking chair*	bercer	*to rock*
bétonneuse	*cement mixer*	béton	*cement*
broyeuse	*crusher*	broyer	*to crush*
coiffeuse	*dressing table*	coiffer	*to style hair*
colleuse	*splicer*	coller	*to glue on*
dépanneuse	*tow truck*	dépanner	*to tow*
écrémeuse	*cream separator*	écrémer	*to skim*
éplucheuse	*peeler*	éplucher	*to peel*
friteuse	*fryer*	frite	*fry*
moissonneuse	*harvester*	moissonner	*to harvest*
poinçonneuse	*punch press*	poinçonner	*to punch holes*
tondeuse	*lawn mower*	tondre	*to mow the lawn*
tronçonneuse	*chain saw*	tronçonner	*to saw*
veilleuse	*night-light*	veiller	*to stay up*

EXERCICE
61·1

Vrai ou faux? *Indicate whether each statement is true or false, using* **V** *for* **vrai** *true or* **F** *for* **faux** *false.*

1. _____ Une poinçonneuse sert à écrire.

2. _____ Une moissonneuse est indispensable à l'agriculteur.

3. _____ Une écrémeuse sert à ajouter de la crème.

4. _____ Une bétonneuse est un camion qui porte le béton.

5. _____ Une broyeuse sert à broyer les plantes.

6. _____ Une tronçonneuse sert à planter des arbres.

7. _____ Une tondeuse sert à tondre les cheveux.

8. _____ Une friteuse sert à frire les frites.

9. _____ Une veilleuse est une petite lampe.

10. _____ Une éplucheuse sert à cuire les pommes de terre.

11. _____ Une balayeuse sert à laver la voiture.

12. _____ Une dépanneuse sert à donner de l'aide lors d'une panne de voiture.

13. _____ Une coiffeuse est une table de pique-nique.

14. _____ Une colleuse sert à joindre deux bouts.

15. _____ Une berceuse est un fauteuil qui balance.

16. _____ Une agrafeuse sert à détacher des agrafes.

◆ 62 ◆ -eur/-euse

MEANING	Exhibiting a quality/trait
ENGLISH EQUIVALENT	—
PART OF SPEECH	Adjective, noun
GENDER	Masculine/feminine

A French adjective ending in the suffix **-eur** (feminine: **-euse**) may denote a personal quality. The base word is a verb that indicates the nature of the quality. For example, the base word for **boudeur** is the verb **bouder** *to sulk*, and the suffixed adjective denotes a sulking quality. The regular formation for this type of adjective consists in replacing the infinitive ending of the base verb with **-eur/-euse**. Some of these adjectives also function as nouns; for example, in the phrase **un grand blagueur** *a big joker*, **blagueur** is a noun, but in the sentence **Il a un ton blagueur** *He has a teasing tone*, it is an adjective. Words with this dual function have both the adjective and noun meanings given in the following charts.

ADJECTIVE/NOUN ENDING IN **-eur/-euse**	ENGLISH EQUIVALENT	BASE WORD	ENGLISH EQUIVALENT
batailleur	*aggressive/fighter*	(se) batailler	*to fight*
blagueur	*joking, teasing / joker*	blaguer	*to joke*
boudeur	*sulky/sulker*	bouder	*to sulk*
brailleur	*yelling / yeller, complainer*	brailler	*to yell, complain*
cajoleur	*affectionate/cajoler*	cajoler	*to cajole*
charmeur	*charming/charmer*	charmer	*to charm*
chicaneur	*quibbling/quibbler*	chicaner	*to quibble*
complimenteur	*complimentary/flatterer*	complimenter	*to compliment*
demandeur	*requesting/requester*	demander	*to ask*
dragueur	*flirtatious / pick-up artist*	draguer	*to womanize*

EXERCICE 62·1

Définitions! *Provide the noun that matches each description.*

1. Un homme criard   _____

2. Une femme qui cherche à séduire   _____

3. Un garçon qui a tendance à être mécontent   _____

4. Une fille qui critique et conteste tout le temps   _____

5. Un homme qui flatte et complimente   _____

6. Une fille qui aime la lutte et les débats   _____

7. Un garçon qui aime blaguer   _____

8. Une fille qui cherche toujours un petit ami   _____

9. Un homme qui cherche asile   _____ d'asile

10. Une fille qui aime caresser et être tendre   _____

The following chart contains two exceptions of formation. The base word for **tapageur** *rowdy* is the noun **tapage** *noise*, where the suffix **-eur/-euse** replaces the **-e** ending of the noun. The word **vengeur** has the irregular feminine ending **-eresse**. (See No. 46.)

ADJECTIVE/NOUN ENDING IN **-eur/-euse**	ENGLISH EQUIVALENT	BASE WORD	ENGLISH EQUIVALENT
ensorceleur	*bewitching/bewitcher*	ensorceler	*to bewitch*
menteur	*lying/liar*	mentir	*to lie*
moqueur	*mocking/teaser*	(se) moquer	*to mock*
pêcheur	*fishing/fisherman*	pêcher	*to fish*
rieur	*cheerful/laugher*	rire	*to laugh*
tapageur	*rowdy/brawler*	tapage	*noise*
trompeur	*deceptive/cheater*	tromper	*to deceive*
vengeur	*vengeful/avenger*	venger	*to avenge*

EXERCICE 62·2

Amusons-nous! *To reconstitute this short story, complete each sentence with the masculine or feminine form of the appropriate adjective.*

1. C'est un homme de paix qui n'a jamais dit une seule parole _____ envers ses agresseurs.

2. C'est un homme qui n'a jamais commis d'actes _____ ou hypocrites.

3. Il a un sourire _____ et irrésistible.

4. Il est heureux; même ses yeux sont _____.

5. Il a un entourage _____ et bruyant.

6. Ses amis ne sont pas _____ ; ils disent la vérité.

7. Ses amis ne sont pas non plus _____ ; ils sont sérieux.

8. Ce sont des martins-_____ (petits oiseaux marins).

63 ◆ -isme

MEANING	Faith, belief
ENGLISH EQUIVALENT	*-ism*
PART OF SPEECH	Noun
GENDER	Masculine

Nouns ending in the suffix **-isme** are prevalent in French. They are grouped by theme in Nos. 63–66. Since most of these French nouns have English cognates, they tend to be easily recognized; once you are familiar with them, you will be able to use them in French as easily as in English.

A French noun ending in **-isme** usually denotes a faith or a system of personal belief. For example, the base word for the noun **chauvinisme** is **Chauvin**, the name of a legendary, nationalistic young man who served in Napoleon's army. The noun **chauvinisme** has evolved from its original meaning, *nationalistic*, to a meaning of bigotry or bias. Other **-isme** nouns in the following chart denote a faith, philosophy, or ideology; the base word **libéral** indicates that **libéralisme** denotes a belief in liberal ideas.

NOUN ENDING IN -isme	ENGLISH EQUIVALENT	BASE WORD	ENGLISH EQUIVALENT
anticléricalisme	*anticlericalism*	[anti-] + clérical	*against + clerical*
athéisme	*atheism*	athée	*atheist*
bouddhisme	*Buddhism*	Bouddha	*Buddha*
calvinisme	*Calvinism*	Calvin	*Calvin*
catholicisme	*Catholicism*	catholique	*Catholic*
chauvinisme	*chauvinism*	Chauvin	*Chauvin*
christianisme	*Christianity*	Christ	*Christ*
idéalisme	*idealism*	idéal	*ideal*
libéralisme	*liberalism*	libéral	*liberal*
luthéranisme	*Lutheranism*	Luther	*Luther*
nationalisme	*nationalism*	national	*national*
patriotisme	*patriotism*	patriotique	*patriotic*
protestantisme	*Protestantism*	protestant	*Protestant*
psychisme	*psyche*	psyche [GRK.]	*soul, mind*
sionisme	*Zionism*	Sion	*hill in Jerusalem*
théisme	*theism*	theos [GRK.]	*god, deity*

Des synonymes! *Provide the noun corresponding to each description.*

1. Courant de pensée que les pragmatistes trouvent naïf _____

2. Fierté et amour de son pays _____

3. Contraire du conservatisme _____

4. Mouvement favorable à l'établissement d'un état juif en Palestine _____

5. Ensemble des caractères qui définissent la personnalité _____

6. Ensemble des religions chrétiennes _____

7. Croyance en Dieu _____

8. Croyance dans les préceptes de Calvin _____

9. Ensemble des courants protestants _____

10. Mouvement d'opposition à l'intervention du clergé dans la vie publique _____

11. Patriotisme excessif _____

12. Religion et philosophie orientales _____

13. Doctrine qui nie l'existence de Dieu _____

14. Doctrine qui préconise l'intérêt national _____

15. Religion des chrétiens qui reconnaissent le pape _____

16. Doctrine de Luther _____

64 ▸ -isme

MEANING	Political/social/economic system/doctrine
ENGLISH EQUIVALENT	*-ism*
PART OF SPEECH	Noun
GENDER	Masculine

A French noun ending in the suffix **-isme** may denote a particular political, social, or economic system. For example, the base word for the noun **capitalisme** is **capital**, and the suffixed noun denotes an economic system based on capital.

NOUN ENDING IN -isme	ENGLISH EQUIVALENT	BASE WORD	ENGLISH EQUIVALENT
abolitionnisme	*abolitionism*	abolition	*abolition*
américanisme	*Americanism*	américain	*American*
capitalisme	*capitalism*	capital	*capital*
colonialisme	*colonialism*	colonial	*colonial*
communisme	*communism*	commun	*common*
coopératisme	*cooperatism*	coopératif	*cooperative*
despotisme	*despotism*	despotique	*despotic*
existentialisme	*existentialism*	existence	*existence*
isolationnisme	*isolationism*	isolation	*isolation*
mercantilisme	*mercantilism*	mercari [LAT.]	*to trade*
monarchisme	*monarchism*	monarchique	*monarchical*
mondialisme	*internationalism*	mondial	*international*
provincialisme	*provincialism*	province	*province*
séparatisme	*separatism*	séparation	*separation*
socialisme	*socialism*	social	*social*

Vrai ou faux? *Indicate whether each statement is true or false, using* **V** *for* **vrai** *true or* **F** *for* **faux** *false.*

1. _____ Le provincialisme est une vision étroite et insulaire des choses.

2. _____ Le mondialisme consiste à percevoir tous les dangers du monde.

3. _____ Cuba subit le despotisme depuis seulement quelques années.

4. _____ Le président Lincoln a combattu l'abolitionnisme.

5. _____ Le coopératisme veut généraliser la coopération industrielle entre pays.

6. _____ Le Québec est connu pour ses tendances de séparatisme.

7. _____ Le mercantilisme est une doctrine économique du 17e siècle basée sur l'or et l'argent d'Amérique.

8. _____ L'isolationnisme est la politique d'un état qui consiste à opposer toute intervention de l'extérieur.

9. _____ Le communisme est encore à la base de l'économie et de la politique chinoises.

10. _____ Le colonialisme préconise le développement de pays dépendants et soumis.

11. _____ L'américanisme est enseigné dans les universités partout dans le monde.

12. _____ Le monarchisme constitutionnel est en vigueur en France.

13. _____ Le capitalisme est bien vu en Russie.

14. _____ L'existentialisme est une philosophie explorée par Jean-Paul Sartre et Albert Camus.

15. _____ Le socialisme vise à socialiser les groupes ethniques différents.

65 ▸ -isme

MEANING	Adherence/appreciation (of values)
ENGLISH EQUIVALENT	*-ism*
PART OF SPEECH	Noun
GENDER	Masculine

A French noun ending in the suffix **-isme** may denote adherence to a system of personal views or values represented by the base word. For example, the base word for the noun **conformisme** is the adjective **conforme** *conforming*, and the suffixed noun denotes an appreciation of conformism. The values embodied by these nouns may be moral, immoral, or amoral. The word **masochisme** is based on the name of an Austrian writer known for his masochistic novels. Similarly, the word **sadisme** is based on **de Sade**, the name of the notorious 18th-century marquis and novelist whose works meshed sexuality with violence and criminal behavior. See Nos. 67 and 68 for nouns ending in **-iste** that denote adherents of these *-isms*.

NOUN ENDING IN -isme	ENGLISH EQUIVALENT	BASE WORD	ENGLISH EQUIVALENT
conformisme	*conformism*	conforme	*conforming*
culturalisme	*culturalism*	culture	*culture*
égocentrisme	*egocentrism*	[ego-] + centre	*ego + center*
fétichisme	*fetishism*	fétiche	*fetish*
hédonisme	*hedonism*	hedone [GRK.]	*pleasure*
masochisme	*masochism*	von Sacher-Masoch	*Austrian writer*
nudisme	*nudism*	nu	*nude*
optimisme	*optimism*	optimus [LAT.]	*best*
pessimisme	*pessimism*	pessimus [LAT.]	*worst*
racisme	*racism*	race	*race*
sadisme	*sadism*	Marquis de Sade	*French writer*
satanisme	*Satanism*	satan	*Satan*
stoïcisme	*stoicism*	stoïque	*stoic*
traditionalisme	*traditionalism*	traditionnel	*traditional*
végétarisme	*vegetarianism*	végétarien	*vegetarian*

EXERCICE 65·1

Définitions! *Provide the noun that corresponds to each description.*

1. Disposition d'esprit qui incline à prendre les choses du bon côté _____

2. Tendance qui consiste à ne voir que ses propres intérêts _____

3. Style de vie où on passe une grande partie de son temps dans un état de nudité _____

4. Style de vie où on ne cherche qu'à se faire plaisir _____

5. Tendance à se conformer aux usages et aux normes sociales _____

6. Hostilité envers un groupe ou une race _____

7. Régime alimentaire qui exclue la viande
   _____

8. Attachement aux coutumes traditionnelles
   _____

9. Impassibilité devant le malheur
   _____

10. Culte de Satan
    _____

11. Plaisir à faire souffrir
    _____

12. Disposition d'esprit qui incline à prendre les choses du mauvais côté
    _____

13. Croyance que chaque culture modèle une personnalité typique
    _____

14. Comportement de quelqu'un qui recherche les situations qui font souffrir
    _____

15. Admiration sans réserve de quelque chose
    _____

66 ◆ -isme

MEANING	Artistic/literary/musical movement/style
ENGLISH EQUIVALENT	*-ism*
PART OF SPEECH	Noun
GENDER	Masculine

A French noun ending in the suffix **-isme** may denote a particular movement in art, literature, or music. Imagination is sometimes required to comprehend the composite meaning of the base word and suffix. For example, the base word for the noun **cubisme** is the adjective **cube**; the noun **cubisme** denotes a movement in painting that has multiple viewpoints. (Georges Braque and Pablo Picasso were pioneers of this movement.)

NOUN ENDING IN -isme	ENGLISH EQUIVALENT	BASE WORD	ENGLISH EQUIVALENT
cubisme	*cubism*	cube	*cube*
existentialisme	*existentialism*	existence	*existence*
fauvisme	*fauvism*	fauve	*wild animal*
futurisme	*futurism*	futur	*future*
humanisme	*humanism*	humain	*human*
impressionnisme	*impressionism*	impression	*impression*
modernisme	*modernism*	moderne	*modern*
réalisme	*realism*	réel	*real*
romantisme	*romanticism*	romantique	*romantic*
scientisme	*scientism*	science	*science*
surréalisme	*surrealism*	surréel	*surreal*
symbolisme	*symbolism*	symbole	*symbol*

Complétez! *Choose the best completion for each sentence.*

1. _____ L'impressionnisme

2. _____ Le scientisme

3. _____ Le modernisme s'oppose

4. _____ Le romantisme consiste à

5. _____ Matisse et Braque sont des peintres

6. _____ Le surréalisme comprend des formes

7. _____ Le réalisme s'oppose

8. _____ Le symbolisme est un système

9. _____ L'existentialisme est une doctrine

10. _____ Le futurisme est un mouvement

11. _____ L'humanisme place

12. _____ On attribue surtout les débuts

a. de symboles destinés à interpréter des faits.

b. au romanticisme.

c. qu'on associe au fauvisme.

d. est un art qui capture des impressions.

e. au traditionalisme.

f. basé sur les notions du monde futur.

g. les valeurs humaines au centre de tout.

h. se laisser dominer par l'imagination.

i. du cubisme à Picasso.

j. d'expression comme l'écriture automatique.

k. basée sur l'expérience du vécu.

l. consiste à croire que la science explique la vie.

67 ◆ -iste

MEANING	Believer (in a personal viewpoint/value)
ENGLISH EQUIVALENT	*-ist*
PART OF SPEECH	Noun
GENDER	Masculine/feminine

Nouns ending in the suffix **-iste** are prevalent in French. They are grouped by theme in Nos. 67–70 and correspond, for the most part, to nouns ending in **-isme**. (See Nos. 63–66.) These suffixed nouns may also function as adjectives. Since most of them have English cognates, they tend to be easily recognized; once you are familiar with them, you will be able to use them in French as easily as in English.

A French noun ending in the suffix **-iste** may denote a believer in a personal viewpoint or value. For example, the base word for the noun **pacifiste** is the noun **paix** *peace*, and the suffixed noun denotes a person (male or female) who values peace. Included in the following chart is the noun **je-m'en-foutiste** *I-don't-give-a-damn type*, based on the expression **je m'en fou** *I don't give a damn*; the suffixed noun is often used as an adjective.

NOUN ENDING IN -iste	ENGLISH EQUIVALENT	BASE WORD	ENGLISH EQUIVALENT
alarmiste	*alarmist*	alarme	*alarm*
altruiste	*altruist*	alter [LAT.]	*other*
anticonformiste	*anticonformist*	[anti-] + conforme	*against + conforming*
conformiste	*conformist*	conforme	*conforming*
élitiste	*elitist*	élite	*elite*
fantaisiste	*fantasist*	fantaisie	*fantasy*
je-m'en-foutiste	*I-don't-give-a-damn type*	je m'en fou	*I don't give a damn*
matérialiste	*materialist*	matériel	*material*
naturiste	*naturist*	nature	*nature*
nihiliste	*nihilist*	nihil [LAT.]	*nothing*
pacifiste	*pacifist*	paix	*peace*
perfectionniste	*perfectionist*	parfait	*perfect*
puriste	*purist*	pure	*pure*
utopiste	*utopian*	utopie	*utopia*

EXERCICE

67·1

Vrai ou faux? *Indicate whether each statement is true or false, using* **V** *for* **vrai** *true or* **F** *for* **faux** *false.*

1. _____ Les matérialistes aiment les richesses et les possessions matérielles.

2. _____ Les naturistes n'aiment pas la nudité.

3. _____ Les je-m'en-foutistes sont traditionnels.

4. _____ Les utopistes croient qu'il est possible de forger une société idéale.

5. _____ Les altruistes n'aiment pas la société.

6. _____ Les anticonformistes s'opposent aux usages et aux normes.

7. _____ Les puristes veulent purifier l'eau dans le monde.

8. _____ Les conformistes s'adaptent mal à la vie moderne.

9. _____ Les perfectionnistes veulent tout faire minutieusement.

10. _____ Les nihilistes ne veulent pas d'anarchisme.

11. _____ Les pacifistes préconisent la paix avant tout.

12. _____ Les fantaisistes ne sont pas sérieux.

13. _____ Les élitistes croient à la monarchie absolue.

14. _____ Les alarmistes ont tendance à répandre des mensonges.

68 ◆ -iste

MEANING	Proponent, follower
ENGLISH EQUIVALENT	*-ist*
PART OF SPEECH	Noun
GENDER	Masculine/feminine

A French noun ending in the suffix **-iste** may denote a proponent or follower of a particular movement. For example, the base word for the noun **royaliste** is the noun **roi** *king*, and the suffixed noun denotes a person (male or female) who supports a particular king. Many of the nouns in the following chart are related to nouns ending in **-isme**; for example, **activiste** is *activist* and **activisme** is *activism*. (See Nos. 64 and 66.)

NOUN ENDING IN **-iste**	ENGLISH EQUIVALENT	BASE WORD	ENGLISH EQUIVALENT
abolitionniste	*abolitionist*	abolition	*abolition*
activiste	*activist*	agir	*to act*
anticommuniste	*anticommunist*	[anti-] + commun	*against + common*
capitaliste	*capitalist*	capital	*capital*
contre-terroriste	*counterterrorist*	terreur	*terror*
existentialiste	*existentialist*	existence	*existence*
extrémiste	*extremist*	extrême	*extreme*
féministe	*feminist*	féminin	*feminine*
helléniste	*Hellenist*	Hellas [GRK.]	*Greece*
humaniste	*humanist*	humain	*human*
intégrationniste	*integrationist*	intégration	*integration*
protectionniste	*protectionist*	protection	*protection*
royaliste	*royalist*	roi	*king*
sécessionniste	*secessionist*	sécession	*secession*
socialiste	*socialist*	social	*social*

EXERCICE
68·1

Définitions! *Provide the noun that corresponds to each phrase.*

1. Contre l'esclavage   _____

2. Contre le communisme   _____

3. Pour le respect des droits des femmes   _____

4. Fana de la culture grecque   _____

5. Pour la séparation d'un état   _____

6. Pour le roi   _____

7. Pour l'entreprise privée   _____

8. Pour des mesures radicales   _____

9. Pour les valeurs humaines   _____

10. Contre la concurrence étrangère   _____

11. Pour un système politique qui protège les droits des travailleurs _____

12. Partisan de l'égalité raciale ou politique _____

13. Pour le sens de la vie par le vécu _____

14. Partisan de l'action _____

69 ◆ -iste

MEANING	Expert/specialist (in a skill or art form)
ENGLISH EQUIVALENT	*-ist*
PART OF SPEECH	Noun
GENDER	Masculine/feminine

A French noun ending in the suffix **-iste** may denote a person who specializes in a skill or art form. For example, the base word for the noun **caricaturiste** is the noun **caricature**, and the suffixed noun denotes a person who exaggerates features of subjects in his or her drawing or writing. Similarly, the base word for **alpiniste** *mountain climber* is **Alpes**, the name of one of the longest mountain ranges in Europe; the Alps are indeed a heaven for mountain climbers. The regular formation for this type of noun consists in replacing the **-e** ending of the base noun with **-iste**. If the base noun ends in a consonant, the suffix is directly attached to it; for example, **violon** yields **violoniste**.

Some of the nouns in the following chart are related to nouns ending in **-isme** that denote a set of skills; for example, **alpiniste** is *mountain climber* and **alpinisme** is *mountain climbing*. Others examples are **automobiliste/automobilisme, illusionniste/illusionnisme,** and **motocycliste/motocyclisme**. (See No. 66 for more information about such nouns.) Note that the noun **encyclopédiste** exists only in the masculine form, because it refers to exclusively male 18th-century thinkers like Denis Diderot, who drafted the first French encyclopedia.

NOUN ENDING IN **-iste**	ENGLISH EQUIVALENT	BASE WORD	ENGLISH EQUIVALENT
alpiniste	*mountain climber*	Alpes	*Alps*
automobiliste	*automobilist*	automobile	*automobile*
caricaturiste	*caricaturist*	caricature	*caricature*
céramiste	*ceramist*	céramique	*ceramic*
clarinettiste	*clarinetist*	clarinette	*clarinet*
concertiste	*concert artist*	concert	*concert*
cycliste	*cyclist*	cyclisme	*cycling*
duettiste	*duettist*	duo	*duet*
encyclopédiste	*encyclopedist*	encyclopédie	*encyclopedia*
fabuliste	*fable writer*	fable	*fable*
flûtiste	*flutist*	flûte	*flute*
humoriste	*humorist*	humour	*humor*
illusionniste	*illusionist*	illusion	*illusion*
maquettiste	*model maker*	maquette	*model*
motocycliste	*motorcyclist*	motocycle	*motorcycle*

▶

NOUN ENDING IN **-iste**	ENGLISH EQUIVALENT	BASE WORD	ENGLISH EQUIVALENT
organiste	*organist*	orgue	*organ*
paysagiste	*landscaper*	paysage	*landscape*
soliste	*soloist*	solo	*solo*
sopraniste	*soprano*	soprano [ITAL.]	*high voice*
styliste	*fashion designer*	style	*style*
urbaniste	*urban planner*	urbain	*urban*
violoniste	*violinist*	violon	*violin*

EXERCICE
69·1

Le jeu des catégories! *Answer each question, using the names of specialists. There are at least two answers for each question.*

1. Qui dessine?

_____ _____ _____ _____

2. Qui joue d'un instrument?

_____ _____ _____ _____

3. Qui offre des spectacles divertissants et drôles?

_____ _____ _____ _____

4. Qui est expert en activités sportives?

_____ _____ _____ _____

5. Qui chante?

_____ _____ _____

6. Quel artiste musical donne une performance individuelle?

_____ _____

7. Qui est expert de la langue?

_____ _____ _____

8. Qui a une expertise artisanale et manuelle?

_____ _____ _____

70 ◆ -iste

MEANING	Technician/specialist (in medicine/health/science)
ENGLISH EQUIVALENT	*-ist*
PART OF SPEECH	Noun
GENDER	Masculine/feminine

A French word ending in the suffix **-iste** may denote a person who has a career in medicine, health, or science. The base word denotes the field of expertise. For example, the base word for the noun **dentiste** is the noun **dent** *tooth*, and the suffixed noun denotes the person (male or female) who practices dentistry.

NOUN ENDING IN **-iste**	ENGLISH EQUIVALENT	BASE WORD	ENGLISH EQUIVALENT
algébriste	*algebraist*	algèbre	*algebra*
anesthésiste	*anesthetist*	[an-] + esthésie	*no + sensitivity*
botaniste	*botanist*	botanique	*botany*
chimiste	*chemist*	chimie	*chemistry*
dentiste	*dentist*	dent	*tooth*
diététiste	*dietician*	diète	*diet*
exorciste	*exorcist*	exorcisme	*exorcism*
génétiste	*geneticist*	gène	*gene*
herboriste	*herbalist*	herbe	*herb*
hygiéniste	*hygienist*	hygiène	*hygiene*
nutritionniste	*nutritionist*	nutrition	*nutrition*
oculiste	*eye doctor*	oculus [LAT.]	*eye*
orthodontiste	*orthodontist*	orthos + odous [GRK.]	*straight + tooth*
orthopédiste	*orthopedist*	orthos + pais/paidos [GRK.]	*straight + child*
secouriste	*first-aid worker*	secours	*aid, help*

EXERCICE 70·1

De qui s'agit-il? *Provide the name of the specialist described in each sentence.*

1. Il/Elle vous guide dans vos régimes alimentaires. _____

2. Il/Elle vous guide dans votre hygiène dentaire. _____

3. Il/Elle vous endort pendant une opération. _____

4. Il/Elle vous corrige des anomalies de position dentaire. _____

5. Il/Elle étudie les effets de la structure génétique. _____

6. Il/Elle fait des expériences et des études de chimie. _____

7. Il/Elle vous corrige les imperfections de la vue. _____

8. Il/Elle est expert en matière d'algèbre. _____

9. Il/Elle soigne vos dents: les caries etc. _____

10. Il/Elle vous vient en aide lors d'un accident. _____

11. Il/Elle se spécialise dans les difformités du corps. _____

12. Il/Elle étudie les matières végétales. _____

13. Il/Elle se spécialise dans les plantes médicinales. _____

14. Il/Elle chasse les démons. _____

15. Il/Elle traite les patients par des moyens diététiques. _____

71 ◆ -ologiste

MEANING	Technician/specialist (in medicine/health/science)
ENGLISH EQUIVALENT	*-ologist*
PART OF SPEECH	Noun
GENDER	Masculine/feminine

The suffix **-ologiste**, as well as the suffixes **-ologue** and **-ologie** (Nos. 72 and 73, respectively), evolved from the Greek noun **logos**, whose meaning evolved from *speech* to *a principle of knowledge or science*.

A French noun ending in the suffix **-ologiste** denotes a person (male or female) who has a career in medicine, health, or science. For example, the base word for the noun **anesthésiologiste** is the noun **anesthésie** *absence of sensitivity*, and the suffixed noun denotes the medical specialist in charge of anesthesia. The noun **anesthésiste** (see No. 70) can be regarded as *one who puts people to sleep* but without the larger responsibilities of **anesthésiologiste**. A similar distinction can be made between the nouns **oculiste** *eye doctor* and **ophtalmologiste** *ophthalmologist*. Since most of these French nouns have English cognates, they tend to be easily recognized.

NOUN ENDING IN **-ologiste**	ENGLISH EQUIVALENT	BASE WORD	ENGLISH EQUIVALENT
allergologiste	*allergist*	allergie	*allergy*
anesthésiologiste	*anesthesiologist*	anesthésie	*anesthesia*
bactériologiste	*bacteriologist*	bactérie	*bacteria*
biologiste	*biologist*	biologie	*biology*
cosmétologiste	*cosmetologist*	cosmétique	*cosmetic*
dermatologiste	*dermatologist*	derma [GRK.]	*skin*
embryologiste	*embryologist*	embryon	*embryo*
généalogiste	*genealogist*	gène	*gene*
immunologiste	*immunologist*	immune	*immune*
laryngologiste	*laryngologist*	larynx	*larynx*
neurologiste	*neurologist*	neuron [GRK.]	*nerve*
ophtalmologiste	*ophthalmologist*	ophthalmos [GRK.]	*eye*
pathologiste	*pathologist*	pathos [GRK.]	*disease*
pharmacologiste	*pharmacologist*	pharmacie	*pharmacy*
radiologiste	*radiologist*	radio	*radio*
virologiste	*virologist*	virus	*virus*

Charade! *Provide the name of the specialist associated with each item.*

1. Les nerfs _____

2. Les virus _____

3. Le système immunitaire _____

4. Le larynx _____

5. La cosmétique _____

6. Les soins de la peau _____

7. Les embryons _____

8. Les causes et les symptômes d'une maladie _____

9. La pharmacie _____

10. Les allergies _____

11. Les rayons X _____

12. La suppression de la sensibilité corporelle _____

13. Les yeux _____

14. Les bactéries _____

15. Les organismes vivants _____

16. Les gènes _____

72 ◆ -ologue

MEANING	Specialist (in a global discipline)
ENGLISH EQUIVALENT	*-ologist*
PART OF SPEECH	Noun
GENDER	Masculine/feminine

A French noun ending in the suffix **-ologue** denotes a person with expertise in a medical specialty or a global discipline. The base word represents the area of expertise. For example, the base word for the noun **cancérologue** is the noun **cancer**, and the suffixed noun denotes the medical specialist who treats cancer. For some of these nouns, the meaning has extended or shifted. For example, the base word for the noun **météorologue** is the noun **météore**; the ancient Greeks studied meteors, and their modern counterparts forecast weather. (See No. 73 for the areas in which these specialists operate.) Since most of these French nouns have English cognates, they tend to be easily recognized.

NOUN ENDING IN -ologue	ENGLISH EQUIVALENT	BASE WORD	ENGLISH EQUIVALENT
anthropologue	*anthropologist*	anthropos [GRK.]	*human being*
archéologue	*archaeologist*	archaios [GRK.]	*ancient*
cancérologue	*oncologist*	cancer	*cancer*
cardiologue	*cardiologist*	kardia [GRK.]	*heart*
climatologue	*climatologist*	climat	*climate*
criminologue	*criminologist*	crime	*crime*
géologue	*geologist*	geos [GRK.]	*earth*
gynécologue	*gynecologist*	gyne [GRK.]	*woman*
hydrologue	*hydrologist*	hydor [GRK.]	*water*
météorologue	*meteorologist*	météore	*meteor*
musicologue	*musicologist*	musique	*music*
océanologue	*oceanologist*	océan	*ocean*
philologue	*philologist*	philos [GRK.]	*lover*
pneumologue	*pneumologist*	pneuma [GRK.]	*breath*
politologue	*political analyst*	politique	*politics*
psychologue	*psychologist*	psyche [GRK.]	*soul, mind*
sexologue	*sexologist*	sexe	*sex*
sociologue	*sociologist*	société	*society*
spéléologue	*speleologist*	spelaion [GRK.]	*cave*
volcanologue	*vulcanologist*	volcan	*volcano*

EXERCICE
72·1

Le jeu des catégories! *Answer each question, using the names of specialists. There are at least two answers for each question.*

1. Qui étudie les conditions naturelles associées au temps?

   _____   _____

2. Qui étudie les états d'esprit et les états mentaux?

   _____   _____

3. Qui étudie la terre?

   _____   _____   _____

   _____   _____

4. Qui sont les experts de la politique et de la société?

   _____   _____

5. Qui soigne des maladies très graves?

   _____   _____   _____

6. Qui sont les experts des anciens temps et des anciennes civilisations?

   _____   _____

7. Qui sont les experts en matière de troubles sexuels et en gynécologie?

_____   _____

8. Qui a une expertise de l'expression musicale et linguistique?

_____   _____

73 -ologie

MEANING	Area of study/research
ENGLISH EQUIVALENT	*-ology*
PART OF SPEECH	Noun
GENDER	Feminine

A French noun ending in the suffix **-ologie** denotes an area of study or research. For example, the prefix **bio-** *life*, which is a Greek root, is the base word for the noun **biologie** *biology*, and the suffixed noun denotes the study of things that are alive. There are numerous words ending in this suffix; the following chart presents only a sampling. Since these French nouns have English cognates, they are easily recognized. (See Nos. 71 and 72 for related nouns ending in **-ologiste** and **-ologue**; these nouns denote specialists in the areas of study.)

NOUN ENDING IN **-ologie**	ENGLISH EQUIVALENT	BASE WORD	ENGLISH EQUIVALENT
astrologie	*astrology*	astre	*celestial body*
bactériologie	*bacteriology*	bactérie	*bacteria*
biologie	*biology*	[bio-]	*life*
cancérologie	*oncology*	cancer	*cancer*
climatologie	*climatology*	climat	*climate*
cosmologie	*cosmology*	kosmos [GRK.]	*world*
criminologie	*criminology*	crime	*crime*
embryologie	*embryology*	embryon	*embryo*
géologie	*geology*	geos [GRK.]	*earth*
gynécologie	*gynecology*	gyne [GRK.]	*woman*
idéologie	*ideology*	idée	*idea*
météorologie	*meteorology*	météore	*meteor*
microbiologie	*microbiology*	[micro-] + [bio-]	*micro + life*
morphologie	*morphology*	morphe [GRK.]	*form, shape*
mythologie	*mythology*	mythe	*myth*
neurologie	*neurology*	neuron [GRK.]	*nerve*
psychologie	*psychology*	psyche [GRK.]	*soul, mind*
théologie	*theology*	theos [GRK.]	*god*
toxicologie	*toxicology*	toxicum [LAT.]	*poison*
volcanologie	*vulcanology*	volcan	*volcano*

Lesquels ont quelque chose en commun? *Name the specialties associated with each item. There are at least two specialties for each item.*

1. Le fœtus

_____ _____

2. La cellule en transformation

_____ _____

3. Les couches géologiques de la terre

_____ _____

4. L'ensemble d'idées et de croyances

_____ _____ _____

5. L'univers et les astres

_____ _____

6. Les bactéries

_____ _____

7. Ce qui est nuisible et criminel

_____ _____

8. Les états du système nerveux et ceux d'esprit

_____ _____

9. La prévision du temps

_____ _____

10. La forme des êtres vivants

_____ _____

74 ◆ -ite

MEANING	Inflammation
ENGLISH EQUIVALENT	*-itis*
PART OF SPEECH	Noun
GENDER	Feminine

A French noun ending in the suffix **-ite** may denote an inflammation of animal tissue. The base word, a part of the anatomy, represents the tissue or organ that is inflamed. For example, the base word for the noun **otite** is the Greek root **otos** *ear*, and the suffixed noun means inflammation of the ear, or *otitis*. Since these French nouns have English cognates, they are easily recognized, even though they are technical words.

NOUN ENDING IN -ite	ENGLISH EQUIVALENT	BASE WORD	ENGLISH EQUIVALENT
amygdalite	*tonsillitis*	amygdale	*tonsil*
appendicite	*appendicitis*	appendice	*appendix*
artérite	*arteritis*	artère	*artery*
arthrite	*arthritis*	arthron [GRK.]	*joint*
bronchite	*bronchitis*	bronches	*bronchi*
cardite	*carditis*	kardia [GRK.]	*heart*
colite	*colitis*	côlon	*colon*
cystite	*cystitis*	kustis [GRK.]	*bladder*
dermatite	*dermatitis*	derma [GRK.]	*skin*
encéphalite	*encephalitis*	encéphale	*encephalon*
entérite	*enteritis*	enteron [GRK.]	*intestine*
gastrite	*gastritis*	gaster [GRK.]	*stomach*

EXERCICE

74·1

Vrai ou faux? *Indicate whether each statement is true or false, using* **V** *for* **vrai** *true or* **F** *for* **faux** *false.*

1. _____ On développe parfois une bronchite après un rhume.

2. _____ Il suffit de prendre des aspirines pour guérir une appendicite.

3. _____ La colite est l'inflammation du gros intestin.

4. _____ Une artérite est une rupture de l'artère.

5. _____ L'entérite est l'inflammation de l'intestin grêle.

6. _____ L'amygdalite est une infection de la gorge.

7. _____ La dermatite est un procédé esthétique.

8. _____ La cardite est une inflammation du cerveau.

9. _____ L'encéphalite est l'inflammation d'une partie du cerveau.

10. _____ La gastrite est un cancer de l'estomac.

11. _____ La cystite est un problème de vessie.

12. _____ La colite se manifeste par une tumeur dans le côlon.

NOUN ENDING IN -ite	ENGLISH EQUIVALENT	BASE WORD	ENGLISH EQUIVALENT
gingivite	*gingivitis*	gingiva [LAT.]	*gum*
laryngite	*laryngitis*	larynx	*larynx*
lymphangite	*lymphangitis*	lymphe	*lymph*
méningite	*meningitis*	méninges	*meninges*
myosite	*myositis*	mys [GRK.]	*muscle*
otite	*otitis*	otos [GRK.]	*ear*
pancréatite	*pancreatitis*	pancréas	*pancreas*
poliomyélite	*poliomyelitis*	polios + myelos [GRK.]	*grayish + marrow*
sinusite	*sinusitis*	sinus	*sinus*
tendinite	*tendonitis*	tendon	*tendon*

EXERCICE 74·2

De quelle inflammation s'agit-il? *Provide the name of the inflammation for each type of tissue.*

1. Celle des sinus _____

2. Celle des méninges _____

3. Celle des lymphes _____

4. Celle des gencives _____

5. Celle des muscles _____

6. Celle des tendons _____

7. Celle du larynx _____

8. Celle du pancréas _____

9. Celle des oreilles _____

10. Celle de la substance grise de la moelle épinière _____

75 ◆ -manie

MEANING	Addiction
ENGLISH EQUIVALENT	*-mania*
PART OF SPEECH	Noun
GENDER	Feminine

A French word ending in the suffix **-manie** denotes an addiction; the Greek word **mania** means *madness.* For example, the base word for the noun **anglomanie** is **anglo-**, and the suffixed noun denotes an addiction to all things English. Related nouns denoting people who are dependent or addicted are **pyromane** *fire addict* and **claustromane** *one addicted to closed spaces.* The Greek root **eros** *love* plus the suffix **-manie** yield **érotomanie** *erotomania,* which is the false conviction that one is loved by a stranger (frequently a celebrity). Since many of these French words have English cognates, they tend to be easily recognized.

NOUN ENDING IN -manie	ENGLISH EQUIVALENT	BASE WORD	ENGLISH EQUIVALENT
anglomanie	*anglomania*	anglo	*Anglo*
bibliomanie	*bibliomania*	biblion [GRK.]	*book*
claustromanie	*claustromania*	claustrer	*to lock up*
cocaïnomanie	*cocaine addiction*	cocaïne	*cocaine*
démonomanie	*demon mania*	démon	*demon*
érotomanie	*erotomania*	eros [GRK.]	*love*
kleptomanie	*kleptomania*	kleptes [GRK.]	*thief*
mégalomanie	*megalomania*	megas [GRK.]	*grand*
morphinomanie	*morphine addiction*	morphine	*morphine*
mythomanie	*mythomania*	mythe	*myth*
nymphomanie	*nymphomania*	nymphe	*nymph*
opiomanie	*opium addiction*	opium	*opium*
pharmacomanie	*pharmacomania*	pharmakeia [GRK.]	*medication*
pyromanie	*pyromania*	pyr [GRK.]	*fire*
tabacomanie	*tobacco addiction*	tabac	*tobacco*
toxicomanie	*drug addiction*	toxicum [LAT.]	*poison*

EXERCICE
75·1

Faites le bon choix! *Choose the best word in the second column to complete each sentence in the first column.*

1. _____ La mégalomanie est une manie de la _____.

2. _____ La cocaïnomanie est une dépendance de la _____.

3. _____ L'anglomanie est une obsession pour tout ce qui est _____.

4. _____ L'érotomanie est la conviction illusoire d'être _____.

5. _____ La kleptomanie est une impulsion qui pousse à _____.

6. _____ La démonomanie paraît souvent dans des films d'_____ à Halloween.

7. _____ La bibliomanie consiste à collectionner un nombre infini de _____.

8. _____ La mythomanie empêche de distinguer le _____ de l'imaginaire.

9. _____ La pyromanie pousse les pyromanes à allumer des _____.

10. _____ La tabacomanie est finalement en _____.

11. _____ La pharmacomanie est la cause du _____ d'un certain nombre de personnes.

12. _____ L'opiomanie est la dépendance de l'_____.

13. _____ La toxicomanie est l'_____ de consommer des substances qui engendrent un état de dépendance.

14. _____ La nymphomanie est l'exacerbation du désir _____ chez la femme.

15. _____ La morphinomanie est la dépendance de la _____.

16. _____ La claustromanie pousse les claustromanes à s'_____.

a. anglais

b. enfermer

c. grandeur

d. aimé

e. habitude

f. opium

g. voler

h. déclin

i. livres

j. cocaïne

k. feux

l. vécu

m. horreur

n. sexuel

o. décès

p. morphine

76 -phobie

MEANING	Obsessive fear
ENGLISH EQUIVALENT	*-phobia*
PART OF SPEECH	Noun
GENDER	Feminine

A French noun ending in the suffix **-phobie** denotes an irrational or obsessive fear of something. The base word represents the object of the fear. For example, the base word for the noun **arachnophobie** is the Greek word **arachne** *spider*, and the suffixed noun denotes a fear of spiders. Related nouns denoting people afflicted by these fears are **acrophobe** *one fearful of heights* and **agoraphobe** *one fearful of public places*.

NOUN ENDING IN **-phobie**	ENGLISH EQUIVALENT	BASE WORD	ENGLISH EQUIVALENT
acrophobie	*acrophobia*	akros [GRK.]	*high*
agoraphobie	*agoraphobia*	agora [GRK.]	*public place*
arachnophobie	*arachnophobia*	arachne [GRK.]	*spider*
claustrophobie	*claustrophobia*	claustrer	*to lock up*
émétophobie	*emetophobia*	emetos [GRK.]	*vomit*
gymnophobie	*gymnophobia*	gymnos [GRK.]	*naked*
logophobie	*logophobia*	logos [GRK.]	*speech*
ochlophobie	*ochlophobia*	ochlos [GRK.]	*crowd*

EXERCICE
76·1

Quel cauchemar! *Provide the name of the phobia expressed by each exclamation.*

1. « Monter à la Tour Eiffel! Ah non! » _____

2. « Me baigner tout nu sur la Côte d'Azur! Ah non! » _____

3. « Sortir le 4 juillet pour voir les feux d'artifice! Ah non! » _____

4. « Nous promener en forêt avec tous les insectes! Ah non! » _____

5. « Faire un discours devant une audience! Ah non! » _____

6. « Être infirmier et laver les vomissures! Ah non! » _____

7. « Rester coincé dans un petit ascenseur! Ah non! » _____

8. « Sortir tout seul dans un café! Ah non! » _____

77 ▸ -itude

MEANING	State, condition
ENGLISH EQUIVALENT	*-itude*
PART OF SPEECH	Noun
GENDER	Feminine

A French word ending in the suffix **-itude** denotes a state or condition. The base word is usually an adjective or a Latin root. For example, the adjective **exact** yields the noun **exactitude**. If an adjective ends in **-e**, this ending is replaced by the suffix **-itude**; for example, the adjective **ample** yields the noun **amplitude**. Since these French words have English cognates, they are easily recognized.

NOUN ENDING IN **-itude**	ENGLISH EQUIVALENT	BASE WORD	ENGLISH EQUIVALENT
altitude	*altitude*	altus [LAT.]	*high*
amplitude	*amplitude*	ample	*ample*
aptitude	*aptitude*	apte	*apt*
certitude	*certitude*	certain	*certain*
décrépitude	*decrepitude*	décrépit	*decrepit*
exactitude	*exactitude, accuracy*	exact	*accurate*
gratitude	*gratitude*	gratus [LAT.]	*grateful*
habitude	*habit*	habitudo [LAT.]	*habit*
inexactitude	*inaccuracy*	[in-] + exact	*not + accurate*
ingratitude	*ingratitude*	[in-] + gratus [LAT.]	*not + grateful*

EXERCICE 77·1

Complétez! *Complete each sentence with the appropriate noun.*

1. Il faut montrer de la _____ aux gens qui vous aident.

2. La _____ de ces vieux immeubles est lamentable.

3. Les candidats présidentiels ont toujours la _____ qu'ils gagneront.

4. Il vaut mieux prendre la bonne _____ de finir le travail avant de partir.

5. L'_____ quand on arrive à un rendez-vous est toujours appréciée.

6. Les enfants ont toutes sortes d'_____ qu'il faut encourager.

7. L'_____ des changements climatiques est sous-estimée.

8. L'_____ vis à vis de la générosité n'est pas appropriée.

9. Les journalistes font parfois la faute de transmettre une _____.

10. Il y a moins d'oxygène à une grande _____.

NOUN ENDING IN **-itude**	ENGLISH EQUIVALENT	BASE WORD	ENGLISH EQUIVALENT
lassitude	*lassitude, tiredness*	las	*tired*
multitude	*multitude*	[multi-]	*many*
prélude	*prelude*	[pre-] + ludere [LAT.]	*before + play*
promptitude	*promptness*	prompt	*prompt, quick*
servitude	*servitude*	servus [LAT.]	*slave*
similitude	*similitude, likeness*	similis [LAT.]	*similar*
solitude	*solitude*	solus [LAT.]	*alone*
sollicitude	*solicitude, concern*	sollicitus [LAT.]	*concerned*
turpitude	*turpitude, depravity*	turpis [LAT.]	*ugly, nasty*
vicissitude	*vicissitude*	vicis [LAT.]	*change*

EXERCICE 77·2

Soyons logiques! *Choose the best completion for each sentence.*

1. _____ Les bons vendeurs montrent
2. _____ La vicissitude des saisons
3. _____ La similitude est naturelle
4. _____ La lassitude est normale
5. _____ La turpitude morale est
6. _____ La promptitude de votre réponse
7. _____ La multitude des symptômes
8. _____ Les pêcheurs recherchent
9. _____ Quel dommage que certains
10. _____ Ce prélude musical annonce

a. un magnifique concert.
b. rend le diagnostic difficile.
c. est requise.
d. doivent vivre en état de servitude.
e. la solitude.
f. entre des jumeaux ou des jumelles.
g. n'est pas banale.
h. un défaut.
i. après une maladie.
j. beaucoup de sollicitude.

78 ◆ -aison

MEANING	Action, result of an action
ENGLISH EQUIVALENT	—
PART OF SPEECH	Noun
GENDER	Feminine

A French noun ending in the suffix **-aison** denotes an action or the result of an action. The base word is usually a verb. For example, the base word for the noun **comparaison** *comparison* is the verb **comparer** *to compare*, and the suffixed noun is the act or result of comparing. The regular formation for this type of noun consists in replacing the infinitive ending of the verb with the suffix **-aison**. Note that base words for botanical and farming words are nouns; for example, the noun **fronde** *large leaf* is the base word for **frondaison** *foliage*, the noun **feuille** *leaf* is the base word for **feuillaison** *leafing out*, and the noun **foin** *hay* is the base word for **fenaison** *haymaking*.

NOUN ENDING IN -aison	ENGLISH EQUIVALENT	BASE WORD	ENGLISH EQUIVALENT
cargaison	*cargo*	charger	*to load*
combinaison	*combination*	combiner	*to combine*
comparaison	*comparison*	comparer	*to compare*
conjugaison	*conjugation*	conjuguer	*to conjugate*
couvaison	*brooding, incubation*	couver	*to hatch*
crevaison	*perforation*	crever	*to perforate*
cuvaison	*fermentation of grape skins*	cuver	*to ferment*
défleuraison	*shedding flowers*	(se) défleurir	*to shed flowers*
démangeaison	*itch*	démanger	*to itch*

EXERCICE
78·1

Qu'est-ce qui est évoqué? *Provide the noun associated with the two items in each line.*

1. Raisins, vin _____

2. Poule, œuf _____

3. Urticaire, inflammation _____

4. Rosier, pétales _____

5. Verbes, terminaisons _____

6. Panne, pneu _____

7. Bateau, transport _____

8. Plus, moins _____

9. Arrangement, assemblage _____

NOUN ENDING IN -aison	ENGLISH EQUIVALENT	BASE WORD	ENGLISH EQUIVALENT
exhalaison	*exhalation*	exhaler	*to exhale*
fenaison	*haymaking*	foin	*hay*
feuillaison	*leafing out*	feuille	*leaf*
floraison	*blooming*	fleurir	*to bloom*
flottaison	*flotation*	flotter	*to float*
frondaison	*foliage*	fronde	*large leaf*
inclinaison	*slope*	incliner	*to incline*
livraison	*delivery*	livrer	*to deliver*
pendaison	*hanging*	pendre	*to hang*
terminaison	*ending*	terminer	*to finish*

Complétez! *Complete each sentence with the appropriate noun.*

1. La _____ du nouveau lit est remise à demain.

2. La _____ d'un hors la loi dans le Wild West était publique.

3. La _____ est la coupe d'herbe dans les pâturages.

4. La _____ d'un verbe change selon le sujet.

5. La _____ dans ce jardin a lieu régulièrement chaque printemps.

6. L'_____ du terrain protège du vent.

7. Le temps de la _____ dépend un peu du temps.

8. Un corps qui se décompose dégage une _____ malodorante.

9. La _____ des chênes se fait après celles d'autres arbres.

10. La _____ des troncs d'arbre permet d'économiser en transport.

79 ▸ -ure

MEANING	Result/outcome of an action
ENGLISH EQUIVALENT	—
PART OF SPEECH	Noun
GENDER	Feminine

A French noun ending in the suffix **-ure** denotes the result or outcome of an action. The base word is frequently a verb that represents the nature of the action. For example, the base word for the noun **blessure** *wound* is the past participle **blessé** *wounded*. The base word for the noun **embrasure** *opening* is the past participle **embrasé** *lit up*. Opening a door or window lights up a room, hence the meaning of the suffixed noun in **l'embrasure de la porte** *the doorway*. The regular formation for this type of noun consists in replacing the past participle ending with **-ure**, as in the **blessé ~ blessure** and **embrasé ~ embrasure** examples, or adding **-ure** to a past participle ending in **-t**; for example, **couvert** *covered* yields **couverture** *cover*.

NOUN ENDING IN **-ure**	ENGLISH EQUIVALENT	BASE WORD	ENGLISH EQUIVALENT
blessure	*wound*	blessé	*wounded*
brûlure	*burn*	brûlé	*burnt*
cassure	*break*	cassé	*broken*
chaussure	*shoe*	chaussé	*with shoes on*
clôture	*fence*	clos	*closed*
coiffure	*hair style*	coiffé	*styled* (hair)
confiture	*jam*	confit	*crystallized fruit*
coupure	*cut*	coupé	*cut*

▶

NOUN ENDING IN -ure	ENGLISH EQUIVALENT	BASE WORD	ENGLISH EQUIVALENT
couverture	*cover*	couvert	*covered*
créature	*creature*	créé	*created*
écriture	*handwriting*	écrit	*written*
embrasure	*opening*	embrasé	*lit up*

EXERCICE
79·1

Complétez! *Choose the best completion for each sentence.*

1. _____ Les Françaises semblent préférer
2. _____ Une invitation écrite à la main
3. _____ Une cassure dans un objet de cristal
4. _____ Les Français aiment les tartines
5. _____ Les blessures sérieuses
6. _____ Il vaut mieux porter
7. _____ Il vaut mieux ne pas s'approcher d'un feu
8. _____ Il y a toutes sortes de créatures immondes
9. _____ La couverture de ce livre
10. _____ Se faire une petite coupure au doigt
11. _____ La clôture du jardin doit rester fermer
12. _____ Il fait plus clair

a. des chaussures de cuir en hiver.
b. dans le film *Le Hobbit*.
c. laissent des cicatrices.
d. pour éviter les brûlures.
e. en diminue la valeur.
f. les coiffures courtes.
g. n'est pas très grave.
h. exige une belle écriture.
i. à cause du chien.
j. au beurre et à la confiture.
k. dans l'embrasure d'une fenêtre.
l. a une illustration intrigante.

NOUN ENDING IN -ure	ENGLISH EQUIVALENT	BASE WORD	ENGLISH EQUIVALENT
fêlure	*crack*	fêlé	*cracked*
fermeture	*closing*	fermé	*closed*
foulure	*sprain*	foulé	*sprained*
fourrure	*fur*	fourré	*stuffed*
lecture	*reading*	lectus [LAT.]	*read* [PAST PART.]
moisissure	*mold*	moisi	*turned moldy*
nourriture	*nourishment*	nourri	*nourished*
ouverture	*opening*	ouvert	*open*
peinture	*painting*	peint	*painted*
pourriture	*rot*	pourri	*rotted*
sculpture	*sculpture*	sculpté	*sculpted*
signature	*signature*	signé	*signed*
tournure	*turn (of events)*	tourné	*turned*
vomissure	*vomit*	vomi	*vomited*

Complétez! *Complete each sentence with the appropriate noun.*

1. Pour guérir une _____ de l'os, il faut un plâtre.

2. La _____ peut être à l'huile ou à l'eau.

3. Ce contrat exige la _____ du banquier.

4. Les femmes d'aujourd'hui ne portent plus très souvent les manteaux de

   _____.

5. Rodin était un maître de _____.

6. La _____ rend les bananes immangeables.

7. Il y a des gens qui restent dans les bars jusqu'à l'heure de _____.

8. Les étudiants doivent faire beaucoup de _____.

9. Les gymnastes se font quelquefois une _____ à la main ou à la cheville.

10. La _____ est un rejet de ce qu'on a mangé.

11. La _____ animale est exclue d'un régime végétarien.

12. L'_____ des grands magasins est généralement à 9 heures.

13. La _____ des événements dans ce film est surprenante.

14. La _____ sur ce pain est dégoûtante.

80 ◆ -ure

MEANING	Made of/for
ENGLISH EQUIVALENT	—
PART OF SPEECH	Noun
GENDER	Feminine

A French noun ending in the suffix **-ure** may denote a component or a purpose. The base word may be a noun, an adjective, or even a preposition that represents the component or the purpose. For example, the base word for the noun **encolure** *neckline* is the noun **col** *neck*, and the suffixed noun characterizes something as made for the neck, like the neckline of a sweater. The base word for the noun **devanture** *display window* is the preposition **devant** *in front*, and the suffixed noun denotes an item intended to be *in front*, like a shop or display window. Imagination is sometimes required to connect a base word with the suffixed word.

NOUN ENDING IN **-ure**	ENGLISH EQUIVALENT	BASE WORD	ENGLISH EQUIVALENT
acupuncture	*acupuncture*	acus + punctus [LAT.]	*needle + punctured*
architecture	*architecture*	architectura [LAT.]	*architecture*
candidature	*candidacy*	candidat	*candidate*
ceinture	*belt*	ceint	*buckled*
chevelure	*(head of) hair*	chevel [OLD FR.]	*hair*
dentelure	*jaggedness*	dent	*tooth*
denture	*denture*	dent	*tooth*
désinvolture	*casualness*	désinvolte	*casual, offhanded*
devanture	*display window*	devant	*in front*
droiture	*righteousness*	droit	*right*

EXERCICE

80·1

Vrai ou faux? *Indicate whether each statement is true or false, using* **V** *for* **vrai** *true or* **F** *for* **faux** *false.*

1. _____ Il y a des mannequins dans les devantures des boutiques de vêtements.

2. _____ Il faut remplir une fiche de candidature pour acheter une voiture.

3. _____ L'acupuncture est une branche de la médecine traditionnelle chinoise.

4. _____ Les vieilles feuilles de parchemin peuvent avoir une dentelure tout autour.

5. _____ Une personne indifférente agit parfois avec désinvolture.

6. _____ L'architecture de la cathédrale de Notre Dame à Paris est gothique.

7. _____ Les chevelures des chevaux servent à faire des éponges.

8. _____ Une ceinture se met autour du cou.

9. _____ La denture remplace les vraies dents.

10. _____ La droiture est une vertu.

NOUN ENDING IN **-ure**	ENGLISH EQUIVALENT	BASE WORD	ENGLISH EQUIVALENT
emmanchure	*armhole*	manche	*sleeve*
encolure	*neckline*	col	*collar*
imposture	*imposture, deception*	impostura [LAT.]	*imposture*
mantelure	*top coat* (dog)	manteaux	*coat*
mésaventure	*misadventure*	[més-] + aventure	*bad + adventure*
ossature	*bone structure*	os	*bone*
pointure	*size* (gloves, shoes)	punctum [LAT.]	*hole, puncture*
progéniture	*offspring, progeny*	progenies [LAT.]	*progeny*
sépulture	*grave*	sepultura [LAT.]	*grave*
température	*temperature*	temps	*weather*
texture	*texture*	textura [LAT.]	*texture, weaving*
voilure	*sails*	voile	*sail*

Charade! *Provide the noun associated with each pair of items.*

1. 30 degrés, chaud   _____

2. Manteau, poil   _____

3. Surface, matériel   _____

4. Cou, pull-over   _____

5. Enfants, petits   _____

6. Manche, chemise   _____

7. Bateau, voile   _____

8. Tombe, mort   _____

9. Prendre la place, faux roi _____

10. Squelette, os   _____

11. Mauvais moment, malheur   _____

81 ▸ -son

MEANING	Outcome/product of an action
ENGLISH EQUIVALENT	—
PART OF SPEECH	Noun
GENDER	Feminine

A French noun ending in the suffix -**son** often denotes the outcome or product of an action. The base word is a verb; for example, the base word for the noun **boisson** *beverage* is the verb **boire** *to drink*. In the noun **façon** *manner*, the medial **s** is replaced by **ç**.

NOUN ENDING IN -**son**	ENGLISH EQUIVALENT	BASE WORD	ENGLISH EQUIVALENT
boisson	*beverage*	boire	*to drink*
chanson	*song*	chanter	*to sing*
cloison	*partition*	clausus [LAT.]	*closed*
cuisson	*cooking*	cuire	*to cook*
façon	*manner, fashion*	facere [LAT.]	*to make*
floraison	*blossoming*	fleurir	*to blossom*
garnison	*garrison*	garnir	*to fill*
guérison	*recovery*	guérir	*to cure*
maison	*house*	manere [LAT.]	*to stay*
raison	*reason*	reri [LAT.]	*to think*
saison	*season*	serere [LAT.]	*to sow*
trahison	*treason*	trahir	*to betray*
unisson	*unison*	unir	*to unite*

Vrai ou faux? *Indicate whether each statement is true or false, using* **V** *for* **vrai** *true or* **F** *for* **faux** *false.*

1. _____ Beaucoup de gens comptent sur leur médecin pour assurer leur guérison.

2. _____ Les membres d'une chorale doivent chanter en unisson.

3. _____ La limonade est une boisson alcoolisée.

4. _____ Faire de l'espionnage n'est pas toujours une trahison.

5. _____ Tout être vivant a besoin d'une raison d'être.

6. _____ L'automne est la saison de la floraison.

7. _____ Le temps de cuisson n'est pas important pour la viande rouge.

8. _____ Il faut des cloisons entre les bureaux pour assurer un espace privé pour chacun.

9. _____ Il vaut mieux quitter la maison quand on est malade.

10. _____ Différentes cultures ont des façons différentes de faire la cuisine.

11. _____ Il n'y avait pas de villes de garnison à l'époque de la guerre civile.

12. _____ Tout le monde aime les chansons d'amour.

82 ◆ -ail

MEANING	Made for, consisting of
ENGLISH EQUIVALENT	—
PART OF SPEECH	Noun
GENDER	Masculine

A French noun ending in the suffix **-ail** may denote purpose. For example, the base word for the noun **bercail** *home, fold* is the noun **brebis** *ewe*, and the suffixed noun is a place intended as a home for sheep. Purpose is also denoted if the base word is a verb. The base word for the noun **épouvantail** *scarecrow* is the verb **épouvanter** *to scare*, and the suffixed noun is an object intended to scare crows. Sometimes, the suffixed noun is a collective noun, of which the base word represents an individual component; for example, the base word for the noun **bétail** *cattle* is **bête** *animal*, and the suffixed noun denotes a group of large farm animals.

NOUN ENDING IN **-ail**	ENGLISH EQUIVALENT	BASE WORD	ENGLISH EQUIVALENT
attirail	*gear, attire*	tirer	*to pull*
bercail	*home, fold*	brebis	*ewe*
bétail	*cattle*	bête	*animal*
corail	*coral*	corallum [LAT.]	*coral*
émail	*enamel*	smalt [OLD FR.]	*to smelt*

▶

NOUN ENDING IN -ail	ENGLISH EQUIVALENT	BASE WORD	ENGLISH EQUIVALENT
épouvantail	*scarecrow*	épouvanter	*to scare*
éventail	*fan*	éventer	*to fan*
portail	*gate, portal*	porte	*door*
travail	*work*	tripalium [LAT.]	*instrument of torture*

EXERCICE
82·1

Complétez! *Complete each sentence with the appropriate noun.*

1. Le _____ au fond des océans est en danger à cause de la pollution.

2. L'_____ est un matériau de verre ou de cristal très affiné.

3. Le _____ est une nécessité pour tous et une passion pour certains.

4. Le _____ reste dans les champs quand il fait beau.

5. Les bricoleurs ont tout un _____ pour leurs projets.

6. On dit que les agneaux reviennent toujours au _____.

7. La reine Cléopâtre était toujours entourée de femmes avec des _____.

8. Il faut fermer le _____ de la basse-cour pour que les animaux ne sortent pas.

9. L'_____ effraie les corbeaux et les empêchent de venir picorer les semences.

83 ◆ -aire

MEANING	Agent, dealer
ENGLISH EQUIVALENT	—
PART OF SPEECH	Noun
GENDER	Masculine/feminine

There are numerous adjectives ending in the suffix -**aire** in French (see No. 85); the same ending is used to indicate or modify both masculine and feminine nouns.

A French noun ending in the suffix -**aire** may denote an agent, a dealer, or a person involved in a specific activity. The base word may be a noun, a verb, or an adjective that represents the activity. For example, the base word for the noun **libraire** *bookstore owner/manager* is the Latin noun **liber** *book*. The base word for **signataire** *signatory* is the verb **signer** *to sign*. Since these suffixed nouns denote persons of both sexes, they may be masculine or feminine. An exception is **légionnaire** *legionnaire*, which, because it describes men only, is masculine.

NOUN ENDING IN -aire	ENGLISH EQUIVALENT	BASE WORD	ENGLISH EQUIVALENT
actionnaire	*shareholder*	action	*stock*
adversaire	*adversary*	adversarius [LAT.]	*adversary*
antiquaire	*antique dealer*	antique	*antique*
apothicaire [ARCHAIC/ PEJORATIVE]	*apothecary*	apothecarius [LAT.]	*shopkeeper*
bibliothécaire	*librarian*	bibliothèque	*library*
célibataire	*bachelor*	célibat	*single status*
contestataire	*protester*	contester	*to protest*
dépositaire	*agent*	déposer	*to deposit*
légionnaire	*legionnaire*	légion	*legion*
libraire	*bookseller*	liber/libri [LAT.]	*book*
locataire	*renter*	louer	*to rent*
millionnaire	*millionaire*	million	*million*
pétitionnaire	*petitioner*	pétition	*petition*
propriétaire	*owner*	propriété	*property*
secrétaire	*secretary*	secretus [LAT.]	*confidential*
signataire	*signatory*	signer	*to sign*
stagiaire	*trainee, intern*	stage	*internship*
vétérinaire	*veterinarian*	veterinarius [LAT.]	*veterinary*

EXERCICE
83·1

Vrai ou faux? *Indicate whether each statement is true or false, using* **V** *for* **vrai** *true or* **F** *for* **faux** *false.*

1. _____ Le signataire d'un document légal doit être majeur.

2. _____ Il y a généralement un contestataire à un mariage.

3. _____ Les millionnaires sont tous des philanthropes.

4. _____ Un actionnaire a généralement droit à des intérêts.

5. _____ L'antiquaire vend de vieilles choses sans valeur.

6. _____ Les libraires vous laissent emprunter des livres.

7. _____ Chaque équipe de football américain veut battre son adversaire.

8. _____ Un immeuble avec des appartements a généralement des locataires.

9. _____ Le propriétaire d'un immeuble peut vendre sa propriété.

10. _____ Le secrétaire de bureau prend toutes les décisions administratives et financières.

11. _____ Un stagiaire est toujours expérimenté et bien payé.

12. _____ Un pétitionnaire fait un procès à la cour de justice.

13. _____ Les vétérinaires ne soignent que les animaux domestiques.

14. _____ Les grandes entreprises automobiles ont des dépositaires agréés.

15. _____ Les légionnaires romains se battaient avec des lions.

16. _____ Les bibliothécaires vendent des livres.

17. _____ Les célibataires sont de jeunes personnes de moins de vingt-cinq ans.

18. _____ Les apothicaires préparaient et vendaient autrefois des médicaments.

84 ◆ -aire

MEANING	Organizational tool, event
ENGLISH EQUIVALENT	—
PART OF SPEECH	Noun
GENDER	Masculine

A French noun ending in the suffix **-aire** may denote an organizational tool or an event. The base word may be a noun, a verb, or an adjective. For example, the base word for the noun **annuaire** *directory* is the noun **année** *year*, and the suffixed noun denotes an inventory tool based on information for the year. The base word for the noun **anniversaire** *birthday, anniversary* is also the noun **année** *year*, and the suffixed noun denotes an event during the year.

NOUN ENDING IN -aire	ENGLISH EQUIVALENT	BASE WORD	ENGLISH EQUIVALENT
Organizational tools			
annuaire	*directory*	année	*year*
formulaire	*form*	formule	*formula*
glossaire	*glossary*	glossa [LAT.]	*glossary*
inventaire	*inventory*	inventarium [LAT.]	*inventory*
questionnaire	*questionnaire*	question	*question*
sommaire	*contents, summary*	summa [LAT.]	*summary*
vestiaire	*cloakroom, locker room*	vestiarium [LAT.]	*cloakroom*
vocabulaire	*vocabulary*	vocabularium [LAT.]	*vocabulary*
Cyclical events			
anniversaire	*birthday, anniversary*	année	*year*
bicentenaire	*bicentennial*	[bi-] + centenaire	*two + centennial*
centenaire	*centennial*	cent	*one hundred*
millénaire	*millennium*	mille	*one thousand*

EXERCICE
84·1

Définitions! *Provide the noun(s) corresponding to each description.*

1. Le résumé du contenu d'une dissertation _____

2. L'endroit où on laisse son manteau au théâtre _____

3. La liste annuelle des abonnés à un service Internet _____

4. Une période de mille ans _____

5. La commémoration d'un événement d'il y a cent ans _____

6. La célébration de sa naissance _____

7. La commémoration d'un événement d'il y a deux cents ans _____

8. Une fiche avec des questions _____

9. Description détaillée du contenu d'une maison ou d'un commerce _____

10. Ensemble ou liste de mots _____

_____

◆ 85 ◆ -aire

MEANING	Pertaining to
ENGLISH EQUIVALENT	*-ary*
PART OF SPEECH	Adjective
GENDER	Masculine/feminine

A French adjective ending in the suffix **-aire** may denote a characteristic pertaining to the base word, which is a noun. For example, the base word for the adjective **héréditaire** *hereditary* is the noun **hérédité** *heredity*, and the suffixed adjective describes something in terms of heredity. The regular formation for this type of adjective consists in adding the suffix to the base noun if it ends in **-t** (for example, **aliment** yields **alimentaire**) or replacing the **-e** or **-é** ending of the base noun with the suffix (for example, **autorité** yields **autoritaire**). Since many of these French adjectives have English cognates, they tend to be easily recognized.

ADJECTIVE ENDING IN **-aire**	ENGLISH EQUIVALENT	BASE WORD	ENGLISH EQUIVALENT
alimentaire	*alimentary*	aliment	*food*
ancillaire	*relative to servants*	ancilla [LAT.]	*servant*
angulaire	*angular*	angle	*angle*
arbitraire	*arbitrary*	arbitre	*referee*
autoritaire	*authoritarian*	autorité	*authority*
bancaire	*banking*	banque	*bank*
bénéficiaire	*beneficiary*	bénéfice	*benefice*
binaire	*binary*	[bi-]	*two*
budgétaire	*budgetary*	budget	*budget*
communautaire	*community*	communauté	*community*
consulaire	*consular*	consulat	*consulate*
dentaire	*dental*	dent	*tooth*

Complétez! *Choose the best completion for each sentence.*

1. _____ Une équation binaire a

2. _____ Une personne autoritaire

3. _____ Presque tous les adultes

4. _____ Beaucoup de pays ont un

5. _____ Les juges ne sont pas censés prendre

6. _____ Tous les gouvernements doivent avoir

7. _____ L'art roman n'a pas beaucoup de

8. _____ Un cabinet dentaire

9. _____ Certains quartiers de villes ont des

10. _____ Les produits alimentaires

11. _____ Les personnes bénéficiaires d'une assurance-vie

12. _____ Des amours ancillaires avaient parfois

a. sont contrôlés en France.

b. des décisions arbitraires.

c. une certaine restreinte budgétaire.

d. jardins communautaires.

e. donne beaucoup d'ordres.

f. corps consulaire à New York.

g. ont un compte bancaire.

h. lieu dans les familles nobles.

i. formes angulaires.

j. sont nommées dans la police d'assurance.

k. deux éléments.

l. donne des soins dentaires.

ADJECTIVE ENDING IN **-aire**	ENGLISH EQUIVALENT	BASE WORD	ENGLISH EQUIVALENT
héréditaire	*hereditary*	hérédité	*heredity*
humanitaire	*humanitarian*	humanité	*humanity*
majoritaire	*majority*	majorité	*majority*
minoritaire	*minority*	minorité	*minority*
nucléaire	*nuclear*	nucleus [LAT.]	*nucleus*
publicitaire	*publicity, advertising*	publicité	*publicity*
quadragénaire	*forty-year-old*	quadragenarius [LAT.]	*forty-year-old*
rectangulaire	*rectangular*	rectangle	*rectangle*
révolutionnaire	*revolutionary*	révolution	*revolution*
scolaire	*school, academic*	schola [LAT.]	*school*
supplémentaire	*supplementary*	supplément	*supplement*
vestimentaire	*clothing*	vestiment [OLD FR.]	*clothing*

Complétez! *Complete each sentence with the correct form of the appropriate adjective.*

1. Qu'un enfant soit nommé d'après son père était une fois une tradition

_____ .

2. La France a des centrales _____ qui produisent de l'électricité.

3. Les _____ d'aujourd'hui se sentent encore jeunes.

4. Les styles _____ varient parfois d'une culture à l'autre.

5. Il y a beaucoup d'annonces _____ à la télévision.

6. Une fraction _____ de la population de notre pays est xénophobe.

7. Des visites _____ au cours d'un voyage ont un tarif séparé.

8. Toute crise _____ demande un effort global.

9. La vie _____ aux États-Unis comprend les activités sportives.

10. La conception du sous-marin par Jules Vernes était une idée _____.

11. Un bac à glace a une forme _____.

12. Les actionnaires _____ d'une société prennent les grandes décisions.

86 ◆ -ence

MEANING	Action, result of an action, state
ENGLISH EQUIVALENT	*-ence*
PART OF SPEECH	Noun
GENDER	Feminine

A French noun ending in the suffix **-ence** denotes the action, the result of an action, or the state represented by its base word, which is an adjective. For example, the base word for the noun **absence** is the adjective **absent**, and the suffixed noun is the state of being absent. The regular formation for this type of adjective consists in replacing the **-ant** or **-ent** ending of a base adjective with **-ence**; thus, **absent** yields **absence**. Since almost all of these French nouns, which are numerous and prevalent, have English cognates, they tend to be easily recognized. (See No. 87 for adjectives related to these nouns.)

NOUN ENDING IN **-ence**	ENGLISH EQUIVALENT	BASE WORD	ENGLISH EQUIVALENT
absence	*absence*	absent	*absent*
abstinence	*abstinence*	abstinent	*abstinent*
adolescence	*adolescence*	adolescent	*adolescent*
apparence	*appearance*	apparent	*apparent*
cohérence	*coherence*	cohérent	*coherent*
compétence	*competence*	compétent	*competent*
concurrence	*competition*	concurrent	*competitive, rival*
conscience	*consciousness, conscience*	conscient	*conscious*
corpulence	*corpulence*	corpulent	*corpulent*
divergence	*divergence*	divergent	*divergent*
effervescence	*effervescence*	effervescent	*effervescent*
éloquence	*eloquence*	éloquent	*eloquent*
éminence	*eminence*	éminent	*eminent*
fluorescence	*fluorescence*	fluorescent	*fluorescent*
fréquence	*frequency*	fréquent	*frequent*

Vrai ou faux? *Indicate whether each statement is true or false, using* **V** *for* **vrai** *true or* **F** *for* **faux** *false.*

1. _____ Un dégagement gazeux provoque une effervescence.

2. _____ L'adolescence précède la puberté.

3. _____ L'abstinence sexuelle est importante dans certains groupes religieux.

4. _____ La conscience morale distingue le bien du mal.

5. _____ La compétence linguistique n'est pas importante dans le monde actuel.

6. _____ L'éloquence peut être verbale ou écrite.

7. _____ L'absence aux cours n'empêche pas les élèves médiocres d'exceller.

8. _____ La divergence d'opinion est basée sur des perspectives différentes.

9. _____ Une éminence anormale de la peau ou de l'os peut être un signe de maladie.

10. _____ La corpulence d'une personne montre sa force.

11. _____ La fréquence des atterrissages d'avions exige beaucoup de précautions.

12. _____ Les boîtes de nuit et les discothèques ont des lumières fluorescentes.

NOUN ENDING IN **-ence**	ENGLISH EQUIVALENT	BASE WORD	ENGLISH EQUIVALENT
excellence	*excellence*	excellent	*excellent*
existence	*existence*	existant	*existing*
impatience	*impatience*	impatient	*impatient*
indifférence	*indifference*	indifférent	*indifferent*
indulgence	*indulgence*	indulgent	*indulgent*
innocence	*innocence*	innocent	*innocent*
insolence	*insolence*	insolent	*insolent*
intelligence	*intelligence*	intelligent	*intelligent*
négligence	*negligence*	négligent	*negligent*
prudence	*prudence*	prudent	*prudent*
somnolence	*somnolence*	somnolent	*somnolent*
transparence	*transparency*	transparent	*transparent*
urgence	*urgency*	urgent	*urgent*
violence	*violence*	violent	*violent*

Des synonymes! *Provide the best synonym for each item.*

1. Perfection _____

2. Énervement _____

3. Intellect _____

4. Effronterie   _____

5. Léthargie   _____

6. Opacité   _____

7. Vie   _____

8. Impératif   _____

9. Naïveté   _____

10. Précaution   _____

11. Apathie   _____

12. Excès de force   _____

13. Inattention   _____

14. Clémence   _____

◆ 87 ◆ -ent/-ente

MEANING	Possessing a quality
ENGLISH EQUIVALENT	-ent
PART OF SPEECH	Adjective
GENDER	Masculine/feminine

A French adjective ending in the suffix **-ent** (feminine: **-ente**) denotes a quality represented by the base word, which may be a verb, an adjective, a noun, or a Latin root. For example, the base word for the adjective **abstinent** is the verb **abstenir** *to abstain*, and the suffixed adjective denotes the quality or condition of abstinence. The regular formation for this type of adjective consists in replacing the infinitive ending of the base verb with **-ent**; thus, **abhorrer** yields **abhorrent**. Since most of these French adjectives, which are numerous, have English cognates, they tend to be easily recognized. (See No. 86 for nouns related to these adjectives.)

ADJECTIVE ENDING IN -ent/-ente	ENGLISH EQUIVALENT	BASE WORD	ENGLISH EQUIVALENT
abhorrent	*abhorrent*	abhorrer	*to abhor*
abstinent	*abstinent*	abstenir	*to abstain*
ambivalent	*ambivalent*	[ambi-] + valens [LAT.]	*both + strong*
apparent	*apparent*	apparaître	*to appear*
éloquent	*eloquent*	eloquens [LAT.]	*eloquent*
éminent	*eminent*	eminens [LAT.]	*eminent*
évident	*evident*	evidens [LAT.]	*evident*
excellent	*excellent*	excellens [LAT.]	*excellent*
fluorescent	*fluorescent*	fluorescer	*to be fluorescent*
grandiloquent	*grandiloquent*	grandiloquus [LAT.]	*grandiloquent*
non-adhérent	*nonstick*	[non-] + adhérer	*not + to adhere*
omnipotent	*omnipotent*	omnipotens [LAT.]	*omnipotent* ▶

ADJECTIVE ENDING IN -ent/-ente	ENGLISH EQUIVALENT	BASE WORD	ENGLISH EQUIVALENT
◀ omniscient	*omniscient*	omnisciens [LAT.]	*omniscient*
opalescent	*opalescent*	opale	*opal*
phosphorescent	*phosphorescent*	phosphore	*phosphorus*
polyvalent	*versatile*	[poly-] + valens [LAT.]	*many + strong*
précédent	*preceding*	praecedens [LAT.]	*preceding*
réticent	*reticent*	reticens [LAT.]	*silent*

EXERCICE

87·1

Soyons logiques! *Complete each sentence with the correct form of the appropriate adjective.*

1. Il sait tout; il est _____.

2. Elle s'abstient de nourriture; elle est _____.

3. Il a tous les pouvoirs; il est _____.

4. Cette surface ne colle pas; elle est _____.

5. Le message est clair et _____.

6. La lumière est brillante et _____.

7. Le liquide est laiteux et _____.

8. Le cheval est prudent et même _____.

9. Cette image est abominable et _____.

10. Il est plurivalent ou _____.

11. C'est la page avant ou _____.

12. Cette projection est luminescente et _____.

13. Ce vocabulaire est pompeux et _____.

14. Cette note est ambigüe et _____.

15. La vérité est vraisemblable et _____.

16. Le discours est bien articulé et _____.

17. Ce personnage est remarquable et _____.

18. Cette glace délicieuse est _____.

88 ◆ -ise

MEANING	Quality, trait, state
ENGLISH EQUIVALENT	—
PART OF SPEECH	Noun
GENDER	Feminine

A French noun ending in the suffix **-ise** denotes a quality, trait, or condition. The base word is usually an adjective or verb, although it may be a noun. For example, the base word for the noun **bêtise** *stupidity, stupid act* is the adjective **bête** *stupid* (which may also function as a noun), and the suffixed noun is the state of being stupid. The base word for the noun **prêtrise** *priesthood* is the noun **prêtre** *priest*, and the suffixed noun is the state of being a priest. (Another base noun, **maître** *master*, yields **maîtrise** *mastery*.) The regular formation for this type of noun consists in adding the suffix **-ise** to a base adjective (for example, **balourd** yields **balourdise**) or replacing the infinitive ending of a base verb with the suffix **-ise** (for example, **convoiter** yields **convoitise**).

NOUN ENDING IN **-ise**	ENGLISH EQUIVALENT	BASE WORD	ENGLISH EQUIVALENT
balourdise	*clumsiness*	balourd	*clumsy*
bâtardise	*illegitimacy* (of birth)	bâtard	*bastard*
bêtise	*stupidity, stupid act*	bête	*stupid*
convoitise	*greed*	convoiter	*to desire*
couardise	*cowardice*	couard	*coward*
débrouillardise	*resourcefulness*	débrouillard	*resourceful*
expertise	*expertise*	expert	*expert*
fainéantise	*idleness*	fainéant	*idle*
franchise	*frankness*	franc/franche	*frank*
gaillardise	*bawdy remark*	gaillard	*bawdy*

EXERCICE
88·1

Des antonymes! *Provide the appropriate antonym(s) for each set of nouns.*

1. Passion, activité   _____

2. Apathie, modestie   _____

3. Intelligence, subtilité   _____

4. Maladresse, incompétence   _____   _____

5. Inaptitude, manque de reflexes   _____

6. Duplicité, hypocrisie   _____

7. Courage, bravoure   _____

8. Adresse, tact   _____

9. Sérieux, finesse   _____

NOUN ENDING IN **-ise**	ENGLISH EQUIVALENT	BASE WORD	ENGLISH EQUIVALENT
hantise	*obsession*	hanter	*to haunt*
maîtrise	*mastery*	maître	*master*
mignardise	*affectation; delicacies, sweets*	mignard	*sweet, cute*
paillardise [PEJORATIVE]	*bawdiness*	paillard	*bawdy*
prêtrise	*priesthood*	prêtre	*priest*
roublardise [PEJORATIVE]	*craftiness*	roublard	*cunning*
sottise	*nonsense, silliness*	sot/sotte	*silly*
surprise	*surprise*	surpris	*surprised*
traîtrise	*betrayal*	traître	*traitor*
vantardise	*boastfulness*	vantard	*boaster*

EXERCICE
88·2

Complétez! *Complete each sentence with the correct form of the appropriate noun.*

1. Les enfants sont parfois punis quand ils font des _____.

2. Il faut démontrer la _____ de certaines compétences quand on se présente à un emploi.

3. La _____ dont faisaient preuve les Gaulois ne serait pas appréciée par les femmes d'aujourd'hui.

4. La _____ est pour ceux qui ont une vraie vocation.

5. Il vaut mieux ne pas avoir la _____ de la mort; c'est trop morbide.

6. Gagner à la loterie serait une belle _____.

7. Il ne fait pas croire ceux qui sont connus pour leur _____.

8. La _____ de la part d'un ami ne se pardonne pas facilement.

9. Quelques _____ pour accompagner un bon café ne seront pas refusées.

10. Certaines personnes ont la _____ de croire qu'elles savent tout.

89 ◆ -ard/-arde

MEANING	Pejorative quality (familiar register)
ENGLISH EQUIVALENT	—
PART OF SPEECH	Adjective, noun
GENDER	Masculine/feminine

A French adjective ending in the suffix **-ard** (feminine: **-arde**) conveys a pejorative connotation about a quality or trait. The base word is a noun or verb that represents the quality or trait that is disparaged. For example, the base word for the adjective **froussard** *cowardly* is the noun **frousse** *strong fear, fright*, and the suffixed adjective describes a chronically cowardly person. The base word for the adjective **criard** *loud, shrill* is the verb **crier** *to shout, yell*, and the suffixed adjective means unpleasantly shrill or loud. The regular formation for this type of adjective consists in replacing the **-e** ending of a feminine base noun with **-ard/-arde**, as in the **frousse/froussard** example. If the base word is a verb, as in the **crier/criard** example, the regular formation consists in replacing the **-er** infinitive ending of the verb with the suffix.

These adjectives can function as nouns; for example, **bâtard** may be inoffensively applied to animals, although it is a pejorative noun when applied to people. In the sentence **C'est un bâtard** *He's a bastard*, **bâtard** is a noun, while in the phrase **un enfant bâtard** *an illegitimate child*, it is an adjective. Both adjectives and nouns are given in the English equivalents of these suffixed words.

ADJECTIVE/NOUN ENDING IN **-ard/-arde**	ENGLISH EQUIVALENT	BASE WORD	ENGLISH EQUIVALENT
bâtard	*illegitimate/bastard*	bastardus [LAT.]	*bastard*
braillard	*loud-mouthed/yeller*	brailler	*to yell*
criard	*loud, shrill / yeller*	crier	*to shout, yell*
flemmard	*lazy/lazybones*	flemme [SLANG]	*laziness*
froussard	*cowardly/chicken*	frousse	*fright*
grognard	*grumbling/grumbler*	grogner	*to grumble*
pleurnichard	*whining/whiner*	pleurnicher	*to whine*
soûlard	*drinking/drunkard*	saoul	*drunk*
vantard	*boastful/braggart*	se (vanter)	*to brag*
veinard	*lucky / lucky devil*	veine [SLANG]	*luck*

EXERCICE
89·1

Des synonymes! *Provide the best synonym for each description.*

1. Enfant né en dehors d'une union légale (anciens temps) _____

2. Peureux _____

3. Qui crie d'une voix aigüe et sifflante _____

4. Paresseux _____

5. Qui parle trop fort _____

6. Qui a beaucoup de chance _____

7. Qui se vante tout le temps _____

8. Qui pleure pour un rien _____

9. Qui grogne et boude _____

10. Qui boit trop d'alcool _____

90 ▸ -et

MEANING	Diminutive
ENGLISH EQUIVALENT	—
PART OF SPEECH	Noun
GENDER	Masculine

A French noun with the suffix **-et** conveys a diminutive connotation. The base word for the noun **agnelet** is the noun **agneau** *lamb*, and the suffixed noun represents a little lamb. If applied to children or small animals, **mon agnelet** *my little lamb* is a term of endearment. If applied to an adult, however, the person may feel belittled and demeaned. The title **baronet** was historically the lowest rank in British nobility and did not allow its bearer to be a member of the House of Lords. Similarly, the noun **blondinet** *fair-haired boy* may have a literal, affectionate connotation, but it can also be used in a scathing manner and convey a sense of weakness.

The meanings of most of these nouns are easy to figure out, but some are brainteasers. The noun **cadet** comes from a dialect spoken in Gascony, a province in the southwest of France and home to the famous French Musketeers. In the 15th century, the youngest sons of noble families served as captains in the army, and the word was applied to them. **Cadet** is the only word in the following chart that can be both a noun and an adjective. In the sentence **C'est le cadet** *He is the youngest child*, **cadet** is a noun, whereas in the phrase **le fils cadet** *the youngest son*, it is an adjective. **Cadet** is also one of the few words in the charts that have feminine counterparts; these are indicated by an asterisk (*). **Cadette** is the youngest daughter. (See No. 92 for nouns ending in the feminine diminutive suffix **-ette**.)

NOUN ENDING IN **-et**	ENGLISH EQUIVALENT	BASE WORD	ENGLISH EQUIVALENT
agnelet	*little lamb*	agneau	*lamb*
balconnet	*little balcony*	balcon	*balcony*
ballonnet	*little balloon*	ballon	*balloon*
baronet	*baronet*	baron	*baron*
basset	*basset* (dog)	bas	*low*
bâtonnet	*short stick*	bâton	*stick*
blondinet*	*fair-haired boy*	blond	*blond*
bonnet	*small hat/cap*	abonnis [MED. LAT.]	*headdress*
bourrelet	*little roll*	bourre	*stuffing material*
bourriquet	*little donkey*	bourrique	*donkey*
bracelet	*bracelet*	bras	*arm*
cadet*	*youngest (child)*	capdet	*15th-century French captain*
cervelet	*cerebellum*	cerveau	*brain*
châtelet	*little castle*	château	*castle*
cochonnet	*piglet, jack* (game)	cochon	*pig*

EXERCICE 90·1

Définitions! *Provide the noun that corresponds to each phrase.*

1. une partie du cerveau _____

2. un petit chien _____

3. un petit âne _____

4. un petit agneau _____

5. un petit château _____

6. un petit balcon _____

7. le plus jeune des frères _____

8. un petit ballon _____

9. un petit bâton _____

10. un tricot pour la tête _____

11. une petite boule (dans un jeu de boules) _____

12. une petite boule de graisse à la taille ou dans la cuisse _____

13. un petit garçon blond _____

14. un noble britannique (entre chevalier et baron) _____

15. petite chaîne autour du bras _____

NOUN ENDING IN -et	ENGLISH EQUIVALENT	BASE WORD	ENGLISH EQUIVALENT
coquelet	*cockerel*	coq	*rooster*
corselet	*corselet*	corset	*corset*
coussinet	*small cushion*	coussin	*cushion*
gantelet	*gauntlet, specialized glove*	gant	*glove*
garçonnet	*little boy*	garçon	*boy*
gobelet	*tumbler*	gobel [OLD FR.]	*cup*
godet	*small jar, vase*	kodde [DUTCH]	*cylindrical wood*
jardinet	*little garden*	jardin	*garden*
mantelet	*capelike coat*	manteau	*coat*
martelet	*scutch, little hammer*	marteau	*hammer*
minet*	*kitty* (term of endearment)	mine	*look*
oiselet	*little bird*	oiseau	*bird*
osselet	*knuckle bone, jack* (game)	os	*bone*
poissonnet	*little fish*	poisson	*fish*
ruisselet	*little stream*	ruisseau	*stream*
tabouret	*stool*	tambour	*drum*

EXERCICE

90·2

Garfield à la ferme! *To reconstitute this little story about little things, complete the following sentences with the appropriate nouns.*

La fermière trait les vaches, assise sur un (1) _____. Pour être plus

à l'aise, elle a mis un (2) _____ dessus. Elle récolte le lait dans

un (3) _____. Elle verse un peu de lait frais dans un

(4) _____ pour Louis, son (5) _____.

Louis porte un (6) _____ par-dessus sa chemise parce qu'il fait

un peu froid. Il caresse Garfield, son (7) _____ qui ronronne près de lui. Garfield décide d'aller jouer avec son (8) _____.

Puis Louis sort dans son (9) _____ couvert de neige blanche.

Il n'y a pas (10) d'_____ aujourd'hui, seulement un

(11) _____ qui cherche des graines à picorer. Même le

(12) _____ d'eau limpide est couvert de glace; Louis prend un

(13) _____ pour faire un trou dans la glace; il veut pêcher! Son petit

chien Martin l'accompagne; il porte un (14) _____ bien chaud qui

lui couvre le corps comme un (15) _____. Bonne pêche! Garfield

attend son (16) _____.

◆ 91 ◆ -et/-ette

MEANING	Approximate, diminutive
ENGLISH EQUIVALENT	—
PART OF SPEECH	Adjective
GENDER	Masculine/feminine

A French adjective ending in the suffix **-et** (feminine: **-ette**) denotes an approximate or diminutive quality. The base word is an adjective that indicates the quality, such as color of hair, look, or taste, that is being approximated or diminished. For example, the base word for the adjective **aigrelet** is the adjective **aigre** *bitter*, and the suffixed adjective means *sort of bitter*. The regular formation for this type of adjective consists in replacing the **-e** ending of a feminine base adjective with **-et** or **-ette**. In the following chart, the feminine form of base adjectives is included if it differs from the masculine form. (See also No. 90 for nouns ending in **-et** and No. 92 for nouns ending in **-ette**.)

ADJECTIVE ENDING IN -et/-ette	ENGLISH EQUIVALENT	BASE WORD	ENGLISH EQUIVALENT
aigrelet	*sort of bitter*	aigre	*bitter*
brunet	*with brownish hair*	brun/brune	*brown*
clairet	*thin* (voice)	clair/claire	*light*
doucet	*sweetish*	doux/douce	*sweet*
douillet	*cozy*	doux/douce	*gentle, soft*
fluet	*thin, scraggy*	flou/floue	*fuzzy*
follet	*a bit crazy*	fou/folle	*crazy*
gentillet	*sort of nice*	gentil/gentille	*nice*
grassouillet	*sort of fat*	gras/grasse	*fat, fatty*
mignonnet	*sort of cute*	mignon/mignonne	*cute*
pauvret	*sort of poor*	pauvre	*poor*
propret	*sort of clean*	propre	*clean*
rondelet	*sort of round*	rond/ronde	*round*
simplet	*sort of simple*	simple	*simple*
verdelet	*sort of green*	vert/verte	*green*

Un conte! *To reconstitute this tale about a mommy lark and two baby larks, complete the following sentences with the correct forms of the appropriate adjectives.*

Il y avait une fois une mère alouette qui était plutôt (1) _____

à cause de la rigueur de sa vie. Elle avait deux oiselets adorables bien

(2) _____ et (3) _____. Le plumage de

la mère était (4) _____ comme une feuille desséchée alors que

la couleur des oiselets était (5) _____ comme une feuille d'été.

La maman alouette avait fait un nid (6) _____ et confortable; le nid

était aussi (7) _____ (sans aucune saleté). Mais la vie est difficile

quand le temps froid arrive trop tôt: la (8) _____ ne trouvait pas

de vermisseaux ni d'insectes pour nourrir ses oiselets. La maman elle-même était encore

(9) _____ et (10) _____ parce qu'elle avait

bien mangé quand il faisait beau. Malheureusement, ses oiselets étaient bien maigres

et (11) _____. Que faire? Tout d'un coup, elle entend une voix

(12) _____ qui murmure d'un ton (13) _____ :

«Voilà une mangeoire avec des graines pour toi et tes oiselets!» Un acte aussi

(14) _____ que cela peut rendre l'espoir à une maman désespérée!

92 ◆ -ette

MEANING	Diminutive
ENGLISH EQUIVALENT	—
PART OF SPEECH	Noun
GENDER	Feminine

A French noun ending in the suffix **-ette** conveys a diminutive connotation. The base word for the noun **amourette** *infatuation* is the noun **amour** *love*, and the suffixed noun signifies a moderate degree of love. The regular formation for this type of noun consists in attaching the suffix directly to a base noun, as in the **amour/amourette** example, or replacing the **-e** ending of a base noun with the suffix **-ette**; for example, **fille** *girl* yields **fillette** *little girl*. (See No. 90 for nouns ending in the masculine diminutive suffix **-et**.)

NOUN ENDING IN -ette	ENGLISH EQUIVALENT	BASE WORD	ENGLISH EQUIVALENT
aiguillette	*little needle, small hand* (clock)	aiguille	*needle, hand* (clock)
amourette	*infatuation*	amour	*love*
banquette	*small seat/bench*	banc	*seat, bench*
barbichette	*small goatee*	barbiche	*goatee*
blondinette	*fair-haired girl*	blonde	*fair-haired girl*
bouclette	*little curl*	boucle	*curl*
boulette	*little ball*	boule	*ball*
camionnette	*little truck*	camion	*truck*
chansonnette	*little song*	chanson	*song*
couchette	*bunk*	coucher	*to put to bed*
dînette	*tea party* (child)	dîner	*dinner*
épaulette	*shoulder pad*	épaule	*shoulder*
épinglette	*little pin*	épingle	*pin*
fléchette	*dart*	flèche	*arrow*

EXERCICE 92·1

Complétez! *Choose the best completion for each sentence.*

1. _____ Les uniformes militaires ont parfois

2. _____ Les gens qui attendent l'autobus

3. _____ Une dînette est un beau cadeau

4. _____ Il faut une épinglette pour empêcher

5. _____ Les mousquetaires avaient des moustaches

6. _____ Les jeunes gens ont souvent

7. _____ On peut recoudre une déchirure avec

8. _____ Tout le monde peut interpréter

9. _____ Une blondinette a quelquefois

10. _____ Certains enfants ont des bouclettes

11. _____ Dans les trains de nuit,

12. _____ Il y a des boulettes de viande

13. _____ Le livreur de lait conduit

14. _____ La fléchette doit atteindre

a. tout à fait naturelles.

b. une chansonnette.

c. une aiguillette.

d. des amourettes passagères.

e. pour un jeune enfant.

f. un chemisier déboutonné de s'ouvrir.

g. et des barbichettes.

h. peuvent s'asseoir sur des banquettes.

i. dans certaines sauces tomates.

j. une camionnette.

k. le centre de la cible.

l. des points de rousseur.

m. il y a des couchettes.

n. des épaulettes.

NOUN ENDING IN -ette	ENGLISH EQUIVALENT	BASE WORD	ENGLISH EQUIVALENT
fillette	*little girl*	fille	*girl*
gaufrette	*cookie*	gaufre	*waffle*
gommette	*sticker*	gommer	*to erase*
kitchenette	*little kitchen*	kitchen [ENG.]	*kitchen*
maisonnette	*little house*	maison	*house*
montagnette	*little mountain*	montagne	*mountain*
moulinette	*vegetable processor*	moulin	*mill*
pincette	*tweezers*	pincer	*to pinch*
pirouette	*pirouette, spin*	pirouetter	*to spin*
pommette	*cheekbone*	pomme	*apple*
poulette	*chick*	poule	*chicken*
poussette	*stroller*	pousser	*to push*
sandalette	*little sandal*	sandale	*sandal*
sœurette	*little sister*	sœur	*sister*

EXERCICE 92·2

Vrai ou faux? *Indicate whether each statement is true or false, using* **V** *for* **vrai** *true or* **F** *for* **faux** *false.*

1. _____ Une poulette a deux roues.

2. _____ Une moulinette sert à faire de la farine.

3. _____ Une fillette pleure tout le temps.

4. _____ Les gaufrettes sont des petits gâteaux.

5. _____ Les acrobates font des pirouettes.

6. _____ Le Mont Blanc est une montagnette.

7. _____ On peut donner des gommettes comme prix aux enfants.

8. _____ Un studio est souvent équipé d'une kitchenette.

9. _____ On a froid en sandalettes sur le sable chaud.

10. _____ Une sœurette est toujours pénible pour un frère.

11. _____ On peut s'épiler les sourcils avec une pincette.

12. _____ La pommette est une petite pomme.

13. _____ Un enfant de huit ans n'a pas besoin de poussette.

14. _____ Les Sctroumpfs (smurfs) habitent dans des maisonnettes.

93 ▸ -in/-ine

MEANING	Diminutive, pejorative (people)
ENGLISH EQUIVALENT	—
PART OF SPEECH	Noun
GENDER	Masculine/feminine

A French noun with the suffix **-in** (feminine: **-ine**) often denotes the origin or nationality of a person; an example is **un Argentin / une Argentine** *a person from Argentina*. The suffix may also denote other personal characteristics, for example, **capucin/capucine** *Capuchin monk/nun*. (See No. 12.)

A French noun with this suffix may also have a pejorative connotation for the base word, which represents the person being diminished or mocked. The following chart contains nouns of this type. The base word for the noun **ignorantin** is the noun **ignorant** *ignoramus*, and the suffixed noun denotes someone who is worse than ignorant. The noun **cabotin** *bad actor* is thought to come from the name of a notoriously bad comedian in the time of King Louis XIII.

Some nouns ending in the suffix **-in/-ine** are derived directly from Latin, Italian, or Romansh (a language spoken in the Swiss Alps). Some nouns (for example, **assassin**, **babouin**, **bourrin**, **brigantin**, **cabotin**, **diablotin**, **galopin**, and **plaisantin**) do not have a feminine **-ine** counterpart. Some nouns (for example, **blondin** and **rouquin**) may also function as adjectives; these are indicated by an asterisk (*). For example, in the sentence **C'est une rouquine** *She is a redhead*, **rouquine** is a noun, while in the phrase **une fille rouquine** *a redheaded girl*, it is an adjective.

NOUN ENDING IN **-in/-ine**	ENGLISH EQUIVALENT	BASE WORD	ENGLISH EQUIVALENT
assassin	*murderer*	assassino [ITAL.]	*murderer*
babouin	*badly behaved child*	babouin	*baboon*
blondin*	*blondie*	blond	*blond*
bourrin	*clod, coarse person*	bourrique	*donkey*
brigantin	*bandit*	brigand	*bandit*
cabotin	*bad actor/actress*	Cabotin	*17th-century actor*
coquin*	*rascal*	coquinus [LAT.]	*beggar*
crétin*	*moron*	crétin [ROMANSH]	*cretin*
diablotin	*little devil*	diable	*devil*
galopin	*ragamuffin*	galoper	*to gallop*
ignorantin	*utter fool*	ignorant	*ignoramus*
plaisantin	*smart aleck*	plaisanter	*to joke*
rouquin*	*redhead*	roux	*red* (hair)

Less frequently, a French noun ending in the suffix **-in** (feminine: **-ine**) denotes a childish person (for example, **bambin**) or one who is innocent and pure (for example, **chérubin**). This type of suffixed noun may denote a person who is younger in a family. The noun **dauphin** referred to the royal child who was to succeed the king, because the southeastern province of Dauphiné was ruled by the king of France and his heirs, who called themselves **dauphins**. This noun has no feminine counterpart.

NOUN ENDING IN **-in/-ine**	ENGLISH EQUIVALENT	BASE WORD	ENGLISH EQUIVALENT
bambin	*little child*	bambino [ITAL.]	*child*
benjamin	*youngest child*	Benjamin	*a biblical name*
chérubin	*cherub*	kerub [HEBREW]	*angel*
cousin	*cousin*	consobrinus [LAT.]	*cousin*
dauphin	*prince* (king's heir)	Dauphiné	*a French province*

Des synonymes! *Provide an appropriate synonym for each word or phrase.*

1. Gamin _____

2. Espiègle _____

3. Petit garçon qui court les rues _____

4. Fils d'une tante _____

5. Petit ange _____

6. Petit diable _____

7. Petit singe _____

8. Meurtrier _____

9. Lourd comme un cheval _____

10. Prince héritier _____

11. Petit blond _____

12. Bandit _____

13. Idiot _____

14. Aux cheveux roux _____

15. Dernier-né _____

16. Mauvais acteur _____

17. Stupide _____

18. Farceur _____

94 ▸ -in

MEANING	Diminutive, pejorative (things)
ENGLISH EQUIVALENT	—
PART OF SPEECH	Noun
GENDER	Masculine

A French noun ending in the suffix **-in** denotes a diminutive aspect, literal or figurative, of the base word, which is typically a masculine noun and represents a thing. One exception is the noun **bottine** *bootie*; its base word is the feminine noun **botte** *boot*, and the suffixed noun retains the gender of the base noun: **botte** yields **bottine**. The base word for some of these nouns is a verb, for example, **déclin** (from **décliner** *to decline*). Many of these nouns have a foreign word as a base, notably Italian diminutives like **biscottino** *little biscuit* and **cordina** *little cord formerly used to* *beat convicts*. The base noun may also be Dutch or German; for example, the base word for the noun **butin** *loot* (literally, *small prey*) is the German noun **Beute** *prey*.

NOUN ENDING IN **-in**	ENGLISH EQUIVALENT	BASE WORD	ENGLISH EQUIVALENT
baladin	*wandering entertainer*	ballade	*ballad*
bassin	*basin, bowl*	baccinus [LAT.]	*basin*
biscotin	*little biscuit*	biscottino [ITAL.]	*little biscuit*
bottine	*bootie*	botte	*boot*
boudin	*blood sausage*	bodine [OLD FR.]	*sausage*
bouquin [FAMILIAR]	*book*	boeckin [DUTCH]	*little book*
bulletin	*bulletin*	bulle	*seal, decree*
butin	*loot*	Beute [GER.]	*prey*
chemin	*path*	camminus [LAT.]	*path*
couffin	*bassinet*	cophinus [LAT.]	*basket*
coussin	*pillow*	coxinus [LAT.]	*pillow*
crottin	*dung*	crotte	*dog excrement*
déclin	*decline*	décliner	*to decline*
engin	*machinery*	ingenium [LAT.]	*creative genius*

EXERCICE
94·1

Complétez! *Complete each sentence with the appropriate noun.*

1. Il y a un _____ à explorer dans cette forêt.

2. Dans le _____ de l'association, on apprend les dernières nouvelles.

3. Il faut ramasser le _____ des chevaux après la promenade.

4. Les bouquinistes le long de la Seine vendent des vieux _____.

5. Les vainqueurs d'une bataille rentraient chez eux avec un _____.

6. Une des spécialités du terroir alsacien est le _____.

7. Un nouveau-né rentre parfois chez lui dans un _____.

8. Paris est situé dans un _____.

9. Le _____ est délicieux, trempé dans une tasse de thé.

10. Il a construit un _____ qui vole.

11. Le _____ de la Renaissance était apprécié par les nobles de la cour.

12. Les causes du _____ de l'empire romain sont controversées.

13. On a besoin de _____ sur les divans.

14. Les femmes aiment porter de jolies _____ en hiver.

NOUN ENDING IN -in	ENGLISH EQUIVALENT	BASE WORD	ENGLISH EQUIVALENT
escarpin	*light shoe*	scarpino [ITAL.]	*dancing shoe*
festin	*feast*	festino [ITAL.]	*little feast*
gourdin	*club, bludgeon*	cordina [ITAL.]	*little cord*
gradins [PL.]	*bleachers*	gradino [ITAL.]	*little step*
gratin	*gratin*	gratter	*to scrape*
larcin	*petty theft*	latrocinium [LAT.]	*robbery*
moulin	*mill*	molinum [LAT.]	*mill*
patin	*skate, floor pad*	patte	*paw, leg*
romarin	*rosemary*	rosmarinus [LAT.]	*rosemary*
sous-marin	*submarine*	[sub-] + mare [LAT.]	*under + sea*
tremplin	*springboard*	trempellino [ITAL.]	*springboard*
vaccin	*vaccine*	vacciner	*to vaccinate*
vacherin	*cream cake*	vache	*cow*
venin	*venom*	venenum [LAT.]	*poison*

EXERCICE
94·2

Vrai ou faux? *Indicate whether each statement is true or false, using* **V** *for* **vrai** *true or* **F** *for* **faux** *false.*

1. _____ Un agent de police français porte un gourdin.

2. _____ Une soupe à l'oignon est toujours au gratin.

3. _____ Il est recommandé de prendre le vaccin contre la grippe.

4. _____ Un larcin est un crime au niveau fédéral.

5. _____ Le venin d'un serpent n'est pas toujours fatal.

6. _____ Le romarin est une herbe.

7. _____ Les escarpins sont des bottines.

8. _____ Au stade de foot, les spectateurs sont assis sur des gradins.

9. _____ La Hollande est connue pour ses moulins à vent.

10. _____ On sert parfois du vacherin comme hors d'œuvre.

11. _____ On porte des patins à la patinoire.

12. _____ Les courses de ski démarrent sur un tremplin.

13. _____ Aux mariages, il y a généralement un grand festin dans la rue.

14. _____ Le premier sous-marin date du 14e siècle.

95 ▶ -on

MEANING	Diminutive (animals and things)
ENGLISH EQUIVALENT	—
PART OF SPEECH	Noun
GENDER	Masculine

A French noun ending in the suffix **-on** denotes a diminutive aspect, literal or figurative, of the base word, which is typically a masculine noun and represents an animal or a thing. The base noun for **aiglon** is the noun **aigle** *eagle*, and the suffixed noun is a young eagle. The regular formation for this type of noun consists in replacing the **-e** ending of the base noun with the suffix **-on**, as in the **aigle ~ aiglon** example. The base word for some of these nouns is a verb.

NOUN ENDING IN -on	ENGLISH EQUIVALENT	BASE WORD	ENGLISH EQUIVALENT
aiglon	*eaglet*	aigle	*eagle*
aiguillon	*stinger*	aiguille	*needle*
aileron	*fin* (shark), *wing* (plane)	aile	*wing*
ânon	*little donkey*	âne	*donkey*
ballon	*ball, balloon*	balle	*ball*
balluchon	*bundle of clothes*	balle	*ball*
blouson	*jacket*	blouse	*blouse*
boulon	*(nut and) bolt*	boule	*ball*
caneton	*little duck*	cane	*female duck*
capuchon	*hoodie*	capuche	*hood*
carillon	*bell*	quadrinio [LAT.]	*group of four bells*
ceinturon	*belt*	ceinture	*belt*
chaînon	*link*	chaîne	*chain*

EXERCICE

95·1

Charade! *Provide the noun associated with each clue.*

1. Cet oiseau fait coin coin.   Le _____

2. On en porte un en cuir quand on fait de la moto.   Le _____

3. Le petit chaperon rouge en porte un.   Le _____

4. La chaîne est cassée s'il manque en un.   Le _____

5. Aux fêtes d'anniversaire, il y en a pour décorer et jouer.   Les _____

6. On l'entend sonner aux mariages ou aux fêtes religieuses.   Le _____

7. C'est un oiseau qui a servi de symbole à des souverains.   L' _____

8. Il faut l'enlever quand on a été piqué par une abeille.   L' _____

9. Ce sont des gouvernes aérodynamiques.   Les _____

10. Il aide à unir deux pièces.   Le _____

11. Les sans-abri en ont parfois un contenant quelques vêtements. Le _____

12. On en porte un pour serrer la taille d'un pantalon ou
    d'une robe.   Le _____

13. C'est un petit animal à quatre pattes qui ressemble
    à un poney.   Le _____

NOUN ENDING IN -on	ENGLISH EQUIVALENT	BASE WORD	ENGLISH EQUIVALENT
chaton	*kitten*	chat	*cat*
croûton	*crouton*	croûte	*crust*
dindon	*turkey* (cock)	dinde	*turkey*
échelon	*rung, step*	échelle	*ladder, scale*
fourgon	*van*	forgon [OLD FR.]	*carriage*
glaçon	*ice cube*	glace	*ice*
harpon	*harpoon*	harper	*to catch*
jupon	*underskirt*	jupe	*skirt*
maillon	*link*	maille	*stitch*
médaillon	*medallion*	médaille	*medal*
plongeon	*dive*	plonger	*to dive*
poêlon	*skillet*	poêle	*pan*
portillon	*gate*	porte	*door*
réveillon	*Christmas dinner, New Year's Eve dinner*	réveiller	*to wake up*

EXERCICE

95·2

Complétez! *Complete each sentence with the appropriate noun.*

1. On peut louer un _____ pour déménager un ou deux meubles.

2. Un _____ contient parfois des cheveux ou le portrait de quelqu'un.

3. Les esquimaux se servent d'un _____ pour pêcher.

4. Pour toucher le fond de la piscine, il faut faire un _____.

5. La chatte errante a souvent des _____.

6. Le repas de la Saint Sylvestre s'appelle le _____.

7. Certains aiment les _____ de pain dans leur salade.

8. Un _____ de la chaîne qui tient l'ancre du bateau est rompue.

9. Le _____ du jardin était ouvert et le chien est sorti.

10. On fait l'omelette dans un _____.

11. Les femmes ne portent plus que rarement un _____ sous leur robe.

12. Les Américains adorent les _____ dans leurs boissons.

13. Cette échelle a vingt _____.

14. Le _____ est la viande traditionnelle du repas de la Thanksgiving.

MEANING	Diminutive, condescension (people)
ENGLISH EQUIVALENT	—
PART OF SPEECH	Noun, adjective
GENDER	Masculine/feminine

A French noun ending in the suffix **-on** (feminine: **-onne**) denotes a diminutive or pejorative aspect, literal or figurative, of the base word, which is typically a masculine noun and represents a person. Some of these nouns have no feminine counterpart; examples are **chaperon** *old-fashioned lady's hat*, *chaperone*, **forgeron** *blacksmith* (who was historically male), and **marmiton** *assistant cook* (who was historically male, like his boss). The base word for the noun **marmiton** is the noun **marmite** *pot*, and this suffixed noun designates an assistant cook. The regular formation for this type of noun consists in replacing the -**e** ending of a base noun with the suffix -**on**: **marmite** yields **marmiton**. The base word may also be a verb; for example, the base word for **forgeron** is the verb **forger**. The regular formation for this type of noun consists in replacing the infinitive ending of the verb with the suffix: **friper** yields **fripon**. Some of these suffixed nouns may also function as adjectives; examples are **bouffon**, **félon**, **forgeron**, and **fripon**. In the sentence **C'est un grand fripon** *He's a big rascal*, **fripon** is a noun, while in the sentence **Ce garçon est plutôt fripon** *This boy is rather rascally*, it is an adjective.

NOUN/ADJECTIVE ENDING IN **-on/-onne**	ENGLISH EQUIVALENT	BASE WORD	ENGLISH EQUIVALENT
avorton	*runt*	avorter	*to abort*
bouffon	*buffoon*	buffone [ITAL.]	*joker, buffoon*
chaperon	*hat, chaperone*	chape [OLD FR.]	*headdress*
félon	*felon*	fel [OLD FR.]	*traitor*
forgeron	*blacksmith*	forger	*to forge*
fripon	*rascal*	friper	*to crease, crumple*
grognon	*grouch*	grogner	*to growl*
maigrichon	*scrawny creature*	maigre	*scrawny*
marmiton	*assistant cook*	marmite	*pot*
mitron	*baker's boy*	mitre	*miter, baker's hat*
moucheron	*kid*	mouche	*fly*
vigneron	*wine grower*	vigne	*vine*

EXERCICE 96·1

Complétez! *Complete each sentence with the appropriate noun.*

1. Il est encore de mauvaise humeur. Quel _____!

2. Elle ne mange rien. Quelle _____!

3. Ne lui faites pas confiance! Quel _____!

4. Elle est vigilante et surveille sa protégée. Quel _____!

5. Il est si minuscule. Quel _____!

6. Elle nous a encore trompés. Quelle _____!

7. Il se lève à quatre heures du matin pour cuire le pain. Quel _____!

8. Il faisait des épées pour les chevaliers. Quel _____!

9. Il suit tous les ordres du cuisinier à la lettre. Quel _____!

10. Ses vins gagnent toujours des prix. Quelle _____!

11. Il ne fait que des plaisanteries et des bêtises. Quel _____!

12. Ce petit canard est né fluet et maigrichon. C'est un _____ pourtant adorable.

97 ◆ -eau

MEANING	Diminutive (animals)
ENGLISH EQUIVALENT	—
PART OF SPEECH	Noun
GENDER	Masculine

A French noun ending in the suffix **-eau** denotes a young animal if the base word is an animal. For example, the base word for the noun **éléphanteau** is the noun **éléphant**, and the suffixed noun is a young elephant. These nouns are masculine and have no feminine counterparts.

NOUN ENDING IN -eau	ENGLISH EQUIVALENT	BASE WORD	ENGLISH EQUIVALENT
chevreau	*young goat, kid*	chèvre	*goat*
cigogneau	*young stork*	cigogne	*stork*
éléphanteau	*young elephant, calf*	éléphant	*elephant*
faisandeau	*young pheasant, chick*	faisan	*pheasant*
lionceau	*lion cub*	lion	*lion*
louveteau	*wolf cub*	loup	*wolf*
pigeonneau	*young pigeon*	pigeon	*pigeon*
renardeau	*fox cub*	renard	*fox*
souriceau	*young mouse*	souris	*mouse*
vermisseau	*little worm*	ver	*worm*

Charade! *Provide the noun associated with each clue.*

1. Il hurle à la pleine lune. _____

2. Il a une crinière comme son père. _____

3. Il aime le fromage. _____

4. Il aime sauter et courir; il donnera un jour du lait. _____

5. C'est un oiseau qu'on trouve dans toutes les places publiques. _____

6. Il a la réputation d'être rusé et malin. _____

7. C'est le petit d'un oiseau que les chasseurs aiment bien. _____

8. Il est tout petit et se glisse dans la terre. _____

9. C'est le petit d'un oiseau qui aime faire son nid sur les cheminées. _____

10. Bien que jeune, il est très grand et gros. _____

98 ◆ -ot/-ote

MEANING	Diminutive (familiar, pejorative)
ENGLISH EQUIVALENT	—
PART OF SPEECH	Noun
GENDER	Masculine/feminine

A French noun ending in the suffix **-ot** (feminine: **-ote**) often adds a diminutive meaning to its base noun. For example, the base word for the noun **chiot** *puppy* is the noun **chien** *dog*. More often than not, though, this suffix assigns a pejorative or—at the very least—a familiar connotation to the base word. The noun **parigot**, based on the name of the city of **Paris**, describes someone who lives in Paris, but is extremely familiar and considered slang. Similarly, the word **soûlot** is a pejorative characterization of an alcoholic. While the nouns **parigot**, **poivrot**, and **soûlot** have feminine counterparts ending in **-ote**, the remainder of the words in the following chart do not. The masculine noun **boulot** is slang for *work*; however, it may also refer to a plump person, in which case it also functions as an adjective (with a feminine form ending in **-otte**).

NOUN ENDING IN -ot/-ote	ENGLISH EQUIVALENT	BASE WORD	ENGLISH EQUIVALENT
asticot	*small white worm, maggot*	asticoter	*to annoy, needle*
bachot	*secondary studies exam*	baccalauréat	*exam*
boulot	*job*	boulotter [FAMILIAR]	*to eat*
boulot(te)	*plump person*	boule	*ball*
bourricot	*small donkey*	bourrique	*donkey*
chariot	*wagon, cart*	char	*cart* (farm)
chiot	*puppy*	chien	*dog*
ciboulot	*small onion*	ciboule	*onion*
cuissot	*haunch* (venison)	cuisse	*thigh*
îlot	*small island*	île	*island*
loupiot	*young wolf*	loup	*wolf*
mendigot	*beggar*	mendiant	*beggar*
parigot(e)	*Parisian*	Paris	*Paris*
poivrot(e)	*drunkard*	poivre	*pepper*
soûlot(e)	*drunkard*	soûl	*drunk*

EXERCICE 98·1

En toute familiarité! *Provide the noun(s) associated with each clue.*

1. Un jeune animal _____ _____

2. Quelqu'un qui boit trop d'alcool _____ _____

3. Ça se mange. _____ _____

4. Quelqu'un qui demande de l'argent aux passants _____

5. Un Parisien _____

6. Il faut travailler dur pour l'obtenir. _____ _____

7. Un peu potelé avec des formes bien rondelettes _____

8. Sert d'appas à la pêche _____

9. Entouré de plages _____

10. Sert à porter les provisions au supermarché _____

99 ▸ -ot/-ote

MEANING	Diminutive (familiar; affectionate or pejorative)
ENGLISH EQUIVALENT	—
PART OF SPEECH	Adjective
GENDER	Masculine/feminine

Many French adjectives ending in the suffix **-ot** (feminine: **-ote**) have a diminutive connotation, which can be intended in an affectionate or pejorative manner. For example, the base word for the adjective **bellot** is the feminine adjective **belle** *beautiful*, and the suffixed adjective means *bonny*. Applied to children, this is an affectionate term; applied to adults, it has a pejorative connotation. The regular formation for this type of adjective consists in replacing the **-e** ending of a feminine base adjective with **-ot** or **-ote**. For this reason, the feminine form of a base adjective is included in the following chart if it differs from the masculine form.

ADJECTIVE ENDING IN -ot/-ote	ENGLISH EQUIVALENT	BASE WORD	ENGLISH EQUIVALENT
bellot	bonny	beau/belle	beautiful
falot	dull	fellow [ENG.]	fellow
fiérot	sort of proud	fier/fière	proud
jeunot	youngish	jeune	young
maigriot	sort of skinny	maigre	skinny
pâlot	sort of pale	pâle	pale
petiot	sort of small	petit/petite	small
vieillot(te)	sort of old	vieux/vieille	old

EXERCICE 99·1

Décrivez! *Complete each sentence with the correct form of the appropriate adjective.*

1. Marie, tu ne fais que parler de tes richesses. Tu es plutôt _____!

2. Guy, tu n'as que la peau et les os. Tu es plutôt _____!

3. Marie, avec cet accoutrement de grand-mère, tu as l'air plutôt _____!

4. Guy, avec ce visage de bébé, tu as l'air plutôt _____!

5. Marie, avec tes quatre pieds de grandeur, tu es bien _____!

6. Guy, avec ces beaux yeux et ces cheveux longs, tu as l'air plutôt _____!

7. Marie, avec ces joues sans couleur, tu es plutôt _____!

8. Guy, tu n'as pas d'opinion; tu es plutôt _____!

100 -âtre

MEANING	Pejorative, approximate
ENGLISH EQUIVALENT	—
PART OF SPEECH	Adjective
GENDER	Masculine/feminine

A French adjective ending in the suffix **-âtre** imparts a pejorative connotation to a quality or an approximate value to a color. For example, the base word for the adjective **opiniâtre** is the noun **opinion**, and the suffixed adjective has the negative meaning *stubborn, opinionated*. The base word for the adjective **rougeâtre** is the adjective **rouge** *red*, and the suffixed adjective means *reddish*. The regular formation for this type of adjective consists in adding the suffix **-âtre** to the masculine form of an adjective: **noir** yields **noirâtre**. There are, however, some irregularities designed to preserve the soft **c** and **g** sounds, as in **douceâtre** and **rougeâtre**; similarly, **blanc** yields **blanchâtre** to facilitate its pronunciation.

ADJECTIVE ENDING IN -âtre	ENGLISH EQUIVALENT	BASE WORD	ENGLISH EQUIVALENT
acariâtre	*grouchy*	âcre	*grouchy*
blanchâtre	*whitish*	blanc	*white*
bleuâtre	*bluish*	bleu	*blue*
brunâtre	*brownish*	brun	*brown*
douceâtre	*sicky-sweet*	doux/douce	*sweet*
folâtre	*frolicsome, worry-free*	folâtrer	*to frolic*
grisâtre	*grayish*	gris	*gray*
jaunâtre	*yellowish*	jaune	*yellow*
noirâtre	*blackish*	noir	*black*
opiniâtre	*stubborn, opinionated*	opinion	*opinion*
rougeâtre	*reddish*	rouge	*red*
verdâtre	*greenish*	vert	*green*

EXERCICE
100·1

Complétez la description! *Complete each phrase with the appropriate adjective.*

1. Une voix gentille et _____

2. Un bambin enjoué et _____

3. Un vieux papier _____

4. Une personne irascible et _____

5. Une peau _____ à force d'être exposée au soleil

6. Une belle eau _____ sous un ciel bleu

7. Une peau de banane bien mûrie et _____

8. Une potion magique _____ comme les algues

9. Une substance huileuse et _____

10. Ni noir ni blanc mais plutôt _____

11. Têtu et _____ comme une mule

12. Une écume _____ sur les hautes vagues

French prefixes

Many French prefixes have English equivalents. Since these prefixes usually derive from the same Latin or Greek root, their meanings tend to be easily recognized. Some French prefixes, however, have no English counterpart; learning these prefixes will enhance your understanding of word formation by revealing whole new sets of vocabulary.

The charts of prefixed words show at a glance how a prefix attached to a base word creates a new, related word. Usually, the prefix is attached to an existing French word; for example, the prefix **re-** attached to **naissance** *birth* forms **renaissance** *rebirth*. Sometimes, however, a French prefix is attached to a Latin or Greek root, which may have, over time, become a French suffix. For example, the French suffix **-gène** derives from the Greek word **genos** *birth*, *origin*, *type*. The noun **homogène** comprises the prefix **homo-** *same* and the suffix **-gène**, and the prefixed noun means of the same origin or type, or *homogeneous*. You will recognize these words more easily as you become familiar with common Latin and Greek roots, especially as you use the words in each chart and work the accompanying exercises.

Some French suffixes, such as **-graphe**, **-gramme**, and **-pathe**, appear as base words in this section and are included in Part I. Others, such as **-phone** and **-naute**, are not included in Part I; they are presented here because they are easy to recognize and are in common usage.

The charts of prefixed words also facilitate an awareness of how families of words can expand vocabulary. As an example, the words **découvrir** *to discover*, **découvert** *discovered*, and **découverte** *discovery* are members of the family of words that share the prefix **dé-** and the base word **couvrir** *to cover*.

If the base word for a prefixed noun is also a noun, the prefixed noun has the same gender as its base noun. Adjectives are listed in their masculine form; those ending in **-e** have the same masculine and feminine forms.

The prefixes are generally organized in semantic categories; for an overview of the organization, consult the Contents or Appendix B. Where possible, the charts of prefixed words alternately focus on nouns and verbs; this allows you to practice using both parts of speech in the exercises.

Use of a **trait d'union** *hyphen* after a prefix sometimes seems arbitrary. The orthographic reforms of 1990 include recommendations (not mandates) against the use of hyphens after prefixes derived from Latin (for example, **extra-**, **infra-**, **intra-**, and **ultra-**), as well as scientific prefixes (for example, **aéro-**, **audio-**, and **auto-**). The current trend is to eliminate a hyphen unless its omission impairs pronunciation.

3
Beginning prefixes

 **101** ◆ **non-**

MEANING	No, not
ENGLISH EQUIVALENT	*non-*
PART OF SPEECH	Noun, adjective

The French prefix **non-** is found in many nouns and some adjectives. Although it has an exact English equivalent, its use has increased in French in recent years. It is recommended to use a hyphen in nouns, but hyphen use in adjectives is undecided. For consistency, both nouns and adjectives prefixed with **non-** are hyphenated in the following charts. English does not use a hyphen with *non-*.

NOUN/ADJECTIVE BEGINNING IN **non-**	ENGLISH EQUIVALENT	BASE WORD	ENGLISH EQUIVALENT
non-acceptation [F.]	*nonacceptance*	acceptation	*acceptance*
non-activité [F.]	*nonactivity*	activité	*activity*
non-agression [F.]	*nonaggression*	agression	*aggression*
non-alignement [M.]	*nonalignment*	alignement	*alignment*
non-assistance [F.]	*nonassistance*	assistance	*assistance*
non-belligérance [F.]	*nonbelligerence*	belligérance	*belligerence*
non-combattant [M./ADJ.]	*noncombatant*	combattant	*combatant*
non-conciliation [F.]	*nonconciliation*	conciliation	*conciliation*
non-concurrence [F.]	*noncompetition*	concurrence	*competition*
non-conformisme [M.F.]	*nonconformism*	conformisme	*conformism*
non-croyant(e) [M.F./ADJ.]	*nonbeliever*	croyant(e)	*believer*
non-discrimination [F.]	*nondiscrimination*	discrimination	*discrimination*
non-endettement [M.]	*no debt*	endettement	*getting into debt*
non-lieu [M.]	*dismissed case*	lieu	*place*
non-retour [M.]	*no return*	retour	*return*
non-violence [F.]	*nonviolence*	violence	*violence*
non-voyant(e) [M.F./ADJ.]	*visually impaired*	voyant(e)	*seeing* (person)

Adjectives related to nouns in the preceding chart are as follows.

non-actif	*inactive*
non-agressé	*not attacked*
non-aligné	*unaligned*
non-assisté	*unassisted*
non-belligérant	*not belligerent*
non-conformiste	*nonconformist*
non-discriminé	*not discriminated against, undifferentiated*
non-endetté	*not in debt*
non-violent	*nonviolent*

Charade! *Provide the noun(s) corresponding to each pair of clues.*

1. Disculpation, tribunal _____

2. Sans armes, employé civil _____

3. Impasse, stop _____

4. Pause, vacances _____

5. Pacifisme, idéalisme _____ _____

   _____

6. Autonomie, autodirection _____ _____

7. Vues opposées, entêtement _____

8. Économies, stabilité financière _____

9. Privé du sens de la vue, presque
   aveugle _____

10. Refus d'aider, isolationnisme _____

11. Impartialité, équité _____

12. Refus, récalcitrance _____

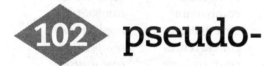

102 ◆ pseudo-

MEANING	False, would-be
ENGLISH EQUIVALENT	*pseudo-*
PART OF SPEECH	Adjective, noun

The French prefix **pseudo-**, used to form adjectives and nouns, is a Greek root meaning *false*, *untrue*. The base word prefixed with **pseudo-** indicates what is false. For example, the adjective **pseudo-classique** denotes a close resemblance to a classical quality; it may also signify a pretended but unauthentic resemblance to the quality. The noun **pseudonyme** *pen name* is a name adopted by an author for his or her writings, but not his or her real name. If the base word is a French adjective, a hyphen is mandatory after this prefix.

ADJECTIVE BEGINNING IN **pseudo-**	ENGLISH EQUIVALENT	BASE WORD	ENGLISH EQUIVALENT
pseudo-alpin	*pseudoalpine*	alpin	*alpine*
pseudo-artistique	*pseudoartistic*	artistique	*artistic*
pseudo-classique	*pseudoclassical*	classique	*classical*
pseudo-démentiel	*pseudoinsane*	démentiel	*insane*
pseudo-élastique	*pseudoelastic*	élastique	*elastic*
pseudo-épique	*pseudoepic*	épique	*epic*
pseudo-objectif	*pseudo-objective*	objectif	*objective*
pseudo-original	*pseudo-original*	original	*original*
pseudo-philosophique	*pseudophilosophical*	philosophique	*philosophical*
pseudo-scientifique	*pseudoscientific*	scientifique	*scientific*

Nouns related to adjectives in the preceding chart are as follows.

pseudo-art [M.]	*pseudoart*
pseudo-classicisme [M.]	*pseudoclassicism*
pseudo-démence [F.]	*pseudoinsanity*
pseudo-élasticité [F.]	*pseudoelasticity*
pseudo-épopée [F.]	*pseudoepic*
pseudo-objectivité [F.]	*pseudo-objectivity*
pseudo-originalité [F.]	*pseudo-originality*
pseudo-philosophie [F.]	*pseudophilosophy*
pseudo-science [F.]	*pseudoscience*

EXERCICE
102·1

Complétez! *Choose the best completion for each sentence.*

1. _____ L'œuvre d'un artiste est pseudo-originale

2. _____ L'expérimentation sur les jumeaux

3. _____ Une escalade des Rockies est une

4. _____ Certains pensent que le graffiti est une

5. _____ Nous pouvons tous décrire nos

6. _____ Les films d'action comportent des

7. _____ L'architecture pseudo-classique

8. _____ Stephen Colbert adopte souvent une

9. _____ Les journalistes font

10. _____ Il y a des matériaux pseudo-élastiques

a. prétention pseudo-artistique.

b. courses de voiture pseudo-épiques.

c. des reportages pseudo-objectifs.

d. s'il n'admet pas que c'est une copie.

e. de certains bâtiments laisse à désirer.

f. qui reprennent leur forme après s'être détendus.

g. pensées pseudo-philosophiques.

h. n'était que pseudo-scientifique.

i. montée pseudo-alpine.

j. attitude pseudo-démentielle.

 **quasi-**

MEANING	To some degree
ENGLISH EQUIVALENT	*quasi-*
PART OF SPEECH	Noun, adjective

The French prefix **quasi-**, used to form nouns and adjectives, denotes the presence or existence of the base word *to some degree*. The Latin word **quasi** means *as if*. The hyphen is mandatory in nouns formed with this prefix, but not in adjectives. For consistency, both nouns and adjectives prefixed with **quasi-** are hyphenated in the following chart and list.

NOUN BEGINNING IN **quasi-**	ENGLISH EQUIVALENT	BASE WORD	ENGLISH EQUIVALENT
quasi-certitude [F.]	*quasi-certainty*	certitude	*certainty*
quasi-contrat [M.]	*quasi-contract*	contrat	*contract*
quasi-crime [M.]	*quasi-crime*	crime	*crime*
quasi-fraternité [F.]	*quasi-fraternity*	fraternité	*fraternity*
quasi-légalité [F.]	*quasi-legality*	légalité	*legality*
quasi-monopole [M.]	*quasi-monopoly*	monopole	*monopoly*
quasi-morbidité [F.]	*quasi-morbidity*	morbidité	*morbidity*
quasi-sororité [F.]	*quasi-sorority*	sororité	*sorority*
quasi-totalité [F.]	*quasi-totality*	totalité	*totality*
quasi-unanimité [F.]	*quasi-unanimity*	unanimité	*unanimity*

Adjectives related to nouns in the preceding chart are as follows.

quasi-certain	*quasi-certain*
quasi-criminel	*quasi-criminal*
quasi-fraternel	*quasi-brotherly*
quasi-légal	*quasi-legal*
quasi-morbide	*quasi-morbid*
quasi-total	*quasi-total*
quasi-unanime	*quasi-unanimous*

EXERCICE

103·1

Complétez! *Provide the appropriate noun to complete each sentence.*

1. La _____ des autopsies dans les feuilletons me donnent la chair de poule.

2. La _____ de la vente de substances autrefois illégales est un fait accompli dans certains états.

3. La _____ entre amis proches est remarquable.

4. Nous avons un _____ avec nos voisins concernant l'emplacement de nos clôtures.

5. C'est un _____ de laisser ses bêtes dehors pendant de grands froids.

6. Certains pays ont le _____ des médias.

7. C'est une _____ que la Floride va sombrer dans l'océan à moins que le gouvernement intervienne.

8. La _____ des États-Unis était anglophone au 19ᵉ siècle.

9. Il y a une _____ entre les femmes victimes du viol.

10. La _____ des avis montre que cette décision est la bonne.

104 ◆ archi-

MEANING	Extremely
ENGLISH EQUIVALENT	—
PART OF SPEECH	Adjective

The French prefix **archi-** may be attached to almost any French adjective to denote intensity or an extreme quality. Although it is translated *super-* in the following chart, it has no equivalent in English. Use of the hyphen is inconsistent and undecided with **archi-**. For consistency, adjectives prefixed with **quasi-** are hyphenated in the chart.

ADJECTIVE BEGINNING IN **archi-**	ENGLISH EQUIVALENT	BASE WORD	ENGLISH EQUIVALENT
archi-beau	*superbeautiful*	beau	*beautiful*
archi-connu	*super-well-known*	connu	*known*
archi-ennuyeux	*superboring, superannoying*	ennuyeux	*boring, annoying*
archi-faux	*superfalse*	faux	*false*
archi-généreux	*supergenerous*	généreux	*generous*
archi-glacial	*supericy*	glacial	*icy*
archi-humide	*superhumid*	humide	*humid*
archi-pluvieux	*superrainy*	pluvieux	*rainy*
archi-sérieux	*superserious*	sérieux	*serious*
archi-tenace	*supertenacious*	tenace	*tenacious*

EXERCICE
104·1

Une actualité archi-courante! *To interpret the following pseudo–news event, complete each sentence with the correct form of the appropriate adjective.*

C'est un fait (1) _____ que le climat équatorial peut être

(2) _____ surtout pendant la saison des pluies où il fait un temps

(3) _____ . Cela devient (4) _____ quand

les sentiers sont inondés et les rivières débordent. Mais les habitants de ces zones qui

ont beaucoup d'endurance sont (5) _____ . Ils sont aussi

(6) _____ avec leurs provisions qu'ils partagent volontiers. Cela dit,

il est quand même (7) _____ qu'ils ne puissent quitter leurs refuges

en hauteur. Ils sont impatients de pouvoir jouir de nouveau de leur habitat qui est

normalement (8) _____ . Il est (9) _____

de croire qu'ils ne souhaiteraient pas parfois le temps (10) _____

du Pôle Nord.

105 néo-

MEANING	New
ENGLISH EQUIVALENT	*neo-*
PART OF SPEECH	Noun, adjective

The French prefix **néo-** is found primarily in nouns and adjectives ending in the suffixes **-isme** and **-iste**; the former denotes a faith, an ideology, or an artistic/literary/musical movement or style, and the latter denotes an adherent or practitioner of the faith, ideology, or movement. An example is **néo-classicisme** *neoclassicism*. (For the suffixes **-isme** and **-iste**, see Nos. 63–70 in Part I.) The base word may also be the name of the inhabitant of a country or region, for example, **Néo-Zélandais** *New Zealander*. In the following chart, note the consistent use of the hyphen before the base word except in **néonazi** and **néonazisme**.

NOUN/ADJECTIVE BEGINNING IN **néo-**	ENGLISH EQUIVALENT	BASE WORD	ENGLISH EQUIVALENT
néo-capitalisme [M.]	*neocapitalism*	capitalisme	*capitalism*
néo-capitaliste [M.F./ADJ.]	*neocapitalist*	capitaliste	*capitalist*
néo-classicisme [M.]	*neoclassicism*	classicisme	*classicism*
néo-classiciste [M.F./ADJ.]	*neoclassicist*	classiciste	*classicist*
néo-colonialisme [M.]	*neocolonialism*	colonialisme	*colonialism*
néo-colonialiste [M.F./ADJ.]	*neocolonialist*	colonialiste	*colonialist*
néo-évolutionnisme [M.]	*neoevolutionism*	évolutionnisme	*evolutionism*
néo-évolutionniste [M.F./ADJ.]	*neoevolutionist*	évolutionniste	*evolutionist*
néonazi(e) [M.F./ADJ.]	*neo-Nazi*	nazi	*Nazi*
néonazisme [M.]	*neo-Nazism*	nazisme	*Nazism*
Néo-Indien(ne) [M.F.]	*Neo-Indian*	Indien	*Indian*
Néo-Québécois(e) [M.F.]	*Neo-Quebecois*	Québécois(e)	*Quebecois*
Néo-Zélandais(e) [M.F.]	*New Zealander*	Zélandais(e)	*Zealander*

Adjectives related to nouns in the preceding chart are as follows.

néoclassique	*neoclassical*
néo-indien	*neo-Indian*
néo-québécois	*neo-Quebecois*
néo-zélandais	*New Zealand*

EXERCICE
105·1

Définitions! *Provide the appropriate word for each description.*

1. Adjectif qui décrit les habitants de la Nouvelle-Zélande   _____

2. Adjectif qui décrit les nouvelles populations de l'Inde   _____

3. Adjectif qui décrit les nouveaux habitants du Québec   _____

4. Celui ou celle qui croit au renouveau du colonialisme   _____

5. Celui ou celle qui croit au renouveau du capitalisme   _____

6. Le mouvement qui veut faire renaître le classicisme   _____

7. La nouvelle théorie de l'évolutionnisme   _____

8. Le nouveau mouvement d'extrême droite en Allemagne   _____

106 ⬧ aéro-

MEANING	Related to air/aeronautics
ENGLISH EQUIVALENT	*aero-*
PART OF SPEECH	Noun, adjective

The French prefix **aéro-**, like English *aero-*, indicates a relationship of the base word to air or aeronautics. For example, the base word for the noun **aérophagie** is the Greek root **phagein** *to eat*, and the prefixed noun denotes excessive swallowing of air. The base word for the noun **aérogare** is the French noun **gare** *(train) station*, and the prefixed noun denotes an airport terminal. Since many of these prefixed nouns have English cognates, they tend to be easily recognized. Some of the words in the following chart function both as nouns and as adjectives; compare the phrases **un aérosol** (noun) and **un produit aérosol** (adjective).

NOUN/ADJECTIVE BEGINNING IN **aéro-**	ENGLISH EQUIVALENT	BASE WORD	ENGLISH EQUIVALENT
aéroclub [M.]	*flying club*	club	*club*
aérodrome [M.]	*airfield*	dromos [GRK.]	*race*
aérodynamique [F./ADJ.]	*aerodynamics/aerodynamic*	dynamique	*dynamic*
aérogare [F.]	*air terminal*	gare	*(train) station*
aéronaute [M.F.]	*balloonist*	[-naute]	*navigator*
aéronautique [F./ADJ.]	*aeronautics/aeronautical*	[-naute]	*navigator*
aéronaval [ADJ.]	*air-sea*	naval	*by sea*
aérophagie [F.]	*aerophagy*	phagein [GRK.]	*to eat*
aéroport [M.]	*airport*	port	*port*
aérosol [M./ADJ.]	*spray, aerosol*	solidus [LAT.]	*three-dimensional*
aérospatial [ADJ.]	*aerospace*	spatial	*spatial*
aéroterrestre [ADJ.]	*air-land*	terre	*land*
aérothermique [ADJ.]	*aerothermic*	thermique	*thermic, thermal*
aérotrain [M.]	*hover train*	train	*train*
aérotransport [M.]	*air transportation*	transport	*transportation*

Complétez! *Provide the appropriate word to complete each sentence.*

1. L'Airbus 380 est actuellement le plus gros avion civil de transport de passagers dans l'histoire de l'_____.

2. Les États-Unis ont une force _____ importante; elle dépend du secrétaire à la Marine.

3. Les États-Unis ont passé le programme _____ de NASA au secteur privé.

4. L'_____ est un véhicule qui glisse sur un coussin d'air au-dessus des rails.

5. L'_____ est le moyen de transportation le plus rapide.

6. L'industrie de défense terrestre et _____ est en croissance.

7. Il y a plusieurs _____ autour de Paris pour les avions de plaisance.

8. Les aviateurs amateurs font partie d'un _____.

9. Charles de Gaulle est le plus grand _____ de Paris.

10. Quand un aéroport devient trop petit, on agrandit les _____.

11. L'_____ pratique l'aérostation en ballon libre.

12. L'_____ est l'étude et l'analyse des écoulements d'air.

13. Les panneaux solaires _____ sont bénéfiques à l'environnement.

14. Certains _____ sont responsables de la diminution de la couche d'ozone.

15. L'_____ pose des problèmes gastriques bénins.

 **anti-**

MEANING	Against
ENGLISH EQUIVALENT	*anti-*
PART OF SPEECH	Adjective, noun

The French prefix **anti-**, used to form adjectives and nouns, means *against*. Although this prefix is used mostly with adjectives, some words in the following chart function both as nouns and as adjectives; compare the phrases **un antiacide** (noun) and **un produit antiacide** (adjective).

ADJECTIVE/NOUN BEGINNING IN anti-	ENGLISH EQUIVALENT	BASE WORD	ENGLISH EQUIVALENT
antiacide [M./ADJ.]	*antacid*	acide	*acid*
antiadhésif [M./ADJ.]	*nonstick*	adhésif	*adhesive*
antibiotique [M./ADJ.]	*antibiotic*	biotique	*biotic*
antibrouillard [M./ADJ.]	*fog-proof*	brouillard	*fog*
anticommunisme [M.]	*anticommunism*	communisme	*communism*
anticorps [M.]	*antibody*	corps	*body*
antidopage [M./ADJ.]	*antidoping*	dope [ENG.]	*illegal drug*
antidote [M.]	*antidote*	dote [GRK.]	*what is given*
antihistaminique [M.]	*antihistamine*	histamine	*histamine*
antimatière [F.]	*antimatter*	matière	*matter*
antiphrase [F.]	*antiphrasis*	phrase	*sentence*
antisémite [M.F./ADJ.]	*antisemite/antisemitic*	sémite	*semitic*
antiseptique [M./ADJ.]	*antiseptic*	septique	*septic*
antithèse [F.]	*antithesis*	thèse	*thesis*
antivol [M./ADJ.]	*antitheft*	vol	*theft*

EXERCICE

107·1

Complétez! *Choose the best completion for each sentence.*

1. _____ Les anticorps désactivent

2. _____ Les antihistaminiques

3. _____ L'antidopage est une politique

4. _____ Un gel antiseptique est recommandé

5. _____ Les scientifiques croient à

6. _____ Les bananes ont un effet

7. _____ Un micro-organisme peut devenir résistant

8. _____ Le progrès économique est l'antidote

9. _____ L'anticommunisme était exacerbé

10. _____ La philosophie hégélienne

11. _____ Beaucoup de voitures sont munies

12. _____ Il faut une poêle antiadhésive

13. _____ Il ne faut pas allumer ses feux

14. _____ L'antiphrase exprime

15. _____ L'antisémite n'admet pas toujours

a. qui vise les infractions sportives.

b. ses préjugés.

c. de dispositifs antivol.

d. aux antibiotiques.

e. les antigènes.

f. combattent les réactions allergiques.

g. pour soigner une coupure.

h. est basée sur la thèse et l'antithèse.

i. le contraire de ce qu'on pense.

j. l'existence de l'antimatière.

k. antiacide.

l. pour faire les crêpes.

m. à l'époque du maccarthisme.

n. au chômage.

o. antibrouillard quand il fait beau.

The following chart presents additional adjectives with the prefix **anti-**; since all of them have English cognates, they are easily recognized. Note the hyphen that separates the prefix **anti-** from a base word that begins in **i-**, for example, **anti-infectieux** and **anti-inflammatoire**.

ADJECTIVE BEGINNING IN anti-	ENGLISH EQUIVALENT	BASE WORD	ENGLISH EQUIVALENT
antiaérien	*antiaircraft*	aérien	*airbound*
antialcoolique	*antialcohol*	alcoolique	*alcoholic*
antiallergique	*antiallergenic*	allergique	*allergic*
antibruit	*soundproof*	bruit	*noise*
anticancéreux	*anticancer*	cancéreux	*cancerous*
antichoc	*shockproof*	choc	*shock*
anticlérical	*anticlerical*	clérical	*clerical*
anticommuniste	*anticommunist*	communiste	*communist*
anticonformiste	*anticonformist*	conformiste	*conformist*
anti-infectieux	*anti-infective*	infectieux	*infectious*
anti-inflammatoire	*anti-inflammatory*	inflammatoire	*inflammatory*
antisocial	*antisocial*	social	*social*
antitabac	*anti-tobacco*	tabac	*tobacco*
antivenimeux	*antivenomous*	venimeux	*poisonous*

EXERCICE
107·2

Vrai ou faux? *Indicate whether each statement is true or false, using* **V** *for* **vrai** *true or* **F** *for* **faux** *false.*

1. _____ Les médicaments anti-infectieux sont particulièrement dangereux.

2. _____ Tous les Cubains sont anticommunistes.

3. _____ Il faut administrer un médicament antivenimeux aux serpents.

4. _____ Il y a des groupes sociaux antialcooliques organisés.

5. _____ Les passagers d'un avion doivent porter des casques antibruit.

6. _____ Les pharmacies offrent une variété de produits antiallergiques.

7. _____ Les extraits de la plante aloès peuvent avoir un effet anti-inflammatoire.

8. _____ Les voitures sont équipées de systèmes antichocs.

9. _____ Il n'existe pas encore de systèmes de défense antiaériens en Europe.

10. _____ Les victimes du cancer suivent des traitements anticancéreux.

11. _____ Les chefs de la révolution française étaient plutôt anticléricaux.

12. _____ Tous les adultes sont anticonformistes de nos jours.

13. _____ Une attitude antisociale n'est pas agréable, surtout lors des célébrations.

14. _____ Les fanatiques antitabac ne sont pas accueillis dans les bons hôtels.

 **108** **auto-**

MEANING   Self
ENGLISH EQUIVALENT   *auto-*
PART OF SPEECH   Noun, adjective

The French prefix **auto-**, used to form nouns and adjectives, means *self* or *by itself.* Note that some words in the following chart function both as nouns and as adjectives.

NOUN/ADJECTIVE BEGINNING IN **auto-**	ENGLISH EQUIVALENT	BASE WORD	ENGLISH EQUIVALENT
autoallumage [M.]	*autoignition*	allumage	*ignition*
autoanalyse [F.]	*self-analysis*	analyse	*analysis*
autobiographie [F.]	*autobiography*	biographie	*biography*
autocensure [F.]	*self-censorship*	censure	*censorship*
autochtone [M.F.]	*native*	chthon [GRK.]	*land*
autocollant [M./ADJ.]	*sticker/self-adhesive*	collant	*sticky*
autodéfense [F.]	*self-defense*	défense	*defense*
autodestruction [F.]	*self-destruction*	destruction	*destruction*
autodidacte [M.F./ADJ.]	*self-taught*	didaschein [GRK.]	*to teach*
autographe [M.]	*autograph*	graphein [GRK.]	*to write*
automate [M.]	*automation*	motus [LAT.]	*movement*
autonomie [F.]	*autonomy*	nomos [GRK.]	*law, rule*
autonomiste [M.F.]	*autonomist*	nomos [GRK.]	*law, rule*
autoportrait [M.]	*self-portrait*	portrait	*portrait*

Verbs related to nouns in the preceding chart are as follows.

s'autocensurer	*to censor oneself*
s'autocoller	*to self-adhere*
s'autodétruire	*to self-destruct*
autographier	*to autograph*
s'autonomiser	*to become self-reliant*

Adjectives related to nouns in the preceding chart are as follows.

autobiographique	*autobiographical*
autocensuré	*self-censored*
autodétruit	*self-destroyed*
autographié	*autographed*
automatique	*automatic*
automatisé	*automated*

EXERCICE
108·1

Complétez! *Provide the appropriate word to complete each sentence.*

1. L'ingénieur allemand Rudolf Diesel a inventé le premier moteur diesel à

_____ .

2. La province du Québec a une certaine _____ au Canada.

3. Les présidents écrivent souvent des _____ ou des mémoires.

4. Les institutions scolaires font souvent des _____ de leurs méthodes pédagogiques.

5. Les grands artistes signent des _____ à leurs fans.

6. Maya Angelou et Albert Einstein sont des _____ célèbres.

7. Il y a des _____ au Pays Basque et en Corse.

8. L'artiste Norman Rockwell a peint un _____.

9. Un objet programmé et doté d'une mémoire est un _____.

10. Certains psychopathes ont une tendance à l'_____.

11. Le judo enseigne des techniques d'_____.

12. Les _____ du Québec comprennent les Inuits et les tribus amérindiennes.

13. Les enfants adorent les _____ représentant des animaux.

14. La peur des répercussions sociales peut encourager l'_____ parmi les journalistes.

109 ▸ auto-

MEANING	Related to automobiles
ENGLISH EQUIVALENT	*auto-*
PART OF SPEECH	Noun

The French prefix **auto-**, used to form nouns, relates the base word to an automobile. Since **auto-** can also mean *self*, context helps determine which meaning of **auto-** is intended. Note that the word **automobile** may function both as a noun and as an adjective.

NOUN BEGINNING IN **auto-**	ENGLISH EQUIVALENT	BASE WORD	ENGLISH EQUIVALENT
auto-école [F.]	*driving school*	école	*school*
automobile [F./ADJ.]	*automobile*	mobile	*movable*
automobilisme [M.]	*motoring, driving*	mobile	*movable*
automobiliste [M.F.]	*motorist, driver*	mobile	*movable*
autoneige [F.] (Canada)	*snowmobile*	neige	*snow*
autorail [M.]	*railcar*	rail	*rail*
autoroute [F.]	*highway*	route	*road*
auto-stop [M.]	*hitchhiking*	stop	*stop*
auto-stoppeur [M.]	*hitchhiker* (male)	stop	*stop*
auto-stoppeuse [F.]	*hitchhiker* (female)	stop	*stop*

Vive l'automobile! *Provide the appropriate word(s) to complete each sentence of the paragraph.*

Un (1) _____ voit un (2) _____ et une

(3) _____ au bord de (4) l'_____. Il s'arrête

et les fait monter dans son (5) _____. Il leur dit que le cyclisme ou

(6) l'_____ est beaucoup mieux que (7) l'_____.

Les passagers répondent que d'habitude ils prennent (8) l'_____ de

leur père pour venir passer le week-end chez leurs grands-parents, mais elle est en panne;

ils demandent que le monsieur les dépose près de (9) l'_____ le

plus proche.

110 ▸ bio-

MEANING	Life, existence, nature
ENGLISH EQUIVALENT	*bio-*
PART OF SPEECH	Noun, adjective

The French prefix **bio-**, used to form nouns and adjectives, relates the base word to living organisms. Since the following French words have English cognates, they are easily recognized.

NOUN BEGINNING IN **bio-**	ENGLISH EQUIVALENT	BASE WORD	ENGLISH EQUIVALENT
biochimie [F.]	*biochemistry*	chimie	*chemistry*
bioclimatologie [F.]	*bioclimatology*	climatologie	*climatology*
biodiversité [F.]	*biodiversity*	diversité	*diversity*
bioénergie [F.]	*bioenergy*	énergie	*energy*
biographie [F.]	*biography*	[-graphie]	*written/visual representation*
biologie [F.]	*biology*	[-ologie]	*science, study*
biologiste [M.F.]	*biologist*	[-ologiste]	*expert in a science/study*
biométrie [F.]	*biometry*	[-métrie]	*measurement*
biosynthèse [F.]	*biosynthesis*	synthèse	*synthesis*
biotechnologie [F.]	*biotechnology*	technologie	*technology*
biothérapeute [M.F.]	*biotherapist*	thérapeute	*therapist*
biothérapie [F.]	*biotherapy*	thérapie	*therapy*

Adjectives related to nouns in the preceding chart are as follows.

biochimique	*biochemical*
biographique	*biographical*
biologique	*biological*
biométrique	*biometrical*
biosynthétique	*biosynthetic*
biotechnologique	*biotechnological*
biothérapeutique	*biotherapeutic*

Another common adjective with this prefix is **biodégradable** *biodegradable*.

EXERCICE 110·1

Vrai ou faux? *Indicate whether each statement is true or false, using* **V** *for* **vrai** *true or* **F** *for* **faux** *false.*

1. _____ La biosynthèse est la formation de substances par un être vivant.

2. _____ La biologie recouvre toutes les sciences naturelles.

3. _____ La biotechnologie peut modifier les caractéristiques d'une plante.

4. _____ La dégradation des ressources marines menace la biodiversité des océans.

5. _____ Les sacs en plastique sont biodégradables.

6. _____ Les biothérapies sont efficaces contre les rhumatismes.

7. _____ La biothérapeute donne des massages.

8. _____ La biométrie est l'analyse des caractéristiques biologiques d'une personne.

9. _____ La bioclimatologie est l'étude des effets du climat sur le développement des êtres vivants.

10. _____ Les biologistes sont des spécialistes de l'anatomie humaine.

11. _____ La biochimie est la science qui étudie l'automation.

12. _____ Les bioénergies sont dérivées de la conversion de l'énergie solaire.

111 co-/col-

MEANING	Jointly, sharing, together
ENGLISH EQUIVALENT	*co-*
PART OF SPEECH	Noun, adjective, verb

The French prefix **co-** and its variant **col-** (used before a base word beginning in **l-**) denotes a state of togetherness or sharing. This common prefix is used in nouns and adjectives, as well as in a few verbs.

NOUN/ADJECTIVE BEGINNING IN **co-/col-**	ENGLISH EQUIVALENT	BASE WORD	ENGLISH EQUIVALENT
coaccusé(e) [M.F.]	*codefendant*	accusé(e)	*defendant*
coauteur [M.F.]	*coauthor*	auteur	*author*
collaborateur(-trice) [M.F.]	*collaborator*	labor [LAT.]	*work*
collection [F.]	*collection*	legere [LAT.]	*to collect*
collectionneur(-euse) [M.F.]	*collector*	legere [LAT.]	*to collect*
collectivité [F.]	*collectivity*	legere [LAT.]	*to collect*
colocataire [M.F.]	*cotenant*	locataire	*tenant*
colocation [F.]	*houseshare*	location	*rental*
coopérateur(-trice) [M.F./ADJ.]	*cooperator/cooperative*	opérateur	*operator*
coopération [F.]	*cooperation*	opération	*operation*
copain [M.]/copine [F.]	*buddy*	pain	*bread*
copilote [M.F.]	*copilot*	pilote	*pilot*
copropriétaire [M.F.]	*co-owner*	propriétaire	*owner*
cosignataire [M.F.]	*cosignatory*	signataire	*signatory*

Verbs related to nouns in the preceding chart, including past participles that serve as adjectives, are as follows. (See Appendix A for information on present and past participles.)

collaborer	*to collaborate*
collectionner/collectionné	*to collect / collected*
collectiviser/collectivisé	*to collectivize / collectivized*
colouer/coloué	*to corent / corented*
coopérer	*to cooperate*
copiloter/copiloté	*to copilot / copiloted*
cosigner/cosigné	*to cosign / cosigned*

Other verbs formed with the prefix **co-/col-** are as follows.

coadministrer	*to coadminister*
coexister	*to coexist*
cogérer	*to comanage*
cohabiter	*to cohabit*
coïncider	*to coincide*
coordonner	*to coordinate*

EXERCICE 111·1

Définitions! *Provide an appropriate noun for each description.*

1. Celui ou celle qui loue un studio ensemble _____

2. Un ami _____

3. Un ensemble d'objets regroupés selon un thème commun _____

4. Le contraire d'un comportement concurrentiel _____

5. Celui ou celle qui assiste dans le pilotage _____

6. Celui ou celle qui partage les droits de la propriété _____

7. Celui ou celle qui signe un document avec une autre personne _____

8. L'une des deux personnes qui doivent se défendre en cour de justice _____

9. Un groupe d'individus qui ont le même intérêt _____

10. L'une des deux personnes qui ont écrit un livre ensemble _____

11. Un associé dans une entreprise _____

12. Celui ou celle qui opère avec quelqu'un _____

13. La condition et l'accord de louer ensemble _____

14. Celui ou celle qui fait la collection de quelque chose _____

 **com-**

MEANING   Jointly, sharing, together
ENGLISH EQUIVALENT *com-*
PART OF SPEECH   Noun, verb, adjective

The French prefix **com-** denotes a state of togetherness or sharing. This prefix is used in nouns, as well as in a few verbs and adjectives. It is a variant of **co-**, **col-**, and **con-** and is affixed to a base word that begins in **b-**, **m-**, or **p-**. (See Nos. 111 and 113.)

NOUN BEGINNING IN **com-**	ENGLISH EQUIVALENT	BASE WORD	ENGLISH EQUIVALENT
combat [M.]	*combat*	(se) battre	*to fight*
combattant(e) [M.F.]	*combatant*	(se) battre	*to fight*
commémoration [F.]	*commemoration*	mémoire	*memory*
commisération [F.]	*commiseration*	misère	*misery*
communicateur(-trice) [M.F.]	*communicator*	munus [LAT.]	*task*
comparaison [F.]	*comparison*	paraître	*to appear*
compassion [F.]	*compassion*	pâtir	*to endure*
compère [M.]	*acolyte*	père	*father*
compétition [F.]	*competition*	petere [LAT.]	*to seek*
complaisance [F.]	*kindness*	plaisant	*pleasing*
comportement [M.]	*behavior*	port	*bearing*

Verbs related to nouns in the preceding chart, including present and past participles that serve as adjectives, are as follows. (See Appendix A for information on present and past participles.)

combattre/combattu	*to fight / fought*
commémorer/commémoré	*to commemorate / commemorated*
commisérer	*to commiserate*
communiquer/communiqué	*to communicate / communicated*
compatir/compatissant	*to empathize / empathetic*
complaire/complaisant	*to please / pleasing*
comporter/comporté	*to include / included*

Quel nom est évoqué? *Provide the noun(s) associated with the clue(s) in each line.*

1. Guerre, bataille   _____   _____

2. Anniversaire d'un traité   _____

3. Façon de faire, contenance   _____

4. Pitié, miséricorde   _____   _____

5. Discuteur, négociateur   _____

6. Échange, message   _____

7. Championnat, épreuve   _____

8. Complice, acolyte   _____

9. Indulgence, désir de satisfaire   _____

113 ▸ con-

MEANING	Jointly, sharing, together
ENGLISH EQUIVALENT	*con-*
PART OF SPEECH	Noun, verb, adjective

The French prefix **con-** denotes a state of togetherness or sharing. This prefix is used in nouns, as well as in a few verbs and adjectives. It is a variant of **co-**, **col-**, and **com-** and is affixed to a base word that begins in a consonant other than **b**, **l**, **m**, or **p**. (See Nos. 111 and 112.)

NOUN BEGINNING IN **con-**	ENGLISH EQUIVALENT	BASE WORD	ENGLISH EQUIVALENT
conciliateur(-trice) [M.F.]	*conciliator*	calare [LAT.]	*to call, summon*
conciliation [F.]	*conciliation*	calare [LAT.]	*to call, summon*
concurrence [F.]	*competition*	currere [LAT.]	*to run*
concurrent(e) [M.F.]	*competitor*	currere [LAT.]	*to run*
condoléances [F.PL.]	*condolences*	doléance	*grievance*
confrère [M.]	*colleague*	frère	*brother*
confrérie [F.]	*brotherhood*	frère	*brother*
congrégation [F.]	*congregation*	gregare [LAT.]	*to assemble*
consolidateur(-trice) [M.F.]	*consolidator*	solide	*solid*
consolidation [F.]	*consolidation*	solide	*solid*
convive [M.F.]	*guest*	vivere [LAT.]	*to live*
convivialité [F.]	*conviviality*	convivial	*friendly*

Verbs related to nouns in the preceding chart, including past participles that serve as adjectives, are as follows.

concilier/concilié	*to conciliate / conciliated*
concurrencer/concurrencé	*to challenge / challenged*
consolider/consolidé	*to consolidate / consolidated*

EXERCICE
113·1

Définitions! *Provide the appropriate noun for each description.*

1. Affrontement et compétition   _____

2. Action de mettre ensemble   _____

3. Membre de sa profession   _____

4. Témoignage de sympathie après un décès   _____

5. Celle qui tente de rapprocher des personnes en désaccord   _____

6. Ensemble de rapports chaleureux   _____

7. Association de fidèles   _____

8. Invité(e) à un dîner   _____

9. Celui qui consolide   _____

10. Ensemble de personnes unies par des liens professionnels   _____

 **ex-**

MEANING	Outside, outward, beyond
ENGLISH EQUIVALENT	*ex-*
PART OF SPEECH	Verb, adjective, noun

The French and English prefix **ex-** means *outside*, *outward*, or *beyond*. It is used in verbs, in their past participles, and in related nouns. These are presented side by side in the following charts to promote awareness of these as families of words. All of the nouns are feminine except **excès** and **exposé**. The base words are omitted, since they are all Latin roots shared by the French and English words.

VERB/ADJECTIVE/NOUN BEGINNING IN **ex-**	ENGLISH EQUIVALENTS
exagérer, exagéré, exagération [F.]	*to exaggerate, exaggerated, exaggeration*
exalter, exalté, exaltation [F.]	*to exalt, exalted, exaltation*
exaspérer, exaspéré, exaspération [F.]	*to exasperate, exasperated, exasperation*
excaver, excavé, excavation [F.]	*to excavate, excavated, excavation*
excéder, excédé, excès [M.]	*to exceed, exceeded, excess*
exceller, —, excellence [F.]	*to excel, —, excellence*
excepter, excepté, exception [F.]	*to except, excepted, exception*
exciter, excité, excitation [F.]	*to excite, excited, excitement*
exclure, exclu, exclusion [F.]	*to exclude, excluded, exclusion*
exhaler, exhalé, exhalaison [F.]	*to exhale, exhaled, exhalation*
exhorter, exhorté, exhortation [F.]	*to exhort, exhorted, exhortation*
exonérer, exonéré, exonération [F.]	*to exonerate, exonerated, exoneration*

EXERCICE

114·1

Vrai ou faux? *Indicate whether each statement is true or false, using* **V** *for* **vrai** *true or* **F** *for* **faux** *false.*

1. _____ Les grands génies sont des exceptions.

2. _____ Se trouver dans un lieu mythique ou religieux peut causer une grand exaltation.

3. _____ Un tribunal de justice ne peut pas accorder l'exonération d'un accusé.

4. _____ Les fanas du sport détestent l'excitation fiévreuse d'un grand public.

5. _____ Un euphémisme est une exagération.

6. _____ Une grande frustration mène à l'exaspération.

7. _____ Un excès de vitesse est permis sur les autoroutes.

8. _____ L'excellence académique est appréciée des professeurs.

9. _____ L'exhortation est un faible encouragement.

10. _____ Le parfum et le déodorant aident à couvrir l'exhalaison corporelle.

11. _____ L'exclusion d'une personne à cause de sa race est légale en France.

12. _____ Il y a encore des excavations archéologiques en France de nos jours.

VERB/ADJECTIVE/NOUN BEGINNING IN **ex-**	ENGLISH EQUIVALENTS
exhumer, exhumé, exhumation [F.]	*to exhume, exhumed, exhumation*
expectorer, expectoré, expectoration [F.]	*to expectorate, expectorated, expectoration*
expédier, expédié, expédition [F.]	*to expedite, expedited, expedition*
expérimenter, expérimenté, expérimentation [F.]	*to experiment, experimented, experimentation*
expliquer, expliqué, explication [F.]	*to explain, explained, explanation*

VERB/ADJECTIVE/NOUN BEGINNING IN **ex-**	ENGLISH EQUIVALENTS
explorer, exploré, exploration [F.]	*to explore, explored, exploration*
exploser, explosé, explosion [F.]	*to explode, exploded, explosion*
exporter, exporté, exportation [F.]	*to export, exported, export*
exposer, exposé, exposé [M.]	*to expose, exposed, exposé*
exprimer, exprimé, expression [F.]	*to express, expressed, expression*
exproprier, exproprié, expropriation [F.]	*to expropriate, expropriated, expropriation*
expulser, expulsé, expulsion [F.]	*to expel, expelled, expulsion*

EXERCICE

114·2

Complétez! *Provide the infinitive or correct past participle form of the appropriate verb to complete each sentence.*

1. Si un locataire ne paie pas son loyer, il peut être _____.

2. Attention! Cette bouteille de soda congelée peut _____.

3. En chimie, on doit constamment _____ avec des produits gazeux.

4. C'est urgent! Il faut _____ ce paquet immédiatement.

5. Quelquefois, il faut faire une autopsie sur un corps _____.

6. Il vaut mieux _____ ses émotions.

7. Les gens qui ont la grippe doivent _____ souvent.

8. Il suffit d'_____ ses motifs pour obtenir l'indulgence d'autrui.

9. Samuel de Champlain est allé _____ les territoires du Québec.

10. L'objectif d'une galerie d'art est d'_____ des œuvres d'art.

11. Pour avoir une bonne économie, un pays doit _____ des produits.

12. Si on ne paie pas l'hypothèque sur sa maison à sa banque, on risque d'être

    _____.

 **extra-**

MEANING	Outside, beyond
ENGLISH EQUIVALENT	*extra-*
PART OF SPEECH	Adjective, noun, verb

The French prefix **extra-** means *outside* or *beyond*. It is used to form many adjectives and, occasionally, nouns and verbs. The base word is generally an adjective or a Latin root. In the following chart of adjectives beginning in **extra-**, the words **extra-terrestre** *extraterrestrial* and **extraverti** *extroverted* may also function as nouns, meaning *extraterrestrial being* and *extrovert*, respectively.

ADJECTIVE BEGINNING IN **extra-**	ENGLISH EQUIVALENT	BASE WORD	ENGLISH EQUIVALENT
extrabudgétaire	*extrabudgetary*	budget	*budget*
extra-fin	*superfine*	fin	*fine*
extra-fort	*superstrong*	fort	*strong*
extra-lucide	*extralucid*	lucide	*lucid*
extraordinaire	*extraordinary*	ordinaire	*ordinary*
extraplat	*slimline, thin*	plat	*flat*
extrapolé	*extrapolated*	pôle	*pole*
extra-scolaire	*extracurricular*	scolaire	*school-related*
extra-sensible	*ultrasensitive*	sensible	*sensitive*
extra-sensoriel	*extrasensory*	sensoriel	*sensory*
extra-terrestre	*extraterrestrial*	terrestre	*terrestrial*
extravagant	*wild, excessive*	vagari [LAT.]	*to wander*
extraverti	*extroverted*	vertere [LAT.]	*to turn*

Nouns related to adjectives in the preceding chart are as follows; both nouns are feminine.

extrapolation	*extrapolation*
extravagance	*eccentricity*

Verbs related to adjectives in the preceding chart are as follows.

extrapoler	*to extrapolate*
extravaguer	*to rave*

EXERCICE 115·1

Quel adjective convient le mieux? *Provide the adjective that corresponds to each clue.*

1. Un voyant _____

2. Un grand artiste capricieux et excentrique _____

3. Un homme sociable avec beaucoup d'amis _____

4. Un écran de télévision très mince _____

5. Un parfum _____

6. Une personne qui pleure pour un rien _____

7. Le don d'une personne avec des pouvoirs télépathiques _____

8. Une activité estudiantine comme l'excursion ou le sport _____

9. Un message sous-entendu _____

10. Un hasard inattendu _____

11. Une dépense urgente et imprévue _____

12. Le palais d'un gourmet _____

13. Un habitant de Mars ou Pluton _____

116 ▷ hyper-

MEANING	Above, beyond
ENGLISH EQUIVALENT	*hyper-*
PART OF SPEECH	Adjective, noun

The prefix **hyper-** is of Greek origin and means *above, beyond* in both French and English; it confers intensity to the meaning of the word to which it is affixed. French words with this prefix may be adjectives or nouns, and some prefixed words may function as both, for example, **hyper-réaliste** *hyperrealistic* (adjective) and *hyperrealist* (noun).

ADJECTIVE BEGINNING IN **hyper-**	ENGLISH EQUIVALENT	BASE WORD	ENGLISH EQUIVALENT
hyperactif	*hyperactive*	actif	*active*
hyperbolique	*hyperbolic*	ballein [GRK.]	*to throw*
hypercritique	*supercritical*	critique	*critical*
hypernerveux	*high-strung*	nerveux	*nervous*
hyperréaliste	*hyperrealistic*	réaliste	*realistic*
hypersensible	*hypersensitive*	sensible	*sensitive*
hypersonique	*supersonic*	son	*sound*
hypertrophique	*hypertrophic*	trophe [GRK.]	*nourishment, growth*

Nouns related to adjectives in the preceding chart are as follows.

hyperactivité [F.]	*hyperactivity*	hypersensibilité [F.]	*hypersensitivity*
hyperbole [F.]	*hyperbole*	hypertrophie [F.]	*hypertrophy*
hyperréalisme [M.]	*hyperrealism*		

Other nouns beginning in **hyper-** are as follows.

hypermarché [M.]	*superstore*
hypertension [F.]	*hypertension*
hypertexte [M.]	*hypertext*

EXERCICE
116·1

Définitions! *Provide the appropriate adjective for each noun phrase.*

1. Un missile _____

2. La peau après un coup de soleil _____

3. Un enfant qui bouge constamment _____

4. Une cicatrice ou un nerf _____

5. Une trajectoire _____

6. Une personne qui critique systématiquement _____

7. Un artiste qui interprète d'une façon photographique _____

8. Un patient qui a les nerfs à fleur de peau _____

---

117 ▸ hypo-

MEANING	Below, under
ENGLISH EQUIVALENT	*hypo-*
PART OF SPEECH	Noun, adjective

The prefix **hypo-** is of Greek origin and means *below, under* in both French and English; it confers a negative intensity to the meaning of the word to which it is affixed.

NOUN BEGINNING IN **hypo-**	ENGLISH EQUIVALENT	BASE WORD	ENGLISH EQUIVALENT
hypocentre [M.]	*hypocenter*	centre	*center*
hypocondrie [F.]	*hypochondria*	chondros [GRK.]	*ribs*
hypocrisie [F.]	*hypocrisy*	krisis [GRK.]	*judgment*
hypocrite [M.F.]	*hypocrite*	krisis [GRK.]	*judgment*
hypoderme [M.]	*hypodermic*	derma [GRK.]	*skin*
hypoglycémie [F.]	*hypoglycemia*	glykos [GRK.]	*sweet*
hyposécrétion [F.]	*hyposecretion*	sécrétion	*secretion*
hypotension [F.]	*hypotension*	tension	*blood pressure*
hypothermie [F.]	*hypothermia*	thermos [GRK.]	*heat*
hypothèse [F.]	*hypothesis*	thèse	*thesis*
hypotrophie [F.]	*hypotrophy*	trophe [GRK.]	*nourishment, growth*

Adjectives related to nouns in the preceding chart are as follows.

hypocondriaque	*hypochondriac*	hypoglycémique	*hypoglycemic*
hypocrite	*hypocritical*	hypothermique	*hypothermic*
hypodermique	*hypodermic*	hypotrophique	*hypotrophic*

EXERCICE 117·1

Complétez! *Choose the best completion for each sentence.*

1. _____ On fait généralement une hypothèse
2. _____ L'hypoglycémie est l'excessive diminution
3. _____ L'hyposécrétion peut être
4. _____ L'hypotrophie peut être un
5. _____ L'hypocentre d'un séisme est
6. _____ L'hypoderme est directement
7. _____ L'anesthésie est accompagnée
8. _____ L'hypochondrie consiste à
9. _____ L'hypocrite dit souvent
10. _____ La flatterie peut être

a. craindre les maladies.

b. sous la peau.

c. d'hypotension.

d. attribuée à une glande.

e. le contraire de ce qu'il pense.

f. du taux de glucose.

g. sous-développement du corps.

h. avant de faire des expériences.

i. une forme d'hypocrisie.

j. l'endroit où l'énergie est libérée sous terre.

118 ▶ micro-

MEANING	Very small
ENGLISH EQUIVALENT	*micro-*
PART OF SPEECH	Noun, adjective

The prefix **micro-** is used in both French and English, especially in scientific and technological words, and means *very small.*

The prefix **macro-**, in both French and English, means *very large.* Used in words like **macrocosme** *macrocosm* and **macro-économique** *macroeconomics*, the prefix **macro-** is affixed to many of the same base words as the prefix **micro-**.

NOUN BEGINNING IN **micro-**	ENGLISH EQUIVALENT	BASE WORD	ENGLISH EQUIVALENT
microanalyse [F.]	*microanalysis*	analyse	*analysis*
microbiologie [F.]	*microbiology*	biologie	*biology*
microbiologiste [M.F.]	*microbiologist*	biologie	*biology*
microchimie [F.]	*microchemistry*	chimie	*chemistry*
microclimat [M.]	*microclimate*	climat	*climate*
microélectronique [F.]	*microelectronics*	électronique	*electronics*
microfilm [M.]	*microfilm*	film	*film*
microflore [F.]	*microflora*	flore	*flora*
micro-ondes [M.]	*microwave oven*	onde	*wave*
micro-ordinateur [M.]	*microcomputer*	ordinateur	*computer*
micro-organisme [M.]	*microorganism*	organisme	*organism*
microphone [M.]	*microphone*	[-phone]	*sound, voice*
microscope [M.]	*microscope*	skopein [GRK.]	*to look at*
microseconde [F.]	*microsecond*	seconde	*second*

Adjectives related to nouns in the preceding chart are as follows.

microbiologique	*microbiological*
microchimique	*microchemical*
microscopique	*microscopic*

EXERCICE
118·1

Complétez! *Provide the appropriate noun to complete each sentence.*

1. On crée un _____ pour les plantes en serre.

2. Il est plus rapide de réchauffer un repas en _____.

3. Autrefois, on mettait des documents sur _____ pour les préserver.

4. Le virus de la grippe est étudié dans le laboratoire national de _____.

5. On utilise son smartphone comme _____.

6. La _____ est l'identification quantitative de petites quantités de matière.

7. La _____ est l'ensemble des êtres vivants non animaux.

8. La _____ est l'étude de matière de l'ordre du milligramme.

9. De très petits organismes s'appellent _____ .

10. Les chanteurs se servent de _____ sur scène.

11. Grâce aux progrès en _____ , les micro-ordinateurs et les puces électroniques deviennent de plus en plus petits.

12. Les chercheurs ont des _____ très avancés en laboratoire.

13. La _____ est une unité de mesure du temps.

14. Pasteur est un _____ célèbre.

119 il-/ir-

MEANING	Not, without
ENGLISH EQUIVALENT	*il-, ir-*
PART OF SPEECH	Adjective, noun

The French prefix **il-** is affixed to adjectives that begin in **l-**; similarly, the prefix **ir-** is affixed to adjectives that begin in **r-**. The prefixed adjective means the opposite of the base adjective. For example, the prefix **il-** affixed to the base word **lettré** *literate* forms the adjective **illettré** *illiterate*. Note that the word **illettré(e)** may also function as a noun: *an illiterate person*. Since most of these adjectives are cognates, they tend to be easily recognized.

ADJECTIVE BEGINNING IN il-	ENGLISH EQUIVALENT	BASE WORD	ENGLISH EQUIVALENT
illégal	*illegal*	légal	*legal*
illégitime	*illegitimate*	légitime	*legitimate*
illettré	*illiterate*	lettré	*well-read*
illicite	*illicit*	licitum [LAT.]	*permissible*
illimité	*unlimited*	limité	*limited*
illisible	*illegible*	lisible	*legible*
illogique	*illogical*	logique	*logical*
illusoire	*unreal*	illudere [LAT.]	*to trick, fool*

Nouns related to adjectives in the preceding chart are as follows.

illégalité [F.]	*illegality*
illégitimité [F.]	*illegitimacy*
illettrisme [M.]	*illiteracy*
illogisme [M.]	*non sequitur*
illusion [F.]	*illusion*

Les antonymes *Provide the masculine form of the antonym of each adjective.*

1. lettré _____

2. lisible _____

3. logique _____

4. réel _____

5. limité _____

6. légitime _____

7. légal _____

8. permis _____

French adjectives formed with the prefix **ir-** are numerous, and most have English cognates.

ADJECTIVE BEGINNING IN **ir-**	ENGLISH EQUIVALENT	BASE WORD	ENGLISH EQUIVALENT
irrationnel	*irrational*	rationnel	*rational*
irréalisable	*unrealizable*	réalisable	*realizable*
irréalisé	*unrealized*	réalisé	*realized*
irréconciliable	*irreconcilable*	réconciliable	*reconcilable*
irrécusable	*unimpeachable*	récusable	*impeachable*
irréductible	*irreducible*	réductible	*reducible*
irréel	*unreal*	réel	*real*
irréfléchi	*thoughtless*	réfléchi	*thought out*
irréfutable	*irrefutable*	réfutable	*refutable*
irrégulier	*irregular*	régulier	*regular*
irrémédiable	*unmendable*	remédiable	*mendable*
irremplaçable	*irreplaceable*	remplaçable	*replaceable*
irréparable	*irreparable*	réparable	*reparable*
irréprochable	*irreproachable*	reprochable	*reproachable*
irrésistible	*irresistible*	résistible	*resistible*
irrésolu	*irresolute*	résolu	*resolute*
irrespectueux	*disrespectful*	respectueux	*respectful*
irrespirable	*unbreathable*	respirable	*breathable*
irresponsable	*irresponsible*	responsable	*responsible*
irréversible	*irreversible*	réversible	*reversible*

Nouns related to adjectives in the preceding chart are as follows; all nouns are feminine.

irréalité	*unreality*
irréductibilité	*irreducibility*
irrégularité	*irregularity*
irrésistibilité	*irresistibility*
irrésolution	*indecision*
irresponsabilité	*irresponsibility*
irréversibilité	*irreversibility*

Définitions! *Provide the correct form of the appropriate adjective for each description.*

1. Quelqu'un qui manque de respect _____
2. Un projet qui ne sera jamais réalisé _____
3. Quelqu'un qui est déraisonnable _____
4. Une preuve qu'on ne peut pas réfuter _____
5. Un guerrier qu'on ne peut pas vaincre _____
6. Un homme qui ne peut pas prendre de décision _____
7. Une femme qu'on ne peut pas réconcilier avec son mari _____
8. Un objet brisé qu'on ne peut plus réparer _____
9. Une personne sur qui on ne peut pas compter _____
10. Une action spontanée et dangereuse _____
11. Une prononciation qui ne suit pas les règles _____
12. Un fait accompli _____
13. Un air super-pollué _____
14. Quelqu'un de terriblement charmant _____
15. Quelque chose d'indiscutable _____
16. Un rêve qui ne s'est pas réalisé _____
17. Une personne de qui on ne peut pas se passer _____
18. Le patron parfait _____
19. Une sensation qui ne paraît pas réelle _____
20. Une erreur qu'on ne peut pas corriger _____

120 im-/in-

MEANING   Not, without
ENGLISH EQUIVALENT   *im-, in-*
PART OF SPEECH   Adjective, noun

The prefixes **im-** and **in-** are found in numerous French and English adjectives. The prefixed adjective means the opposite of the base word.

    Im- is affixed to base words beginning in **b-**, **m-**, or **p-**; for example, the prefix **im-** affixed to the adjective **mature** *mature* yields the adjective **immature** *immature*. Most of these French adjectives have English cognates. There are, however, words in which the prefix **im-** means *into, inward,* or *toward*. (See No. 121.) The first two charts list words prefixed with **im-**, while the third and fourth charts list words prefixed with **in-**.

ADJECTIVE BEGINNING IN **im-**	ENGLISH EQUIVALENT	BASE WORD	ENGLISH EQUIVALENT
imbattable	*unbeatable*	battable	*beatable*
imbuvable	*undrinkable*	buvable	*drinkable*
immangeable	*inedible*	mangeable	*edible*
immatériel	*immaterial, intangible*	matériel	*material*
immature	*immature*	mature	*mature*
immobile	*motionless*	mobile	*mobile*
immoral	*immoral*	moral	*moral*
immortel	*immortal*	mortel	*mortal*
impardonnable	*unforgivable*	pardonnable	*forgivable*
impartial	*impartial*	partial	*partial*
impatient	*impatient*	patient	*patient*
impraticable	*impracticable, impassable*	praticable	*feasible, passable*

EXERCICE

120·1

Définitions! *Provide the correct form of the appropriate adjective for each description.*

1. Une équipe qui gagne chaque match _____

2. Une statue _____

3. Un meurtrier _____

4. Un aliment pourri et couvert de moisi _____

5. Un juge très juste _____

6. Un dieu mythologique comme Zeus _____

7. Un sentier couvert de troncs d'arbres _____

8. Le bonheur _____

9. Un enfant qui veut aller aux toilettes _____

10. Un homme qui agit comme un enfant _____

11. Une personne incestueuse _____

12. De l'eau acide _____

ADJECTIVE BEGINNING IN **im-**	ENGLISH EQUIVALENT	BASE WORD	ENGLISH EQUIVALENT
impensable	*unthinkable*	pensable	*thinkable*
imperméable	*impermeable*	perméable	*permeable*
impersonnel	*impersonal*	personnel	*personal*
impoli	*rude*	poli	*polite*

▶

ADJECTIVE BEGINNING IN im-	ENGLISH EQUIVALENT	BASE WORD	ENGLISH EQUIVALENT
◀ impossible	*impossible*	possible	*possible*
imprécis	*imprecise*	précis	*precise*
imprévisible	*unpredictable*	prévisible	*predictable*
imprévu	*unforeseen*	prévu	*foreseen*
improductif	*unproductive*	productif	*productive*
imprudent	*imprudent*	prudent	*prudent*
impuissant	*powerless*	puissant	*powerful*
impur	*impure*	pur	*pure*

EXERCICE 120·2

Complétez! *Provide the correct form of the appropriate adjective to complete each sentence.*

1. Il est _____ de prévoir son avenir.

2. Les contours des personnes sont _____ dans ce tableau.

3. Il faut filtrer tout ce qui est _____ dans cette eau.

4. Un acte immoral est souvent _____ pour les gens ordinaires.

5. Il est _____ de pousser les gens.

6. Un jeune enfant est _____ à se défendre d'un adulte.

7. Un sac en plastique est _____.

8. Il y a toujours un moment _____ pendant les vacances.

9. Un cadeau d'argent peut être un peu _____.

10. Il est _____ de faire la grève.

11. Il est _____ de traverser la rue sans regarder des deux côtés.

12. Ce qui se passera sur terre et dans l'espace dans un millénaire est encore _____.

Nouns related to adjectives in the preceding charts are as follows; all nouns are feminine, as indicated by their suffixes.

immaturité	*immaturity*	impolitesse	*rudeness*
immobilité	*immobility*	impossibilité	*impossibility*
immoralité	*immorality*	imprécision	*imprecision*
immortalité	*immortality*	improductivité	*unproductiveness*
impartialité	*impartiality*	imprudence	*imprudence*
impatience	*impatience*	impuissance	*powerlessness*
imperméabilité	*impermeability*	impureté	*impurity*

The prefix **in-** has the same meaning as the prefix **im-**; it is affixed to a base word that does not begin in **b-**, **l-**, **m-**, **p-**, or **r-**. It is found in numerous adjectives as well as some nouns.

ADJECTIVE BEGINNING IN **in-**	ENGLISH EQUIVALENT	BASE WORD	ENGLISH EQUIVALENT
inaccoutumé	*unaccustomed*	accoutumé	*accustomed*
inactif	*inactive*	actif	*active*
inadmissible	*inadmissible*	admissible	*admissible*
inanimé	*inanimate*	animé	*animated*
inattendu	*unexpected*	attendu	*expected*
inattentif	*inattentive*	attentif	*attentive*
incomparable	*incomparable*	comparable	*comparable*
incompatible	*incompatible*	compatible	*compatible*
incompétent	*incompetent*	compétent	*competent*
incomplet	*incomplete*	complet	*complete*
incompréhensible	*incomprehensible*	compréhensible	*comprehensible*
inconnu	*unknown*	connu	*known*
inconscient	*unconscious*	conscient	*conscious*
inconsolable	*inconsolable*	consolable	*consolable*
incorrect	*incorrect*	correct	*correct*
incorrigible	*incorrigible*	corrigible	*corrigible*
incorruptible	*incorruptible*	corruptible	*corruptible*
incroyable	*incredible*	croyable	*credible*
indésirable	*undesirable*	désirable	*desirable*
indestructible	*indestructible*	destructible	*destructible*
indiscret	*indiscreet*	discret	*discreet*

EXERCICE
120·3

Définitions! *Provide the appropriate adjective for each description.*

1. Ce qu'on ne peut pas croire _____

2. Ce qu'on ne peut pas détruire _____

3. Ce qui n'est pas correct _____

4. Celui qui n'a pas la compétence requise _____

5. Celui qui ne sait pas garder un secret _____

6. Celui qui ne fait pas attention _____

7. Ce qui ne va pas avec quelque chose _____

8. Ce qu'on ne peut pas comprendre _____

9. Ce qu'on n'attendait pas _____

10. Ce qui n'est pas fini _____

11. Celui qui n'a pas l'habitude de quelque chose _____

12. Ce qui n'a pas de vie _____

13. Ce qu'on ne peut pas comparer à quoi que ce soit _____

14. Celle qu'on ne peut pas consoler _____

15. Celui qui ne fait rien _____

16. Une personne ou une chose qu'on ne peut pas accepter _____

17. Celui qui est dans le coma _____

18. Ce qu'on ne peut pas corriger _____

19. Ce que personne ne connaît _____

20. Ce dont personne ne veut _____

21. Celui ou celle qu'on ne peut pas corrompre _____

In the following chart, the words **infidèle** _unfaithful_ and **infini** _infinite_ may function both as adjectives and as nouns.

ADJECTIVE BEGINNING IN **in-**	ENGLISH EQUIVALENT	BASE WORD	ENGLISH EQUIVALENT
inégal	_unequal_	égal	_equal_
inexpérimenté	_inexperienced_	expérimenté	_experienced_
infertile	_infertile_	fertile	_fertile_
infidèle	_unfaithful_	fidèle	_faithful_
infini	_infinite_	fini	_finished_
infréquent	_infrequent_	fréquent	_frequent_
inhabité	_uninhabited_	habité	_inhabited_
inhabituel	_unusual_	habituel	_habitual_
inhospitalier	_inhospitable_	hospitalier	_hospitable_
inimaginable	_unimaginable_	imaginable	_imaginable_
inimitable	_inimitable_	imitable	_imitable_
injustifiable	_unjustifiable_	justifiable	_justifiable_
inlassable	_tireless_	las	_tired_
inodore	_odorless_	odorant	_scented_
inoubliable	_unforgettable_	oublié	_forgotten_
insalubre	_unsanitary_	salubre	_sanitary_
insatiable	_insatiable_	satiable	_satiable_
insensible	_insensitive_	sensible	_sensitive_
inséparable	_inseparable_	séparable	_separable_
insignifiant	_insignificant_	signifiant	_significant_
insouciant	_unconcerned_	soucieux	_concerned_
insurmontable	_insurmountable_	surmontable	_surmountable_

EXERCICE
120·4

Vrai ou faux? _Indicate whether each statement is true or false, using_ **V** _for_ **vrai** _true_ _or_ **F** _for_ **faux** _false._

1. _____ La planète Mars est inhabitée.

2. _____ Les gens aiment les chiens parce qu'ils sont infidèles.

3. _____ Les élèves surdoués ont généralement un talent insignifiant.

4. _____ Les grandes fortunes sont inimaginables pour certains.

5. _____ La construction de grandes tours comme l'Empire State Building est inimitable.

6. _____ Les meilleurs ou les pires souvenirs sont souvent inoubliables.

7. _____ Un problème de santé comme la grippe est insurmontable.

8. _____ Les écrivains romantiques du 19ᵉ siècle étaient particulièrement insensibles.

9. _____ La distribution des biens matériels dans le monde est inégale.

10. _____ Il ne faut pas de personnes inexpérimentées pour soigner les maladies graves.

11. _____ Les meilleurs parents sont les parents insouciants.

12. _____ Les microbes se développent mieux dans des conditions insalubres.

13. _____ Les terres volcaniques sont infertiles.

14. _____ Les TGV font des stops infréquents.

15. _____ Il y a un symbole mathématique pour ce qui est infini.

16. _____ Les amoureux sont inséparables.

17. _____ Les savons sont toujours inodores.

18. _____ Un appétit insatiable peut causer des problèmes de poids.

19. _____ Une personne avec de l'hypotension est inlassable.

20. _____ La malhonnêteté des personnes religieuses est injustifiable.

21. _____ Les régions arctiques offrent généralement des habitats inhospitaliers.

22. _____ La ponctualité chez les personnes disciplinées est inhabituelle.

Nouns related to adjectives in the preceding charts are as follows; all nouns are feminine, as indicated by their suffixes.

inactivité	*inactivity*
inadmissibilité	*inadmissibility*
inattention	*inattention*
incompatibilité	*incompatibility*
incompétence	*incompetence*
indiscrétion	*indiscretion*
inégalité	*inequality*
infidélité	*infidelity*
insatiabilité	*insatiability*
insensibilité	*insensitivity*
insouciance	*lack of concern*

121 ◆ im-/in-

MEANING	Into, inward, toward
ENGLISH EQUIVALENT	*im-, in-*
PART OF SPEECH	Verb, adjective, noun

The French prefixes **im-** and **in-**, when used to form verbs, convey a sense of movement or effect into, inward, or toward. For example, the verb **immatriculer** *to register*, formed with the prefix **im-** and the base word **matriculer** *to register*, conveys the idea of putting something into a register. Many of the verbs formed with the prefix **im-** or **in-** are related to adjectives and nouns that include the same base word and prefix. Because of the two possible meanings of the prefixes **im-** and **in-** (see No. 120), it is essential to use context to determine which meaning is correct.

Most of the base words for the verbs in the following charts are Latin roots; a few are nouns. The base word for the verb **immoler** requires a stroll down history lane: in Roman times, a lamb was rolled in **mola** *flour* before being offered as a sacrifice. Other base words are less obscure. For example, the base word for the verb **imbiber** is the Latin verb **bibere** *to drink*, and the prefixed verb means *to soak in*.

The prefix **im-** is affixed to base words beginning in **b-**, **m-**, or **p-**. In the following chart, verbs are presented as infinitives along with their past participles, which function as adjectives. As an example, the past participle of the verb **immatriculer** is **immatriculé**, which functions as an adjective in the phrase **la personne immatriculée** *the registered person*, or *registrant*. (For more information about past participles used as adjectives, see Appendix A.)

VERB/ADJECTIVE BEGINNING IN **im-**	ENGLISH EQUIVALENT	BASE WORD	ENGLISH EQUIVALENT
imbiber/imbibé	to soak in / soaked in	bibere [LAT.]	to drink
immatriculer/immatriculé	to register / registered	matriculer	to register
immerger/immergé	to immerse / immersed	mergere [LAT.]	to plunge
immigrer/immigré	to immigrate / immigrated	migrare [LAT.]	to move
immoler/immolé	to immolate / immolated	mola [LAT.]	flour
impartir/imparti	to grant / granted	partire [LAT.]	to distribute
implanter/implanté	to implant / implanted	planter	to plant
impliquer/impliqué	to imply / implied, to implicate / implicated	plicare [LAT.]	to fold
implorer/imploré	to implore / implored	plorare [LAT.]	to cry over
importer/importé	to import / imported	porter	to carry
imposer/imposé	to impose / imposed	poser	to put down
impressionner/ impressionné	to impress / impressed	pression [F.]	pressure
imprimer/imprimé	to print / printed	premere [LAT.]	to press
improviser/improvisé	to improvise / improvised	providere [LAT.]	to provide

EXERCICE 121·1

Complétez! *Provide the correct form of the appropriate adjective to complete each sentence.*

1. Ces tapis persans sont _____.

2. Cette citation est _____ dans les livres d'histoire.

3. Un patron est _____ par un CV complet.

4. Il y a encore des vaisseaux pirates _____ dans l'océan.

5. Cette éponge est _____ de jus.

6. Un complice est _____ dans cette affaire criminelle.

7. Cette pièce _____ est magnifique.

8. Une taxe est souvent _____ sur un héritage.

9. Chopin était un artiste _____ de Pologne.

10. Les érables sont des arbres bien _____ au Canada.

11. Un secours urgent est _____ lors d'une catastrophe naturelle.

12. Le message _____ aux parents était clair.

13. Une voiture _____ à Strasbourg porte le numéro 67.

14. Un agneau était _____ comme sacrifice par les païens.

Most of the words in the preceding chart are related to nouns with the same prefix and base word; all of these nouns are feminine, as indicated by their suffix.

immatriculation	*registration*
immersion	*immersion*
immigration	*immigration*
immolation	*immolation*
implantation	*implantation*
implication	*implication*
imploration	*supplication*
importation	*import*
imposition	*imposition*
impression	*impression*
improvisation	*improvisation*

The prefix **in-** has the same meaning as the prefix **im-**. It is affixed to base words that do not begin in **b-**, **l-**, **m-**, **p-**, or **r-**.

VERB/ADJECTIVE BEGINNING IN **in-**	ENGLISH EQUIVALENT	BASE WORD	ENGLISH EQUIVALENT
incarcérer/incarcéré	*to incarcerate / incarcerated*	carcer [LAT.]	*jail*
incarner/incarné	*to personify / personified*	carnis [LAT.]	*flesh*
incendier/incendié	*to set on fire / set on fire*	cendre	*ashes*
incinérer/incinéré	*to incinerate / incinerated*	cendre	*ashes*
inciter/incité	*to incite / incited*	citare [LAT.]	*to urge on*
inclure/inclus	*to include / included*	cludere [LAT.]	*to close*
indiquer/indiqué	*to indicate / indicated*	dicere [LAT.]	*to state*
industrialiser/ industrialisé	*to industrialize / industrialized*	industrie	*industry*
infiltrer/infiltré	*to infiltrate / infiltrated*	filtre	*filter*
infliger/infligé	*to inflict / inflicted*	fligere [LAT.]	*to beat*

VERB/ADJECTIVE BEGINNING IN **in-**	ENGLISH EQUIVALENT	BASE WORD	ENGLISH EQUIVALENT
informer/informé	*to inform / informed*	former	*to form*
infuser/infusé	*to infuse / infused*	fundere [LAT.]	*to pour*
inhumer/inhumé	*to bury / buried*	humare [LAT.]	*to bury*
injurier/injurié	*to insult / insulted*	injure	*insult*
inonder/inondé	*to flood / flooded*	undare [LAT.]	*to flood*
inscrire/inscrit	*to inscribe / inscribed*	écrire	*to write*
insinuer/insinué	*to insinuate / insinuated*	sinus [LAT.]	*curve, cavity*
inspecter/inspecté	*to inspect / inspected*	spectare [LAT.]	*to look at*
inspirer/inspiré	*to inspire / inspired*	spirare [LAT.]	*to breathe, live*

EXERCICE
121·2

Vrai ou faux? *Indicate whether each statement is true or false, using* **V** *for* **vrai** *true or* **F** *for* **faux** *false.*

1. _____ Le criminel qui est trouvé coupable est incarcéré.

2. _____ Une punition est infligée à la victime d'un cambriolage.

3. _____ Les corps des décédés sont inhumés ou incinérés.

4. _____ En France, le service au restaurant est inclus et indiqué sur l'addition.

5. _____ L'hymne national américain était inspiré de l'hymne français.

6. _____ Les valises sont inspectées par les douaniers à l'aéroport.

7. _____ Le Canada est un pays industrialisé.

8. _____ Une personne injuriée doit s'excuser.

9. _____ Des hectares de terre ont été incendiés en Californie à cause de la sécheresse.

10. _____ Un virus infiltré dans un logiciel peut causer une panne.

11. _____ Pendant un incendie de forêt, la terre est inondée d'eau des rivières.

12. _____ Une accusation insinuée est punissable par la loi.

13. _____ Une personne informée est plus lucide.

14. _____ Une tisane doit être infusée pendant des heures.

15. _____ Une foule incitée à manifester paisiblement est dangereuse.

16. _____ Une notion abstraite peut être incarnée dans une illustration.

Nouns related to adjectives in the preceding chart are as follows. **Incendie** is the only masculine noun in the list.

incarcération	*incarceration*
incarnation	*incarnation, embodiment*
incendie	*fire*
incinération	*incineration*
incitation	*incentive*
inclusion	*inclusion*
indication	*indication*
industrialisation	*industrialization*
infiltration	*infiltration*
information	*information*
infusion	*infusion*
inhumation	*burial*
injure	*insult*
inondation	*flood*
inscription	*inscription*
insinuation	*insinuation*
inspection	*inspection*
inspiration	*inspiration*

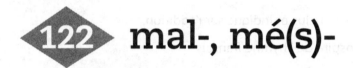

122 ▸ mal-, mé(s)-

MEANING	Bad, mean, evil, not
ENGLISH EQUIVALENT	*mal-, mis-*
PART OF SPEECH	Noun, adjective

The French prefixes **mal-** and **mé(s)-** usually convey the sense of *bad*, *mean*, or *evil*. For example, the noun **maladresse**, formed with the prefix **mal-** and the base word **adresse** *skill, dexterity*, means *clumsiness* or *awkwardness*.

NOUN BEGINNING IN **mal-/me(s)-**	ENGLISH EQUIVALENT	BASE WORD	ENGLISH EQUIVALENT
maladresse [F.]	*awkwardness, clumsiness*	adresse	*skill, dexterity*
malaise [M.]	*malaise*	aise	*ease*
malchance [F.]	*bad luck*	chance	*luck*
malédiction [F.]	*curse*	diction	*speaking*
malentendu [M.]	*misunderstanding*	entendre	*to hear*
malfaiteur [M.]	*wrongdoer*	fait	*done*
malformation [F.]	*malformation*	formation	*formation*
malheur [M.]	*misfortune*	heure	*hour, time*
malhonnêteté [F.]	*dishonesty*	honnêteté	*honesty*
maltraitement [M.]	*mistreatment*	traitement	*treatment*
malveillance [F.]	*ill will*	veiller	*to ensure*
mécontentement [M.]	*dissatisfaction*	contentement	*satisfaction*
médisance [F.]	*bad-mouthing*	dire	*to tell*
mésentente [F.]	*disagreement*	entente	*agreement*

Complétez! *Choose the best completion for each sentence.*

1. _____ Les malformations des os		a.	est cruel.
2. _____ Les allergies causent		b.	est aussi un scélérat.
3. _____ Le maltraitement des animaux		c.	sont parfois génétiques.
4. _____ Perdre son smartphone deux fois de suite,		d.	par un léger oubli.
5. _____ Il est malheureux que les gens		e.	se laissent aller à la médisance.
6. _____ Quel malheur qu'il y ait tant		f.	la malédiction de Montezuma.
7. _____ Les attentats terroristes démontrent		g.	dans une famille.
8. _____ La mésentente entre travailleurs		h.	des malaises.
9. _____ Un salaire minimum et stagnant		i.	la première marche de l'escalier.
10. _____ Quelle maladresse de tomber de		j.	mène au mécontentement.
11. _____ Il y a des gens qui croient à		k.	c'est de la malchance.
12. _____ Un malfaiteur		l.	la pure malveillance.
13. _____ Un malentendu s'explique parfois		m.	de désastres naturels.
14. _____ La malhonnêteté n'a pas de place		n.	n'est pas productive.

Adjectives related to nouns in the preceding chart are as follows.

maladroit	*awkward, clumsy*
malchanceux	*unlucky*
malformé	*malformed*
malheureux	*unhappy*
malhonnête	*dishonest*
maltraité	*mistreated*
malveillant	*malevolent*
maudit	*damned, cursed*
mécontent	*dissatisfied*
médisant	*slanderous*

The following chart includes adjectives with the prefix **mal-** or **mé(s)-** that are unrelated to nouns in the preceding chart. All are formed with an adjective as the base word. Some of these words, indicated by an asterisk (*), function both as adjectives and as nouns.

ADJECTIVE BEGINNING IN **mal-/me(s)-**	ENGLISH EQUIVALENT	BASE WORD	ENGLISH EQUIVALENT
mal-aimé*	*unpopular / unpopular person*	aimé	*liked, loved*
malaisé	*uncomfortable*	aisé	*comfortable*
malappris*	*uncouth/boor*	appris	*learned*
maléfique	*evil*	fait	*done*
malhabile	*clumsy*	habile	*skillful*

ADJECTIVE BEGINNING IN **mal-/me(s)-**	ENGLISH EQUIVALENT	BASE WORD	ENGLISH EQUIVALENT
mal-jugé*	*misjudged / bad decision*	jugé	*judged*
malmené	*badly treated*	mené	*led*
malodorant	*ill-smelling*	odorant	*nice-smelling*
méjugé	*misjudged*	jugé	*judged*
mépris*	*mistaken/contempt*	pris	*taken*
mésallié	*married beneath oneself*	allié	*allied*
mésestimé	*underestimated, misjudged*	estimé	*estimated*

Verbs related to adjectives in the preceding chart are as follows.

malmener	*to mistreat*
méjuger	*to misjudge*
(se) méprendre	*to be mistaken (about)*
(se) mésallier	*to form the wrong alliance, marry beneath oneself*
mésestimer	*to underestimate*

EXERCICE 122·2

Complétez! *Choose the best completion for each sentence.*

1. _____ Une personne que peu de personnes apprécient

2. _____ S'il est malmené,

3. _____ Les personnes se sentent méjugées

4. _____ Mépris de tous,

5. _____ Il faut montrer de l'indulgence

6. _____ Aucune femme ne sortira avec

7. _____ Un démon jette un sort

8. _____ Des élèves avec du génie sont parfois

9. _____ Autrefois, une princesse et un paysan

10. _____ Une exhalaison malodorante

11. _____ La qualité d'une œuvre est malheureusement

12. _____ L'accès aux toilettes ne devrait jamais

a. maléfique à ses victimes.

b. auraient été considérés mésalliés.

c. si on ne leur fait pas quelques compliments.

d. être malaisé.

e. un malappris.

f. mésestimés par leurs profs.

g. est mal-aimée.

h. aux personnes malhabiles.

i. un employé va donner sa démission.

j. parfois méjugée.

k. les gens n'ont plus aucun amour-propre.

l. peut faire évanouir une personne.

123 ◆ para-/pare-

MEANING	Protection against
ENGLISH EQUIVALENT	*para-*
PART OF SPEECH	Noun

A French noun formed with the prefix **para-** or **pare-** denotes an object that offers protection from a menace or danger, as represented by the base word. For example, the noun **parachute** is formed with the prefix **para-** and the base word **chute** *fall* and describes an object designed to protect against a fatal fall from, say, an aircraft. The variant **pare-** is separated from the base word by a hyphen. Note that the prefixed nouns in the following chart are masculine, even though their base words may be feminine.

NOUN BEGINNING IN **para-/pare-**	ENGLISH EQUIVALENT	BASE WORD	ENGLISH EQUIVALENT
parachute [M.]	*parachute*	chute [F.]	*fall*
parapluie [M.]	*umbrella*	pluie [F.]	*rain*
parasol [M.]	*parasol*	soleil [M.]	*sun*
paratonnerre [M.]	*lightning rod*	tonnerre [M.]	*thunder*
paravent [M.]	*screen*	vent [M.]	*wind*
pare-brise [M.]	*windshield*	brise [F.]	*breeze*
pare-chocs [M.]	*bumper*	choc [M.]	*shock*
pare-feu [M.]	*firewall*	feu [M.]	*fire*
pare-soleil [M.]	*sun visor*	soleil [M.]	*sun*

A common adjective is also formed with the prefix **para-**.

parasismique   *earthquake-resistant*   (< sismique *seismic*)

EXERCICE
123·1

Qu'est-ce que c'est? *Provide the appropriate word for each description.*

1. Il vous protège du vent, des cailloux sur la route quand vous êtes en voiture. _____

2. Ils sont devant et derrière la voiture et absorbent le choc d'une collision. _____

3. Cet écran orientable vous protège du soleil quand vous conduisez. _____

4. Cette ombrelle de plage vous protège des rayons du soleil. _____

5. Il était conçu pour protéger du vent mais il est maintenant plutôt décoratif dans les maisons. _____

6. C'est un logiciel qui permet de protéger la sécurité d'un réseau informatique. _____

7. Ce type de construction prévoit les conséquences des tremblements de terre. _____

8. C'est une tige placée en hauteur et connectée à la terre par un conducteur d'électricité. _____

9. Vous le portez quand vous sortez par un temps pluvieux. _____

10. Vous le mettez avant de sauter d'un avion. _____

As in English, the prefix **para-** may sometimes mean *next to* or *parallel*; an example is the noun/adjective **parascolaire** *extracurricular (activity)*, which represents an activity that is outside the curriculum but related to it. Many of these French words have English cognates. This fact, plus common sense, help differentiate this meaning of **para-** from that of *protection against*.

paramètre [M.]	*parameter*
paramilitaire [ADJ.]	*paramilitary*
paranormal [M./ADJ.]	*paranormal*
paraphrase [F.]	*paraphrase*

 **124 ▶ post-**

MEANING	After
ENGLISH EQUIVALENT	*post-*
PART OF SPEECH	Adjective, noun

The French prefix **post-**, used to form adjectives and nouns, means *after*. Due to the orthographic reforms of 1990, many hyphens have been omitted in prefixed words; there are exceptions, however, especially if the base word is a Latin root.

ADJECTIVE/NOUN BEGINNING IN **post-**	ENGLISH EQUIVALENT	BASE WORD	ENGLISH EQUIVALENT
postambule [M.]	*afterword*	ambulare [LAT.]	*to walk*
post-combustion [F.]	*postcombustion*	combustion	*combustion*
postcommunisme [M.]	*postcommunism*	communisme	*communism*
postdate [F.]	*postdate*	date	*date*
postface [F.]	*conclusion, afterword*	facia [LAT.]	*portrait*
postglaciaire [ADJ.]	*postglacial*	glaciaire	*glacial*
posthume [ADJ.]	*posthumous*	humare [LAT.]	*to bury*
postlude [M.]	*postlude*	ludere [LAT.]	*to play*
postmoderne [ADJ.]	*postmodern*	moderne	*modern*
post-mortem [M.]	*postmortem*	mortem [LAT.]	*death*
postnatal [ADJ.]	*postnatal*	natal	*natal*
postopératoire [ADJ.]	*postoperative*	opératoire	*operative*
postproduction [F.]	*postproduction*	production	*production*
postromantisme [M.]	*postromanticism*	romantisme	*romanticism*
postscolaire [ADJ.]	*after-school*	scolaire	*school*
post-scriptum [M.]	*postscript*	scriptum [LAT.]	*written*
post-test [M.]	*post test*	test [ENG.]	*test*
post-traumatique [ADJ.]	*posttraumatic*	trauma [GRK.]	*wound*

Complétez! *Provide the correct form of the appropriate word to complete each sentence.*

1. L'appréciation _____ des œuvres de Van Gogh est ironique.

2. Beaucoup de gens ont une formation professionnelle _____.

3. La _____ d'une création audiovisuelle comporte des promotions.

4. Le _____ publicitaire est l'évaluation d'une campagne publicitaire.

5. Le _____ est destiné à clore une œuvre musicale.

6. En philosophie, le mouvement _____ conteste les idées majeures de la modernité.

7. Le trouble de stress _____ est commun parmi les anciens combattants.

8. Le _____ est le mouvement artistique qui a suivi le romantisme.

9. La période _____ commence à l'hôpital où l'enfant est né.

10. Il y a parfois un _____ à la fin d'une lettre.

11. Le protocole _____ doit être suivi à la lettre par le personnel de santé.

12. Une autopsie est un examen _____.

13. Le _____ suit le corps du texte.

14. La _____ est un procédé visant à augmenter la poussée d'un réacteur.

15. Une date postérieure à la vraie date d'un acte est une _____.

16. La période _____ se caractérise par un réchauffement climatique sur terre.

17. Beaucoup de livres ont une _____, c'est-à-dire un commentaire à la fin du livre.

18. Un évènement important qui a marqué le _____ en Europe est la réunification allemande.

 **pré-**

MEANING	Before
ENGLISH EQUIVALENT	*pre-*
PART OF SPEECH	Noun, verb, adjective

The prefix **pré-**, used to form nouns, verbs, and adjectives, means *before*.

NOUN BEGINNING IN **pré-**	ENGLISH EQUIVALENT	BASE WORD	ENGLISH EQUIVALENT
préaccord [M.]	*preagreement*	accord	*agreement*
préadolescence [F.]	*preadolescence*	adolescence	*adolescence*
préambule [M.]	*foreword*	ambulare [LAT.]	*to walk*
préapprentissage [M.]	*preapprenticeship*	apprentissage	*apprenticeship*
prédestination [F.]	*predestination*	destination	*destination*
prédisposition [F.]	*predisposition*	disposition	*disposition*
préenregistrement [M.]	*prerecording*	enregistrement	*recording*
préexistence [F.]	*preexistence*	existence	*existence*
préfabrication [F.]	*prefabrication*	fabrication	*fabrication*
préfinancement [M.]	*prefinancing*	financement	*financing*
préhistoire [F.]	*prehistory*	histoire	*history*
préjugé [M.]	*prejudice*	juger	*to judge*
préméditation [F.]	*premeditation*	méditation	*meditation*
prémolaire [F.]	*premolar*	molaire	*molar*
prénom [M.]	*first name*	nom	*name*
préoccupation [F.]	*preoccupation*	occupation	*occupation*
présage [M.]	*omen*	sagus [LAT.]	*prophetic*
présomption [F.]	*presumption*	sumere [LAT.]	*to suppose*

EXERCICE

125·1

Charade! *Provide the appropriate noun for each description.*

1. Avant la vie   _____

2. Une supposition sans preuve   _____

3. Avant la confection   _____

4. Une intention mauvaise   _____

5. Les très anciens temps   _____

6. Le nom familier d'une personne   _____

7. Un penchant naturel   _____

8. Un jugement préconçu   _____

9. L'annonce d'une chose à venir   _____

10. La dent située entre une canine et une molaire   _____

11. Le crédit accordé à une entreprise avant la mise   _____
    en place d'une production

12. Une inquiétude   _____

13. L'enregistrement fait à l'avance   _____

14. Le caractère fatal du destin   _____

15. Formation pratique qui précède l'apprentissage   _____

16. Période entre l'enfance et l'adolescence   _____

17. L'avant-propos d'un texte   _____

18. Contrat liant deux parties préalablement   _____

Verbs and adjectives related to nouns in the preceding chart are as follows. (For more information about past participles used as adjectives, see Appendix A.)

prédestiner/prédestiné	*to predestine / predestined*
prédisposer/prédisposé	*to predispose / predisposed*
préenregistrer/ préenregistré	*to prerecord / prerecorded*
préfabriquer/préfabriqué	*to prefabricate / prefabricated*
préfinancer/préfinancé	*to prefinance / prefinanced*
préjuger/préjugé	*to prejudge / prejudged*
préméditer/prémédité	*to premeditate / premeditated*
prénommer/prénommé	*to name / named*
préoccuper/préoccupé	*to preoccupy / preoccupied*
présager/présagé	*to foresee / foreseen*

126 anté-

MEANING   Before
ENGLISH EQUIVALENT   *ante-*
PART OF SPEECH   Noun, adjective, verb

The French prefix **anté-** affixed to a French adjective or noun means *before*. The English counterpart of this prefix is found in a few nouns, such as *antechamber*, and rarely in adjectives, such as *antediluvian*. The prefix **anté-** is exceptionally found in the verb **antéposer** *to place before*. Note that in the French noun **antéchrist** *Antichrist*, the prefix conveys the sense of **anti-** *against*.

NOUN/ADJECTIVE/VERB BEGINNING IN **anté-**	ENGLISH EQUIVALENT	BASE WORD	ENGLISH EQUIVALENT
antécédence [F.]	*antecedence*	cedere [LAT.]	*to go*
antécédent [M./ADJ.]	*antecedent / preceding*	cedere [LAT.]	*to go*
antéchrist [M.]	*Antichrist*	Christ	*Christ*
antédiluvien [ADJ.]	*antediluvian*	déluge	*deluge*
antéislamique [ADJ.]	*pre-Islamic*	islam	*Islam*
anténatal [ADJ.]	*prenatal*	natal	*natal*
antéposer	*to place before*	poser	*to place*
antéposition [F.]	*anteposition*	position	*position*
antérieur [ADJ.]	*previous*	anterior [LAT.]	*before*
antériorité [F.]	*precedence*	anterior [LAT.]	*before*

Complétez! *Choose the best completion for each sentence.*

1. _____ La construction de l'arche de Noé

2. _____ L'histoire de l'Arabie antéislamique

3. _____ Le personnage de l'antéchrist paraît

4. _____ L'antéposition de l'adjectif relativement

5. _____ Le diagnostic anténatal est un sujet

6. _____ L'antécédence d'une rêverie peut

7. _____ L'antécédent est souvent le nom

8. _____ Le principe de l'antériorité d'une

9. _____ L'invention du téléphone est

10. _____ Il faut antéposer les priorités

a. au substantif est rare en français.

b. reposer sur un fait réel.

c. auquel se rapporte un pronom relatif.

d. date de la période antédiluvienne.

e. antérieure à celle de la télévision.

f. date de l'Antiquité.

g. dans un agenda.

h. stipulation de contrat doit être respecté.

i. assez controversé.

j. dans des films genre « Vendredi, 13 ».

127 ◆ mono, uni-; bi(s)-; tri(s)-

MEANING   One, single, mono-; two, dual, bi-; three, triple, tri-
ENGLISH EQUIVALENT   *mono-, uni-; bi-; tri-*
PART OF SPEECH   Adjective, noun

The French prefixes **mono-/uni-**, **bi(s)-**, and **tri(s)-**, used to form French adjectives and nouns, denote one, two, or three, respectively. For example, the noun **monocycle** is formed with the prefix **mono-** and the base word **cycle** and denotes a unicycle. The noun **bicyclette** is formed with the prefix **bi-** and the suffix **-cyclette** and denotes a bicycle. The noun **tricycle** is formed with the prefix **tri-** and the base word **cycle** and denotes a tricycle. Usually, the prefix **bi-** becomes **bis-** and the prefix **tri-** becomes **tris-** before a base word beginning in a vowel sound.

ADJECTIVE/NOUN BEGINNING IN **mono-**	ENGLISH EQUIVALENT	BASE WORD	ENGLISH EQUIVALENT
monochrome [M./ADJ.]	*monochrome*	chroma [GRK.]	*color*
monocycle [M.]	*unicycle*	cycle	*cycle*
monogame [ADJ.]	*monogamous*	gamos [GRK.]	*marriage, union*
monogramme [M.]	*monogram*	[-gramme]	*letter, sign*
monolingue [ADJ.]	*monolingual*	langue	*language*
monolithique [ADJ.]	*monolithic*	lithos [GRK.]	*stone*
monologue [M.]	*monologue*	logos [GRK.]	*speech*
mononucléaire [ADJ.]	*mononuclear*	nucleus [LAT.]	*nucleus*

▶

ADJECTIVE/NOUN BEGINNING IN **mono-**	ENGLISH EQUIVALENT	BASE WORD	ENGLISH EQUIVALENT
monopole [M.]	*monopoly*	polein [GRK.]	*to sell*
monospace [F./ADJ.]	*minivan*	espace	*space*
monosyllabique [ADJ.]	*monosyllabic*	syllabe	*syllable*
monothéiste [ADJ.]	*monotheist*	theos [GRK.]	*deity, god*

Vrai ou faux? *Indicate whether each statement is true or false, using* **V** *for* **vrai** *true or* **F** *for* **faux** *false.*

1. _____ En France, le gouvernement a le monopole de la vente du tabac.

2. _____ Dans les grandes tragédies classiques, il y a des monologues.

3. _____ Les acrobates se servent de monocycles.

4. _____ Les Européens sont généralement monolingues.

5. _____ L'union monogame est interdite aux États-Unis.

6. _____ Le parti républicain aux États-Unis est monolithique.

7. _____ Les cultures anciennes étaient toujours monothéistes.

8. _____ Le monogramme de Louis Vuitton comprend ses initiales.

9. _____ La structure familiale américaine est mononucléaire.

10. _____ Une œuvre artistique réalisée en une seule couleur est un monochrome.

In the following chart, note that **unijambiste** may function as a noun or as an adjective.

ADJECTIVE/NOUN BEGINNING IN **uni-**	ENGLISH EQUIVALENT	BASE WORD	ENGLISH EQUIVALENT
unicellulaire [ADJ.]	*unicellular*	cellule	*cell*
unicolore [ADJ.]	*plain*	couleur	*color*
unidimensionnel [ADJ.]	*unidimensional*	dimension	*dimension*
unidirectionnel [ADJ.]	*unidirectional*	direction	*direction*
uniforme [ADJ.]	*uniform*	forme	*form*
uniformité [F.]	*uniformity*	forme	*form*
unijambiste [M.F./ADJ.]	*one-legged (person)*	jambe	*leg*
unilatéral [ADJ.]	*unilateral*	latéral	*lateral*
unisexe [ADJ.]	*unisex*	sexe	*sex*
unitaire [ADJ.]	*unit, joint*	unité	*unit*
univalent [ADJ.]	*univalent*	valeur	*value*
univers [M.]	*universe*	versus [LAT.]	*turning*
universalité [F.]	*universality*	versus [LAT.]	*turning*
universel [ADJ.]	*universal*	versus [LAT.]	*turning*
univoque [ADJ.]	*unequivocal*	vox [LAT.]	*voice*

Définitions! *Provide the appropriate word for each description.*

1. Synonyme de monovalent, valence chimique de 1 _____

2. Caractéristique d'un mot qui garde le même sens dans tous ses emplois _____

3. Caractéristique d'une décision prise par une seule personne ou un seul groupe _____

4. Caractéristique des organismes vivants constitués d'une seule cellule _____

5. Indiquant une seule direction _____

6. Ayant une seule couleur _____

7. Avec une jambe amputée _____

8. Caractéristique d'un vêtement ou d'une coiffure convenable aux deux sexes _____

9. Qui est le même pour tous _____

10. Qui s'applique à tous les cas ou à toute la terre _____

11. Qui tend à l'unité d'action _____

12. Qui a une seule dimension _____

In the following chart, note that **bicentenaire** may function as a noun or an adjective.

ADJECTIVE/NOUN BEGINNING IN **bi(s)-/tri(s)-**	ENGLISH EQUIVALENT	BASE WORD	ENGLISH EQUIVALENT
biathlète [M.F.]	*biathlete*	athlète	*athlete*
bicentenaire [M./ADJ.]	*bicentennial*	centenaire	*centennial*
bicolore [ADJ.]	*two-colored*	couleur	*color*
biculturel [ADJ.]	*bicultural*	culture	*culture*
bicyclette [F.]	*bicycle*	cycle	*cycle*
bifocal [ADJ.]	*bifocal*	focus [LAT.]	*hearth*
bigame [ADJ.]	*bigamous*	gamos [GRK.]	*marriage, union*
bilingue [ADJ.]	*bilingual*	langue	*language*
bimensuel [ADJ.]	*bimonthly*	mensis [LAT.]	*month*
biréacteur [M.]	*twin-engine jet*	réacteur	*reactor*
bisannuel [ADJ.]	*biennial*	annuel	*annual*
bisexuel [ADJ.]	*bisexual*	sexe	*sex*
triangle [M.]	*triangle*	angle	*angle*
triathlète [M.F.]	*triathlete*	athlète	*athlete*
tricentenaire [M.]	*tricentennial*	centenaire	*centennial*
tricolore [ADJ.]	*three-colored*	couleur	*color*
tricycle [M.]	*tricycle*	cycle	*cycle*
trilingue [ADJ.]	*trilingual*	langue	*language*
trisannuel [ADJ.]	*triennial*	annuel	*annual*

Quels sont les mots apparentés? *Complete each one-two(-three) series with the appropriate word(s).*

1. monolingue, _____, _____

2. mensuel, _____

3. monofocal, _____

4. monocycle, _____, _____

5. monoréacteur, _____

6. annuel, _____, _____

7. monosexuel, _____

8. monogame, _____

9. centenaire, _____, _____

10. angle, —, _____

11. athlète, _____, _____

12. unicolore, _____, _____

13. monoculturel, _____

French also uses the prefixes **multi-** and **poly-**; examples follow.

multicolore	*multicolored*
multimillionnaire	*multimillionaire*
polycopier	*to duplicate*
polygamie	*polygamy*

 **128 pro-**

MEANING   Forward, in favor of
ENGLISH EQUIVALENT   *pro-*
PART OF SPEECH   Verb, adjective, noun

The French prefix **pro-** affixed to a verb conveys the sense of *forward* or *in favor of*. Most words formed with this prefix may be spelled with or without a hyphen; for example, both **pro-actif** and **proactif** are currently used. A hyphen must be used, however, if the base word begins in **i-** or **u-** or if the base word is a proper noun, such as **pro-Europe or pro-Américain**. Proper nouns are not included in the chart of words prefixed with **pro-**.

The following chart presents verbs and their past participles. (For information about past participles used as adjectives, see Appendix A.)

VERB/ADJECTIVE BEGINNING IN **pro-**	ENGLISH EQUIVALENT	BASE WORD	ENGLISH EQUIVALENT
procéder	*to proceed*	céder	*to pass, yield*
proclamer/proclamé	*to proclaim / proclaimed*	clamer	*to claim*
procurer/procuré	*to provide / provided*	curare [LAT.]	*to care for*
projeter/projeté	*to project / projected*	jeter	*to throw*
prolonger/prolongé	*to prolong / prolonged*	long	*long*
promouvoir/promu	*to promote / promoted*	mouvoir	*to move*
pronostiquer/pronostiqué	*to forecast / forecast*	noscere [LAT.]	*to know*
propager/propagé	*to propagate / propagated*	pangere [LAT.]	*to compose*
prophétiser/prophétisé	*to prophesy / prophesied*	phemi [GRK.]	*to show*
proposer/proposé	*to propose / proposed*	ponere [LAT.]	*to put down, set*
provenir/provenu	*to originate / originated*	venir	*to come*

French adjectives not related to verbs in the preceding chart are as follows.

proactif	*proactive*
pronucléaire	*pronuclear*

Nouns related to verbs in the preceding chart are as follows; all nouns are feminine, as indicated by their suffixes, except for **procédé** and **pronostic**.

procédé	*procedure, process*
procession	*procession*
proclamation	*proclamation*
projection	*projection*
prolongation	*prolongation*
promotion	*promotion*
pronostic	*forecast*
propagation	*propagation*
prophétie	*prophecy*
proposition	*proposition*
provenance	*origin*

EXERCICE
128·1

Complétez! *Complete each sentence with the correct form of the appropriate past participle.*

1. Il faut démontrer une grande compétence pour être _____ dans une société d'entreprise.

2. L'itinéraire _____ semble bien planifié.

3. Le voyage _____ est tombé à l'eau parce que tout le monde était malade.

4. La nouvelle qui vient d'être _____ a surpris le public.

5. Le gagnant de la course avait été _____ par ce joueur professionnel.

6. La mort du roi de France, _____ par Nostradamus, a eu lieu à un tournoi.

7. L'attente _____ de l'arrivée des secours était interminable.

8. La laine _____ de Nouvelle Zélande est de haute qualité.

9. Une calomnie _____ peut causer de grands troubles.

10. Après avoir _____ à la vérification des papiers, les douaniers nous ont laissé passer.

◆129◆ psych(o)-

MEANING	Mind
ENGLISH EQUIVALENT	*psycho-*
PART OF SPEECH	Noun, adjective

The French prefix **psych(o)-**, used to form French nouns and adjectives, is a Greek root signifying the mind and mental activities. Before a vowel, the prefix **psych-** is used; before a consonant, the prefix **psycho-** is used. Many nouns are formed with the prefix **psych(o)-** and a base word or a suffix such as **-iatre** or **-ologie** (see Part I for information about suffixes). Since most French words prefixed with **psych(o)-** have English cognates, they tend to be easily recognized.

NOUN BEGINNING IN **psych(o)-**	ENGLISH EQUIVALENT	BASE WORD	ENGLISH EQUIVALENT
psychanalyse [F.]	*psychoanalysis*	analyse	*analysis*
psychiatre [M.F.]	*psychiatrist*	[-iatre]	*-iatrist*
psychisme [M.]	*psyche*	[-isme]	*-ism*
psychodrame [M.]	*psychodrama*	drame	*drama*
psychologie [F.]	*psychology*	[-ologie]	*-ology*
psychologue [M.F.]	*psychologist*	[-ologue]	*-ologist*
psychonévrose [F.]	*psychoneurosis*	névrose	*neurosis*
psychopathe [M.F.]	*psychopath*	[-pathe]	*-path*
psychopathologie [F.]	*psychopathology*	pathologie	*pathology*
psychose [F.]	*psychosis*	[-ose]	*-osis*
psychothérapeute [M.F.]	*psychotherapist*	thérapeute	*therapist*
psychothérapie [F.]	*psychotherapy*	thérapie	*therapy*

Adjectives related to nouns in the preceding chart are as follows.

psychanalytique	*psychoanalytical*
psychiatrique	*psychiatric*
psychodramatique	*psychodramatic*
psychique	*psychological*
psychologique	*psychological*
psychopathique	*psychopathic*
psychothérapique	*psychotherapeutic*

The French verb **psychanalyser** has an English cognate, *to psychoanalyze*.

Vrai ou faux? *Indicate whether each statement is true or false, using* **V** *for* **vrai** *true or* **F** *for* **faux** *false.*

1. _____ La psychothérapeute administre des traitements.

2. _____ La psychose est une condition normale.

3. _____ La psychonévrose désigne un trouble psychique sans cause organique démontrable.

4. _____ La psychologie est le redressement des comportements négatifs.

5. _____ Le/la psychiatre diagnostique et traite les maladies mentales.

6. _____ Le psychisme est l'ensemble des traitements alternatifs.

7. _____ La psychothérapie réussit dans tous les cas.

8. _____ La psychopathie est un trouble de la personnalité.

9. _____ Le psychopathe est un médecin spécialisé.

10. _____ Le psychodrame est une forme de thérapie qui utilise le jeu de rôle.

11. _____ La psychologue se sert de médicaments pour traiter ses patients.

12. _____ La psychanalyse doit beaucoup à Sigmund Freud.

130 re-/r(é)-

MEANING	Again, back
ENGLISH EQUIVALENT	*re-*
PART OF SPEECH	Verb, adjective, noun

The French prefixes **re-** and **r(é)-** convey a sense of repetition or restoration, withdrawal, or return to a previous condition. Almost any verb can be the base word for a verb formed with this prefix. However, verbs that indicate a state of being (for example, *to be, to have, to hope, to want,* and *to be able to*) cannot take the prefix **re-/r(é)-**. The prefix **re-** becomes **r-** or **ré-** before a base word beginning in a vowel. In the following chart, a sampling of such verbs, along with their past participles, is presented. (For information about past participles used as adjectives, see Appendix A.)

VERB/ADJECTIVE BEGINNING IN **re-/r(é)-**	ENGLISH EQUIVALENT	BASE WORD	ENGLISH EQUIVALENT
rappeler/rappelé	*to call back / called back*	appeler	*to call*
rapporter/rapporté	*to bring back / brought back*	apporter	*to bring*
rassembler/rassemblé	*to assemble / assembled*	assembler	*to assemble*
rassurer/rassuré	*to reassure / reassured*	assurer	*to assure*
recompter/recompté	*to recount / recounted*	compter	*to count*
reconstituer/reconstitué	*to reconstitute / reconstituted*	constituer	*to constitute*

VERB/ADJECTIVE BEGINNING IN **re-/r(é)-**	ENGLISH EQUIVALENT	BASE WORD	ENGLISH EQUIVALENT
reconstruire/reconstruit	to rebuild / rebuilt	construire	to build
récrire/récrit	to rewrite / rewritten	écrire	to write
recycler/recyclé	to recycle / recycled	cycler	to cycle
redire/redit	to repeat / repeated	dire	to say
réécouter/réécouté	to listen to again / listened to again	écouter	to listen to
refaire/refait	to redo / redone	faire	to do
réhabituer/réhabitué	to reaccustom / reaccustomed	habituer	to accustom
remonter/remonté	to go back up / reascended	monter	to go up
rendormir/rendormi	to put back to sleep / put back to sleep	endormir	to put to sleep
reprendre/repris	to take back / taken back, to begin again / begun again	prendre	to take
reproduire/reproduit	to reproduce / reproduced	produire	to produce
réunir/réuni	to reunite / reunited	unir	to unite
réutiliser/réutilisé	to reuse / reused	utiliser	to use
revenir/revenu	to come back / sent back	venir	to come

Nouns related to verbs and adjectives in the preceding chart are as follows.

rappel [M.]	recall, reminder
rapport [M.]	report
rassemblement [M.]	gathering
reconstitution [F.]	reconstitution
reconstruction [F.]	reconstruction
recyclage [M.]	recycling
remontée [F.]	climb up
reprise [F.]	resumption
reproduction [F.]	reproduction
réunion [F.]	reunion
réutilisation [F.]	reuse

EXERCICE
130·1

Tout retourne à la normale! *Complete each sentence with the infinitive of the appropriate verb.*

1. Après les vacances, il faut _____ le travail.

2. Après avoir quitté la maison, il est habituel de _____ chez soi.

3. Après avoir prêté un bijou, il faut le _____ .

4. Après avoir démoli la tour de Legos, il faut la _____ .

5. Après avoir réparé l'aspirateur, on peut le _____ .

6. Quand un interlocuteur ne répond pas au téléphone, il faut le

   _____ .

7. Quand on se trompe en comptant l'argent, il faut le _____ .

8. Après avoir emprunté quelque chose, il faut le _____.

9. Après un tremblement de terre, il faut _____ les maisons détruites.

10. Après la récréation, il faut _____ tous les enfants.

11. Après une panne d'ordinateur, il faut _____ certains documents.

12. Après avoir vécu à l'étranger, il faut se _____ à sa propre culture.

13. Après avoir mangé un bon gâteau, il faut en _____ un autre.

14. Si on n'est pas entendu la première fois, il faut tout _____.

15. Pour aider l'environnement, il faut _____.

16. Quand on aime une chanson à la folie, il faut la _____.

17. Quand on a oublié quelque chose dans sa chambre, il faut _____ en haut.

18. Quand le bébé se réveille la nuit, il faut le _____.

19. Après une grande peur, il faut _____ l'enfant.

20. Quand l'inventaire d'un produit est épuisé, il faut le _____.

4
Intermediate/advanced prefixes

 **131** ◆ **sous-, sub-**

MEANING	Under, insufficient
ENGLISH EQUIVALENT	*under-, sub-*
PART OF SPEECH	Verb, adjective, noun

The French prefixes **sous-** and **sub-**, used to form verbs, adjectives, and nouns, add the meaning *under* to the base word. The prefix **sous-** is separated from the base word by a hyphen.

VERB BEGINNING IN **sous-, sub-**	ENGLISH EQUIVALENT	BASE WORD	ENGLISH EQUIVALENT
sous-alimenter	*to undernourish*	alimenter	*to nourish*
sous-développer	*to underdevelop*	développer	*to develop*
sous-employer	*to underemploy*	employer	*to employ*
sous-entendre	*to imply*	entendre	*to hear*
sous-estimer	*to underestimate*	estimer	*to value*
sous-exploiter	*to underuse*	exploiter	*to make use of*
sous-louer	*to sublet*	louer	*to rent*
sous-titrer	*to subtitle*	titrer	*to title*
subjuguer	*to subjugate, captivate*	jugare [LAT.]	*to bind together*
submerger	*to submerge*	mergere [LAT.]	*immerse*
subordonner	*to subordinate*	ordonner	*to command*
subventionner	*to subsidize, provide*	venire [LAT.]	*to come*

Adjectives (past participles) related to verbs in the preceding chart are as follows. (For more information about past participles used as adjectives, see Appendix A.)

sous-alimenté	*undernourished*
sous-entendu	*implied*
subjugué	*subjugated, captivated*
subvenu	*provided*

Nouns related to verbs in the preceding chart are as follows.

sous-alimentation [F.]	*malnutrition*
sous-développement [M.]	*underdevelopment*
sous-emploi [M.]	*underemployment*
sous-entendu [M.]	*innuendo*
sous-estimation [F.]	*underestimation*
sous-exploitation [F.]	*underuse*
sous-location [F.]	*sublet*
sous-titre [M.]	*subtitle*
subjugation [F.]	*subjugation, fascination*

submersion [F.]	submersion
subordination [F.]	subordination
subvention [F.]	subsidy

EXERCICE
131·1

Complétez! *Complete each sentence with the correct form of the appropriate past participle.*

1. Dans une mauvaise économie, les travailleurs sont _____.

2. Les films étrangers sont souvent _____.

3. Les appartements universitaires sont parfois _____.

4. Les nouvelles industries doivent parfois être _____ par le gouvernement.

5. Une région _____ a besoin d'aide.

6. Une personne peut être _____ par la beauté de quelque chose.

7. Il y a des personnes _____ dans les pays pauvres.

8. Beaucoup d'artistes ont été fortement _____ par leurs contemporains.

9. L'autorité du secrétaire est _____ à celle du ministre.

10. Dans une fable, il y a des références historiques _____.

11. Un sous-marin ne reste pas tout le temps _____.

12. Certains services sociaux sont _____ parce qu'on ne les connaît pas.

The following chart consists of nouns formed with the prefix **sous-** or **sub-** and a base word that is a noun or adjective. Note that **subalterne** and **subconscient** may function both as nouns and as adjectives.

NOUN/ADJECTIVE BEGINNING IN **sous-, sub-**	ENGLISH EQUIVALENT	BASE WORD	ENGLISH EQUIVALENT
sous-chef [M.]	*sous-chef*	chef	*chef*
sous-comité [M.]	*subcommittee*	comité	*committee*
sous-marin [M.]	*submarine*	marin	*marine*
sous-officier [M.]	*noncommissioned officer*	officier	*officer*
sous-secrétaire [M.F.]	*undersecretary*	secrétaire	*secretary*
sous-titre [M.]	*subtitle*	titre	*title*
sous-vêtement [M.]	*underwear*	vêtement	*item of clothing*
subalterne [M.F./ADJ.]	*subordinate*	alter [LAT.]	*other*
subconscient [M./ADJ.]	*subconscious*	conscient	*conscious*
subdivision [F.]	*subdivision*	division	*division*

EXERCICE
131·2

Définitions! *Provide the appropriate noun for each description.*

1. Il est dans le militaire.   _____

2. C'est une section administrative.   _____

3. C'est un titre secondaire.   _____

4. Il/Elle occupe une fonction peu élevée.   _____

5. Cela se porte au-dessous des pulls et des robes.   _____

6. L'assistant du chef   _____

7. Un bateau de guerre qui peut combattre en plongée   _____

8. Ensemble des états psychiques non-conscients   _____

9. Un groupe nommé par un autre groupe pour étudier
   certaines questions   _____

10. Il/Elle travaille pour la secrétaire d'État ou un ministre.   _____

132 ◆ sur-

MEANING	Over, above, in excess
ENGLISH EQUIVALENT	—
PART OF SPEECH	Noun, adjective, verb

The French prefix **sur-**, used to form nouns, adjectives, and verbs, conveys the sense of excess. Unlike words with the prefix **sous-**, words prefixed with **sur-** are not hyphenated. In the following chart, nouns prefixed with **sur-** have nouns for base words. Note that **surnaturel** *supernatural* may also function as an adjective.

NOUN/ADJECTIVE BEGINNING IN **sur-**	ENGLISH EQUIVALENT	BASE WORD	ENGLISH EQUIVALENT
surabondance [F.]	*overabundance*	abondance	*abundance*
surchauffe [F.]	*overheating*	chauffe	*heating*
surclassement [M.]	*upgrade*	classement	*ranking*
surdose [F.]	*overdose*	dose	*dose*
suremploi [M.]	*overemployment, overuse*	emploi	*employment, use*
surexcitation [F.]	*overexcitement*	excitation	*excitement*
surgélateur [M.]	*deep freezer*	gel	*ice*
surgélation [F.]	*deep freeze*	gel	*ice*
surhomme [M.]	*superman*	homme	*man*
surlendemain [M.]	*day after tomorrow*	lendemain	*next day*
surnaturel [M./ADJ.]	*supernatural*	naturel	*natural*
surproduction [F.]	*overproduction*	production	*production*
surréservation [F.]	*overbooking*	réservation	*reservation*

▶

NOUN/ADJECTIVE BEGINNING IN **sur-**	ENGLISH EQUIVALENT	BASE WORD	ENGLISH EQUIVALENT
sursaut [M.]	*jolt, jerk*	saut	*jump*
surtaxe [F.]	*surcharge*	taxe	*tax*
survêtement [M.]	*jogging suit*	vêtement	*item of clothing*
survie [F.]	*survival*	vie	*life*
survol [M.]	*flight over, overview*	vol	*flight*

EXERCICE
132·1

Vrai ou faux? *Indicate whether each statement is true or false, using* **V** *for* **vrai** *true or* **F** *for* **faux** *false.*

1. _____ Le surlendemain de la fête du Nouvel An, les gens se reposent.

2. _____ Une grande surprise peut causer un sursaut.

3. _____ On ne trouve un surhomme que dans les films.

4. _____ La surréservation en avion est illégale.

5. _____ L'instinct de survie peut donner de grandes forces.

6. _____ La surchauffe de la planète fait fondre les glaciers.

7. _____ Le suremploi d'une machine peut la faire tomber en panne.

8. _____ La surgélation des aliments existe depuis la préhistoire.

9. _____ Certains habitués d'une ligne aérienne peuvent bénéficier d'un surclassement.

10. _____ Prendre trop de bagages en avion peut mener à une surtaxe.

11. _____ On installe le surgélateur à la salle de bains.

12. _____ La surabondance des fruits entraîne un coût plus élevé.

13. _____ Quand on révise en profondeur un chapitre, on en fait le survol.

14. _____ Une surdose de drogues peut être fatale.

15. _____ Un moment de surexcitation demande des soins sérieux.

16. _____ Il y a des crises journalières de surproduction de marchandise dans notre société.

17. _____ On met son survêtement pour nager.

18. _____ Le surnaturel échappe aux lois de la nature.

Verbs and their past participles related to nouns in the preceding chart are as follows. (For information about past participles used as adjectives, see Appendix A.)

surabonder	*to abound*
surchauffer/surchauffé	*to overheat / overheated*
surclasser/surclassé	*to upgrade / upgraded*
suremployer/suremployé	*to overemploy / overemployed*
surexciter/surexcité	*to overexcite / overexcited*

surgeler/surgelé	*to deep-freeze / deep-frozen*
surproduire/surproduit	*to overproduce / overproduced*
surréserver/surréservé	*to overbook / overbooked*
sursauter	*to jump*
surtaxer/surtaxé	*to surcharge / surcharged*
survivre/survécu	*to survive / survived*
survoler/survolé	*to fly over / flown over, to skim through / skimmed through*

133 ▸ super-, ultra-

MEANING	Over, above, in excess
ENGLISH EQUIVALENT	*super-, ultra-*
PART OF SPEECH	Adjective, noun

The French prefixes **super-** and **ultra-**, used to form adjectives as well as nouns, convey the sense of great power, with the meaning *intense, great, mighty,* or *superior*. The first chart presents adjectives formed with the prefix **super-** and base adjectives or Latin roots.

ADJECTIVE BEGINNING IN **super-**	ENGLISH EQUIVALENT	BASE WORD	ENGLISH EQUIVALENT
superacide	*superacidic*	acide	*acidic*
superchic	*supercool, superelegant*	chic	*cool, elegant*
superflu	*superfluous*	fluere [LAT.]	*to flow*
superlatif	*superlative*	superlatus [LAT.]	*exaggerated*
superléger	*superlight*	léger	*light*
super-mignon	*supercute*	mignon	*cute*
supersonique	*supersonic*	sonique	*sonic*
super-transparent	*supertransparent*	transparent	*transparent*

EXERCICE
133·1

Devinez la caractéristique! *Provide the appropriate adjective for each set of items.*

1. Un vin très jeune, un citron   _____

2. Une plume, un brin d'herbe   _____

3. Un plastique, un cristal   _____

4. De trop, surabondant   _____

5. Un chapeau, une toilette   _____

6. Un petit garçon, un joli dessin   _____

7. Exagéré, excessif   _____

8. Un avion, une vitesse   _____

The following chart presents nouns formed with the prefix **super-**.

NOUN BEGINNING IN **super-**	ENGLISH EQUIVALENT	BASE WORD	ENGLISH EQUIVALENT
supercarburant [M.]	*premium gas*	carburant	*gas*
superchampion [M.]	*superchampion*	champion	*champion*
super-héroïne [F.]	*superwoman*	héroïne	*heroine*
super-héros [M.]	*superman*	héros	*hero*
supermarché [M.]	*supermarket*	marché	*market*
superordinateur [M.]	*supercomputer*	ordinateur	*computer*
superpuissance [F.]	*superpower*	puissance	*power*
super-remise [F.]	*super discount*	remise	*discount*
superstar [F.]	*superstar*	star	*star*
superviseur [M.]	*supervisor*	videre [LAT.]	*to see*

EXERCICE
133·2

Complétez! *Provide the appropriate word to complete each sentence.*

1. Un _____ est un type de justicier dans les bandes dessinées.

2. Un _____ permet de faire des calculs à haute performance.

3. Elvis Presley était indubitablement une _____.

4. En automne il y a des _____ sur la marchandise d'été.

5. Wonder Woman est une _____.

6. Les États-Unis sont une _____ remarquable.

7. Un _____ contrôle tous ses employés et leurs activités.

8. Un magasin de grande surface en libre-service est un _____.

The following chart presents adjectives formed with the prefix **ultra-** and base adjectives. **Ultra-** conveys a sense of even greater intensity than **super-**.

ADJECTIVE BEGINNING IN **ultra-**	ENGLISH EQUIVALENT	BASE WORD	ENGLISH EQUIVALENT
ultrablanc	*ultrawhite*	blanc	*white*
ultrachic	*ultrachic*	chic	*chic*
ultralourd	*ultraheavy*	lourd	*heavy*
ultramoderne	*ultramodern*	moderne	*modern*
ultrapropre	*ultraclean*	propre	*clean*
ultraroyaliste	*ultraroyalist*	royaliste	*royalist*
ultrasensible	*ultrasensitive*	sensible	*sensitive*
ultraviolet	*ultraviolet*	violet	*violet*

133·3

Cherchez la caractéristique! *Provide the appropriate adjective to describe each noun.*

1. Un rayon _____

2. Un membre de la noblesse _____

3. Des sous-vêtements _____

4. Des romantiques _____

5. Des draps _____

6. Une tablette _____

7. D'anciens meubles _____

8. Un pendentif _____

134 télé-

MEANING	Remote, distant
ENGLISH EQUIVALENT	*tele-*
PART OF SPEECH	Noun, verb, adjective

The French prefix **télé-**, used to form nouns, verbs, and adjectives, conveys the sense of remoteness or distance. Since most of these French words have English cognates, they tend to be easily recognized.

NOUN BEGINNING IN **télé-**	ENGLISH EQUIVALENT	BASE WORD	ENGLISH EQUIVALENT
téléachat [M.]	*home shopping*	achat	*shopping*
téléchargement [M.]	*download*	chargement	*load, cargo*
télécommande [F.]	*remote control*	commande	*order*
téléconférence [F.]	*teleconference*	conférence	*conference*
télécopie [F.]	*fax*	copie	*copy*
télédiffusion [F.]	*television broadcasting*	diffusion	*broadcasting*
téléenseignement [M.]	*distance education*	enseignement	*instruction*
télégestion [F.]	*teleprocessing*	gestion	*management*
télékinésie [F.]	*telekinesis*	kinesis [GRK.]	*movement*
télémarketing [M.]	*telemarketing*	marketing	*marketing*
téléobjectif [M.]	*telephoto lens*	objectif	*lens*
téléphone [M.]	*telephone*	[-phone]	*sound, voice*
téléportation [F.]	*teleportation*	porter	*to carry*
téléréalité [F.]	*reality TV*	réalité	*reality*
télescope [M.]	*telescope*	skopein [GRK.]	*to look at*
télésiège [M.]	*ski lift*	siège	*seat*
télévision [F.]	*television*	vision	*viewing*

Verbs and adjectives related to nouns in the preceding chart are as follows. (For more information about past participles used as adjectives, see Appendix A.)

télécharger/téléchargé	*to download / downloaded, to upload / uploaded*
télécommander/télécommandé	*to operate remotely / remotely operated*
télécopier/télécopié	*to fax / faxed*
télédiffuser/télédiffusé	*to broadcast / broadcast*
téléphoner/téléphoné	*to telephone / telephoned*
téléporter/téléporté	*to teleport / teleported*
téléviser/télévisé	*to televise / televised*

EXERCICE
134·1

Vrai ou faux? *Indicate whether each statement is true or false, using* **V** *for* **vrai** *true or* **F** *for* **faux** *false.*

1. _____ La télécommande permet de zapper d'une émission à l'autre.

2. _____ La télévision ne transmet que les nouvelles.

3. _____ Dans les films de science-fiction, la téléportation est de rigueur.

4. _____ La télédiffusion encourage les membres des réseaux sociaux à se voir.

5. _____ Le télescope se trouve uniquement dans les laboratoires.

6. _____ Le téléachat n'est pas très populaire.

7. _____ La téléréalité permet de suivre la vie quotidienne de certaines personnes.

8. _____ Il y a aujourd'hui des logiciels de télémarketing très efficaces.

9. _____ Le téléobjectif permet de photographier de petits sujets à grande distance.

10. _____ Le télésiège est le seul moyen de monter au sommet d'une montagne.

11. _____ Le téléphone sans fil est une invention du 19e siècle.

12. _____ Le téléenseignement comprend souvent des programmes de radio et de télévision.

13. _____ La télégestion permet de travailler chez soi.

14. _____ Les téléconférences sont nécessaires et courantes parmi les lycéens.

15. _____ La télékinésie peut s'apprendre facilement.

135 ▸ trans-

MEANING	Across, beyond
ENGLISH EQUIVALENT	*trans-*
PART OF SPEECH	Noun, verb, adjective

The French prefix **trans-**, used to form nouns, verbs, and adjectives, means *across* or *beyond*. Most of these words have a French noun or a Latin root for the base word. Since French words with this prefix have English cognates, they are easily recognized. In the following chart, all nouns are feminine except **transfert** and **transport**.

NOUN BEGINNING IN **trans-**	ENGLISH EQUIVALENT	BASE WORD	ENGLISH EQUIVALENT
transaction [F.]	*transaction*	action	*action*
transcendance [F.]	*transcendence*	scandere [LAT.]	*ascend*
transcription [F.]	*transcript*	scriptus [LAT.]	*written*
transfert [M.]	*transfer*	ferre [LAT.]	*to carry*
transfiguration [F.]	*transfiguration*	figure	*face*
transformation [F.]	*transformation*	formation	*formation*
transfusion [F.]	*transfusion*	fusion	*merger*
transgression [F.]	*transgression*	gressus [LAT.]	*step*
transmission [F.]	*transmission*	mittere [LAT.]	*to send*
transmutation [F.]	*transmutation*	mutation	*mutation*
transparence [F.]	*transparency*	parere [LAT.]	*to appear*
transplantation [F.]	*transplantation*	planter	*to plant*
transport [M.]	*transport*	portare [LAT.]	*to carry*
transportation [F.]	*transportation*	portare [LAT.]	*to carry*
transposition [F.]	*transposition*	position	*position*
transsexualité [F.]	*transsexuality*	sexualité	*sexuality*

Verbs and adjectives related to nouns in the preceding chart are as follows. (For more information about past participles used as adjectives, see Appendix A.)

transactionnel	*transactional*
transcender/transcendé	*to transcend / transcended*
transcrire/transcrit	*to transcribe / transcribed*
transférer/transferé	*to transfer / transferred*
transfigurer/transfiguré	*to transfigure / transfigured*
transformer/transformé	*to transform / transformed*
transfuser/transfusé	*to transfuse / transfused*
transgresser/transgressé	*to transgress / transgressed*
transmettre/transmis	*to transmit / transmitted*
transmuter/transmuté	*to transmute / transmuted*
transplanter/transplanté	*to transplant / transplanted*
transporter/transporté	*to transport / transported*
transposer/transposé	*to transpose / transposed*

Other adjectives with the prefix **trans-** are as follows.

transafricain	*trans-African*
transalpine	*transalpine*
transatlantique	*transatlantic*
transculturel	*transcultural*

Complétez! *Choose the best completion for each sentence.*

1. _____	Pendant une opération chirurgicale, il faut	a.	très utilisé en Europe.
2. _____	Le train est un mode de transport	b.	ont été transposées dans un contexte contemporain.
3. _____	La chirurgie esthétique peut	c.	afin d'être promu.
4. _____	Certaines cellules biologiques sont	d.	des centaines de passagers.
5. _____	Certaines œuvres cinématographiques	e.	parfois faire une transfusion de sang.
6. _____	Un grand paquebot peut transporter	f.	transmis en direct.
7. _____	La réalité peut transcender	g.	être transparents.
8. _____	La transsexualité consiste à avoir	h.	accompagnent parfois un CV.
9. _____	La transportation d'un groupe de Roms	i.	capables de transmuter.
10. _____	Désobéir aux ordres d'un supérieur	j.	financières à la banque.
11. _____	Les matchs de football sont	k.	peut être un détriment à l'écologie.
12. _____	Les actes politiques devraient	l.	a causé un grand scandale en France.
13. _____	La transplantation d'une espèce animale	m.	causer une vraie transfiguration.
14. _____	Il vaut mieux faire ses transactions	n.	l'imagination.
15. _____	Il faut parfois accepter un transfert	o.	est une transgression.
16. _____	Des lettres de recommandation	p.	une identité sexuelle non conforme à son sexe.

136 ▶ a-/an-

MEANING	Lack, deprivation
ENGLISH EQUIVALENT	*a-*
PART OF SPEECH	Adjective, noun

The French prefix **a-/an-**, used to form adjectives and nouns, is of Greek origin and is called **a-privatif** in French; it denotes absence, lack, or deprivation. **An-** is used if the base word begins in a vowel or **h-**. This prefix should not be confused with the prefix **a-** (and its many variants: **ac-**, **ad-**, **af-**, and so on) that derives from the Latin preposition **ad**, which means *toward* (a direction or goal), for example, **affirmer** *to assert*. (For this prefix, see No. 146.) The base word for an **a-privatif** prefix may be a French word, but it is often a Greek or Latin root. Since many of these prefixed words have English cognates, they tend to be easily recognized.

ADJECTIVE BEGINNING IN **a-/an-**	ENGLISH EQUIVALENT	BASE WORD	ENGLISH EQUIVALENT
alogique	*lacking logic*	logos [GRK.]	*reason*
amoral	*amoral*	moral	*moral*
analphabète	*illiterate*	alphabet	*alphabet*
anarchique	*anarchical*	arche [GRK.]	*hierarchy*
anarchiste	*anarchist*	arche [GRK.]	*hierarchy*
anonyme	*anonymous*	nom	*name*
anormal	*abnormal*	norme	*norm*
apatride	*stateless*	patrie	*homeland*
apolitique	*apolitical*	politique	*politics*
asexué	*asexual*	sexe	*sex*
asocial	*asocial*	société	*society*
asymétrique	*asymmetrical*	symétrique	*symmetrical*
atone	*lifeless, sluggish*	tonos [GRK.]	*accent*
atoxique	*nonpoisonous*	toxicum [LAT.]	*poison*

Nouns related to adjectives in the preceding chart are as follows.

amoralisme [M.]	*amoral attitude*
amoralité [F.]	*amorality*
analphabète [M.F.]	*illiterate person*
analphabétisme [M.]	*illiteracy*
anarchie [F.]	*anarchy*
anarchisme [M.]	*anarchism*
anarchiste [M.F.]	*anarchist*
anonymat [M.]	*anonymity*
anormalité [F.]	*abnormality*
apatride [M.F.]	*stateless person*
asymétrie [F.]	*asymmetry*
atonie [F.]	*lifelessness, sluggishness*

EXERCICE
136·1

Trouvez l'adjectif! *Complete each sentence with the correct form of the appropriate adjective.*

1. Une attitude _____ et hors-la-loi ne convient pas à un politicien.

2. On aurait du mal à trouver des gens _____ pendant une élection présidentielle.

3. Le nombre de personnes _____ décroit au fur et à mesure qu'un pays se développe.

4. Une personne _____ n'a aucun code de moralité.

5. Des organismes _____ se reproduisent sans l'intervention d'organismes de sexe opposé.

6. Des immigrants non-reconnus et non-identifiés sont quasi-_____.

7. Un essai avec de bons arguments bien organisés et défendus n'est pas

_____.

8. Il faut absolument que les jouets soient _____.

9. Un hermite est jugé _____.

10. Un estomac ou un intestin qui ne fonctionne pas bien est _____.

11. Il existe pas mal d'artistes de graffiti _____ et inconnus.

12. Dans un bureau sans patron ni patronne, il règne un désordre _____.

13. Une coiffure _____ peut être charmante.

14. Une attitude surprenante est souvent jugée _____.

137 ► contre-

MEANING	Opposition, reaction
ENGLISH EQUIVALENT	*counter-*
PART OF SPEECH	Noun, adjective, verb

The French prefix **contre-**, used to form nouns, adjectives, and verbs, conveys a contrary or opposing sense. The base word is usually a noun, but may be an adjective or verb.

NOUN BEGINNING IN **contre-**	ENGLISH EQUIVALENT	BASE WORD	ENGLISH EQUIVALENT
contradiction [F.]	*contradiction*	dire	*to say*
contre-attaque [F.]	*counterattack*	attaque	*attack*
contrebande [F.]	*contraband*	bande	*group*
contrebandier [M.]	*smuggler*	bande	*group*
contrechoc [M.]	*countershock*	choc	*shock*
contrecoup [M.]	*rebound, recoil*	coup	*blow, shot*
contrecourant [M.]	*countercurrent*	courant	*current*
contre-exemple [M.]	*counterexample*	exemple	*example*
contrefaçon [F.]	*forgery, counterfeiting*	façon	*way, manner*
contre-indication [F.]	*contraindication, counterargument*	indication	*indication*
contre-interrogatoire [M.]	*cross-examination*	interrogatoire	*interrogation*
contrespionnage [M.]	*counterespionage*	espionnage	*espionage*

Verbs and adjectives related to nouns in the preceding chart are as follows. (For more information about past participles used as adjectives, see Appendix A.)

contre-attaquer/contre-attaqué	*to counterattack / counterattacked*
contredire/contredit	*to contradict / contradicted*
contrefaire/contrefait	*to counterfeit / counterfeit*
contre-indiquer/contre-indiqué	*to warn against / warned against*

EXERCICE

137·1

Définitions et synonymes! *Provide the appropriate noun for each description.*

1. Une répercussion   _____

2. Une réaction en sens inverse   _____

3. Une objection   _____

4. Un conseil contraire   _____

5. Un exemple de ce qu'il ne faut pas faire   _____

6. Un second interrogatoire visant à juger de la fiabilité des réponses   _____

7. Un choc en retour   _____

8. Recherche d'espions étrangers   _____

9. Commerce clandestin   _____

10. Reproduction illégale   _____

11. Une personne qui se livre à un commerce illégal   _____

12. Une contre-offensive   _____

NOUN/ADJECTIVE BEGINNING IN **contre**-	ENGLISH EQUIVALENT	BASE WORD	ENGLISH EQUIVALENT
contre-offensive [F.]	*counteroffensive*	offensive	*offensive*
contre-ordre [M.]	*counterorder*	ordre	*order*
contreperformance [F.]	*below-average performance*	performance	*performance*
contrepoison [M.]	*antidote*	poison	*poison*
contreproposition [F.]	*counterproposal*	proposition	*proposal*
contrerévolution [F.]	*counterrevolution*	révolution	*revolution*
contrerévolutionnaire [M.F./ADJ.]	*counterrevolutionary*	révolution	*revolution*
contresens [M.]	*misinterpretation*	sens	*meaning, direction*
contretemps [M.]	*delay*	temps	*time*
contre-terrorisme [M.]	*counterterrorism*	terrorisme	*terrorism*
contre-terroriste [M.F.]	*counterterrorist*	terroriste	*terrorist*
contrevent [M.]	*shutter* (window)	vent	*wind*

Verbs and adjectives prefixed with **contre**- are as follows.

contresigner/contresigné	*to countersign / countersigned*
contrevenir/contrevenu	*to infringe / infringed*

Vrai ou faux? *Indicate whether each statement is true or false, using* **V** *for* **vrai** *true or* **F** *for* **faux** *false.*

1. _____ Un délai dans le départ d'un vol est un contretemps fâcheux.

2. _____ L'apprenant de la langue étrangère fait rarement un contresens.

3. _____ Le contre-terroriste initie la violence.

4. _____ Une contre-performance aux Jeux Olympiques peut malheureusement arriver.

5. _____ On n'a pas besoin de contrevents aux fenêtres quand on habite à la plage.

6. _____ Un contrepoison peut sauver la vie.

7. _____ Il y avait bien des contrerévolutionnaires à l'époque de Mao Tse Toung.

8. _____ Le contre-terrorisme est une réaction.

9. _____ La révolution française n'était pas sans contrerévolution.

10. _____ Au football américain, il y a des attaques offensives et des attaques contre-offensives.

11. _____ Lors de l'achat d'une maison, une contre-proposition n'est jamais indiquée.

12. _____ Un contre-ordre affirme un premier ordre.

138 ▸ dé(s)-

MEANING	Undoing, separation, deprivation, reversal of an action
ENGLISH EQUIVALENT	—
PART OF SPEECH	Verb, adjective, noun

The French prefix **dé(s)-** denotes a sense of undoing, separating, depriving, or reversing an action. **Dé-** becomes **dés-** before a base word beginning in a vowel or **h-**. Although this prefix is sometimes found in English words, it is best to consider the meaning of the prefix and that of the base word to deduce the English meaning of the French word; for example, the base word for **dépeigner** *to ruffle hair* is the verb **peigner** *to comb hair*, and it can be deduced that the action of **dépeigner** produces the opposite effect of **peigner**. The list of verbs that include the prefix **dé(s)-** is extensive, so two charts of verbs, along with their past participles functioning as adjectives, are presented. (See Appendix A.)

VERB/ADJECTIVE BEGINNING IN **dé(s)-**	ENGLISH EQUIVALENT	BASE WORD	ENGLISH EQUIVALENT
débloquer/débloqué	*to free / freed*	bloquer	*to block*
débrancher/débranché	*to unplug / unplugged*	brancher	*to plug in*
déconseiller/déconseillé	*to advise against / not recommended*	conseiller	*to advise*
déformer/déformé	*to distort / distorted*	former	*to form*
démêler/démêlé	*to disentangle / disentangled*	mêler	*to mix*
déménager/déménagé	*to move / moved*	ménage	*household*
démentir/démenti	*to deny / denied*	mentir	*to lie*
démoraliser/démoralisé	*to demoralize / demoralized*	moraliser	*to moralize*
dénicher/déniché	*to find / found*	nicher	*to nest*
dépanner/dépanné	*to help out / helped*	panne	*breakdown*
dépasser/dépassé	*to go past / outmoded, outdated*	passer	*to pass*
dépeigner/dépeigné	*to ruffle hair / ruffled*	peigner	*to comb hair*
dépister/dépisté	*to detect / detected*	pister	*to track*
déplacer/déplacé	*to move, displace / displaced*	placer	*to place*
déposséder/dépossédé	*to rob / robbed*	posséder	*to possess*

EXERCICE 138·1

Complétez! *Complete each sentence with the appropriate infinitive or the correct form of the appropriate past participle.*

1. L'eau ne s'écoule pas dans ce lavabo; il faut le _____.

2. Nous avons besoin d'un couteau; il faut en _____ un quelque part.

3. Il y a un automobiliste en panne sur l'autoroute; il faut le _____.

4. Il y a un court-circuit dans ce sèche-cheveux; il faut le _____.

5. Ce fauteuil empêche la lumière d'entrer; il faut le _____.

6. Ces chaussures sont totalement _____ après avoir été dans la pluie toute la nuit.

7. Certains shampoings aident à _____ les cheveux.

8. Il faut _____ tous ces meubles avant l'arrivée du nouveau locataire.

9. Il est _____ de sortir en montagne pendant la tempête.

10. Certains chiens sont entraînés à _____ les drogues et les explosifs.

11. Nos cheveux sont _____ par le vent.

12. Une mauvaise performance peut vraiment _____ un athlète.

13. Il faut _____ les voitures qui roulent trop lentement.

14. Une personne _____ de ses biens est pitoyable.

15. Il faut absolument _____ les insinuations qui ne sont pas fondées.

VERB/ADJECTIVE BEGINNING IN dé(s)-	ENGLISH EQUIVALENT	BASE WORD	ENGLISH EQUIVALENT
déraciner/déraciné	to uproot / uprooted	racine	root
dérouter/dérouté	to sidetrack / sidetracked	route	road
désaltérer/désaltéré	to quench thirst / quenched	altérer	to make thirsty
désapprouver/désapprouvé	to disapprove / disapproved	approuver	to approve
désembarquer/désembarqué	to deboard / deboarded	embarquer	to board
désenchanter/désenchanté	to disillusion / disillusioned	enchanter	to charm
déséquilibrer/déséquilibré	to throw off balance / unbalanced	équilibrer	to balance
déshabiller/déshabillé	to undress / undressed	habiller	to dress
désherber/désherbé	to weed / weeded	herbe	grass
déshériter/déshérité	to disinherit / disinherited	hériter	to inherit
déshydrater/déshydraté	to dehydrate / dehydrated	hydrater	to hydrate
désintoxiquer/désintoxiqué	to detoxify / detoxified	intoxiquer	to intoxicate
désobéir/désobéi	to disobey / disobeyed	obéir	to obey
désodoriser/désodorisé	to deodorize / deodorized	odeur	odor
déstabiliser/déstabilisé	to destabilize / destabilized	stabiliser	to stabilize

EXERCICE
138·2

Complétez! *Complete each sentence with the correct form of the appropriate past participle/adjective.*

1. L'artiste _____ par son manque de succès abandonne son rêve.

2. Un jardin potager _____ produit plus de légumes.

3. Un coureur du marathon ne doit jamais être _____.

4. Un alcoolique _____ se comporte mieux.

5. Une fois _____, les passagers cherchent leurs bagages.

6. Les arbres _____ par les cyclones jonchent le sol.

7. Un trapéziste _____ tombe dans le filet de sauvetage.

8. Une personne _____ ne doit pas conduire.

9. Une personne _____ par ses parents doit vivre de ses propres moyens.

10. Un sportif _____ est en bonne forme.

11. Un ordre _____ était peut-être inapproprié.

12. L'économie d'un pays est _____ par les problèmes sociaux.

13. Une requête _____ peut être remise en jeu.

14. Une salle de bains _____ est plus agréable.

15. Il ne convient pas de mettre un mannequin _____ dans la devanture du magasin.

Nouns related to verbs in the preceding charts are as follows.

déblocquement [M.]	*clearing, unblocking*
débranchement [M.]	*unplugging, disconnecting*
déformation [F.]	*distortion*
démêlage [M.]	*disentanglement*
déménagement [M.]	*move*
démenti [M.]	*denial*
dénichement [M.]	*unearthing*
dépannage [M.]	*help*
dépassement [M.]	*overreach, passing* (driving)
dépeignement [M.]	*ruffling*
dépistage [M.]	*detection*
déplacement [M.]	*displacement*
dépossession [F.]	*dispossession*
déracinement [M.]	*uprooting*
déroutement [M.]	*rerouting*
désaltération [F.]	*quenching of thirst*
désembarquement [M.]	*deboarding*
désenchantement [M.]	*disillusion*
déséquilibre [M.]	*imbalance*
désherbage [M.]	*weeding*
déshydratation [F.]	*dehydration*
désintoxication [F.]	*detoxification*
désobéissance [F.]	*disobedience*
désodorisation [F.]	*deodorization*
déstabilisation [F.]	*destabilization*

dis-

MEANING	Undoing, separation, deprivation, reversal of an action
ENGLISH EQUIVALENT	*dis-*
PART OF SPEECH	Verb, adjective, noun

The French prefix **dis-** denotes a sense of undoing, separating, depriving, or reversing an action. In the following chart, the base word is a verb except for the Latin noun *culpa*. Past participles may be used as adjectives (see Appendix A).

VERB/ADJECTIVE BEGINNING IN **dis-**	ENGLISH EQUIVALENT	BASE WORD	ENGLISH EQUIVALENT
discontinuer/discontinué	*to discontinue / discontinued*	continuer	*to continue*
disculper/disculpé	*to exonerate / exonerated*	culpa [LAT.]	*fault, guilt*
disjoindre/disjoint	*to break apart / broken apart*	joindre	*to join*
disparaître/disparu	*to disappear / disappeared*	paraître	*to appear*
disperser/dispersé	*to disperse / dispersed*	dispergere [LAT.]	*to spread*
disqualifier/disqualifié	*to disqualify / disqualified*	qualifier	*to qualify*

VERB/ADJECTIVE BEGINNING IN dis-	ENGLISH EQUIVALENT	BASE WORD	ENGLISH EQUIVALENT
disséquer/disséqué	to dissect / dissected	secare [LAT.]	to cut
dissocier/dissocié	to dissociate / dissociated	sociare [LAT.]	to join
dissuader/dissuadé	to dissuade / dissuaded	suadere [LAT.]	to persuade

Nouns related to verbs and adjectives in the preceding chart have English cognates; all nouns are feminine, as indicated by their suffix.

discontinuation	*discontinuation*
disjonction	*disjunction*
disparition	*disappearance*
dispersion	*dispersion*
disqualification	*disqualification*
dissection	*dissection*
dissociation	*dissociation*
dissuasion	*dissuasion*

EXERCICE 139·1

Complétez! *Choose the best completion for each sentence.*

1. _____ Il vaut mieux dissuader l'adolescent

2. _____ Il vaut mieux discontinuer

3. _____ Il faut disculper

4. _____ Il vaut mieux ne pas disjoindre

5. _____ Il vaut mieux faire disparaître

6. _____ Il faut disqualifier

7. _____ Il faut disperser

8. _____ Il faut disséquer un squelette

9. _____ Il faut se dissocier des

a. les graines de fleurs tout le long de la clôture.

b. des billets contrefaits.

c. mauvaises fréquentations.

d. deux cellules compatibles.

e. la vente d'une marchandise peu appréciée.

f. en cours d'anatomie.

g. qui veut expérimenter avec les substances toxiques.

h. les tricheurs.

i. un inculpé innocent.

 **em-**

MEANING	Physical/emotional transformation
ENGLISH EQUIVALENT	—
PART OF SPEECH	Verb, adjective, noun

The French prefix **em-**, used to form verbs, adjectives, and nouns, usually denotes a physical or emotional transformation. The English equivalent may be **em-**, but the rules for forming verbs differ in English and French and it is best to determine the meaning of the prefixed verb based on the original meaning of the prefix. The base word for **embellir** is the adjective **belle** *beautiful*, and the verb **embellir** denotes a transformation to achieve beauty. The base word for **embrouiller** is the verb **brouiller** *to mix up*, and the verb **embrouiller** denotes a transformation to achieve a *real* mix-up. In these cases, the prefix intensifies the meaning of the base word. In the following chart, verbs and their past participles are presented side by side to promote awareness of families of words; past participles may function as adjectives (see Appendix A).

Another meaning of the prefix **em-** is given in No. 142.

VERB/ADJECTIVE BEGINNING IN em-	ENGLISH EQUIVALENT	BASE WORD	ENGLISH EQUIVALENT
embaumer/embaumé	*to embalm / embalmed*	baume	*balm*
embellir/embelli	*to embellish / embellished*	belle	*beautiful*
embêter/embêté	*to bother / bothered*	bête	*dumb*
embrouiller/embrouillé	*to tangle / tangled*	brouiller	*to mix up*
empoisonner/empoisonné	*to poison / poisoned*	poison	*poison*

On rare occasions, the prefix **em-** is attached to a verb of movement; the prefixed verb takes on the meaning *from* or *away*, as in the verb **emporter**.

emporter/emporté   *to carry away / carried away*   (< porter *to carry*)

Nouns related to verbs and adjectives in the preceding chart are masculine.

embaumement	*embalming*
embellissement	*embellishment*
embêtement	*annoyance*
embrouillement	*mix-up*
empoisonnement	*poisoning*

 EXERCICE
140·1

Vrai ou faux? *Indicate whether each statement is true or false, using* **V** *for* **vrai** *true or* **F** *for* **faux** *false.*

1. _____ Un narratif historique doit être embelli pour être authentique.

2. _____ Nous sommes bien embêtés quand il nous arrive un accident.

3. _____ Toutes les rivières sont empoisonnées par la pollution.

4. _____ Les pharaons égyptiens étaient embaumés.

5. _____ Les scandales politiques sont souvent bien embrouillés.

141 ◆ en-

MEANING	Physical/emotional transformation
ENGLISH EQUIVALENT	—
PART OF SPEECH	Verb, adjective, noun

The French prefix **en-**, used to form verbs, adjectives, and nouns, usually denotes a physical or emotional transformation. The English equivalent may be **en-**, but the rules for forming verbs differ in English and French and it is best to determine the meaning of the prefixed verb based on the original meaning of the prefix. When the prefix **en-** and the infinitive ending **-er** are affixed to the French noun **graisse** *fat, grease*, the result is **engraisser** *to fatten*, that is, to transform by adding fat. Note that the prefix **en-** has the opposite meaning of the prefix **dé(s)-**; for example, the verb **engraisser** is the antonym of the verb **dégraisser** *to remove fat*. In the following chart, verbs and their past participles are presented side by side to promote awareness of families of words; past participles may function as adjectives (see Appendix A).

Another meaning of the prefix **en-** is given in No. 143.

VERB/ADJECTIVE BEGINNING IN **en-**	ENGLISH EQUIVALENT	BASE WORD	ENGLISH EQUIVALENT
enchanter/enchanté	to enchant / enchanted	chant	song
encourager/encouragé	to encourage / encouraged	courage	courage
endetter/endetté	to get into debt / in debt	dette	debt
endormir/endormi	to put to sleep / asleep	dormir	to sleep
endurcir/endurci	to toughen / toughened	durcir	to harden
enfanter/enfanté	to give birth / born	enfant	child
enfermer/enfermé	to shut up / shut up, to pen / penned	fermer	to close
engloutir/englouti	to swallow / swallowed	gluttire [LAT.]	to gulp down
engraisser/engraissé	to fatten / fattened, to fertilize / fertilized	graisse	fat
enivrer/enivré	to intoxicate / intoxicated	ivre	drunk
enjamber/enjambé	to step over / stepped over	jambe	leg
enlever/enlevé	to kidnap / kidnapped	lever	to lift, raise
enraciner/enraciné	to implant / implanted	racine	root
enrager/enragé	to enrage / enraged	rage	rage
enrichir/enrichi	to enrich / enriched	riche	rich
ensorceler/ensorcelé	to bewitch / bewitched	sorcellerie	sorcery

Nouns related to verbs and adjectives in the preceding chart are as follows.

enchantement [M.]	*enchantment*
encouragement [M.]	*encouragement*
endurcissement [M.]	*hardening*
enfantement [M.]	*childbirth*
engloutissement [M.]	*engulfing, swallowing*
engrais [M.]	*fertilizer*

engraissage [M.]	*fattening*
enivrement [M.]	*intoxication*
enjambée [F.]	*stride*
enjambement [M.]	*enjambment*
enlèvement [M.]	*kidnapping*
enracinement [M.]	*implantation*
enrichissement [M.]	*enrichment*
ensorcèlement [M.]	*witchcraft*

EXERCICE 141·1

Complétez! *Complete each sentence with the appropriate infinitive.*

1. Pour ne pas se salir les chaussures, il faut _____ les flaques d'eau dans la rue.

2. Les jeunes gens n'aiment pas s'_____ mais ils doivent emprunter de l'argent pour faire leurs études.

3. Il faut bien _____ les jeunes arbres pour qu'ils ne s'envolent pas.

4. Il faut du courage pour _____ sans l'aide du médecin.

5. Les sirènes des contes et légendes chantaient pour _____ les marins.

6. Il faut ouvrir la bouche bien grande pour _____ un gros morceau de gâteau.

7. Il vaut mieux _____ les jeunes chiots quand on n'est pas à la maison.

8. La fête de nouvel An n'est pas une excuse pour s'_____.

9. _____ les enfants à faire les devoirs est fortement conseillé.

10. Il ne faut pas _____ un animal sauvage.

11. Les parents chantent ou lisent pour _____ les bébés.

12. Il y a souvent un sorcier ou une sorcière qui veut _____ quelqu'un dans les contes.

13. Il faut étudier les préfixes pour _____ son vocabulaire.

14. Il faut _____ la terre pour augmenter le rendement.

15. Il faut _____ les jeunes gens en les faisant travailler dur.

142 ◆ em-

MEANING	Putting into
ENGLISH EQUIVALENT	—
PART OF SPEECH	Verb, adjective, noun

The French prefix **em-** often means *into*, especially if the base word is a noun. For example, the verb **embrasser** now means *to kiss*, but it was originally formed with the prefix **em-** *into*, the base word **bras** *arm*, and the infinitive ending -**er**, and meant *to take into one's arms*. In the following chart, verbs and their past participles are presented side by side to promote awareness of families of words; past participles may function as adjectives (see Appendix A).

VERB/ADJECTIVE BEGINNING IN **em-**	ENGLISH EQUIVALENT	BASE WORD	ENGLISH EQUIVALENT
emballer/emballé	*to package / packaged*	balle	*ball*
embarquer/embarqué	*to board / boarded*	barque	*boat*
embaucher/embauché	*to hire / hired*	bauc [OLD FR.]	*beam*
emboîter/emboîté	*to fit together / fit together*	boîte	*box*
(s')embourber/embourbé	*to get stuck in mud / stuck in mud*	bourbe	*mud*
embouteiller/embouteillé	*to bottle / bottled*	bouteille	*bottle*
embrasser/embrassé	*to kiss / kissed*	bras	*arm*
emmagasiner/emmagasiné	*to store / stored*	magasin	*store*
emmailloter/emmailloté	*to swaddle / swaddled*	maillot	*cloth*
emmurer/emmuré	*to wall up / walled up*	mur	*wall*
empaqueter/empaqueté	*to pack / packed*	paquet	*package*
empiéter/empiété	*to encroach / encroached*	pied	*foot*
empiler/empilé	*to pile up / piled up*	pile	*pile*
empocher/empoché	*to pocket / pocketed*	poche	*pocket*
empoigner/empoigné	*to grab / grabbed*	poigne	*grip*
emprisonner/emprisonné	*to imprison / imprisoned*	prison	*prison*

Nouns related to verbs and adjectives in the preceding chart are as follows.

emballage [M.]	*packaging*
embarquement [M.]	*boarding*
embauche [F.]	*hiring*
emboîtement [M.]	*fitting*
embourbement [M.]	*getting stuck in mud*
embouteillage [M.]	*traffic jam*
embrassade [F.]	*hugging and kissing*
emmagasinage [M.]	*warehousing*
emmaillotement [M.]	*swaddling*
emmurement [M.]	*walling up*
empiétement [M.]	*encroachment*
empilement [M.]	*piling up, pile*
empoignade [F.]	*brawl*
emprisonnement [M.]	*imprisonment*

Des synonymes! *Provide the appropriate verb for each description.*

1. Mettre en réserve _____

2. Donner un baiser _____

3. Mettre en paquet _____

4. Envelopper (un achat ou un cadeau) _____

5. Mettre en prison _____

6. S'étendre, usurper _____

7. Mettre en bouteille _____

8. Donner du travail _____

9. Construire un mur autour _____

10. Saisir avec ses mains _____

11. Entasser, faire une pile _____

12. (S')enfoncer dans la boue _____

13. Envelopper un nouveau-né _____

14. Monter à bord d'un bateau ou d'un avion _____

15. Mettre en poche _____

16. Ajuster une chose dans une autre _____

143 ⬧ en-

MEANING	Putting into
ENGLISH EQUIVALENT	—
PART OF SPEECH	Verb, adjective, noun

The French prefix **en-** often means *into*, especially if the base word is a noun. For example, the verb **encadrer** is formed with the prefix **en-** *into*, the base word **cadre** *frame*, and the infinitive ending **-er**, and means *to put into a frame*. In the following chart, verbs and their past participles are presented side by side to promote awareness of families of words; past participles may function as adjectives (see Appendix A).

VERB/ADJECTIVE BEGINNING IN **en-**	ENGLISH EQUIVALENT	BASE WORD	ENGLISH EQUIVALENT
encadrer/encadré	*to frame / framed in*	cadre	*frame*
encaisser/encaissé	*to collect / collected*	caisse	*cash register*
encapuchonner/ encapuchonné	*to put on a hood / hooded*	capuchon	*hood*
encercler/encerclé	*to surround / surrounded*	cercle	*circle* ▶

VERB/ADJECTIVE BEGINNING IN en-	ENGLISH EQUIVALENT	BASE WORD	ENGLISH EQUIVALENT
enchaîner/enchaîné	to chain / in chains	chaîne	chain
enclore/enclos	to enclosed / enclosed	clos	enclosed plot
enregistrer/enregistré	to register / registered	registre	register
enrubanner/enrubanné	to tie with a ribbon / beribboned	ruban	ribbon
ensabler/ensablé	to get stuck in sand / stuck in sand	sable	sand
enterrer/enterré	to bury / buried	terre	ground

Nouns related to verbs and adjectives in the preceding chart are as follows. All of these nouns are masculine.

encadrement	*framing*
encaissement	*collection*
encapuchonnement	*putting on a hood*
encerclement	*encirclement*
enchaînement	*chain, series*
enclos	*enclosure*
enregistrement	*enrollment*
enrubannement	*tying with a ribbon*
ensablement	*getting stuck in sand*
enterrement	*burial*

If the prefix **en-** is attached to verbs of movement, it conveys the sense of *from* or *away*.

VERB/ADJECTIVE BEGINNING IN en-	ENGLISH EQUIVALENT	BASE WORD	ENGLISH EQUIVALENT
enfuir/enfui	*to escape / escaped*	fuir	*to flee*
enlever/enlevé	*to take away / taken away*	lever	*to lift, raise*
envoler/envolé	*to fly away / flown away*	voler	*to fly*

Nouns related to verbs and adjectives in the preceding chart are as follows. Both of these nouns are masculine.

enlèvement	*kidnapping*
envol	*flight*

EXERCICE
143·1

Complétez! *Complete each sentence with the correct form of the appropriate past participle.*

1. Une fois la chanson _____, la chanteuse-compositrice touche ses droits.

2. Les chiens cherchent leurs os _____ dans le jardin.

3. Les esclaves _____ dans les cales des navires étaient sans défense.

4. L'argent _____ par le magasin durant la journée est déposé à la banque.

5. Cette photo _____ dans un cadre antique sera accrochée au salon.

6. On trouve parfois des baleines _____ le long de la côte.

7. La volaille occupe un terrain _____ et entouré d'un barbelé en fer.

8. Quel joli cadeau _____!

9. La petite fille du conte « Le petit chaperon rouge » est _____.

10. La banque où a lieu un cambriolage est rapidement _____ par la police.

11. Des adolescents qui se sont _____ du foyer sont en danger.

12. Les oiseaux _____ du nid sont devenus indépendants.

13. Une fois les obstacles _____, le parcours est facile.

144 ▶ demi-, mi-, semi-

MEANING   Half, mid, semi
ENGLISH EQUIVALENT   —, *mid-*, *semi-*
PART OF SPEECH   Noun, adjective, adverb

The French prefix **demi-**, used to form nouns only, means *half*. It is always separated from the base word by a hyphen. **Demi-** is invariable: it does not agree in gender and number with the noun it is attached to. The prefixed noun has the gender of the base noun.

NOUN BEGINNING IN **demi-**	ENGLISH EQUIVALENT	BASE WORD	ENGLISH EQUIVALENT
demi-bas [M.]	*kneesock*	bas	*sock*
demi-bouteille [F.]	*half a bottle*	bouteille	*bottle*
demi-cercle [M.]	*half a circle*	cercle	*circle*
demi-déesse [F.]	*demigoddess*	dea [LAT.]	*goddess*
demi-dieu [M.]	*demigod*	dieu	*god*
demi-douzaine [F.]	*half a dozen*	douzaine	*dozen*
demi-finale [F.]	*semifinal*	finale	*final*
demi-finaliste [M.F.]	*semifinalist*	finaliste	*finalist*
demi-frère [M.]	*half brother*	frère	*brother*
demi-heure [F.]	*half an hour*	heure	*hour*
demi-jour [M.]	*half-light*	jour	*daylight*
demi-journée [F.]	*half a day*	journée	*day*
demi-litre [M.]	*half a liter*	litre	*liter*
demi-lune [F.]	*half-moon*	lune	*moon*
demi-pension [F.]	*half-board*	pension	*board*
demi-sœur [F.]	*half sister*	sœur	*sister*
demi-tasse [F.]	*half a cup*	tasse	*cup*
demi-tour [M.]	*U-turn*	tour	*turn*

Vrai ou faux? *Indicate whether each statement is true or false, using* **V** *for* **vrai** *true or* **F** *for* **faux** *false.*

1. _____ Des demi-frères n'ont qu'un parent en commun.

2. _____ Une demi-lune est plus brillante qu'une pleine lune.

3. _____ Une demi-tasse est une tasse à peine remplie.

4. _____ Le demi-jour est la lumière de l'aube ou du crépuscule.

5. _____ Un demi-bas monte jusqu'à la cheville.

6. _____ Un demi-litre de lait se boit en une gorgée.

7. _____ La demi-finale de Wimbledon est diffusée à la télévision.

8. _____ Venus Williams était plusieurs fois demi-finaliste en gymnastique aux Jeux Olympiques.

9. _____ Une demi-heure par semaine d'exercice en plein air est suffisante pour les jeunes enfants.

10. _____ Il faut une demi-douzaine d'œufs pour faire une dizaine de crêpes.

11. _____ Dans les familles recomposées, il y a souvent des demi-sœurs et des demi-frères.

12. _____ Si on va dans la mauvaise direction, il faut prudemment faire demi-tour.

13. _____ Les hôtels offrent souvent des forfaits demi-pension.

14. _____ Un travail à temps partiel signifie parfois qu'on fait des demi-journées de travail.

15. _____ Le soleil de midi a la forme d'un demi-cercle.

16. _____ Dans l'*Iliade* et l'*Odyssée*, il y a des demi-dieux.

17. _____ Une très belle femme est parfois comparée à une demi-déesse.

18. _____ Il n'existe plus de demi-bouteilles de nos jours.

The French prefix **mi-** is affixed to a month of the year to denote the half-point of the month, as in **Nous partirons mi-juillet** *We will leave in mid-July*. The prefixed word may also be used as a feminine noun, as in **La mi-août est la période des vacances** *Mid-August is vacation time*.

If the prefix **mi-** is affixed to other nouns or adjectives, it means *half(way)* and is always separated from the base word by a hyphen, for example, **mi-charmeur** *half-charming*.

NOUN/ADJECTIVE/ADVERB BEGINNING IN **mi-**	ENGLISH EQUIVALENT	BASE WORD	ENGLISH EQUIVALENT
mi-agréable [ADJ.]	*half-pleasant*	agréable	*pleasant*
mi-août [F./ADV.]	*mid-August*	août	*August*
mi-course [F.]	*midrace*	course	*race*
mi-cuit [ADJ.]	*semicooked*	cuit	*cooked*
mi-cynique [ADJ.]	*half-cynical*	cynique	*cynical*
mi-figue mi-raisin [ADV.]	*neither here nor there*	figue, raisin	*fig, grape*

NOUN/ADJECTIVE/ADVERB BEGINNING IN **mi-**	ENGLISH EQUIVALENT	BASE WORD	ENGLISH EQUIVALENT
mi-juin [F./ADV.]	*mid-June*	juin	*June*
mi-saison [F./ADV.]	*midseason*	saison	*season*
mi-superstitieux [ADJ.]	*half-superstitious*	superstitieux	*superstitious*
mi-temps [F./ADV.]	*half-time*	temps	*time*

EXERCICE
144·2

Trouvez un qualificatif! *Provide the appropriate word for each phrase.*

1. Un personnage un peu négatif et méprisant _____

2. Une réponse équivoque _____

3. Le moment de l'année où les prix d'hôtel sont les plus élevés _____

4. Le travail à demi-journée _____

5. Celui qui croit que le vert cassé porte malheur _____

6. Le milieu du mois qui marque le début de l'été _____

7. Le milieu du mois où la plupart des Français sont en vacances _____

8. Viande un peu saignante _____

9. Un peu (mais pas trop) aimable _____

10. Moment où on a fait la moitié du parcours _____

The French prefix **semi-** means *half* and is always separated from the base word by a hyphen. It may be used before an adjective (for example, **semi-public** *semipublic*), before a noun (for example, **semi-liberté** *partial release from prison*), or before a word that functions both as an adjective and as a noun. Examples of this dual function are the phrase **arme semi-automatique** *semiautomatic weapon*, where the prefixed word is an adjective, and the sentence **Un semi-automatique est dangereux** *A semiautomatic weapon is dangerous*, where the prefixed word is a noun.

NOUN/ADJECTIVE BEGINNING IN **semi-**	ENGLISH EQUIVALENT	BASE WORD	ENGLISH EQUIVALENT
semi-automatique [M./ADJ.]	*semiautomatic*	automatique	*automatic*
semi-conducteur [M./ADJ.]	*semiconductor*	conducteur	*conductor*
semi-liberté [F.]	*partial release from prison*	liberté	*liberty*
semi-nomade [M.F./ADJ.]	*seminomad/seminomadic*	nomade	*nomad/nomadic*
semi-perméable [ADJ.]	*semipermeable*	perméable	*permeable*
semi-précieux [ADJ.]	*semiprecious*	précieux	*precious*
semi-privé [ADJ.]	*semiprivate*	privé	*private*
semi-professionnel [ADJ.]	*semiprofessional*	professionnel	*professional*
semi-public [ADJ.]	*semipublic*	public	*public*

Complétez! *Complete each sentence with the appropriate word.*

1. L'opale est une pierre _____.

2. Un appartement estudiantin est parfois une résidence _____.

3. Les artistes en herbe se contentent d'une carrière _____.

4. Les pêcheurs mettent les poissons dans des filets _____.

5. Certains prisonniers jouissent d'une _____ sur parole.

6. Certaines entreprises privées s'associent à une fonction d'état et deviennent

_____.

7. Un matériau qui ne conduit pas l'électricité de la même façon selon les conditions

ambiantes est un _____.

8. Les travailleurs agricoles saisonniers mènent une vie _____.

145 inter-

MEANING   Between, across
ENGLISH EQUIVALENT   *inter-*
PART OF SPEECH   Verb, adjective, noun

The French prefix **inter-**, used to form verbs, adjectives, and nouns, means *between* or *across*. The base word is a verb; for example, **intercaler** has as its base word **caler** *to wedge*, and the prefixed verb means *to wedge between*, that is, *to insert*. In the following chart, verbs and their past participles are presented side by side to promote awareness of families of words; past participles may function as adjectives (see Appendix A).

VERB/ADJECTIVE BEGINNING IN **inter-**	ENGLISH EQUIVALENT	BASE WORD	ENGLISH EQUIVALENT
interagir	*to interact*	agir	*to act*
intercaler/intercalé	*to insert / inserted*	caler	*to wedge*
intercéder	*to intercede*	céder	*to yield*
intercepter/intercepté	*to intercept / intercepted*	capter	*to get*
interférer/interféré	*to interfere / interfered*	férir [OLD FR.]	*to strike, hit*
interjeter/interjeté	*to lodge / lodged* (law)	jeter	*to throw*
interpeller/interpellé	*to question / questioned*	interpellare [LAT.]	*to interrupt*
interposer/interposé	*to interpose / interposed*	poser	*to put down*
interpréter/interprété	*to interpret / interpreted*	interpretari [LAT.]	*to interpret*
intervenir	*to intervene*	venir	*to come*
intervertir/interverti	*to invert / inverted*	vertere [LAT.]	*to turn*
interviewer/interviewé	*to interview / interviewed*	view [ENG.]	*to view*

Most nouns related to verbs and adjectives in the preceding chart have English cognates.

interaction [F.]	*interaction*	interpellation [F.]	*questioning*
intercalaire [M.]	*insert, divider*	interposition [F.]	*interposition*
interception [F.]	*interception*	interprétation [F.]	*interpretation*
intercession [F.]	*intercession*	intervention [F.]	*intervention*
interférence [F.]	*interference*	interversion [F.]	*inversion*
interjection [F.]	*interjection*	interview [F.]	*interview*

EXERCICE 145·1

Complétez! *Choose the best completion for each sentence.*

1. _____ Il arrive qu'on vous interpelle
2. _____ Le juge doit intercéder quand
3. _____ Il s'agit d'interpréter
4. _____ Il faut interposer une partition
5. _____ Il vaut mieux ne pas interférer
6. _____ Il est intéressant de voir interagir
7. _____ L'avocat de la défense peut
8. _____ Il suffit d'intercaler un papier
9. _____ Les parents peuvent parfois
10. _____ Les professeurs ne doivent pas
11. _____ Barbara Walters a pu
12. _____ Il est facile d'intervertir par erreur

a. des collaborateurs passionnés.
b. interviewer bon nombre de célébrités.
c. pour témoigner dans un tribunal.
d. les avocats sont belligérants.
e. intercepter des messages de leurs enfants.
f. les numéros dans un mot de passe.
g. entre les deux groupes.
h. intervenir dans la vie privée des étudiants.
i. dans les affaires des autres.
j. entre les deux pages pour marquer l'endroit.
k. interjeter appel pour son client.
l. le message sous-entendu.

146 ◆ a-

MEANING	Aiming at, directed at, rendering
ENGLISH EQUIVALENT	—
PART OF SPEECH	Verb, adjective, noun

The French prefix **a-**, used to form verbs, adjectives, and nouns, conveys a sense of direction toward an aim or goal. A variant of the prefix **a-** is used before a base word beginning in **c-**, **f-**, **l-**, **n-**, **p-**, **r-**, **s-**, or **t-**; in each case, the initial letter of the base word is doubled. For example, the verb **annuler** *to cancel* is formed with the prefix **an-**, the adjective **nul** *useless*, and the infinitive ending **-er**.

In the following charts, verbs and their past participles are presented side by side to promote awareness of families of words; past participles may function as adjectives (see Appendix A). In the first two charts, the base word is an adjective and the prefix **a-** means *to render* or *to make*. As an example, the base word for the verb **appauvrir** is the adjective **pauvre** *poor*, and the prefixed verb means *to render poor*, or *to impoverish*.

VERB/ADJECTIVE BEGINNING IN **a-**	ENGLISH EQUIVALENT	BASE WORD	ENGLISH EQUIVALENT
abaisser/abaissé	*to lower / lowered*	bas	*low*
abrutir/abruti	*to stupefy / stupefied*	brute	*raw*
adoucir/adouci	*to soften / softened*	doux	*soft*
affaiblir/affaibli	*to weaken / weakened*	faible	*weak*
affamer/affamé	*to starve / starved*	faim	*hungry*
affermir/affermi	*to strengthen / strengthened*	ferme	*firm*
affiner/affiné	*to refine / refined*	fin	*fine*
affoler/affolé	*to throw into a panic / thrown into a panic*	fou/folle	*mad*
agrandir/agrandi	*to enlarge / enlarged*	grand	*big*
ajuster/ajusté	*to adjust / adjusted*	juste	*just*
alléger/allégé	*to lighten / lightened*	léger	*light*
allonger/allongé	*to lengthen / lengthened*	long	*long*
alourdir/alourdi	*to weigh down / weighted*	lourd	*heavy*
amaigrir/amaigri	*to make thin / thinner*	maigre	*skinny*

Nouns related to verbs and adjectives in the preceding chart are as follows. All are masculine, as indicated by their suffix.

abaissement	*lowering, reduction*
abrutissement	*exhaustion, daze*
adoucissement	*softening*
affaiblissement	*weakening*
affermissement	*strengthening*
affinement	*refinement*
affolement	*panic*
agrandissement	*enlargement*
ajustement	*adjustment*
allongement	*lengthening*
alourdissement	*weight increase*
amaigrissement	*weight loss*

EXERCICE
146·1

Il faut... ou il ne faut pas... *Begin each sentence with* **Il faut** *or* **Il ne faut pas** *so that the sentence makes sense.*

1. _____ abaisser les ponts de la Seine.

2. _____ alléger notre travail.

3. _____ adoucir les draps du lit.

4. _____ amaigrir les poules.

5. _____ alourdir les livres.

6. _____ affamer les clients au resto.

7. _____ abrutir les étudiants avec trop de devoirs.

8. _____ affermir les muscles.

9. _____ affaiblir les patients à l'hôpital.

10. _____ ajuster le dispositif de la balance.

11. _____ agrandir la belle photo.

12. _____ affiner vos recherches en Français.

13. _____ allonger le pas pour aller plus vite.

14. _____ affoler les enfants qui jouent au parc.

VERB/ADJECTIVE BEGINNING IN **a-**	ENGLISH EQUIVALENT	BASE WORD	ENGLISH EQUIVALENT
amincir/aminci	*to make thinner / thinner*	mince	*thin*
amollir/amolli	*to soften / softened*	mou	*soft*
annoter/annoté	*to annotate / annotated*	note	*note*
annuler/annulé	*to cancel / cancelled*	nul	*useless*
anoblir/anobli	*to make noble / ennobled*	noble	*noble*
appauvrir/appauvri	*to impoverish / impoverished*	pauvre	*poor*
approfondir/approfondi	*to deepen / in-depth*	profond	*deep*
arrondir/arrondi	*to make round / round(ed)*	rond	*round*
atténuer/atténué	*to ease / eased*	ténu	*tenuous*
attiédir/attiédi	*to cool down / cooled down*	tiède	*lukewarm*
attrister/attristé	*to sadden / saddened*	triste	*sad*
avilir/avili	*to vilify / vilified*	vil	*vile*

Nouns related to verbs and adjectives in the preceding chart are as follows. Nearly all are masculine.

annulation [F.]	*cancellation*	atténuation [F.]	*attenuation*
anoblissement [M.]	*ennoblement*	attiédissement [M.]	*cooling*
appauvrissement [M.]	*impoverishment*	attristement [M.]	*saddening*
arrondissement [M.]	*district*	avilissement [M.]	*degradation*

EXERCICE 146·2

Complétez! *Complete each sentence with the correct form of the appropriate past participle.*

1. L'essai _____ par le professeur doit être récrit en tenant compte de ses commentaires.

2. Une forme _____ est plus jolie pour une table.

3. Des bourgeois étaient _____ en échange d'une belle somme d'argent sous Louis XIV.

4. Un personnage de roman _____ par l'auteur est détestable pour le lecteur.

5. On ne se baigne pas dans une eau bouillante; on attend qu'elle soit

_____ .

6. Le pain d'hier va être _____ dans la soupe.

7. Suite à une mauvaise économie, il y a des familles _____ de nos jours.

8. Les symptômes de la grippe peuvent être _____ par certains médicaments.

9. On est naturellement _____ par les souffrances d'autrui.

10. Une personne excessivement _____ peut être malade.

11. Une réflexion _____ est toujours à propos.

12. Un vol _____ est vraiment ennuyeux.

The following chart presents verbs along with their past participles. The prefix **a-** means *to come close to* or *to aim at*, and the base word is a noun. As an example, the base word for the verb **accompagner** is **compagne** *companion*, and the prefixed verb means *to aim at being a companion*, or *to accompany*. To synthesize the meaning of the prefix **a-** with that of the base word may require some inference.

VERB/ADJECTIVE BEGINNING IN **a-**	ENGLISH EQUIVALENT	BASE WORD	ENGLISH EQUIVALENT
accompagner/ accompagné	*to accompany / accompanied*	compagne	*companion*
accoster/accosté	*to draw alongside / drawn alongside*	côte	*coast*
accoucher/accouché	*to give birth / delivered*	couche	*bed*
accourir/accouru	*to rush up / rushed up to*	courir	*to run*
accoutumer/accoutumé	*to accustom / accustomed*	coutume	*custom*
acheminer/acheminé	*to dispatch / dispatched*	chemin	*path*
(s')affairer/affairé	*to be busy / busy*	affaire	*business*
affilier/affilié	*to affiliate / affiliated*	fils	*son*
aguerrir/aguerri	*to toughen / toughened*	guerre	*war*
ajourner/ajourné	*to adjourn / adjourned*	jour	*day*
aligner/aligné	*to align / aligned*	ligne	*line*
allaiter/allaité	*to nurse / nursed*	lait	*milk*
amasser/amassé	*to amass / amassed*	masse	*mass*
apaiser/apaisé	*to appease / appeased*	paix	*peace*
apitoyer/apitoyé	*to move to pity / moved to pity*	pitié	*pity*
approvisionner/ approvisionné	*to supply / supplied*	provision	*supply*
atterrir/atterri	*to land / landed*	terre	*land*

Nouns related to verbs and adjectives in the preceding chart are as follows. Nearly all are masculine.

accompagnement [M.]	*accompaniment*
accostage [M.]	*docking*
accouchement [M.]	*delivery*
accoutumance [F.]	*dependency, addiction*
acheminement [M.]	*transport*
affiliation [F.]	*affiliation*
ajournement [M.]	*adjournment*
alignement [M.]	*alignment*
allaitement [M.]	*nursing*
apaisement [M.]	*appeasement*
apitoiement [M.]	*compassion*
approvisionnement [M.]	*provision of supplies*
atterrissage [M.]	*landing*

EXERCICE
146·3

Définitions et synonymes! *Provide the appropriate noun for each description.*

1. Le moment où l'avion touche la terre _____

2. Le moment où le bateau touche le rivage _____

3. Le transport ou l'envoi du courrier _____

4. L'arrangement d'objets en ligne droite _____

5. L'avitaillement de provisions _____

6. Un sentiment de compassion et de pitié _____

7. Le fait de donner le sein à un bébé _____

8. Le fait de tenir compagnie à un malade _____

9. La consolation et le soulagement _____

10. Une habitude _____

11. L'enfantement _____

12. Le fait d'être membre d'une association _____

13. Le renvoi à une date plus lointaine _____

The following chart presents verbs, along with their past participles, that are formed with the prefix **as-**; this variant of the prefix **a-** is affixed to a base word that begins in **s-**. The prefix, which is usually attached to a French adjective but sometimes to a noun, conveys a sense of rendering or accomplishing. For example, combining the prefix **as-** with the adjective **sec/sèche** *dry* and the infinitive ending **-er** yields the verb **assécher** *to render dry, to dry up.* In the chart, verbs and their past participles are presented side by side to promote awareness of families of words; past participles may function as adjectives (see Appendix A). All base words are adjectives except **saillir**, **saison**, **simulare**, and **serviteur**.

VERB/ADJECTIVE BEGINNING IN **as-**	ENGLISH EQUIVALENT	BASE WORD	ENGLISH EQUIVALENT
assagir/assagi	*to calm / calmed*	sage	*well-behaved, wise*
assaillir/assailli	*to assault / assaulted*	saillir	*to jut out*
assainir/assaini	*to cleanse / cleansed*	sain	*healthy*
assaisonner/assaisonné	*to season / seasoned*	saison	*season*
assécher/asséché	*to dry up / dried up*	sec/sèche	*dry*
assembler/assemblé	*to assemble / assembled*	simulare [LAT.]	*to make similar*
asservir/asservi	*to enslave / enslaved*	serviteur	*servant*
assimiler/assimilé	*to assimilate / assimilated*	similaire	*similar*
associer/associé	*to associate / associated*	sociable	*sociable*
assourdir/assourdi	*to deafen / deafened*	sourd	*deaf*
assujettir/assujetti	*to subject / subjected*	sujet	*subject (to)*
assurer/assuré	*to assure / assured*	sûr	*sure*

Nouns related to verbs and adjectives in the preceding chart denote the act or result of performing the action of the verb; for example, **assurer** means *to ensure* and **assurance** means *assurance* or *insurance*.

assagissement [M.]	*calming down*
assainissement [M.]	*sanitation, clean-up*
assaisonnement [M.]	*seasoning*
assaut [M.]	*assault*
asséchement [M.]	*drying up*
assemblage [M.]	*assembly* (of components)
assemblée [F.]	*assembly, meeting*
assemblement [M.]	*piecing together*
asservissement [M.]	*enslavement*
assimilation [F.]	*assimilation*
association [F.]	*association*
assourdissement [M.]	*deafening*
assujettissement [M.]	*subjection (to)*
assurance [F.]	*assurance, insurance*

EXERCICE

146·4

Vrai ou faux? *Indicate whether each statement is true or false, using* **V** *for* **vrai** *true or* **F** *for* **faux** *false.*

1. _____ Sous le colonialisme, les populations indigènes étaient assujetties.

2. _____ La plupart des gens préfèrent leurs plats sans assaisonnement.

3. _____ L'assurance-vie protège contre les maladies.

4. _____ Après les accidents pétroliers dans l'océan, il faut de grandes opérations d'assainissement.

5. _____ Après un concert de rock, on se sent totalement assourdi.

6. _____ Une terre asséchée portera plus de fruits et de légumes.

7. _____ Certains adolescents difficiles s'assagissent avec l'âge.

8. _____ L'assimilation des nutriments par le corps dépend seulement de l'âge.

9. _____ Certaines œuvres d'art moderne sont des assemblements de pièces disparates.

10. _____ Le président Clinton a subi des assauts concernant sa vie privée.

11. _____ Un pays régi par un dictateur se donne comme but d'asservir les médias.

12. _____ Il ne faut pas s'associer à un projet qui est déjà en place.

 **dia-**

MEANING	Across
ENGLISH EQUIVALENT	*dia-*
PART OF SPEECH	Noun, adjective, verb

The French prefix **dia-** means *across*. It is typically used to form nouns that have a Greek root for a base word. Since most of these nouns have English cognates, they tend to be easily recognized. The prefix is also used to form some adjectives and verbs, which also have English cognates.

NOUN BEGINNING IN **dia-**	ENGLISH EQUIVALENT	BASE WORD	ENGLISH EQUIVALENT
diabète [M.]	*diabetes*	diabetes [LAT.]	*diabetes*
diachronie [F.]	*diachrony*	chronos [GRK.]	*time*
diagnostic [M.]	*diagnostic*	gnostikos [GRK.]	*knowledge*
diagramme [M.]	*diagram*	[-gramme]	*letter, sign*
dialecte [M.]	*dialect*	legein [GRK.]	*to speak*
dialogue [M.]	*dialogue*	logos [GRK.]	*speech*
dialyse [F.]	*dialysis*	luein [GRK.]	*to dissolve, loosen*
diamètre [M.]	*diameter*	[-métrie]	*measurement*
diaphonie [F.]	*crosstalk*	diaphonia [GRK.]	*discordance*
diaphragme [M.]	*diaphragm*	phrattein [GRK.]	*to barricade*
diaspora [F.]	*diaspora*	speirein [GRK.]	*to scatter*
diatribe [F.]	*diatribe*	tribein [GRK.]	*to remain*

Adjectives related to nouns in the preceding chart are as follows.

diabétique	*diabetic*
diachronique	*diachronic*
dialectique	*dialectical*

Verbs related to nouns in the preceding chart are as follows.

diagnostiquer	*to diagnose*
dialoguer	*to dialogue*
dialyser	*to perform dialysis*

EXERCICE
147·1

Charade! *Provide the noun that corresponds to each pair of clues.*

1. Groupe d'expatriés, communauté _____

2. Langue, évolution _____

3. Deux signaux, interférence _____

4. Graphique, tracé géométrique _____

5. Ligne passant par le milieu, cercle _____

6. Entre poitrine et abdomen, muscle _____

7. Langue, patois _____

8. Trouble du métabolisme, glucides _____

9. Épuration du sang, filtration _____

10. Tirade, critique _____

11. Deux personnes, conversation _____

12. Jugement, examen de symptômes _____

 ortho-

MEANING	Straight, correct
ENGLISH EQUIVALENT	*ortho-*
PART OF SPEECH	Noun, adjective

The French prefix **ortho-**, used to form nouns and adjectives, is a Greek root meaning *straight* or *correct*. For example, the prefix **ortho-** attached to the base word **odous** *tooth* yields the noun **orthodontie** *science/skill of straightening teeth*, as well as the noun **orthodontiste** *orthodontist*. Similarly, the nouns **orthopédie** *science/skill of straightening bones* and **orthopédiste** *orthopedic specialist* are formed with the prefix **ortho-**, the Greek root **paidos** *child*, and the suffixes **-ie** and **-iste**, respectively. Using the suffix **-ique** yields the adjective **orthopédique** *orthopedic*; see Part I for the meaning of the suffixes **-ie**, **-iste**, and **-ique**. Note that **orthodoxe** and **orthopédiste** may function both as nouns and as adjectives.

While most of the French prefixed words in the following chart have English cognates, they tend to be scientific terms; an *orthoscope* is an instrument used to examine the superficial parts of the eye and *orthophony* is speech therapy.

NOUN/ADJECTIVE BEGINNING IN **ortho-**	ENGLISH EQUIVALENT	BASE WORD	ENGLISH EQUIVALENT
orthodontie [F.]	*orthodontics*	odous [GRK.]	*tooth*
orthodontiste [M.F.]	*orthodontist*	odous [GRK.]	*tooth*
orthodoxe [M.F./ADJ.]	*orthodox (person)*	doxa [GRK.]	*opinion*
orthodoxie [F.]	*orthodoxy*	doxa [GRK.]	*opinion*
orthographe [F.]	*spelling*	[-graphe]	*written image*
orthographie [F.]	*building profile, elevation*	[-graphe]	*written image*
orthographique [ADJ.]	*spelling*	[-graphe]	*written image*
orthopédie [F.]	*orthopedics*	paidos [GRK.]	*child*
orthopédique [ADJ.]	*orthopedic*	paidos [GRK.]	*child*
orthopédiste [M.F./ADJ.]	*orthopedic specialist*	paidos [GRK.]	*child*
orthophonie [F.]	*orthophony*	[-phone]	*sound, voice*
orthophoniste [M.F.]	*orthophonist*	[-phone]	*sound, voice*
orthoscope [M.]	*orthoscope*	skopein [GRK.]	*to look at*
orthoscopie [F.]	*orthoscopy*	skopein [GRK.]	*to look at*
orthoscopique [ADJ.]	*orthoscopic*	skopein [GRK.]	*to look at*

EXERCICE 148·1

Spécialisons-nous! *Provide the appropriate words to complete each sentence of the paragraph.*

(1) L'_____ est un spécialiste en (2) _____, la rééducation des troubles de l'élocution. L'ophtalmologiste, lui, traite les troubles de l'œil;

il fait un diagnostic basé sur (3) l'_____ (un examen de l'œil)

faite avec un appareil qui s'appelle (4) l'_____. En outre,

(5) l'_____ se spécialise dans (6) l'_____,

la correction des affections des os. La chirurgie (7) _____ vise

à remédier aux malformations de l'appareil locomoteur. Quant à

(8) l'_____, il fait de (9) l'_____ qui

consiste à corriger les malpositions dentaires. Nous devrions tous être spécialisés en

(10) _____, l'art d'écrire correctement, mais probablement pas

en (11) _____—à moins d'être architectes. Finalement, il reste

à dire que (12) l'_____ est le conformisme à une doctrine et

(13) l'_____ est celui ou celle qui suit cette doctrine.

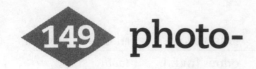 **149** ◆ **photo-**

MEANING	By means of light
ENGLISH EQUIVALENT	*photo-*
PART OF SPEECH	Noun, adjective, verb

The French prefix **photo-**, used to form nouns and adjectives as well as a few verbs, is a Greek root meaning *light*. The base word for the noun **photocopie** is **copie** *copy*, and the prefixed noun means a copy produced by means of light, or *photocopy*. Similarly, the noun **photographie** is formed with the prefix **photo-** and the French suffix **-graphie** (from the Greek root **graphein** *to write, to paint*), and the prefixed noun means a visual representation by means of exposure to light, or *photography*. In the following chart, the nouns are feminine except **photographe**, which may signify a male or female *photographer*.

NOUN BEGINNING IN **photo-**	ENGLISH EQUIVALENT	BASE WORD	ENGLISH EQUIVALENT
photochimie [F.]	*photochemistry*	chimie	*chemistry*
photoconductivité [F.]	*photoconductivity*	conductivité	*conductivity*
photocopie [F.]	*photocopy*	copie	*copy*
photocopieuse [F.]	*photocopier*	copier	*to copy*
photogénie [F.]	*photogenesis*	[-génie]	*creation, production*
photographe [M.F.]	*photographer*	[-graphe]	*written image*
photographie [F.]	*photography*	[-graphe]	*written image*
photogravure [F.]	*photoengraving*	gravure	*engraving*
photométrie [F.]	*photometry*	[-métrie]	*measurement*
photosynthèse [F.]	*photosynthesis*	synthèse	*synthesis*

Adjectives related to nouns in the preceding chart are as follows.

photochimique	*photochemical*
photoconducteur	*photoconductive*
photocopié	*photocopied*
photogénique	*photogenic*
photographié	*photographed*
photographique	*photographic*
photométrique	*photometric*
photosynthétique	*photosynthetic*

Verbs related to nouns in the preceding chart are as follows.

photocopier	*to photocopy*
photographier	*to photograph*
photograver	*to photoengrave*

EXERCICE
149·1

Définitions! *Provide the appropriate noun for each description.*

1. Une machine qui sert à faire des copies   _____

2. La reproduction fidèle d'une image   _____

3. Caractère d'une image photographique de bonne qualité   _____

4. Technique de gravure photochimique   _____

5. Reproduction xérographique   _____

6. La chimie consacrée aux rayonnements lumineux   _____

7. Celui ou celle qui prends des photos   _____

8. Étude de la mesure d'intensité lumineuse   _____

9. Synthèse de glucides dans le monde végétal à partir de l'énergie de la lumière   _____

10. Variation de la conductivité électrique sous l'action du rayonnement lumineux   _____

 **150** épi-

MEANING	Over, toward, focused on
ENGLISH EQUIVALENT	*epi-*
PART OF SPEECH	Noun, adjective

The French prefix **épi-**, used to form nouns and adjectives, means *over*, *toward*, or *focused on*. For example, the base word for the noun **épicentre** is **centre** *center*, and the prefixed noun means *toward* or *at the center*; in geology, it refers to the focal point of an earthquake. Similarly, the noun **épidémie** is formed with the prefix **épi-** and the suffix **-démie** (from the Greek noun **demos** *people*), and the prefixed noun means a rapidly spreading, harmful occurrence that affects a large number of people, or *epidemic*. Although French words formed with the prefix **épi-** have English cognates, some are technical terms and may require interpretation beyond the combination of prefix and base word. For example, the noun **épicycle** denotes a small circle whose center is on the circumference of a larger circle; by extension, it signifies a process occurring within a larger process. Other examples are the noun **épigraphe** (an inscription or a quotation at the beginning of a piece of writing), the noun **épigramme** (a short poem of a pointed or satirical nature), and the noun **épilogue** (the conclusion of a book or play).

NOUN BEGINNING IN **épi-**	ENGLISH EQUIVALENT	BASE WORD	ENGLISH EQUIVALENT
épicentre [M.]	*epicenter*	centre	*center*
épicycle [M.]	*epicycle*	cycle	*cycle*
épidémie [F.]	*epidemic*	demos [GRK.]	*people*
épiderme [M.]	*outer layer of the skin*	derma [GRK.]	*skin*
épigramme [F.]	*epigram*	[-gramme]	*letter, sign*
épigraphe [M.]	*epigraph*	[-graphe]	*written image*
épilepsie [F.]	*epilepsy*	epilambanein [GRK.]	*to seize*
épilogue [M.]	*epilogue*	logos [GRK.]	*speech*
épiphanie [F.]	*epiphany*	epiphaneia [GRK.]	*appearance*
épisode [M.]	*episode*	epeisodion [GRK.]	*episode*

Adjectives related to nouns in the preceding chart are as follows.

épicentrique	*epicentric*
épicyclique	*epicyclical*
épidémique	*epidemic*
épidermique	*epidermic*
épigraphique	*epigraphical*
épileptique	*epileptic*
épiphanique	*epiphanic*
épisodique	*episodic*

EXERCICE
150·1

Une histoire! *Provide the appropriate word(s) to complete each sentence of the paragraph.*

Quand un scénariste écrit les (1) _____ d'un feuilleton qui a lieu

au Moyen Âge, il envisage des fléaux et des (2) _____ . Il doit

aussi y avoir des personnes qui ont l'air démentes mais qui souffrent tout simplement

(3) d'_____ . Il y aura, de plus, de multiples tombes avec des

(4) _____ . Éventuellement, il doit y avoir une

(5) _____ où les gens arrêtent de mourir et tout retourne

à la normalité. Mais non! Malheureusement, il y a alors un séisme avec

(6) l'_____ en plein milieu d'une communauté active

et florissante. Un savant affirme que c'est la conséquence naturelle d'un

(7) _____ , mais on ne le croit pas; on le traite d'hérétique

et on lui brûle (8) l'_____ . Un ménestrel lui dédie une

(9) _____ . Quel est (10) l'_____ de cette

histoire? À vous de l'écrire!

151 ◆ équi-

MEANING	Equal
ENGLISH EQUIVALENT	*equi-*
PART OF SPEECH	Noun, adjective, verb

The French prefix **équi-**, used to form nouns, adjectives, and verbs, means *equal*. For example, the base word for the noun **équilibre** is the Latin noun **libra** *balance*, and the prefixed word means equal balance, or *equilibrium*. Similarly, the base word for the noun **équinoxe** is the Latin noun **nox** *night*, and the prefixed noun denotes the time of year when the length of the day equals that of the night. Another example is the adjective **équidistant**, which is formed with the prefix **équi-** and the base word **distant** and means equally distant, or *equidistant*. Since most French words formed with the prefix **équi-** have English cognates, they tend to be easily recognized.

NOUN/ADJECTIVE/VERB BEGINNING IN **équi-**	ENGLISH EQUIVALENT	BASE WORD	ENGLISH EQUIVALENT
équidistance [F.]	*equidistance*	distance	*distance*
équidistant [ADJ.]	*equidistant*	distant	*distant*
équilatéral [ADJ.]	*equilateral*	latéral	*lateral*
équilibre [M.]	*equilibrium*	libra [LAT.]	*balance*
équilibrer/équilibré	*to balance / balanced*	libra [LAT.]	*balance*
équinoxe [F.]	*equinox*	nox [LAT.]	*night*
équipotent [ADJ.]	*equipotent*	potens [LAT.]	*powerful*
équipotentiel [ADJ.]	*equipotential*	potentiel	*potential*
équitable [ADJ.]	*equitable*	aequitas [LAT.]	*uniformity, fairness*
équité [F.]	*equity*	aequitas [LAT.]	*uniformity, fairness*
équivalent [ADJ.]	*equivalent*	valoir	*to be worth*
équivoque [F./ADJ.]	*ambivalence/equivocal*	vocare [LAT.]	*to name*

EXERCICE
151·1

Définitions et synonymes! *Provide the appropriate word for each description.*

1. Deux termes de la même puissance _____

2. Semblable _____

3. Impartialité _____

4. Malentendu _____

5. Qui a le même potentiel _____

6. Juste _____

7. Situé à égale distance d'un point de référence _____

8. Caractère de ce qui est à égale distance _____

9. Position stable _____

10. Qui est en équilibre   _____

11. Période de l'année où le soleil passe par l'équateur   _____

12. Caractère d'une forme aux côtés égaux   _____

152 ◆ eu-

MEANING	Well, well-being
ENGLISH EQUIVALENT	*eu-*
PART OF SPEECH	Noun, adjective

The French prefix **eu-**, used mostly to form nouns, means *well* or *well-being*. The prefixed words have English cognates, but they may be somewhat technical. For example, the base word for the noun **eugénisme** is the French suffix **-génie** (from a Greek root meaning *creation*, *production*), and the prefixed noun denotes the production of well-being, or *eugenics* (the science of improving humankind by controlled breeding). Other examples are the noun **euphémisme** (whose base word is the Greek noun **pheme** *speech* and which denotes a mild expression as a substitute for a harsh one), the noun **eurythmie** (which is formed with the prefix **eu-** and the Greek root meaning *rhythm* and denotes a system of body movements to the rhythm of spoken words), the noun **euthanasie** (which is formed with the prefix **eu-** and the Greek root for *death* and denotes killing a sick or injured person to prevent further suffering), the noun **eucharistie** (whose base word is the Greek root for *grace* and which denotes a Christian ritual conferring grace), and the noun **euphonie** (whose base word is the Greek root for *sound* and which denotes a sequence of words with a pleasing sound).

NOUN BEGINNING IN **eu-**	ENGLISH EQUIVALENT	BASE WORD	ENGLISH EQUIVALENT
eucharistie [F.]	*eucharist*	eucharistia [LAT.]	*giving thanks*
eugénisme [M.]	*eugenics*	[-génie]	*creation*
eulogie [F.]	*eulogy*	eulogia [GRK.]	*benediction*
euphémisme [M.]	*euphemism*	pheme [GRK.]	*speech*
euphonie [F.]	*euphony*	[-phone]	*sound, voice*
euphorie [F.]	*euphoria*	pherein [GRK.]	*to carry*
eupnée [F.]	*normal breathing*	eupnoia [GRK.]	*normal breathing*
eurythmie [F.]	*eurythmics*	rythme	*rhythm*
euthanasie [F.]	*euthanasia*	thanatos [GRK.]	*death*
eutonie [F.]	*eutonia, eutony*	tonus [LAT.]	*tone*

Adjectives related to nouns in the preceding chart are as follows.

eucharistique	*eucharistic*
eugéniste	*eugenic*
euphonique	*euphonious*
euphorique	*euphoric*
eurythmique	*eurythmic*

Complétez! *Choose the best completion for each sentence.*

1. _____ L'eurythmie est la combinaison
2. _____ L'euphonie est une
3. _____ L'eugénisme vise à
4. _____ Le but de l'euthanasie
5. _____ L'euphorie est une
6. _____ L'eulogie est une
7. _____ L'eutonie est une technique
8. _____ L'eucharistie est un sacrement
9. _____ L'euphémisme consiste à
10. _____ L'eupnée est

a. une respiration normale.

b. est une mort sans souffrance.

c. sensation intense de bien-être.

d. qui commémore le sacrifice du Christ.

e. qui vise à développer un bon état physique et mental.

f. atténuer la grossièreté ou le choc.

g. améliorer le patrimoine génétique.

h. harmonie musicale.

i. bénédiction dans une cérémonie chrétienne.

j. harmonieuse de sons, de gestes ou de couleurs.

 **géo-**

MEANING	Earth
ENGLISH EQUIVALENT	*geo-*
PART OF SPEECH	Noun, adjective

The French prefix **géo-**, used to form many nouns and some adjectives, has a Greek root meaning *earth*. The base word for the noun **géochimie** is **chimie** *chemistry*, and the prefixed noun means chemistry of the earth, or *geochemistry*. Since French nouns formed with **géo-** have English cognates, they are easy to recognize.

NOUN BEGINNING IN **géo-**	ENGLISH EQUIVALENT	BASE WORD	ENGLISH EQUIVALENT
géochimie [F.]	*geochemistry*	chimie	*chemistry*
géochimiste [M.F.]	*geochemist*	chimiste	*chemist*
géographe [M.F.]	*geographer*	[-graphie]	*writing*
géographie [F.]	*geography*	[-graphie]	*writing*
géologie [F.]	*geology*	[-ologie]	*study*
géologiste [M.F.]	*geologist*	[-ologiste]	*expert*
géologue [M.F.]	*geologist*	[-ologue]	*expert*
géomagnétisme [M.]	*geomagnetism*	magnétisme	*magnetism*
géométrie [F.]	*geometry*	[-métrie]	*measurement*
géomorphologie [F.]	*geomorphology*	morphologie	*morphology*
géomorphologiste [M.F.]	*geomorphologist*	morphologie	*morphology*
géophile [M.F.]	*geophile*	[-phile]	*passionate*
géothermie [F.]	*geothermal energy*	therme [GRK.]	*heat*

Adjectives related to nouns in the preceding chart are as follows.

géochimique	*geochemical*
géographique	*geographical*
géologique	*geological*
géomagnétique	*geomagnetic*
géométrique	*geometrical*
géomorphologique	*geomorphological*
géothermique	*geothermic*

EXERCICE
153·1

Améliorons nos connaissances géo! *Provide the appropriate word(s) to complete each sentence of the paragraph.*

Étés-vous passionnées par tout ce qui concerne notre planète? Alors, vous êtes

(1) _____! Vous n'avez peut-être pas étudié les formes

du relief terrestre, c'est-à-dire la (2) _____? Seuls, les

(3) _____ ont fait ce genre d'études. Par contre, vous

n'avez pas besoin d'être (4) _____ pour savoir un peu de

(5) _____; vous connaissez les grandes chaînes de montagne

et les grands fleuves américains, n'est-ce pas? Savez-vous qu'il y a des experts du

(6) _____ terrestre? Ils se spécialisent dans l'étude des champs

(7) _____ et ils étudient l'influence qu'exerce le soleil sur la

planète: c'est une des missions de l'Agence spatiale européenne (ESA). Le centre

nationale de recherches scientifiques (CNRS) fait des études sur l'énergie

(8) _____ pour qu'on puisse disposer d'eau chaude dans sa maison;

la (9) _____ est une forme d'énergie renouvelable. Savez-vous

ce que font les (10) _____? Ces experts de la

(11) _____ étudient les différentes matières qui composent

le globe terrestre. Mais ce sont les (12) _____ qui étudient la

(13) _____, la composition et les réactions chimiques de l'écorce

terrestre. Finalement, il ne reste qu'à mentionner la (14) _____,

cette science qui a pour objet les relations entre points, lignes droites, courbes, surfaces,

volumes et espaces. Ce sera pour une autre fois!

 **154** ⟩ **hélio-**

MEANING	Sun
ENGLISH EQUIVALENT	*helio-*
PART OF SPEECH	Noun, adjective

The French prefix **hélio-**, used to form nouns and adjectives, has a Greek root meaning *sun*. The base word for the noun **héliographe** is the French suffix **-graphe** (from the Greek root **graphein** *to write, to paint*), and the prefixed noun denotes an instrument that measures the amount of sunshine. Other examples are the noun **héliostat** (whose base word is the suffix **-stat**, from the Greek root meaning *stationary*, and which denotes a modern instrument used to produce solar power) and the noun **héliotrope** (whose base word is the Greek noun **tropos** *turn* and which denotes a plant that turns toward the sun).

NOUN BEGINNING IN **hélio-**	ENGLISH EQUIVALENT	BASE WORD	ENGLISH EQUIVALENT
héliocentrisme [M.]	*heliocentrism*	centre	*center*
héliographe [M.F.]	*heliograph*	[-graphe]	*written image*
héliographie [F.]	*heliography*	[-graphe]	*written image*
héliograveur [M.]	*helioengraver*	graveur	*engraver*
héliogravure [F.]	*helioengraving*	gravure	*engraving*
héliophile [M.F.]	*sun lover*	[-phile]	*passionate*
héliostat [M.]	*heliostat*	statos [GRK.]	*stationary*
héliothérapie [F.]	*heliotherapy*	thérapie	*therapy*
héliotrope [M.]	*heliotrope*	tropos [GRK.]	*turn*
héliotropie [M.]	*heliotropism*	tropos [GRK.]	*turn*

Adjectives related to nouns in the preceding chart are as follows.

héliographique	*heliographic*
héliothérapique	*heliotherapeutic*

Other adjectives formed with the prefix **hélio-** are as follows.

hélio-électrique	*helioelectric*
héliofuge	*heliofugal*
héliomarin	*heliotherapeutic by the sea*

 EXERCICE 154·1

Définitions! *Provide the appropriate noun for each description.*

1. Une plante comme le tournesol _____

2. Procédé de gravure par voie photomécanique _____

3. Théorie selon laquelle la terre tourne autour du soleil _____

4. Terme de botanique qui décrit l'acte de tourner _____

5. Traitement de maladie par la lumière solaire _____

6. Celui ou celle qui adore le soleil _____

7. Instrument de mesure de l'intensité du soleil sur un point de la terre _____

8. Étude et description du soleil _____

9. Miroir qui reflète les rayons solaires synchronisé avec la rotation de la terre _____

10. Celui qui fait de l'héliogravure _____

Other prefixes that refer to an element of nature are as follows.

hydro- *water*   hydrogène *hydrogen*   hydrolyse *hydrolysis*
pyro- *fire*   pyrogène *pyrogen*   pyromanie *pyromania*

 **155 hétéro-**

MEANING	Other, different
ENGLISH EQUIVALENT	*hetero-*
PART OF SPEECH	Noun, adjective

The French prefix **hétéro-**, used to form nouns and adjectives, has a Greek root meaning *other* or *different*. It is chiefly used in biological terms. For example, the base word for the noun **hétéro-chromosome** is the noun **chromosome**, and the prefixed noun denotes the sex chromosome. Similarly, the base word for the noun **hétérogamie** is the suffix **-gamie** (from the Greek root meaning *marriage, union*), and the prefixed noun denotes a union between different sexes. In the following chart, note that **hétérosexuel** may function as both a noun and an adjective.

NOUN/ADJECTIVE BEGINNING IN **hétéro-**	ENGLISH EQUIVALENT	BASE WORD	ENGLISH EQUIVALENT
hétérocentrique [ADJ.]	*heterocentric*	centre	*center*
hétérochromosome [M.]	*heterochromosome*	chromosome	*chromosome*
hétéroclite [ADJ.]	*heterogeneous, motley*	heteroclitus [LAT.]	*irregular changes*
hétérocyclique [ADJ.]	*heterocyclic*	cycle	*cycle*
hétérodoxe [ADJ.]	*heterodox*	doxa [GRK.]	*belief*
hétérogamie [F.]	*heterogamy*	[-gamie]	*marriage, union*
hétérogène [ADJ.]	*mixed, miscellaneous*	[-gène]	*creation*
hétérogénéité [F.]	*heterogeneity*	[-gène]	*creation*
hétérologue [ADJ.]	*heterologous*	logos [GRK.]	*speech*
hétéromorphisme [M.]	*heteromorphism*	morphe [GRK.]	*shape*
hétérosexualité [F.]	*heterosexuality*	sexualité	*sexuality*
hétérosexuel(le) [M.F./ADJ.]	*heterosexual*	sexuel	*sexual*
hétérotrophe [ADJ.]	*heterotrophic*	trophe [GRK.]	*nourishment, growth*
hétérotrophie [F.]	*heterotrophy*	trophe [GRK.]	*nourishment, growth*

EXERCICE 155·1

Vrai ou faux? *Indicate whether each statement is true or false, using* **V** *for* **vrai** *true or* **F** *for* **faux** *false.*

1. _____ Les hétérosexuels sont attirés par les personnes du sexe opposé.

2. _____ Un corps hétérologue est différent de tout ce qu'on connaît.

3. _____ L'hétéromorphisme est une affliction médicale.

4. _____ L'hétérogamie est synonyme de bigamie.

5. _____ L'adjectif « hétérocyclique » est relatif à une chaîne fermée de composants organiques.

6. _____ Un organisme hétérotrophe a besoin de nourriture organique.

7. _____ L'hétérogénie est l'apparition de caractères identiques au cours des générations.

8. _____ Une personne hétérocentrique veut être adorée de tous.

9. _____ L'hétérochromosome est celui dont dépend le sexe.

10. _____ Une collection hétéroclite est faite d'articles bien assortis.

11. _____ Une personne hétérodoxe s'écarte de la pensée traditionnelle de son milieu.

12. _____ On trouve un ensemble hétérogène de tournures de style dans les médias.

156 ⬥ homo-

MEANING	Same, common
ENGLISH EQUIVALENT	*homo-*
PART OF SPEECH	Noun, adjective

The French prefix **homo-**, used to form nouns and adjectives, means *same* or *common*. For example, the base word for the noun **homophone** is the Greek root meaning *sound* or *voice*, and the prefixed noun denotes words that sound alike, such as *bear* and *bare*. Other examples are the adjective **homogène** (whose base word is **gène** *creation* and which means *of the same kind*) and the adjective **homologue** (whose base word is the Greek word **logos** *speech* and which denotes similarity in structure, position, or function).

NOUN/ADJECTIVE BEGINNING IN **homo-**	ENGLISH EQUIVALENT	BASE WORD	ENGLISH EQUIVALENT
homocentrique [ADJ.]	*homocentric*	centre	*center*
homocyclique [ADJ.]	*homocyclic*	cycle	*cycle*
homogène [ADJ.]	*homogeneous*	[-gène]	*creation*
homogénéité [F.]	*homogeneity*	[-gène]	*creation*
homologue [M.F./ADJ.]	*homologue/homologous*	logos [GRK.]	*speech*
homonyme [M./ADJ.]	*homonymous*	onoma [GRK.]	*name*
homophone [M./ADJ.]	*homophone*	[-phone]	*sound* ▶

NOUN/ADJECTIVE BEGINNING IN **homo-**	ENGLISH EQUIVALENT	BASE WORD	ENGLISH EQUIVALENT
homophonie [F.]	*homophony*	[-phone]	*sound*
homosexualité [F.]	*homosexuality*	sexualité	*sexuality*
homosexuel(le) [M.F./ADJ.]	*homosexual*	sexuel	*sexual*

Des antonymes! *Provide the word that means the opposite of each item.*

1. L'opposé _____

2. La cacophonie _____

3. Hétérosexualité _____

4. Hétérocyclique _____

5. Hétérogène _____

6. Hétérocentrique _____

7. Personne portant un nom différent du sien _____

8. Des mots de prononciation différente _____

9. Hétérogénéité _____

10. Hétérosexuelle _____

 **allo-**

MEANING	Other
ENGLISH EQUIVALENT	*allo-*
PART OF SPEECH	Noun, adjective

The French prefix **allo-**, used to form nouns and adjectives, means *other*. For example, the base word for the noun **allopathie** is the suffix **-pathie** (from the Greek word **pathos** *suffering*), and the prefixed word denotes a system of medicine that uses remedies with effects different from those produced by the disease, as opposed to homeopathic medicine. Another example is **allogamie**, whose base word is **gamos** *marriage, union* and which means pollination of one flower with another flower's pollen.

NOUN/ADJECTIVE BEGINNING IN **allo-**	ENGLISH EQUIVALENT	BASE WORD	ENGLISH EQUIVALENT
allocentrisme [M.]	*other-directedness*	centrisme	*centrism*
allocentriste [M.F./ADJ.]	*other-directed (person)*	centriste	*centrist*
allochtone [M.F./ADJ.]	*foreign-born (person)*	chtonos [GRK.]	*land*
allogamie [F.]	*allogamy*	gamos [GRK.]	*marriage, union*

NOUN/ADJECTIVE BEGINNING IN **allo-**	ENGLISH EQUIVALENT	BASE WORD	ENGLISH EQUIVALENT
allogène [M.F.]	*nonnative*	allogenes [GRK.]	*born elsewhere*
allopathe [M.]	*allopathic doctor*	[-pathie]	*suffering*
allopathie [F.]	*allopathy*	[-pathie]	*suffering*

EXERCICE 157·1

Vrai ou faux? *Indicate whether each statement is true or false, using* **V** *for* **vrai** *true or* **F** *for* **faux** *false.*

1. _____ L'allopathe est un malade.

2. _____ Les allogènes sont minoritaires dans un pays.

3. _____ L'allopathie est une forme de misogynie.

4. _____ L'allogamie est la pollinisation d'une fleur par le pollen d'une autre fleur.

5. _____ L'allocentrisme est la tendance à centrer son attention sur les autres.

6. _____ Une personne allocentriste est égoïste.

7. _____ Le mot « allochtone » est un synonyme plus moderne du mot « allogène ».

158 holo-

MEANING	Whole
ENGLISH EQUIVALENT	*holo-*
PART OF SPEECH	Noun, adjective

The French prefix **holo-**, used to form nouns and adjectives, is derived from a Greek root meaning *whole*. The base word is usually a Greek root that points to the meaning of the prefixed word.

NOUN/ADJECTIVE BEGINNING IN **holo-**	ENGLISH EQUIVALENT	BASE WORD	ENGLISH EQUIVALENT
holocauste [M.]	*holocaust*	kaustos [GRK.]	*burnt*
holocène [M./ADJ.]	*Holocene* (geological period)	kainos [GRK.]	*new*
holocristalline [ADJ.]	*holocrystal*	cristal	*crystal*
hologramme [M.]	*hologram*	[-gramme]	*letter, sign*
holographie [F.]	*holography*	[-graphie]	*writing, painting*
holographique [ADJ.]	*holographic*	[-graphe]	*visual representation*
holométabole [ADJ.]	*Holometabola* (insect)	metabole [GRK.]	*transformation*
holophrastique [ADJ.]	*holophrastic*	phrase	*sentence*
holoprotéine [F.]	*holoprotein*	protéine	*protein*
holotropique [ADJ.]	*holotropic*	tropos [GRK.]	*turn*

EXERCICE
158·1

Complétez! *Complete each sentence with the appropriate word.*

1. Une langue _____ est une langue dans laquelle une phrase toute entière est contenue dans un seul mot.

2. Une roche _____ est constituée entièrement de cristaux.

3. Les insectes qui ont des métamorphoses complètes sont _____.

4. Un _____ est une image en relief (comme dans Star Trek).

5. La mémoire _____ est une technique de mémoire de masse.

6. La respiration _____ permet d'accéder à une vision unifiée des différents plans de l'être (physique et psychologique).

7. Une _____ est constituée entièrement par des acides aminés.

8. L'_____ est une méthode photographique qui permet de restituer un objet en trois dimensions.

9. On se sert du terme « _____ » pour parler de l'extermination des Juifs par les nazis.

10. La période du quaternaire, 7 000 ans avant notre ère, s'appelle _____.

159 ◆ cosmo-

MEANING	Universe
ENGLISH EQUIVALENT	*cosmo-*
PART OF SPEECH	Noun, adjective

The French prefix **cosmo-**, used to form nouns and adjectives, is derived from a Greek root meaning *universe*. The base word is often a Greek word that points to the meaning of the prefixed word.

NOUN/ADJECTIVE BEGINNING IN **cosmo-**	ENGLISH EQUIVALENT	BASE WORD	ENGLISH EQUIVALENT
cosmodrome [M.]	*cosmodrome*	dromos [GRK.]	*race*
cosmogonie [F.]	*cosmogony*	gonos [GRK.]	*procreation*
cosmographie [F.]	*cosmography*	[-graphie]	*writing, painting*
cosmologie [F.]	*cosmology*	[-ologie]	*science, study*
cosmologiste [M.F.]	*cosmologist*	[-ologiste]	*expert, specialist*
cosmologue [M.F.]	*cosmologist*	[-ologue]	*expert, specialist*
cosmonaute [M.F.]	*cosmonaut*	[-naute]	*navigator*
cosmopolite [M./ADJ.]	*globetrotter / cosmopolitan*	polites [GRK.]	*citizen*
cosmopolitisme [M.]	*cosmopolitanism*	polites [GRK.]	*citizen*

Adjectives related to nouns in the preceding chart are as follows.

cosmogonique   *cosmogonical*
cosmographique *cosmographic*
cosmologique   *cosmological*

EXERCICE
159·1

Définitions! *Provide the appropriate word for each description.*

1. Astronaute   _____

2. Ensemble des mythes sur la naissance de l'univers   _____

3. Domaine métaphysique traitant de l'origine du monde   _____

4. Terrain de lancement d'engins spatiaux   _____

5. Qualité d'une personne ouverte aux autres nations   _____

6. Étude consacrée aux mouvements des corps célestes   _____

7. Spécialiste de l'évolution de l'univers spatial   _____

8. Doctrine de ceux qui se considèrent des « citoyens du   _____
   monde »

 **dys-**

MEANING	Bad, painful, defective
ENGLISH EQUIVALENT	*dys-*
PART OF SPEECH	Noun

The French prefix **dys-**, used to form nouns, is derived from a Greek root meaning *bad*, *painful*, *abnormal*, or *defective*. It is typically found in medical terms. One common exceptional use of the prefix is the adjective **dyslexique** *dyslexic*. The base word is often a Greek word that points to the meaning of the prefixed word.

NOUN BEGINNING IN **dys-**	ENGLISH EQUIVALENT	BASE WORD	ENGLISH EQUIVALENT
dysarthrie [F.]	*dysarthria*	arthron [GRK.]	*joint*
dyschromie [F.]	*dyschromia*	kroma [GRK.]	*color*
dysenterie [F.]	*dysentery*	entera [GRK.]	*bowel*
dysfonctionnement [M.]	*dysfunction*	fonctionnement	*functioning*
dyslexie [F.]	*dyslexia*	legein [GRK.]	*to speak*
dyspepsie [F.]	*dyspepsia*	pepse [GRK.]	*digestion*
dysphonie [F.]	*dysphonia*	[-phone]	*voice, sound*
dysplasie [F.]	*dysplasia*	platis [GRK.]	*growth*
dyspnée [F.]	*dyspnea*	pnein [GRK.]	*to breathe*

Complétez! *Choose the best completion for each sentence.*

1. _____ La dysphonie est la détérioration
2. _____ La dyspepsie est un trouble
3. _____ La dyschromie est un défaut de
4. _____ La dyslexie est un trouble
5. _____ La dyspnée se caractérise par
6. _____ La dysarthrie est un trouble
7. _____ La dysplasia est la malformation
8. _____ Le terme « dysfonctionnement » décrit
9. _____ La personne dyslexique doit surmonter
10. _____ La dysenterie est une

a. d'un organe.
b. qui rend la lecture difficile.
c. des obstacles quant il s'agit de lire.
d. des difficultés respiratoires.
e. du timbre de la voix.
f. de la digestion.
g. inflammation des intestins.
h. de l'articulation.
i. pigmentation de la peau.
j. un mauvais fonctionnement.

APPENDIX A
A crash course in French verbs and adverbs

The infinitive (for example, **aller** *to go* and **faire** *to do*) is the form of the verb found in a dictionary. While an infinitive has its uses, the verb must often be conjugated—a skill taught in grammar books. This appendix, by contrast, focuses on infinitives and specific suffixes that denote two other verbal forms, the present and past participles.

Infinitives

The three categories of regular French verbs are identified by their infinitive endings: **-er**, **-ir**, and **-re**. In addition, there are many types of irregular verbs. Except for the verb **aller** *to go*, a French verb whose infinitive ends in **-er** always has a regular conjugation. There are thousands of **-er** verbs in the French language. Once you memorize the conjugation endings of one of these verbs in a specific time frame (tense), you can attach them to the root or stem of any other regular **-er** verb. Following is a short list of common **-er** verbs, with their roots in bold type.

REGULAR **-er** VERB	ENGLISH EQUIVALENT	IRREGULAR **-er** VERB	ENGLISH EQUIVALENT
arriver	*to arrive*	**all**er	*to go*
chanter	*to sing*		
étudier	*to study*		
habiter	*to inhabit, live*		

French verbs whose infinitives end in **-ir** are not as numerous as **-er** verbs, and some are irregular. Following is a short list of common **-ir** verbs, with their roots in bold type.

REGULAR **-ir** VERB	ENGLISH EQUIVALENT	IRREGULAR **-ir** VERB	ENGLISH EQUIVALENT
accomplir	*to accomplish*	**découvr**ir	*to discover*
choisir	*to choose*	**dorm**ir	*to sleep*
finir	*to finish*	**offr**ir	*to offer*
réfléchir	*to reflect, think*	**part**ir	*to depart*

French verbs whose infinitives end in **-re** are also not as numerous as **-er** verbs, and some are irregular. Following is a short list of common **-re** verbs, with their roots in bold type.

REGULAR **-re** VERB	ENGLISH EQUIVALENT	IRREGULAR **-re** VERB	ENGLISH EQUIVALENT
défendre	*to defend*	**comprend**re	*to understand*
descendre	*to go down*	**être**	*to be*
rendre	*to return*	**plaire**	*to please*
répondre	*to answer*	**rire**	*to laugh*

Past participles

In Part II, many charts and lists of prefixed words include past participles used as adjectives. Because of the high frequency of **-er** verbs in French, the most common past participle in French ends in **-é**.

Past participles are verbal forms; they are used to conjugate verbs in compound tenses, such as the **passé composé**. They are, however, also commonly used as adjectives.

The past participle form of a regular verb is obtained by replacing the infinitive ending as follows.

-er > **-é**
-ir > **-i**
-re > **-u**

Following are a few examples of past participle formations. Two examples of irregular formation are provided, for **prendre** and **recevoir**. The past participle of an irregular verb must be individually memorized.

INFINITIVE	ENGLISH EQUIVALENT	PAST PARTICIPLE	ENGLISH EQUIVALENT
(s')abonner	*to subscribe*	abonné	*subscribed*
choisir	*to choose*	choisi	*chosen*
vendre	*to sell*	vendu	*sold*
prendre	*to take*	pris	*taken*
recevoir	*to receive*	reçu	*received*

In the following examples, the use of the past participle in the passé composé is contrasted with its use as an adjective.

PAST PARTICIPLE IN PASSÉ COMPOSÉ	PAST PARTICIPLE AS AN ADJECTIVE
Elle a **proposé** cette méthode-ci. *She proposed this method.*	La méthode **proposée** est bonne. *The proposed method is good.*
Nous avons **choisi** ces couleurs. *We chose these colors.*	Les couleurs **choisies** sont prêtes. *The chosen colors are ready.*
Il a **vendu** la maison. *He sold the house.*	Voici la liste des maisons **vendues**. *Here is the list of sold houses.*

When a past participle is used as an adjective, it agrees with the noun it describes in gender and number.

Present participles

See affix No. 17 in Part I for words with the suffix **-ant**.

The suffix **-ant** is attached to the stem of the verb to form the present participle. The stem is obtained by dropping the **-ons** ending of the first-person plural of the present tense. There are few exceptions: **avoir** *to have*, **être** *to be*, and **savoir** *to know*, whose irregular stems are **ay-**, **ét-**, and

sach-, respectively. Following is a short list of past participles of common verbs, with their roots in bold type.

PRESENT PARTICIPLE	ENGLISH EQUIVALENT
arrivant	*(while/upon) arriving*
finissant	*(while/upon) finishing*
descendant	*(while/upon) going down*
partant	*(while/upon) leaving*

A present participle is used in French to express *by*, *while*, or *upon* performing an action. But it can also be used as an adjective, in which case it agrees with the noun it describes in gender and number. In the following examples, the use of the present participle in a verbal phrase is contrasted with its use as an adjective.

PRESENT PARTICIPLE IN A VERBAL PHRASE	PRESENT PARTICIPLE AS AN ADJECTIVE
On peut instruire les étudiants en les **amusant**. *One can instruct students while amusing them.*	Nous aimons les chansons **amusantes**. *We like amusing/fun songs.*
La babane mûrit en **jaunissant**. *The banana ripens while turning yellow.*	Ces papiers **jaunissants** sont vieux. *These yellowing papers are old.*
On apprend en **s'intéressant** à tout. *One learns by taking an interest in everything.*	Je veux une leçon **intéressante**. *I want an interesting lesson.*

Adverbs

See affix No. 49 in Part I for words that end in **-(m)ment** and function as adverbs.

Many French adverbs are formed by adding a suffix, usually **-ment**, to the feminine form of an adjective. The suffix **-ment** is the equivalent of *-ly* in English. If the masculine form of the base adjective ends in **-i**, the suffix is attached to the masculine form: **poli** yields **poliment**. If the base adjective ends in **-ant** or **-ent**, the ending is replaced by **-amment** or **-emment**, respectively.

ADVERB	ENGLISH EQUIVALENT	BASE ADJECTIVE	ENGLISH EQUIVALENT
certainement	*certainly*	certain/certaine	*certain*
doucement	*gently, slowly*	doux/douce	*gentle*
élégamment	*elegantly*	élégant	*elegant*
joyeusement	*joyously*	joyeux/joyeuse	*joyous*
patiemment	*patiently*	patient	*patient*
poliment	*politely*	poli/polie	*polite*
probablement	*probably*	probable	*probable*
rapidement	*rapidly*	rapide	*rapid*

APPENDIX B
List of French affixes

Each affix in this book is given with its number reference, meaning, and at least one example.

Suffixes

1	-ain/-aine	*Citizen, inhabitant*	Cubain
2	-ais/-aise	*Citizen, inhabitant*	Français
3	-ois/-oise	*Citizen, inhabitant*	Québécois
4	-ien/-ienne	*Citizen, inhabitant*	Alsacien
5	-ien/-ienne	*Expert, specialist*	musicien
6	-al/-ale	*Like, pertaining to*	amical
7	-el/-elle	*Referring to, pertaining to*	accidentel
8	-if/-ive	*Referring to, pertaining to*	pensif
9	-atif/-ative	*Characterized by a tone/manner*	admiratif
10	-eux/-euse	*Exhibiting a trait*	généreux
11	-eux/-euse	*Possessing a quality*	copieux
12	-in/-ine	*Referring to, pertaining to*	féminin, argentin
13	-ation	*Action, result of an action, condition*	accusation
14	-ateur/-atrice	*Possessing a quality/purpose*	accusateur
15	-ition	*Action, result of an action, condition*	abolition
16	-tion	*Action, result of an action, condition*	dilution
17	-ant/-ante	*Effect*	amusant
18	-ance	*Action, result of an action, state*	alliance
19	-ité	*State, condition*	absurdité
20	-bilité	*Possibility of a state/condition*	accessibilité
21	-able	*Likely to be, worthy of being*	adorable
22	-ible	*Feasible*	audible
23	-té	*Abstract concept, state, condition*	beauté
24	-ie	*State, genre, field*	agonie, chimie
25	-ique	*Pertaining to a field/skill*	acrobatique
26	-ique	*Possessing a quality/belief*	lunatique
27	-sie	*State, condition*	amnésie
28	-gramme	*Tool for print/visual/graphic representation*	cardiogramme
29	-graphie	*Art of print/visual/graphic representation*	cartographie
30	-pathie	*Illness, affliction*	cardiopathie
31	-tie	*State, skill*	diplomatie
32	-crate	*Dedicated to power, seeking power*	démocrate
33	-cratie	*Ruling/governing power*	démocratie
34	-ier	*(Fruit) tree*	pommier
35	-(r)aie	*Patch, orchard, plantation, grove*	cerisaie
36	-culture	*Cultivation, raising*	agriculture

37	-ier/-ière	*Worker*	cuisinier
38	-erie	*Store, shop, factory*	confiserie
39	-erie	*Collection*	argenterie
40	-erie	*Display of behavior, condition*	pruderie
41	-ée	*Action, result of an action*	dictée
42	-ée	*Place, location*	musée
43	-ée	*Physical/natural condition, thought*	marée
44	-ée	*Quantity that fills*	bouchée
45	-esse	*State of being, characteristic*	gentillesse
46	-esse	*Power, title, position*	tigresse
47	-issime	*Possessing a superlative quality (formal and literary registers)*	rarissime
48	-ment	*Action, result of an action*	déplacement
49	-(m)ment	*In a manner pertaining to*	amoureusement
50	-cide	*Killing, killer*	fongicide
51	-ade	*Action, result of an action*	baignade
52	-age	*Action, result of an action*	bavardage
53	-aille	*Action, result of an action*	trouvaille
54	-fère	*Carrying, containing*	salifère
55	-forme	*Of a shape*	difforme
56	-ateur/-atrice	*Worker, performer*	animateur
57	-eur/-euse~-rice	*Engaged in, occupied with*	chanteur, professeur
58	-eur	*Physical state, quality*	pâleur
59	-ateur	*Device, appliance*	congélateur
60	-eur	*Equipment, machinery*	ascenseur
61	-euse	*Equipment, furniture*	agrafeuse
62	-eur/-euse	*Exhibiting a quality/trait*	boudeur
63	-isme	*Faith, belief*	patriotisme
64	-isme	*Political/social/economic system/doctrine*	séparatisme
65	-isme	*Adherence/appreciation (of values)*	hédonisme
66	-isme	*Artistic/literary/musical movement/style*	fauvisme
67	-iste	*Believer (in a personal viewpoint/value)*	pacifiste
68	-iste	*Proponent, follower*	activiste
69	-iste	*Expert/specialist (in a skill or art form)*	alpiniste
70	-iste	*Technician/specialist (in medicine/health/science)*	hygiéniste
71	-ologiste	*Technician/specialist (in medicine/health/science)*	neurologiste
72	-ologue	*Specialist (in a global discipline)*	archéologue
73	-ologie	*Area of study/research*	biologie
74	-ite	*Inflammation*	otite
75	-manie	*Addiction*	kleptomanie
76	-phobie	*Obsessive fear*	acrophobie
77	-itude	*State, condition*	amplitude
78	-aison	*Action, result of an action*	crevaison
79	-ure	*Result/outcome of an action*	blessure
80	-ure	*Made of/for*	devanture
81	-son	*Outcome/product of an action*	trahison
82	-ail	*Made for, consisting of*	bétail, éventail
83	-aire	*Agent, dealer*	actionnaire
84	-aire	*Organizational tool, event*	vestiaire, millénaire
85	-aire	*Pertaining to*	consulaire
86	-ence	*Action, result of an action, state*	urgence
87	-ent/-ente	*Possessing a quality*	omniscient

88	-ise	*Quality, trait, state*	franchise
89	-ard/-arde	*Pejorative quality (familiar register)*	criard
90	-et	*Diminutive*	châtelet
91	-et/-ette	*Approximate, diminutive*	follet
92	-ette	*Diminutive*	amourette
93	-in/-ine	*Diminutive, pejorative (people)*	rouquin
94	-in	*Diminutive, pejorative (things)*	biscotin
95	-on	*Diminutive (animals and things)*	chaînon
96	-on/-onne	*Diminutive, condescension (people)*	maigrichon
97	-eau	*Diminutive (animals)*	chevreau
98	-ot/-ote	*Diminutive (familiar, pejorative)*	îlot, parigot
99	-ot/-ote	*Diminutive (familiar; affectionate or pejorative)*	jeunot
100	-âtre	*Pejorative, approximate*	grisâtre

Prefixes

101	non-	*No, not*	non-agression
102	pseudo-	*False, would-be*	pseudo-épique
103	quasi-	*To some degree*	quasi-légalité
104	archi-	*Extremely*	archi-beau
105	néo-	*New*	néonazisme
106	aéro-	*Related to air/aeronautics*	aéroclub
107	anti-	*Against*	antiacide
108	auto-	*Self*	autoanalyse
109	auto-	*Related to automobiles*	autoroute
110	bio-	*Life, existence, nature*	biochimie
111	co-/col-	*Jointly, sharing, together*	coauteur, collection
112	com-	*Jointly, sharing, together*	comparaison
113	con-	*Jointly, sharing, together*	conciliation
114	ex-	*Outside, outward, beyond*	exagération
115	extra-	*Outside, beyond*	extra-scolaire
116	hyper-	*Above, beyond*	hyperactif
117	hypo-	*Below, under*	hypoderme
118	micro-	*Very small*	micro-organisme
119	il-/ir-	*Not, without*	illégal, irréel
120	im-/in-	*Not, without*	impatient, inactif
121	im-/in-	*Into, inward, toward*	imbiber, incarcérer
122	mal-, mé(s)-	*Bad, mean, evil, not*	malchance
123	para-/pare-	*Protection against*	parachute
124	post-	*After*	posthume
125	pré-	*Before*	préaccord
126	anté-	*Before*	antécédent
127	mono-, uni-; bi(s)-; tri(s)-	*One, single, mono-; two, dual, bi-; three, triple, tri-*	monocycle, bifocal, trilingue
128	pro-	*Forward, in favor of*	propager
129	psych(o)-	*Mind*	psychologie
130	re-/r(é)-	*Again, back*	recycler
131	sous-, sub-	*Under, insufficient*	sous-alimenter, subjuguer
132	sur-	*Over, above, in excess*	surabondance
133	super-, ultra-	*Over, above, in excess*	superchic, ultramoderne
134	télé-	*Remote, distant*	télédiffusion
135	trans-	*Across, beyond*	transaction

136	a-/an-	*Lack, deprivation*	amoral, anonyme
137	contre-	*Opposition, reaction*	contre-attaque
138	dé(s)-	*Undoing, separation, deprivation, reversal of an action*	dépeigner
139	dis-	*Undoing, separation, deprivation, reversal of an action*	disculper
140	em-	*Physical/emotional transformation*	embellir
141	en-	*Physical/emotional transformation*	enrager
142	em-	*Putting into*	embouteiller
143	en-	*Putting into*	encaisser
144	demi-, mi-, semi-	*Half, mid, semi*	demi-tour, mi-juin, semi-privé
145	inter-	*Between across*	interagir
146	a-	*Aiming at, directed at, rendering*	abrutir
147	dia-	*Across*	diamètre
148	ortho-	*Straight, correct*	orthopédie, orthographe
149	photo-	*By means of light*	photographie
150	épi-	*Over, toward, focused on*	épicentre
151	équi-	*Equal*	équinoxe
152	eu-	*Well, well-being*	eulogie
153	géo-	*Earth*	géologue
154	hélio-	*Sun*	héliotrope
155	hétéro-	*Other, different*	hétérosexuel
156	homo-	*Same, common*	homogène
157	allo-	*Other*	allocentrisme
158	holo-	*Whole*	holocauste
159	cosmo-	*Universe*	cosmologie
160	dys-	*Bad, painful, defective*	dyslexie

Answer key

I ♦ **FRENCH SUFFIXES**

1 Beginning suffixes

1·1 1. V 2. V 3. F 4. F 5. F 6. V 7. V 8. F 9. F 10. V

2·1 1. Polonais 2. Français 3. Antillais 4. Portugais 5. Sénégalais 6. Martiniquais
7. New Yorkais 8. Écossais 9. Montréalais 10. Anglais

3·1 1. d 2. g 3. f 4. a 5. h 6. j 7. i 8. e 9. b 10. c

4·1 1. a 2. b 3. b 4. a 5. b 6. b 7. a 8. b 9. b 10. a

5·1 1. généticienne 2. collégien 3. gardien 4. acousticienne 5. grammairien
6. académicienne 7. historien 8. comédienne 9. électricien 10. chirurgienne

5·2 1. informaticiens 2. mathématiciens 3. magiciens 4. pharmaciens 5. mécaniciens
6. logisticiens 7. musiciens 8. lycéens 9. proustiens 10. tragédiens

6·1 1. F 2. V 3. V 4. F 5. F 6. V 7. V 8. V 9. F 10. F 11. V 12. F 13. F
14. F 15. V 16. F 17. F 18. V

7·1 1. présidentielle 2. paternelle 3. intellectuel 4. immortel 5. traditionnelle
6. nutritionnel 7. habituelle 8. textuel 9. transitionnelle 10. artificielle
11. fraternelle 12. accidentelle 13. conventionnelle 14. professionnelle
15. exponentielle 16. exceptionnel 17. annuel 18. éternelle

8·1 1. C 2. G 3. C 4. G 5. C 6. C 7. G 8. G 9 G 10. G

8·2 1. émotive 2. abusif 3. maladive 4. combatif 5. subjective 6. offensif 7. adoptive
8. instinctif 9. pensive 10. expansif 11. compréhensive 12. incisif 13. exécutive

9·1 1. approximatif/estimatif 2. récitatif 3. rébarbatif 4. représentatif 5. vindicatif
6. admiratif 7. démonstratif 8. imaginatif 9. accusatif 10. consultatif

9·2 1. récapitulatif 2. représentatif 3. démonstrative 4. informative 5. défensive
6. approximative/estimative 7. vindicative

10·1 A. 1. PB 2. PB 3. B 4. B 5. B

B. 1. B 2. B 3. B 4. B 5. PB

C. 1. B 2. B 3. B 4. PB 5. PB 6. B 7. B 8. PB 9. PB 10. B

11·1 1. c 2. g 3. a 4. f 5. i 6. d 7. b 8. j 9. e 10. h

11·2 1. nuageux 2. tumultueuse 3. somptueuse 4. poreux 5. savonneuse 6. vertigineux
7. monstrueuse 8. lumineuses

12·1   1. bovine   2. canine   3. chevaline   4. chauvine   5. adultérine   6. anodine   7. cristalline
8. saline   9. masculine   10. féminine   11. estudiantine   12. alpine

12·2   1. g   2. a   3. d   4. f   5. b   6. c   7. e

13·1   1. activation   2. alimentation   3. augmentation   4. annulation   5. argumentation   6. attraction
7. accusation/arrestation   8. abdication   9. accusation/arrestation   10. agitation

13·2   1. V   2. V   3. F   4. F   5. V   6. F   7. V   8. V   9. F   10. V

14·1   1. accusateur   2. approbatrice   3. formateur   4. adoratrice   5. appréciateur   6. provocateur
7. purificatrice   8. dénonciatrice   9. médiatrice   10. accompagnateur   11. exportateur   12. admirateur

14·2   1. usurpateur   2. gladiateur   3. démonstratrice   4. conspiratrice   5. spectateur   6. dictateur
7. programmatrice   8. procurateur   9. préparatrice   10. utilisateur   11. blasphémateur   12. adjudicatrice
13. réformateur   14. évangélisatrice   15. aviatrice

15·1   1. c   2. l   3. d   4. k   5. a   6. i   7. j   8. n   9. b   10. m   11. e   12. f   13. g   14. h

16·1   1. b   2. g   3. j   4. f   5. c   6. h   7. d   8. a   9. e   10. i

16·2   1. R-A   2. A-R   3. R-A   4. R-A   5. A-R   6. R-A

17·1   1. édifiant   2. bienfaisant   3. charmant   4. amusante   5. éblouissante   6. accablante   7. calmante
8. attirante   9. dégradante   10. cinglant

17·2   1. méprisant   2. menaçant   3. terrifiant   4. plaisante   5. séduisante   6. gênante   7. malfaisante
8. pressant   9. passionnante   10. moralisante

18·1   1. V   2. V   3. F   4. F   5. V   6. F   7. V   8. V   9. V   10. F   11. F   12. F

18·2   1. e   2. k   3. a   4. f   5. i   6. d   7. b   8. c   9. h   10. l   11. g   12. j

19·1   1. banalité   2. égalité   3. agressivité   4. austérité   5. efficacité   6. acidité   7. absurdité   8. agilité
9. collégialité   10. affinité

19·2   1. générosité   2. impétuosité   3. vulgarité   4. énormité   5. exclusivité   6. moralité   7. lucidité
8. médiocrité   9. unité   10. ténacité

20·1   1. h   2. g   3. e   4. d   5. k   6. l   7. b   8. a   9. c   10. f   11. i   12. j

20·2   1. irritabilité   2. perfectibilité   3. sociabilité   4. respectabilité   5. susceptibilité   6. instabilité
7. possibilité   8. probabilité   9. invisibilité   10. réversibilité   11. inséparabilité   12. vulnérabilité

21·1   1. admirable, appréciable   2. blâmable, détestable   3. adorable, désirable   4. abordable, discutable
5. buvable, consommable   6. durable, fiable

21·2   1. incassable   2. invariable   3. impensable, inimaginable   4. ingonflable   5. imbuvable   6. indispensable
7. immangeable   8. incomparable   9. incontestable   10. impensable, inimaginable   11. indiscernable
12. imprésentable

22·1   1. compréhensible, corrigible   2. audible, diffusible   3. accessible, compatible   4. combustible,
destructible   5. admissible, crédible   6. comestible, disponible

22·2   1. sensible   2. pénible   3. ostensible   4. lisible   5. tangible   6. traduisible   7. visible   8. paisible
9. possible   10. réversible   11. irréductible   12. invincible

23·1   1. honnêteté   2. beauté   3. fermeté   4. liberté   5. chasteté   6. cruauté   7. ébriété   8. équité   9. bonté
10. fierté

23·2   1. i   2. j   3. e   4. h   5. c   6. g   7. f   8. d   9. a   10. b

24·1   1. V   2. V   3. F   4. F   5. V   6. F   7. F   8. F   9. V   10. V

24·2   1. dynastie   2. économie   3. géographie   4. vilenie   5. décennie   6. comédie   7. chimie   8. tragédie
9. bigamie   10. biologie

25·1   1. calligraphique   2. endémique   3. comique   4. anorexique   5. économique   6. dynastique
7. gastronomiques   8. anatomiques   9. biologique   10. extatique   11. cosmique   12. acrobatique

25·2   1. ludique   2. informatique   3. tragique   4. magique   5. géométrique   6. philosophique   7. théologique
8. zoologique   9. pathologique   10. technologique

26·1   1. lunatique   2. apathique   3. fanatique   4. photogénique   5. aéronautique   6. agnostique   7. romantique
8. magnifique   9. stoïque   10. antipathique   11. antagonique   12. sympathique   13. linguistique

27·1   1. F   2. V   3. V   4. V   5. V   6. F   7. F   8. F   9. V   10. F

28·1   1. encéphalogramme   2. hémogramme   3. oscillogramme   4. audiogramme   5. myogramme
6. cardiogramme   7. spermogramme   8. adénogramme

28·2   1. organigramme   2. histogramme   3. monogramme   4. anagramme   5. idéogramme   6. hologramme
7. épigramme   8. pictogramme   9. calligramme   10. diagramme

29·1   1. V   2. F   3. F   4. F   5. V   6. V   7. V   8. F   9. V   10. F

30·1   1. cardiopathie   2. myopathie   3. psychopathie   4. hémopathie   5. névropathie   6. ostéopathie
7. coronaropathie   8. arthropathie

31·1   1. minutie   2. diplomatie   3. répartie   4. calvitie   5. amnistie   6. prophéties   7. orthodontie
8. modestie   9. suprématie   10. acrobatie

32·1   1. aristocrate   2. phallocrate   3. ploutocrate   4. technocrate   5. physiocrate   6. autocrate   7. démocrate
8. eurocrate   9. bureaucrate   10. théocrate

33·1   1. h   2. g   3. i   4. a   5. j   6. e   7. b   8. d   9. c   10. f

34·1   1. oranger   2. olivier   3. pamplemoussier   4. manguier   5. bananier   6. avocatier   7. figuier   8. cerisier
9. prunier   10. abricotier   11. citronnier   12. amandier   13. poirier   14. pommier

35·1   1. oliveraie   2. roseraie   3. hêtraie   4. bananeraie   5. palmeraie   6. saulaie   7. cocoteraie   8. chênaie
9. cerisaie   10. fraiseraie   11. ronceraie   12. châtaigneraie

36·1   1. sylviculture   2. arboriculture   3. floriculture   4. saliculture   5. aquaculture   6. riziculture
7. puériculture   8. aviculture   9. salmoniculture   10. viticulture   11. sériciculture   12. horticulture
13. agriculture   14. apiculture

37·1   1. V   2. F   3. V   4. V   5. F   6. F   7. F   8. V   9. V   10. V   11. F   12. V   13. V   14. F

37·2   1. chocolatière   2. poissonnier   3. cordonnier   4. boulanger   5. bouchère   6. épicière   7. banquier
8. bijoutière   9. caissier   10. charcutière   11. crémier   12. boutiquier

38·1   1. confiserie   2. blanchisserie   3. brasserie   4. crémerie   5. bijouterie   6. chocolaterie   7. charcuterie
8. boulangerie   9. bouquinerie   10. biscuiterie   11. billetterie   12. boucherie

38·2   1. maroquinerie   2. herboristerie   3. poissonnerie   4. parfumerie   5. sucrerie   6. pâtisserie
7. quincaillerie   8. crêperie   9. fromagerie   10. épicerie   11. ganterie   12. glacerie

39·1   1. soierie   2. tapisserie   3. maçonnerie   4. lingerie   5. ferronnerie   6. boiserie   7. argenterie
8. coutellerie   9. sucrerie   10. armurerie   11. carrosserie   12. pâtisserie   13. verrerie   14. confiserie
15. charcuterie

40·1   1. duperie   2. chicanerie   3. effronterie   4. rêverie   5. ânerie/niaiserie   6. pruderie   7. pleurnicherie
8. flatterie   9. cajolerie   10. niaiserie   11. sorcellerie   12. coquetterie   13. bouderie   14. camaraderie
15. brusquerie

41·1   1. i   2. h   3. j   4. l   5. k   6. g   7. f   8. b   9. a   10. c   11. e   12. d

42·1   1. mosquée   2. entrée   3. musée   4. jetée   5. lycée   6. allée   7. vallée   8. chaussée

43·1   1. V   2. V   3. F   4. V   5. F   6. F   7. F   8. V   9. V   10. F   11. V   12. V

44·1   1. pincée/cuillerée   2. poignée   3. bouchée   4. gorgée   5. pelletée   6. brouettée   7. assiettée   8. brassée
9. fourchetée   10. cuillerée

45·1   1. bassesse   2. allégresse   3. politesse   4. altesse   5. gentillesse   6. noblesse   7. largesse   8. grossesse
       9. adresse   10. jeunesse

45·2   1. sécheresse   2. sagesse   3. promesse   4. tendresse   5. prouesse   6. vieillesse   7. vitesse   8. richesse

46·1   1. V   2. V   3. F   4. V   5. F   6. F   7. V   8. F   9. V   10. V   11. V   12. V   13. F   14. F   15. F

47·1   *Suggested answers:*   1. rarissime   2. richissime   3. urgentissime   4. grandissime   5. éminentissime
       6. bellissime   7. illustrissime   8. sérénissime   9. gravissime   10. célébrissime

48·1   1. dérangement   2. contentement   3. empoisonnements   4. bercement   5. commencement   6. aboiement
       7. déplacement   8. emprisonnement   9. dénouement   10. développement

48·2   1. mouvement   2. vouvoiement   3. paiement   4. sentiment   5. fonctionnement   6. licenciement
       7. tremblement   8. surpeuplement   9. enlèvement   10. plissement

49·1   1. fréquemment   2. finement   3. cyniquement   4. abondamment   5. abusivement   6. amoureusement
       7. activement   8. fièrement   9. éloquemment   10. curieusement   11. absolument   12. catégoriquement

49·2   1. mollement   2. furieusement   3. simplement   4. innocemment   5. verbalement   6. froidement
       7. follement   8. virtuellement   9. insolemment   10. harmonieusement

50·1   1. insecticide   2. matricide   3. herbicide   4. suicide   5. parricide   6. homicide   7. génocide
       8. infanticide   9. fratricide   10. fongicide   11. germicide   12. pesticide

2   Intermediate/advanced suffixes

51·1   1. colonnade   2. embuscade   3. camarade   4. bousculade   5. balade   6. dérobade   7. baignade
       8. ambassade   9. citronnade   10. cavalcade

51·2   1. tornades   2. promenade   3. orangeade   4. parade   5. fusillades   6. rigolades   7. esplanade
       8. peuplades   9. malades   10. galopade   11. grillade   12. nomades

52·1   1. V   2. F   3. V   4. V   5. F   6. F   7. V   8. F   9. F   10. F   11. V   12. V   13. F   14. V   15. V

53·1   1. f   2. a   3. g   4. d   5. c   6. b   7. h   8. e

53·2   1. F   2. F   3. V   4. V   5. F   6. F   7. V   8. V   9. F   10. F   11. V   12. V   13. V   14. V

54·1   1. papillifère   2. humifère   3. somnifère   4. alifère   5. calorifère   6. salifères   7. vaccinifère
       8. fructifères   9. florifères   10. carbonifères

55·1   1. V   2. V   3. F   4. F   5. F   6. V   7. V   8. V   9. F   10. V

56·1   1. coordinatrice   2. collaboratrice   3. admiratrices   4. calomniatrice   5. cultivatrice   6. accusatrice
       7. conspiratrice   8. animatrice   9. agitatrice   10. administratrice   11. accompagnatrice
       12. communicatrice

56·2   1. j   2. g   3. f   4. h   5. k   6. c   7. b   8. d   9. l   10. a   11. e   12. i

57·1   1. dompteur   2. grogneuse   3. balayeur   4. acheteuse   5. flatteur   6. chanteuse   7. éclaireur
       8. auto-stoppeuse   9. bricoleur   10. baigneuse   11. danseur   12. farceuse

57·2   1. tatoueur   2. serveur   3. voleur   4. ronfleur   5. voyageur   6. professeur   7. troqueur   8. visiteur
       9. profiteur   10. rêveur   11. programmeur   12. vendeur

57·3   1. k   2. g   3. m   4. j   5. n   6. h   7. b   8. l   9. f   10. d   11. a   12. i   13. c   14. e

58·1   1. grandeur   2. grosseur   3. douceur   4. apesanteur   5. blondeur   6. blancheur   7. douleur   8. hauteur
       9. aigreur   10. ampleur   11. candeur   12. chaleur

58·2   1. rougeur   2. maigreur, minceur   3. lenteur   4. largeur   5. pesanteur   6. vigueur   7. raideur
       8. pâleur   9. lourdeur   10. profondeur

59·1   1. purificateur   2. adaptateur   3. alternateur   4. commutateur   5. ordinateur   6. aspirateur
       7. ventilateur   8. accélérateur   9. applicateur   10. carburateur   11. congélateur   12. générateur

60·1 1. climatiseur 2. moteur 3. tracteur 4. compacteur 5. classeur 6. ascenseur 7. disjoncteur 8. autocuiseur 9. réacteur 10. conducteur 11. projecteur 12. diffuseur

61·1 1. F 2. V 3. F 4. V 5. V 6. F 7. F 8. V 9. V 10. F 11. F 12. V 13. F 14. V 15. V 16. F

62·1 1. brailleur 2. charmeuse 3. boudeur 4. chicaneuse 5. complimenteur 6. batailleuse 7. blagueur 8. dragueuse 9. demandeur 10. cajoleuse

62·2 1. vengeresse 2. trompeurs 3. ensorceleur 4. rieurs 5. tapageur 6. menteurs 7. moqueurs 8. pêcheurs

63·1 1. idéalisme 2. patriotisme 3. libéralisme 4. sionisme 5. psychisme 6. christianisme 7. théisme 8. calvinisme 9. protestantisme 10. anticléricalisme 11. chauvinisme 12. bouddhisme 13. athéisme 14. nationalisme 15. catholicisme 16. luthéranisme

64·1 1. V 2. F 3. F 4. F 5. F 6. V 7. V 8. V 9. V 10. V 11. F 12. F 13. F 14. V 15. F

65·1 1. optimisme 2. égocentrisme 3. nudisme 4. hédonisme 5. conformisme 6. racisme 7. végétarisme 8. traditionalisme 9. stoïcisme 10. satanisme 11. sadisme 12. pessimisme 13. culturalisme 14. masochisme 15. fétichisme

66·1 1. d 2. l 3. e 4. h 5. c 6. j 7. b 8. a 9. k 10. f 11. g 12. i

67·1 1. V 2. F 3. F 4. V 5. F 6. V 7. F 8. F 9. V 10. F 11. V 12. V 13. F 14. V

68·1 1. abolitionniste 2. anticommuniste 3. féministe 4. helléniste 5. sécessionniste 6. royaliste 7. capitaliste 8. extrémiste 9. humaniste 10. protectionniste 11. socialiste 12. intégrationniste 13. existentialiste 14. activiste

69·1 1. caricaturiste, paysagiste, styliste, urbaniste 2. clarinettiste, flûtiste, organiste, violoniste 3. humoriste, illusionniste 4. alpiniste, cycliste, motocycliste 5. duettiste, sopraniste 6. concertiste, soliste 7. encyclopédiste, fabuliste 8. céramiste, maquettiste

70·1 1. nutritionniste 2. hygiéniste 3. anesthésiste 4. orthodontiste 5. génétiste 6. chimiste 7. oculiste 8. algébriste 9. dentiste 10. secouriste 11. orthopédiste 12. botaniste 13. herboriste 14. exorciste 15. diététiste

71·1 1. neurologiste 2. virologiste 3. immunologiste 4. laryngologiste 5. cosmétologiste 6. dermatologiste 7. embryologiste 8. pathologiste 9. pharmacologiste 10. allergologiste 11. radiologiste 12. anesthésiologiste 13. ophtalmologiste 14. bactériologiste 15. biologiste 16. généalogiste

72·1 1. climatologue, météorologue 2. criminologue, psychologue 3. géologue, hydrologue, océanologue, spéléologue, volcanologue 4. politologue, sociologue 5. cancérologue, cardiologue, pneumologue 6. anthropologue, archéologue 7. gynécologue, sexologue 8. musicologue, philologue

73·1 1. embryologie, gynécologie 2. cancérologie, morphologie 3. géologie, volcanologie 4. idéologie, mythologie, théologie 5. astrologie, cosmologie 6. bactériologie, microbiologie 7. criminologie, toxicologie 8. neurologie, psychologie 9. climatologie, météorologie 10. biologie, morphologie

74·1 1. V 2. F 3. V 4. F 5. V 6. V 7. F 8. F 9. V 10. F 11. V 12. F

74·2 1. sinusite 2. méningite 3. lymphangite 4. gingivite 5. myosite 6. tendinite 7. laryngite 8. pancréatite 9. otite 10. poliomyélite

75·1 1. c 2. j 3. a 4. d 5. g 6. m 7. i 8. l 9. k 10. h 11. o 12. f 13. e 14. n 15. p 16. b

76·1 1. acrophobie 2. gymnophobie 3. ochlophobie 4. arachnophobie 5. logophobie 6. émétophobie 7. claustrophobie 8. agoraphobie

77·1 1. gratitude 2. décrépitude 3. certitude 4. habitude 5. exactitude 6. aptitude 7. amplitude 8. ingratitude 9. inexactitude 10. altitude

77·2 1. j 2. g 3. f 4. i 5. h 6. c 7. b 8. e 9. d 10. a

78·1 1. cuvaison 2. couvaison 3. démangeaison 4. défleuraison 5. conjugaison 6. crevaison 7. cargaison 8. comparaison 9. combinaison

78·2 1. livraison 2. pendaison 3. fenaison 4. terminaison 5. frondaison 6. inclinaison 7. floraison 8. exhalaison 9. feuillaison 10. flottaison

79·1 1. f 2. h 3. e 4. j 5. c 6. a 7. d 8. b 9. l 10. g 11. i 12. k

79·2 1. fêlure 2. peinture 3. signature 4. fourrure 5. sculpture 6. pourriture 7. fermeture 8. lecture 9. foulure 10. vomissure 11. nourriture 12. ouverture 13. tournure 14. moisissure

80·1 1. V 2. F 3. V 4. V 5. V 6. V 7. F 8. F 9. V 10. V

80·2 1. température 2. mantelure 3. texture 4. encolure 5. progéniture 6. emmanchure 7. voilure 8. sépulture 9. imposture 10. ossature 11. mésaventure

81·1 1. V 2. V 3. F 4. F 5. V 6. F 7. F 8. V 9. F 10. V 11. F 12. F

82·1 1. corail 2. émail 3. travail 4. bétail 5. attirail 6. bercail 7. éventails 8. portail 9. épouvantail

83·1 1. V 2. F 3. F 4. V 5. F 6. F 7. V 8. V 9. V 10. F 11. F 12. F 13. F 14. V 15. F 16. F 17. F 18. V

84·1 1. sommaire 2. vestiaire 3. annuaire 4. millénaire 5. centenaire 6. anniversaire 7. bicentenaire 8. questionnaire 9. inventaire 10. glossaire, vocabulaire

85·1 1. k 2. e 3. g 4. f 5. b 6. c 7. i 8. l 9. d 10. a 11. j 12. h

85·2 1. héréditaire 2. nucléaires 3. quadragénaires 4. vestimentaires 5. publicitaires 6. minoritaire 7. supplémentaires 8. humanitaire 9. scolaire 10. révolutionnaire 11. rectangulaire 12. majoritaires

86·1 1. V 2. F 3. V 4. V 5. F 6. V 7. F 8. V 9. V 10. F 11. V 12. V

86·2 1. excellence 2. impatience 3. intelligence 4. insolence 5. somnolence 6. transparence 7. existence 8. urgence 9. innocence 10. prudence 11. indifférence 12. violence 13. négligence 14. indulgence

87·1 1. omniscient 2. abstinente 3. omnipotent 4. non-adhérente 5. évident 6. phosphorescente 7. opalescent 8. réticent 9. abhorrente 10. polyvalent 11. précédente 12. fluorescente 13. grandiloquent 14. ambivalente 15. apparente 16. éloquent 17. éminent 18. excellente

88·1 1. fainéantise 2. convoitise 3. bêtise 4. débrouillardise, expertise 5. débrouillardise 6. franchise 7. couardise 8. balourdise 9. gaillardise

88·2 1. sottises 2. maîtrise 3. paillardise 4. prêtrise 5. hantise 6. surprise 7. roublardise 8. traîtrise 9. mignardises 10. vantardise

89·1 1. bâtard 2. froussard 3. criard 4. flemmard 5. braillard 6. veinard 7. vantard 8. pleurnichard 9. grognard 10. soûlard

90·1 1. cervelet 2. basset 3. bourriquet 4. agnelet 5. châtelet 6. balconnet 7. cadet 8. ballonnet 9. bâtonnet 10. bonnet 11. cochonnet 12. bourrelet 13. blondinet 14. baronet 15. bracelet

90·2 1. tabouret 2. coussinet 3. godet 4. gobelet 5. garçonnet 6. mantelet 7. minet 8. osselet 9. jardinet 10. oiselet 11. coquelet 12. ruisselet 13. martelet 14. corselet 15. gantelet 16. poissonnet

91·1 1. aigrelette 2. gentillets 3. mignonnets 4. brunet 5. verdelette 6. douillet 7. propret 8. pauvrette 9. grassouillette 10. rondelette 11. fluets 12. clairette 13. doucet 14. simplet

92·1 1. n 2. h 3. e 4. f 5. g 6. d 7. c 8. b 9. l 10. a 11. m 12. i 13. j 14. k

92·2 1. F 2. F 3. F 4. V 5. V 6. F 7. V 8. V 9. F 10. F 11. V 12. F 13. V 14. V

93·1 1. bambin 2. coquin 3. galopin 4. cousin 5. chérubin 6. diablotin 7. babouin 8. assassin 9. bourrin 10. dauphin 11. blondin 12. brigantin 13. crétin/ignorantin 14. rouquin 15. benjamin 16. cabotin 17. ignorantin/crétin 18. plaisantin

94·1 1. chemin 2. bulletin 3. crottin 4. bouquins 5. butin 6. boudin 7. couffin 8. bassin 9. biscotin 10. engin 11. baladin 12. déclin 13. coussins 14. bottines

94·2   1. V   2. F   3. V   4. F   5. V   6. V   7. F   8. V   9. V   10. F   11. V   12. V   13. F   14. F

95·1   1. caneton   2. blouson   3. capuchon   4. chaînon   5. ballons   6. carillon   7. aiglon   8. aiguillon
9. ailerons   10. boulon   11. balluchon   12. ceinturon   13. ânon

95·2   1. fourgon   2. médaillon   3. harpon   4. plongeon   5. chatons   6. réveillon   7. croûtons   8. maillon
9. portillon   10. poêlon   11. jupon   12. glaçons   13. échelons   14. dindon

96·1   1. grognon   2. maigrichonne   3. félon   4. chaperon   5. moucheron   6. friponne   7. mitron
8. forgeron   9. marmiton   10. vigneronne   11. bouffon   12. avorton

97·1   1. louveteau   2. lionceau   3. souriceau   4. chevreau   5. pigeonneau   6. renardeau   7. faisandeau
8. vermisseau   9. cigogneau   10. éléphanteau

98·1   1. chiot, loupiot   2. poivrot, soûlot   3. ciboulot, cuissot   4. mendigot   5. parigot   6. bachot, boulot
7. boulot   8. asticot   9. îlot   10. chariot

99·1   1. fiérote   2. maigriot   3. vieillotte   4. jeunot   5. petiote   6. bellot   7. pâlote   8. falot

100·1   1. douceâtre   2. folâtre   3. jaunâtre   4. acariâtre   5. rougeâtre   6. bleuâtre   7. brunâtre   8. verdâtre
9. noirâtre   10. grisâtre   11. opiniâtre   12. blanchâtre

 FRENCH PREFIXES

3   Beginning prefixes

101·1   1. non-lieu   2. non-combattant   3. non-conciliation   4. non-activité   5. non-agression, non-belligérance,
non-violence   6. non-alignement, non-conformisme   7. non-conciliation   8. non-endettement
9. non-voyant   10. non-assistance   11. non-discrimination   12. non-acceptation

102·1   1. d   2. h   3. i   4. a   5. g   6. b   7. e   8. j   9. c   10. f

103·1   1. quasi-morbidité   2. quasi-légalité   3. quasi-fraternité   4. quasi-contrat   5. quasi-crime
6. quasi-monopole   7. quasi-certitude   8. quasi-totalité   9. quasi-sororité   10. quasi-unanimité

104·1   1. archi-connu   2. archi-pluvieux   3. archi-humide   4. archi-sérieux   5. archi-tenaces
6. archi-généreux   7. archi-ennuyeux   8. archi-beau   9. archi-faux   10. archi-glacial

105·1   1. néo-zélandais   2. néo-indiens   3. néo-québécois   4. néo-colonialiste   5. néo-capitaliste
6. néo-classicisme   7. néo-évolutionnisme   8. néonazisme

106·1   1. aéronautique   2. aéronavale   3. aérospatiale   4. aérotrain   5. aérotransport   6. aéroterrestre
7. aérodromes   8. aéroclub   9. aéroport   10. aérogares   11. aéronaute   12. aérodynamique
13. aérothermiques   14. aérosols   15. aérophagie

107·1   1. e   2. f   3. a   4. g   5. j   6. k   7. d   8. n   9. m   10. h   11. c   12. l   13. o   14. i   15. b

107·2   1. F   2. F   3. F   4. V   5. F   6. V   7. V   8. V   9. F   10. V   11. V   12. F   13. V   14. F

108·1   1. autoallumage   2. autonomie   3. autobiographies   4. autoanalyses   5. autographes   6. autodidactes
7. autonomistes   8. autoportrait   9. automate   10. autodestruction   11. autodéfense   12. autochtones
13. autocollants   14. autocensure

109·1   1. automobiliste   2. autostoppeur   3. autostoppeuse   4. autoroute   5. automobile   6. automobilisme
7. autostop   8. autoneige   9. autorail

110·1   1. V   2. F   3. V   4. V   5. F   6. V   7. F   8. V   9. V   10. F   11. F   12. V

111·1   1. colocataire   2. copain   3. collection   4. coopération   5. copilote   6. copropriétaire   7. cosignataire
8. coaccusé(e)   9. collectivité   10. coauteur   11. collaborateur   12. coopérateur/coopératrice
13. colocation   14. collectionneur/collectionneuse

112·1 1. combat, combattant(e) 2. commémoration 3. comportement 4. commisération, compassion 5. communicateur 6. communication 7. compétition 8. compère 9. complaisance

113·1 1. concurrence 2. consolidation 3. confrère 4. condoléances 5. conciliatrice 6. convivialité 7. congrégation 8. convive 9. consolidateur 10. confrérie

114·1 1. V 2. V 3. F 4. F 5. F 6. V 7. F 8. V 9. F 10. V 11. F 12. V

114·2 1. expulsé 2. exploser 3. expérimenter 4. expédier 5. exhumé 6. exprimer 7. expectorer 8. expliquer 9. explorer 10. exposer 11. exporter 12. exproprié

115·1 1. extra-lucide 2. extravagant 3. extraverti 4. extraplat 5. extra-fort 6. extra-sensible 7. extra-sensoriel 8. extra-scolaire 9. extrapolé 10. extraordinaire 11. extrabudgétaire 12. extra-fin 13. extra-terrestre

116·1 1. hypersonique 2. hypersensible 3. hyperactif 4. hypertrophique 5. hyperbolique 6. hypercritique 7. hyperréaliste 8. hypernerveux

117·1 1. h 2. f 3. d 4. g 5. j 6. b 7. c 8. a 9. e 10. i

118·1 1. microclimat 2. micro-ondes 3. microfilm 4. microbiologie 5. micro-ordinateur 6. microanalyse 7. microflore 8. microchimie 9. micro-organismes 10. microphones 11. microélectronique 12. microscopes 13. microseconde 14. microbiologiste

119·1 1. illettré 2. illisible 3. illogique 4. illusoire 5. illimité 6. illégitime 7. illégal 8. illicite

119·2 1. irrespectueux 2. irréalisable 3. irrationnel 4. irréfutable 5. irréductible 6. irrésolu 7. irréconciliable 8. irréparable 9. irresponsable 10. irréfléchie 11. irrégulière 12. irrémédiable/irréversible 13. irrespirable 14. irrésistible 15. irrécusable 16. irréalisé 17. irremplaçable 18. irréprochable 19. irréelle 20. irrémédiable/irréversible

120·1 1. imbattable 2. immobile 3. impardonnable 4. immangeable 5. impartial 6. immortel 7. impraticable 8. immatériel 9. impatient 10. immature 11. immorale 12. imbuvable

120·2 1. impossible 2. imprécis 3. impur 4. impensable 5. impoli 6. impuissant 7. imperméable 8. imprévu 9. impersonnel 10. improductif 11. imprudent 12. imprévisible

120·3 1. incroyable 2. indestructible 3. incorrect 4. incompétent 5. indiscret 6. inattentif 7. incompatible 8. incompréhensible 9. inattendu 10. incomplet 11. inaccoutumé 12. inanimé 13. incomparable 14. inconsolable 15. inactif 16. inadmissible 17. inconscient 18. incorrigible 19. inconnu 20. indésirable 21. incorruptible

120·4 1. V 2. F 3. F 4. V 5. F 6. V 7. F 8. F 9. V 10. V 11. F 12. V 13. F 14. V 15. V 16. V 17. F 18. V 19. F 20. V 21. V 22. F

121·1 1. importés 2. imprimée 3. impressionné 4. immergés 5. imbibée 6. impliqué 7. improvisée 8. imposée 9. immigré 10. implantés 11. imploré 12. imparti 13. immatriculée 14. immolé

121·2 1. V 2. F 3. V 4. V 5. F 6. V 7. V 8. F 9. V 10. V 11. F 12. F 13. V 14. F 15. F 16. V

122·1 1. c 2. h 3. a 4. k 5. e 6. m 7. l 8. n 9. j 10. i 11. f 12. b 13. d 14. g

122·2 1. g 2. i 3. c 4. k 5. h 6. e 7. a 8. f 9. b 10. l 11. j 12. d

123·1 1. pare-brise 2. pare-chocs 3. pare-soleil 4. parasol 5. paravent 6. pare-feu 7. parasismique 8. paratonnerre 9. parapluie 10. parachute

124·1 1. posthume 2. postscolaire 3. postproduction 4. post-test 5. postlude 6. postmoderne 7. post-traumatique 8. postromantisme 9. postnatale 10. post-scriptum 11. postopératoire 12. post-mortem 13. postambule 14. post-combustion 15. postdate 16. postglaciaire 17. postface 18. postcommunisme

125·1 1. préexistence 2. présomption 3. préfabrication 4. préméditation 5. préhistoire 6. prénom 7. prédisposition 8. préjugé 9. présage 10. prémolaire 11. préfinancement 12. préoccupation 13. préenregistrement 14. prédestination 15. préapprentissage 16. préadolescence 17. préambule 18. préaccord

126·1   1. d   2. f   3. j   4. a   5. i   6. b   7. c   8. h   9. e   10. g

127·1   1. V   2. V   3. V   4. F   5. F   6. F   7. F   8. V   9. V   10. V

127·2   1. univalent   2. univoque   3. unilatéral   4. unicellulaire   5. unidirectionnel   6. unicolore   7. unijambiste
       8. unisexe   9. uniforme   10. universel   11. unitaire   12. unidimensionnel

127·3   1. bilingue, trilingue   2. bimensuel   3. bifocal   4. bicyclette, tricycle   5. biréacteur   6. bisannuel,
       trisannuel   7. bisexuel   8. bigame   9. bicentenaire, tricentenaire   10. triangle   11. biathlète, triathlète
       12. bicolore, tricolore   13. biculturel

128·1   1. promu   2. proposé   3. projeté   4. proclamée   5. pronostiqué   6. prophétisée   7. prolongée
       8. provenue   9. propagée   10. procédé

129·1   1. V   2. F   3. V   4. F   5. V   6. F   7. F   8. V   9. F   10. V   11. F   12. V

130·1   1. reprendre   2. revenir   3. reprendre   4. reconstituer/reconstruire   5. réutiliser   6. rappeler
       7. recompter   8. rapporter   9. reconstruire   10. rassembler/réunir   11. récrire   12. réhabituer
       13. refaire   14. redire   15. recycler   16. réécouter   17. remonter   18. rendormir   19. rassurer
       20. reproduire

4   Intermediate/advanced prefixes

131·1   1. sous-employés   2. sous-titrés   3. sous-loués   4. subventionnées   5. sous-développée   6. subjuguée
       7. sous-alimentées   8. sous-estimés   9. subordonnée   10. sous-entendues   11. submergé
       12. sous-exploités

131·2   1. sous-officier   2. subdivision   3. sous-titre   4. subalterne   5. sous-vêtement   6. sous-chef
       7. sous-marin   8. subconscient   9. sous-comité   10. sous-secrétaire

132·1   1. V   2. V   3. F   4. F   5. V   6. V   7. V   8. F   9. V   10. V   11. F   12. F   13. F   14. V   15. F
       16. F   17. F   18. V

133·1   1. superacide   2. superléger   3. super-transparent   4. superflu   5. superchic   6. super-mignon
       7. superlatif   8. supersonique

133·2   1. super-héros   2. superordinateur   3. superstar   4. super-remises   5. super-héroïne   6. superpuissance
       7. superviseur   8. supermarché

133·3   1. ultraviolet   2. ultraroyaliste   3. ultrapropres   4. ultrasensibles   5. ultrablancs/ultrapropres   6. ultrachic/
       ultramoderne   7. ultrachics/ultralourds   8. ultrachic/ultralourd/ultramoderne

134·1   1. V   2. F   3. V   4. F   5. F   6. F   7. V   8. V   9. V   10. F   11. F   12. V   13. V   14. F   15. F

135·1   1. e   2. a   3. m   4. i   5. b   6. d   7. n   8. p   9. l   10. o   11. f   12. g   13. k   14. j   15. c   16. h

136·1   1. anarchiste   2. apolitiques   3. analphabètes   4. amorale   5. asexués   6. apatrides   7. alogique
       8. atoxiques   9. asocial   10. atone   11. anonymes   12. anarchique   13. asymétrique   14. anormale

137·1   1. contrecoup   2. contrecourant   3. contradiction   4. contre-indication   5. contre-exemple
       6. contre-interrogatoire   7. contrechoc   8. contrespionnage   9. contrebande   10. contrefaçon
       11. contrebandier   12. contre-attaque

137·2   1. V   2. F   3. F   4. V   5. F   6. V   7. V   8. V   9. V   10. V   11. F   12. F

138·1   1. débloquer   2. dénicher   3. dépanner   4. débrancher   5. déplacer   6. déformées   7. démêler
       8. déménager   9. déconseillé   10. dépister   11. dépeignés   12. démoraliser   13. dépasser
       14. dépossédée   15. démentir

138·2   1. désenchanté   2. désherbé   3. déshydraté   4. désintoxiqué   5. désembarqués   6. déracinés
       7. déséquilibré   8. déroutée   9. déshéritée   10. désaltéré   11. désobéi   12. déstabilisée   13. désapprouvée
       14. désodorisée   15. déshabillé

139·1   1. g   2. e   3. i   4. d   5. b   6. h   7. a   8. f   9. c

140·1   1. F   2. V   3. F   4. V   5. V

141·1   1. enjamber   2. endetter   3. enraciner   4. enfanter   5. enchanter   6. engloutir   7. enfermer   8. enivrer   9. Encourager   10. enrager   11. endormir   12. ensorceler   13. enrichir   14. engraisser   15. endurcir

142·1   1. emmagasiner   2. embrasser   3. empaqueter   4. emballer   5. emprisonner   6. empiéter   7. embouteiller   8. embaucher   9. emmurer   10. empoigner   11. empiler   12. s'embourber   13. emmailloter   14. embarquer   15. empocher   16. emboîter

143·1   1. enregistrée   2. enterrés   3. enchaînés   4. encaissé   5. encadrée   6. ensablées   7. enclos   8. enrubanné   9. encapuchonnée   10. encerclée   11. enfuis   12. envolés   13. enlevés

144·1   1. V   2. F   3. F   4. V   5. F   6. F   7. V   8. F   9. F   10. F   11. V   12. V   13. V   14. V   15. F   16. V   17. V   18. F

144·2   1. mi-cynique   2. mi-figue mi-raisin   3. mi-saison   4. mi-temps   5. mi-superstitieux   6. mi-juin   7. mi-août   8. mi-cuite   9. mi-agréable   10. mi-course

144·3   1. semi-précieuse   2. semi-privée   3. semi-professionnelle   4. semi-imperméables   5. semi-liberté   6. semi-publiques   7. semi-conducteur   8. semi-nomade

145·1   1. c   2. d   3. l   4. g   5. i   6. a   7. k   8. j   9. e   10. h   11. b   12. f

146·1   1. Il ne faut pas   2. Il faut   3. Il faut   4. Il ne faut pas   5. Il ne faut pas   6. Il ne faut pas   7. Il ne faut pas   8. Il faut   9. Il ne faut pas   10. Il faut   11. Il faut   12. Il faut   13. Il faut   14. Il ne faut pas

146·2   1. annoté   2. arrondie   3. anoblis   4. avili   5. attiédie   6. amolli   7. appauvries   8. atténués   9. attristé   10. amincie   11. approfondie   12. annulé

146·3   1. atterrissage   2. accostage   3. acheminement   4. alignement   5. approvisionnement   6. apitoiement   7. allaitement   8. accompagnement   9. apaisement   10. accoutumance   11. accouchement   12. affiliation   13. ajournement

146·4   1. V   2. F   3. F   4. V   5. V   6. F   7. V   8. F   9. V   10. V   11. V   12. F

147·1   1. diaspora   2. diachronie   3. diaphonie   4. diagramme   5. diamètre   6. diaphragme   7. dialecte   8. diabète   9. dialyse   10. diatribe   11. dialogue   12. diagnostic

148·1   1. orthophoniste   2. orthophonie   3. orthoscopie   4. orthoscope   5. orthopédiste   6. orthopédie   7. orthopédique   8. orthodontiste   9. orthodontie   10. orthographe   11. orthographie   12. orthodoxie   13. orthodoxe

149·1   1. photocopieuse   2. photographie   3. photogénie   4. photogravure   5. photocopie   6. photochimie   7. photographe   8. photométrie   9. photosynthèse   10. photoconductivité

150·1   1. épisodes   2. épidémies   3. épilepsie   4. épigraphes   5. épiphanie   6. épicentre   7. épicycle   8. épiderme   9. épigramme   10. épilogue

151·1   1. équipotents   2. équivalent   3. équité   4. équivoque   5. équipotentiel   6. équitable   7. équidistant   8. équidistance   9. équilibre   10. équilibré   11. équinoxe   12. équilatéral

152·1   1. j   2. h   3. g   4. b   5. c   6. i   7. e   8. d   9. f   10. a

153·1   1. géophile(s)   2. géomorphologie   3. géomorphologistes   4. géographe(s)   5. géographie   6. géomagnétisme   7. géomagnétiques   8. géothermique   9. géothermie   10. géologistes/géologues   11. géologie   12. géochimistes   13. géochimie   14. géométrie

154·1   1. héliotrope   2. héliogravure   3. héliocentrisme   4. héliotropie   5. héliothérapie   6. héliophile   7. héliographe   8. héliographie   9. héliostat   10. héliograveur

155·1   1. V   2. F   3. F   4. F   5. V   6. V   7. F   8. F   9. V   10. F   11. V   12. V

156·1   1. homologue   2. homophonie   3. homosexualité   4. homocyclique   5. homogène   6. homocentrique   7. homonyme   8. homophones   9. homogénéité   10. homosexuelle

157·1   1. F   2. V   3. F   4. V   5. V   6. F   7. V

158·1 1. holophrastique 2. holocristalline 3. holométaboles 4. hologramme 5. holographique 6. holotropique 7. holoprotéine 8. holographie 9. holocauste 10. holocène

159·1 1. cosmonaute 2. cosmogonie 3. cosmologie 4. cosmodrome 5. cosmopolite 6. cosmographie 7. cosmologiste/cosmologue 8. cosmopolitisme

160·1 1. e 2. f 3. i 4. b 5. d 6. h 7. a 8. j 9. c 10. g